Mind's Eye Theatre™

LIVE ACTION STORYTELLING
IN THE WORLD OF DARKNESS

CREDITS

Concept and Design: White Wolf Game Studio

Written by: White Wolf Game Studio and Peter Woodworth

World of Darkness created by Mark Rein•Hagen.

World of Darkness co-created by Stewart Wieck.

The Storytelling System is based on the Storyteller System designed by Mark Rein•Hagen.

Developed by: Alex Teodorescu-Badia and Peter Woodworth

Editor: Ken Cliffe

Art Director: Pauline Benney

Layout & Typesetting: matt milberger

Interior Art: Samuel Araya, Aleksi Briclot, Avery Butterworth, Colleen Denney, Nils Hamm, Becky Jollensten, Brandon Kitkouski, Cosimo Lorenz Panchini, David Seeley, Chris Shy, and Larry Snelly

Front & Back Cover Design: matt milberger

Camarilla Playtesters: Sean Alexander, April Asbury, Bex, Todd Branch, Joe Carron, Wes Contreras, Michael Curnutt, Miguel Duran, Aaron Fenwick, Mark Lewis, Kevin Millard, Hugh Montgomerie, Silja Muller, Randy Ochs, Charlie Rose, Guy Seggev, Jeremiah Spaulding, Nico van Aerde, Jason Walter, Eddy Webb. Additional thanks to the '05 Golden Ticket guinea pi— er, players.

Pete's Playtesters: Scott Adams, Kevin Allen, Fletcher Bennett, Rich Brodsky, Greg Curley, Dan DiFlavis, Jim Fillmore, Matt Florentine, Alyson Gaul, Steve Grabania, Lee Hefner, BJ Hinkle, James Hussiere, Amy Houser, Scott Katinger, Frank Manna, Kirsten Mascioli, Dan Schermond, Andrew J. Scott, Megan Strittmatter, Tim Sullivan, Jackob Thurston, Tome Wilson, Andrew Woodworth.

ACKNOWLEDGEMENT

Thanks to everyone who has ever contributed to and played in **Mind's Eye Theatre**, from the mightiest convention saga to the smallest hometown chronicle. We started a revolution in roleplaying once before. Now it's time to take the next leap forward. So paint your face and shadow smile, and let the play begin!

Poor silly half-brained things

We make our

Oown fortunes

EPT IN ITS ABSOLUTE EFFECT

TABLE OF CONTENTS

Chapter 1: The World of Darkness

No live organism can continue for long to exist sanely under conditions of absolute reality; even larks and katydids are supposed, by some, to dream. Hill House, not sane, stood by itself against its hills, holding darkness within; it had stood so for eighty years and might stand for eighty more. Within, walls continued upright, bricks met neatly, floors were firm, and doors were sensibly shut; silence lay steadily against the wood and stone of Hill House, and whatever walked there, walked alone.

— Shirley Jackson,
The Haunting

Everyone has had the sense at least once in their lives that things are not right with the world, that not everything is at it seems. We sometimes feel that sinister truths hide behind a façade of normality, veiled partially by the rational, orderly "natural laws" taught to us by science. We're told that medieval beliefs in monsters and magic were merely primitive superstitions. We're too wise for that sort of foolishness these days. Or so we assure ourselves. But at night, when the shadows grow long and the wind whistles through the trees, we shudder and remember old truths, the truths of our ancestors, who were right to fear the dark.

We know deep down that the world is a far more terrifying place than we allow our rational minds to acknowledge. To accept this subconscious truth is to invite madness, to succumb to the raw chaos that lurks at the edges of our perception. Best to shut our eyes and pretend it's not there. If we don't see it, *it might not see us.*

Pretending something is not there, however, does not make it go away. It only helps it to hide better — and predators like to hide from their prey, lest it be scared away.

A world where such predators truly exist is a conspiracy theorist's worst nightmare. In such a reality, unseen beings hatch incognito plots against us, pulling our strings like puppeteers looming above, hidden in the darkness beyond the stage lights. Our only protection is ignorance, the obliviousness that allows us to keep going day to day, building toward "something meaningful" — a career, a home, a family. Allegations about secret masters or creatures lurking in the night simply lack evidence. If those things are real, why don't we see them on the evening news? Even Internet sites dedicated to exposing unknown forces in our lives can't produce a single, verifiable picture. It's hard to believe in something we can't see.

Maybe *they* want it that way.

Welcome to the World of Darkness.

MIDNIGHT STORIES

We can't know when humans first started telling stories, or why. But it's a safe bet that the first tale tellers used their craft to explain the mysteries that existed around them. Indeed, some of the most ancient stories that are still told today grapple with the biggest mysteries of all — life, death, creation, redemption and the ongoing struggle of good versus evil. We call the game you hold in your hands a Storytelling game, because it's an opportunity for you to participate in the deeply human endeavor of telling stories. You'll find more about the rules of the game in following chapters.

The stories told in this game are set in the World of Darkness. It's a place very much like our world, sharing the same history, culture and geography. Superficially, most people in this fictional world live the same lives we do. They eat the same food, wear the same clothes, and waste time watching the same stupid TV shows. And yet, in the World of Darkness, shadows are deeper, nights are darker and fog is thicker. If in our world a neighborhood has a rundown house that gives people the creeps, in the World of Darkness that house emits strange sighs on certain nights of the year, and seems to have a human face when seen out of the corner of one's eye. Or so some neighbors say. In our world, there are urban legends. In the World of Darkness, there are urban legends whispered into the ears of autistic children by invisible spiders.

In the world you're about to enter, the horrors and nightmares of legend aren't just scary bedtime stories — they're real, even though most people don't realize it. The truth, or at least some of the truth about this world's hidden terrors, is revealed in other books. But you don't need all the answers to begin exploring. This book gives you everything you need to create your own collaborative tales. Horror stories, ghost stories, wonder tales, adventures or mysteries. Stories of people who suspect the truth about what lurks in the shadows, perhaps only after getting an unwelcome glimpse of it.

This chapter brings you the words of some who've walked the road you're about to take. After that, the rest of this book shows how you and your friends can tell your own stories, with simple but broad rules for doing so. You'll find that this game challenges you not just to draw cards and keep track of numbers, but to inhabit a character who is as real and believable as you can make him. The true measure of success in a Storytelling game is how much your character interacts with the imaginary world he inhabits.

Maybe the character you create will uncover some secrets of his shadowed world. Maybe he'll *become* one of those secrets. Time will tell.

Missing Hikers Found Killed, Mutilated

Watson s Corner, NJ

Following an extensive search involving numerous local and federal law-enforcement agencies, police officials held a press conference this morning to announce that they had found the bodies of five missing college students that disappeared while hiking last week. The students had begun their hike at a local campground on Friday night, but when they failed to return as scheduled Sunday afternoon, concerned friends contacted the police. The grisly remains were discovered late last night. The identities of the victims have been withheld pending notification of their families.

Citing the nature of the ongoing investigation, investigators declined to comment on the specifics of the case, except that they believe the killings were carried out by multiple individuals, possibly ones already familiar with the area. Sources close to the case say that initial investigation efforts have been hampered due to heavy rainfall over the weekend, the extremely brutal trauma inflicted on the victims, and the possibility wild animals may have gotten to the bodies before their discovery.

Anyone who believes they might have information regarding this case is urged contact the authorities. All tips can be made anonymously.

THE ELEMENTS OF MODERN HORROR

This book presents rules for playing a type of live-action roleplaying game called Storytelling. In this type of game, the traditional elements of a story — theme, mood, plot and character — are more important than the rules themselves. The rules serve to help you tell stories about your characters in an interactive experience. They help prevent arguments and provide a solid basis for handling elements of chance, but they don't overshadow the story itself. The triumphs and tragedies of your characters as they try to survive and even thrive in the World of Darkness are the main focus, not cards drawn or lists of traits.

Live-action Storytelling games involve at least two players (for a personal prelude or side session), although most games have 20 to 30 players who attend on a regular basis, and some large games can have more than a hundred players at a time! Everyone involved participates in telling a group story. The players create and act out the roles of their characters, and the Storyteller and her staff creates and reveals the plot, introducing allies and antagonists with which the players' characters interact. The players' choices throughout the course of the Storytelling experience alter the plot. The Storyteller's job isn't to defend his story from any attempt to change it, nor is it the job of the players to "win," but for both sides to work together to help create the best story possible as events unfold, reacting to each other and weaving plots and actions into a greater whole.

Here are some of the key elements that both players and Storytellers should keep in mind when telling stories in the World of Darkness.

THEME – DARK MYSTERY

Every story has its own theme, a summation of what it's about. Sometimes called the "moral" or "lesson" of the story, a theme doesn't have to involve a definitive answer to the questions raised. Merely asking overarching questions is enough to capture a theme.

The overall theme of the World of Darkness is "dark mystery." The world is one of shadows within shadows. Those who participate in these conspiracies should uncover as much of them as they can, lest investigators become unwitting pawns in the games of greater forces. But drawing back the curtain on one mystery reveals even more curtains, each hiding new secrets. It's not possible to uncover them all. Yet, characters can certainly work to reveal more than would otherwise be known, and so free themselves from dark influences.

While each story has its own central theme, the looming theme behind them all explores the dramatic ramifications of a world of supernatural secrets. Storytellers and players alike should be mindful of the "dark mystery" theme when they feel the need to return to the roots of the game.

MOOD — DREAD

People fear what they don't know or understand. On some level, most people suspect that things aren't right, that they're being lied to. Rather than confront this terrible truth ("Who's lying to me? Where are they?"), they choose to repress it. People pretend nothing is out of order and go about their lives as usual. Whether this behavior can be traced back to the ancient depredations of supernatural creatures or to fear of the occult, people refuse to recognize it. They go asleep to the realities around them and refuse to open their eyes.

Even those who do confront the shadows do so with a sense of dread. Exploring the unknown promises rewards, but also risks unforeseen consequences. Are the potential rewards worth the risks? Every step into mystery is onto unsafe ground, and few march boldly into the night.

ATMOSPHERE — THREATENING SYMBOLISM

Combine theme and mood in the fog-bound streets, rave clubs, towering penthouses, midnight woods and cloistered sanctums of the World of Darkness. Add a hint of the otherworldly bleeding through the walls of reality now and then, and you've got the perfect atmosphere for chilling horror Storytelling.

Everything in the World of Darkness has foreboding significance. Nothing is necessarily what it seems. A dead tree might actually harbor a bitter spirit. A car might be a reservoir for magical energies that could kill the unwary. Everything is a cipher for something else, lending mysterious significance to otherwise coincidental events. Is it just chance that you receive a letter from a schoolmate you haven't seen or heard from in years, and you read the next day about his horrifying death by exsanguination. Dare you open the letter?

The World of Darkness rarely communicates its secrets directly. Instead, mysteries can be read in places and things all around — symbols of deeper, unsettling truths. It's easier to ignore these signs than face them. Many people are willfully blind to these messages, fearing what they reveal. "It's just coincidence. Meaningless happenstance." Just keep telling yourself that....

SETTING — A SENSE OF PLACE

The World of Darkness is not about someplace long ago and far away. It's our world today, but different. Looked at from a global perspective, it seems the same. Looking closer, though, the details differ. That house down the street isn't just abandoned, it's haunted. Nobody goes to the old quarry anymore. Some teenagers didn't come back. That new nightclub is so cool, but creepy. Did you see that guy who kept staring at us last night?

The advantage to playing a game of contemporary horror is that it can take place in your own backyard, literally. You can populate your hometown with all manner of secret terrors, imagining how the local convenience-store clerk might really be the thrall of a supernatural creature. Perhaps he helps his master to feed by collecting the corpses of the homeless people who sleep in the alley out back. Or your blowhard mayor might be a member of a secret society dedicated to keeping the spoils of power within a small clique, preventing others from awakening to their true potential.

The drawback here is that you can strike too close to home. Putting horror so near to your daily life can be truly unnerving unless everyone knows to leave their wild imaginations at the game session. It's not a good idea to go around defaming the mayor based on a fictitious conspiracy dreamed up in your game sessions. Remember, the World of Darkness is not our world — it just looks and acts an awful lot like it. Use this resemblance to reality for dramatic effect, not as an excuse to retreat into your basement muttering about *them*.

Of course, this shouldn't prevent *characters* in the World of Darkness from blurring the line between reality and the occult. That's what it's all about. Exploring a world of mystery that tries to keep itself hidden. A world that punishes those who look too deep. But those who refuse to look suffer even worse. They're rocked on seas of conspiracies of which they go unaware. Damned if you do, damned if you don't. There are no easy answers, and knowing is not half the battle. It's only the first shot in a long, grinding war against the shadows.

xJimmyx: im back!

murder_by_beth: so, what happened?

xJimmyx: we finally got in and took some pictures. its *so* weird in there!

murder_by_beth: brrr, i couldn t have gone into an abandoned houses, I d have been too scared.

xJimmyx: thats the weird part   theres still furniture and everything.

murder_by_beth: i thought it was abandoned?

xJimmyx: downstairs was empty, but the rooms on the second floor all had stuff in them, like someones still living there. not like a hobo or anything, either there were all these old books everywhere. it was *totally* creepy.

murder_by_beth: weird!

xJimmyx: yeah it was. Rae kept saying she felt like someone was watching, and she wouldnt let any of us go in the basement at all.

xJimmyx: but thats ok, because we thought heard someone moving around down there when we were coming downstairs. so we got the hell out of there.

murder_by_beth: omg did anyone see you?!?

xJimmyx: i don t think so. there were no lights on, and we didnt see any cars.

murder_by_beth: so what are you going to do now?

xJimmyx: well, we dropped off the film at a one hour place and Tony went to take Rae home, then he and Jack are coming back so we can pick up the pictures and see if any of them turned out ok.

xJimmyx: shit, i think theyre here. i gotta go before they wake up my mom.

xJimmyx: brb

murder_by_beth: be careful Jimmy

User xJimmyx is not available.

"But I Want to Paint it Black!"

One common mistake a lot of inexperienced Storytellers make when adapting their setting for the World of Darkness is connecting absolutely *everything* in town to the supernatural, to the point where everyone and everything is supernatural. While it's sometimes fine for the characters to *feel* as though the supernatural has its hooks in everything, that doesn't mean that it has to be *true*. In fact, it's usually better if it's not. Without a sense of the ordinary to give it some contrast, the supernatural quickly becomes "natural" and loses a lot of its innate horror and alien nature.

Indeed, the more common the supernatural is, the less of an impact it has when it makes its presence known. While juxtaposing otherworldly elements with ordinary settings is an essential part of creating horror — say, trying to act casually when you realize the person ahead of you in line at the bank is actually a blood slave — doing it too often numbs players to the fear everyone tries to create. Players just aren't as frightened of vampires if they see them everywhere they turn. On the other hand, if the *presence* of the undead is suggested through a series of increasingly terrifying clues and encounters, and characters finally encounter the thing, they're bound to be scared out of their wits. They still don't know exactly what to expect.

So, instead of packing your town with supernatural beings of many different varieties and have them populate every prominent industry or location, focus on a lone creature or small group of them. (You can always add more later.) Try to think how they might insinuate themselves in your town to further their sinister agendas. Rather than having monsters control large portions of the population directly, consider "choke points" they might influence, instead. Why go to the trouble of enthralling every business owner in town when a vampire can simply sway the owner of the leasing company that controls the majority of the town's commercial real estate? (Or the vampire can acquire the company itself through proxies.) Doing so gives the nightcrawler an immense amount of clout that doesn't require much effort to maintain. On a story level, the creature's influence is felt around town without him playing his necrotic hand.

Last but not least, remember that as terrifying as monsters are, human beings are responsible for the vast majority of everyday activities in the World of Darkness, not to least of which its crimes and atrocities. Most of these efforts have very little input from the shadow world. If you place supernatural creatures at the head of every political party, big business or crime syndicate in town, you sell your human factor short. Just because vampires *can* control the mayor with their hellish powers doesn't mean that they will. Many creatures find humans more than pliant enough to mundane offers of money and special favors. They resort to outright supernatural control only when they feel they have no other choice. And if you think players' characters are frightened when they learn that some people are compelled to serve dark masters, just wait till they figure out that some people do it without supernatural coercion.

UNRECORDED HISTORY

Once we realize that things are not as we believe, we inevitably conclude that they've *never* been what we thought. History is a lie. If creatures that walk and talk like people exist, how long have they been here? Ancient legends certainly seem to describe some of these beings. Are the superstitious ravings of our ancestors true? Maybe there really are such things as vampires, werewolves and sorcerers — and always have been.

How much of what we're told about history is actual fact and how much is mere conjecture? Are there beings that actively work to falsify the evidence of the past, covering their tracks from all records, written or otherwise? Perhaps the *facts* are right but the *reasons* are wrong. Surely, Columbus discovered America, but maybe his purpose wasn't to seek the Indies to prove the Earth was round. What if he was transporting something away from the Old World and into the New, a land that he knew existed thanks to legends and map fragments? What if this something wasn't a thing at all, but an immortal being who secretly influenced the explorer's mind? Ridiculous, of course. Contemplating these sorts of wacko conspiracies helps us to imagine that all conspiracies are merely the result of overactive imaginations.

But what about less prominent events in history, those that are still shrouded in mystery? For instance, what caused the Tunguska Crater in Siberia? The official explanation is that it was a meteor. And yet, in the World of Darkness, nomadic hunters of the time reportedly swore to a French journalist that strange creatures were sighted in the region. Peasants whispered for years that those who traveled too close to the crater at night would sleepwalk for months afterward. Rubbish, some people say. Clearly it was ground zero for Nicolai Tesla's Death Ray experiments. Case solved.

Viewing history through the lens of supernatural machination allows us to mine the past for stories. The entire tapestry of history, from the invention of agriculture to the nuclear bomb, can be interpreted in a sinister light, with warring forces of occult beings and secret societies using ignorant humans as pawns in their eternal games.

What could we achieve if only we could remove the veil from our eyes and see things as they really are? Human potential is limitless, hampered only by our own unwillingness to question and deal with the ramifications of reality. Beware, however, to whom you address any questions, lest you become enlisted into the armies of the night and wage their wars instead of your own.

GRAND OPENING

CLUB PARADOX

Sick of poser kids slamming into you, and lousy DJ s older than your dad?

Bored with beer-soaked frat boys and second-rate drinks at first-rate prices?

Tired of the same old coffee houses with surly servers and lousy java?

Come experience Club Paradox, the hottest combination nightspot in town!

Club Paradox features three floors of entertainment for a truly amazing nightlife experience.

Main Floor: Forget lame canned music and overcrowded rooms Club Paradox has a nonstop dance party with the best

DJs and live bands on the biggest dance floor in the city, every night of the week!

Downstairs: Feeling thirsty? We've got you covered. Whether from a bottle or a tap, Club Paradox has the largest selection of quality imported and domestic beverages of any club in the city!

Upstairs: Whether you feel like relaxing after a long night of partying, sharing some original verse at our regular open mic nights, or you just want some great conversation outside of the usual club experience, head upstairs to our world-class coffee bar. A true Club Paradox twist of the unexpected!

CLUB PARADOX
Leave Reality Behind and Play

What Is Mind's Eye Theatre?

This game is probably different from any game you've played before. In many ways, this is really not a game at all. **Mind's Eye Theatre** is more concerned with stories than winning, rules, game boards or dice. You'll find that the game has more in common with childhood games of adventure than with card games or *Monopoly*-type board games. This book contains all the information necessary to catapult you into worlds of imagination. You create the action, and you choose your own path. We have a name for this style of game. We call it **Mind's Eye Theatre**.

Playing **Mind's Eye Theatre** is like being in a movie. You and your friends portray the main characters, but the script follows your decisions. The director of this improvisational film is called the Storyteller. Along with her Storytelling staff, often called Narrators, she creates the stage and the minor characters with whom you interact during your adventure. Most scenes are played out in real-time, and always in character. You should break character only when there is a rules dispute or a change of scene that requires adjudication from the Storyteller or a Narrator.

In **Mind's Eye Theatre**, there are no limits to the worlds you can explore.

CHARACTERS

When you play **Mind's Eye Theatre**, you take on the persona of an ordinary person who is totally unaware of the true nature of the world and its darkness. Or you might play a character who is already in over her head with forbidden knowledge and horrible secrets. (Perhaps your character might even become one of the very creatures that stalks the shadows!) No matter where her path ultimately takes your characters, you have to create her first. You decide what she's like and where she comes from, what she is and isn't good at, and then roleplay her over the course of a story and perhaps a chronicle (a series of connected stories). You decide what your character does and says. You decide what risks she accepts or declines.

During the game, you speak as your character. Unless you talk to a member of the Storytelling staff about an out-of-game topic, whatever you say is what your character says. Because most of what a **Mind's Eye Theatre** player perceives depends on the characters around him, players must be vivid and expressive. The characters direct the plot, but at the same time the events of the game guide and develop the characters, helping them to achieve the story's goals. To an extent, as a player in a Storytelling game, you have a responsibility beyond simply portraying your character. You need to consider the story as a whole and your role in making sure that other players enjoy the game.

Creating a character for **Mind's Eye Theatre** is easy and takes only a few moments. A few things are necessary to define a basic character, and then you can play the game. There's another phase to creating a character, though, one that makes playing **Mind's Eye Theatre** all the more rewarding. Your character should be more than just a series of traits and dots. She should be a living, breathing personality with a past, motives, drives, quirks, likes, dislikes — everything you want to see from a character in a movie or a novel, everything people really have. So it's probably a good idea to take time to figure out *who* your character is as well as *what* she is before you start playing. While certain details and personality traits come out while you're playing her, you want to have the basics in place before you begin a game. It's just like an actor establishing his character's motivation before shooting begins.

Characters are the heart and soul of a story. Without them, all the patient efforts of the Storyteller would be for naught. Appreciate the Storyteller's efforts by following the rules and taking an active part in the game.

NARRATORS

In **Mind's Eye Theatre**, Narrators are the people who help the Storyteller present adventures. Narrators are the impartial judges who describe scenes or events that cannot be staged, they adjudicate rules, and they occasionally play the roles of antagonists. Generally, enlisting the aid of one Narrator for every 10 players makes for a good ratio. The best number of Narrators for your game usually depends on the gaming experience of the players. The more experienced the players, in all probability the fewer Narrators they need. Narrators usually play characters of their own, as well as helping out in certain situations. That way they can be a part of the action instead of just trying to correct it from the outside.

Sometimes Narrators may be designated for specific areas only. For example, it's common for some players with expert grasp of the rules to be deputized by the Storytelling staff to act as "combat Narrators" to help ensure that fight scenes run smoothly by assisting other players. These limited Narrators generally have no authority to make decisions regarding the plot or storyline. They simply handle rules arbitration.

username: withered_flower
Subject: since you asked
Date: 8/13/04, 2:08 AM
Entry Status: Locked

Entry: Normally I don t let anyone see it when I write about this, but since you asked, Matt, I ll write it down for you. This entry is locked so only we can see it, so don t tell anyone else, OK? Thanks for listening to me. Here goes.

I had the dream again.

It started with me walking with my parents at the fair, just like it always does. It s bright and sunny, and I m wearing one of my favorite outfits. I m happy and I remember lots of laughing. I see something sparkling, and I let go of Mom s hand to check it out. Mom and Dad aren t paying too much attention, I guess. Not too unusual, dream or not, though those were happier times. Anyway, I m not afraid to be on my own, and I wander off.

I m looking at something in the street, a shiny coin maybe. I can never seem to remember quite what it is. All of a sudden I look up and there s a man standing over me. A dark man, dressed in long dark clothes. They re very old, much older than they should be. When I think about it after I wake up he seems out of place in the bright sunlight and the colorful atmosphere, but in the dream nobody else seems to notice him at all. I can t remember what he looks like, but I always get the feeling he s handsome. He s looking down at me, and I can see his eyes. They re cold blue, like ice, and there s a look to them that makes me break into a cold sweat any time I think about them. It wasn t until recently that I placed exactly where I ve seen it before.

It s the same look my cat gets when he s staring at a bird.

Then the man smiles, and as scary as his eyes are, I feel myself smiling back. He leans down and gently puts something in my hand. I want to look at it, to see what it is, but I can t take my eyes off him. He whispers and I m nodding. He looks at me one more time, very carefully, as though he s making sure of something. I look down. I have a flower in my hands. I have just enough time to see that it s very pretty, and then Mom and Dad are back. They sweep me off my feet and hug me, saying how worried they were that I went missing. The flower falls out of my hand. I reach for it, but they re carrying me away. All I can do is watch as the flower just withers in the sun, getting trampled by people. I cry and cry until I wake up.

I ve had this nightmare at least twice a week ever since, even though my parents insist there was no flower, and for that matter no dark man standing there when they found me after I got lost that day. They say I made him up, because I was frightened. All I know is that I used to love to draw, but now all I can draw is flowers. Dead flowers, like the one in my dream. I can t finish anything else. I know it sounds crazy, since I was a kid and all, but I have this horrible feeling I made some kind of deal that day, and that s why I have the nightmares and all the other problems. The dark man was real somehow, and I gave something up for that flower. Something precious.

But even if he was real, who was he?

And what did I give up?

STORYTELLER

Every game must have a Storyteller, who serves as the ultimate authority and final judge in any game of the **Mind's Eye Theatre** you play. The Storyteller creates the basic elements of the plot, and makes sure that the story unfolds to the entertainment of the players — in addition to doing everything the Narrators do. Storytelling is a demanding job, but also a very rewarding one. It's the Storyteller who creates the framework upon which the players build their experiences.

The Storyteller makes certain the story has content, interesting hooks and a narrative flow. This doesn't mean he should just sit back and dictate the plot — characters who don't have free will are no fun to play. Instead, a Storyteller creates the "framework" elements of the plot, and then turns players loose to see what happens. In large **Mind's Eye Theatre** games, there may even be multiple Storytellers to handle the workload. Make no mistake, running even a small chronicle is fun, but it also takes a lot of time and effort, so multiple Storytellers and Narrators may be necessary to ensure that nobody gets burned out by the demands of the chronicle.

During the game, the Storyteller must be watchful and ready to create new elements to make sure that the story works out well. He is also responsible for safety, ensuring that all of the players have something to do, and that everyone abides by the rules. Although performing all of these tasks simultaneously can be exhausting, the sense of accomplishment gained from creating a successful story makes the whole process worthwhile.

COMMON HAND SIGNALS

Mind's Eye Theatre uses a number of hand signals as a way of conveying information quickly and easily. This alleviates excessive amounts of description tags or "you see" narration. Some of the most common hand signals for all the various **Mind's Eye Theatre** games are included here. It should be noted that they may take on slightly different meanings and mechanics in different games. Players should take care to read up on what each symbol means in the context of each game or each trait. For example, the vampiric power of Sovereignty from **The Requiem** may use the "Imposing Presence" gesture, but it may have an entirely different rules system governing its use than a similar werewolf power found in **The Forsaken**, which uses the same gesture.

Troupes can of course devise their own gestures or similar shortcuts if they desire. These gestures are provided to give all troupes a foundation from which to work. A common language, if you will. If your troupe devises a different signal that works better for your game, carry on.

Abusing these hand signals should be considered a fairly serious offense, depending on the circumstances. ("Oh? Did you think I was invisible? That's weird because, well, I was just standing here with my arms crossed, um, under my neck, because, uh, my neck is cold. It's not my fault if you thought that meant I was invisible!") While a new player or someone from a game that uses different gestures should be forgiven a gaffe or two, deliberate abuse threatens the basis of trust on which the game is played.

Example: Rich and Fletcher's characters are entering a room in a haunted house. As they open the door, they see a Narrator character standing in the corner dressed in ghostly attire — however, the Narrator is holding up a hand at head height, with one finger extended to indicate that she is on the plane of existence occupied by ghosts. Since neither of their characters has the ability to see onto that plane, and the ghost is not using a power which makes its presence known, Rich and Fletcher must roleplay ignorance of the Narrator character's presence until later events somehow make it possible for them to perceive her. Of course, this adds some dramatic tension to the scene since the players are now aware of a threat their characters are oblivious to, but that's part of the fun.

Invisibility
One arm crossed high over chest.

Imposing Presence
One fist held at head-height in the air
next to the player, with no fingers extended.

Out-of-Game
One hand held aloft, with index
and middle fingers crossed.

Telepathy
Index finger of one hand touching the temple.

Speaking Different Language
Hand held out, with thumb and forefinger making an "L" shape.

Enhanced Sight
Index finger of one hand, held close to the face, pointing at the eye.

Enhanced Hearing
Index finger pointing at the ear.

On Different Plane of Existence
One hand held at head-height in the air next to the player, sticking out a number of fingers representing the plane of existence the character is on. Characters on other planes are normally considered invisible to characters on different planes unless otherwise noted.

Storytelling Summary

THE ONLY RULES THAT MATTER

The following are the only **Mind's Eye Theatre** rules that should not be altered and must always be obeyed. These are common-sense rules to keep everyone — other players, yourself, strangers in the area and the authorities — safe and happy with your game. These rules are also designed to limit the opportunities anyone has to destroy the fun of your game. They're not intended to interfere with play or your enjoyment. They're here to make sure that everyone plays sensibly and safely.

Although a superfluous reminder for the 99% of us who are well-adjusted and sensible enough to play by such fundamental guidelines without prompting, it bears noting that these rules deserve particular attention in our world of heightened security and cautious scrutiny. Even something as harmless as a group of friends playing an elaborate game of make-believe can theoretically be construed as something suspicious or even outright dangerous if other people don't know what's going on.

Players new to the game are advised to read the following rules closely and take them to heart, while veterans are encouraged to study them again and remember why they're important.

#1— IT'S ONLY A GAME

This is by far the most important rule. If a character is killed, if a plot falls apart, if a rival wins the day — it's only a game. Don't take things too seriously, as that spoils not only your fun but that of everyone around you. Leave the game behind when it ends. Playing **Mind's Eye Theatre** is a lot of fun; spending time talking about the game is great. And yet, calling the person who plays the reclusive occult scholar at 5:13 A.M. on Sunday to discuss the possible cause of the recent juvenile disappearances at the haunted house is another matter entirely. Maintain perspective.

#2 — NO TOUCHING

Never actually make physical contact with other players, no matter how careful you are or how innocent you believe the gesture is. This goes for so-called "social touches" such as hugs or back rubs as much, if not more than, "combat touches" such as punches or kicks. Accidents happen, intentions are misinterpreted and someone could get hurt. Rely on the rules to cover the physical logistics of your game.

That said, some private troupes have provisions that allow for minor touches such as handshakes or putting a hand on someone's shoulder, or that even allow players to have non-combat, physical contact provided there is explicit, consensual agreement in place. This sort of policy is fine so long as *everyone* agrees to it. But even so, never assume that permission granted in the past still applies to the current scene, and never assume anything about someone you've never played with before. If necessary, quickly describe what you intend to do out-of-character to the person whom you want to touch, getting their consent.

If any doubt exists at all, always assume no touching of any kind is ever allowed without obtaining the explicit consent of another player first. Regardless of troupe policy, violent or sexual touching is *never* allowed in a game. Period.

#3 — NO STUNTS

Never climb, jump, run, leap or swing from anything during a game. Keep the "action" in your action low-key. If you can imagine you're a hard-bitten private detective immersed in a shadowy conspiracy involving sinister creatures and ancient secret societies, you can certainly imagine that you dive across a table, rather than actually feeling compelled to actually do so.

#4 – NO WEAPONS

Real or fake weapons of any sort are absolutely forbidden. Not even obviously fake toy or "boffer" weapons are allowed. Such props give other people the wrong impression as to what you're doing, and they could be mistaken for the real thing in the dark. Use item cards to represent weapons, instead, no matter how cool you think it would be to stash a cap gun in your trenchcoat for the sake of "realism." Police forces around the world have lost the last of what tolerance they ever had regarding people brandishing fake guns, phony bombs or any other such toys.

#5 – NO DRUGS OR DRINKING

This one is a real no-brainer. Drugs and alcohol do not create peak performance. They reduce your ability to think and react, meaning that, among other things, your roleplaying ability is impaired. Simply put, players under the influence of drugs or alcohol are a danger to other players, and to the game as a whole. With explicit Storyteller permission, light social drinking can take place at or before a game, provided no one becomes intoxicated, the game location allows for alcohol to be served, and *all* players present are of proper legal age. (Even though no one should actually get drunk, don't forget to designate drivers for safe rides home if any alcohol at all will be consumed at a session.) There's nothing wrong with playing a *character* who's drunk or stoned, but anyone actually getting even remotely drunk, serving alcohol in the presence of minors, or bringing any sort of illicit substances to a game is in bad taste at best and illegal at worst. It's not being "edgy" or "mature," it's simply foolish. Don't do it.

#6 – BE MINDFUL OF OTHERS

Remember, not everyone you see or who sees you is playing the game. A game can be unnerving or even frightening to passersby. Be considerate of non-players in your vicinity, and make sure your gameplay actions or conversations are not going to alarm anyone in a public area. This is especially important given the heightened security levels around the world, even if you've always been careful about such matters in the past. Trying to explain that you didn't really kill your friend, that your character just chopped off his head "in-game" to a suspicious policeman at 3 A.M. is often an exercise in futility. Likewise, hotel security won't ask if you were discussing building bombs for purely "in-character" reasons before they call the police. Chances are the officers who respond to the call won't see the humor in it, either.

On an average night a relatively normal-looking group of **Mind's Eye Theatre** players may discuss in things like monsters, cults, conspiracies, supernatural powers and other topics that can unnerve ordinary people who don't realize a game is being played. Throw in the fact that your players might wear shocking costumes, be overheard planning all manner of violent acts or describing gruesome things they've "seen," and you have the potential for real trouble. Players should get a Storyteller to handle matters if outsiders look worried, frightened or angry, and more importantly never give in to the temptation to "freak the mundanes." While a certain immature set might find it funny to deliberately disturb onlookers, others realize that doing so only hurts the game, whether by getting everyone ejected from the play area, causing the authorities to intervene or increasing the bad reputation this hobby has in the eyes of many people.

If you can't avoid playing in public or semi-public locations, do your best to keep costuming as inoffensive as possible, make sure nobody carries any suspicious props, and if necessary substitute harmless terms for potentially threatening ones. For example, by substituting words like "dog" and "bark" for words like "gun" and "shoot," you can take a sentence that might set off a panic — "He's got a gun! Shoot him!" — and replace it with the surreal yet far more harmless: "He's got a dog! Bark him!" (If that sounds ridiculous, consider this: What sounds sillier, saying that in a club during a game, or trying to explain to the judge that you were just yelling "in-character" when you accidentally set off a panicked stampede?) While you should enjoy this game and the fun and challenges it presents, never forget that no group plays in a vacuum. What you look like or more importantly what you act like while playing can have serious repercussions on those around you.

#7 — The Rules Are Flexible

In addition to the set of basic rules presented here, **Mind's Eye Theatre** includes a number of optional systems. These additional rules are intended to facilitate more evocative play, cut down on the need for "house rules," and otherwise help customize the game to suit your troupe's style. As always, however, feel free to ignore or adjust any of the rules in this book if it will make your game better. If some rule in this book — with the very notable exception of these most important rules themselves — doesn't work for your troupe, optional or otherwise, *change it*.

Just be consistent, candid and fair with your changes. Nobody likes rules that change every week, that work for only certain players, or that create no-win scenarios. Make sure everyone is aware in advance of any changes that are made, and keep an ear out for unexpected problems with any revisions. That said, if your troupe finds new ways to handle, say, ranged combat or task cards that work better for you than the ones in this book, go for it. The idea is to have fun.

#8 — Make the Game Fun for Everyone

Not "win." Not "Go out and kill everyone else." Just "Make the game fun for everyone." The object of **Mind's Eye Theatre** is not winning. In fact, there are no rules for "victory." It's rather like trying to "defeat" a dinner party or "win" a play. There's nothing wrong with wanting a direct dominate-and-destroy style of experience, but unless the rest of your troupe agrees with you, we recommend that you skip live-action play and fire up the video-game console instead. This isn't elitism, it's simple fact. The two types of games are designed with very different objectives in mind. The goal of live-action roleplaying is to have fun with friends and to tell great stories in a social setting, not to rack up kills, max out your dots or to achieve total numerical superiority over other players.

Indeed, in **Mind's Eye Theatre**, it's not about how the game ends, but about the journey and what happens along the way. It may sound strange, but it's true: If you play for only your own amusement, you not only wind up amusing no one but yourself, but tend to alienate others in the troupe as well. If you play to make the game fun for everyone, all players are rewarded. Remember, everyone has dots on his character sheet. No matter how advanced your character is, someone else could be more powerful.

If your character is a total jerk, there are a number of ways to portray such him that still entertain other players, even if their characters hate yours. Responsible live-action roleplayers do not hide behind excuses like, "I'm a player and my character is a total bastard, so I can do whatever I want and the rest of the group can't complain." Rather, they understand the importance of concepts like, "I'm a player, so even if my character is a bastard — *especially* if he's a bastard — I should make sure what I do makes for a better story *as well as* meeting my own goals." It's a small but absolutely critical difference.

In the end, this final rule is as much a measure of common sense as any other. If you drive away the other players by making the game miserable, you'll soon have no game left in which to demonstrate your bad-ass prowess.

Rules Summary

CARDS

Live-action Storytelling replaces the dice of traditional roleplaying with a hand of 10 ordinary playing cards, using cards 2 to 10 and including an Ace. Neither suit nor style matters. These cards are used to determine the whims of fate. Anytime a character performs an action under adverse conditions or when the outcome is unclear, his player draws a card to see if the task succeeds. Note that the alternate systems don't require cards. If your game makes using cards difficult due to costuming or environmental reasons make sure that every participant is comfortable using one of those systems first.

Each player is normally required to have 10 cards on him while playing, though it is recommended that Storytellers, Narrators and considerate players carry extra sets in order to cover players who forget or do not have costume space to carry their own. Cards can be obtained cheaply at most convenience stores, and since a single deck can supply four characters, the expense isn't terribly great. Players should try to rotate their cards on a regular basis to avoid unintentionally having them acquire bent corners or other telltale marks due to the regular wear and tear of play.

If issues of card marking become a problem, the Storyteller can insist that players obtain new cards for each session, that they rotate cards with other players at random, or even that cards must be submitted for inspection before play begins. The Storyteller can even sign cards to indicate they have been approved for play. If the last case, only cards signed by the Storyteller are considered valid for resolving tests.

Draw Etiquette

Generally, players are required to display their cards to opponents before drawing begins, to show that they have a properly constituted hand. Any time a card is drawn from a hand, the hand must be shuffled before another draw is made. To avoid potential allegations of abuse when drawing for a test, instead of drawing from their own cards, players are expected to draw from an *opponent's* hand (or the hand of a Narrator or nearby player, if the test is not directly opposed). Provided it is not done solely as a delaying tactic, players are within their rights to ask for any of the following at any time: an opponent to shuffle his hand, an opponent to display his hand again to ensure that it's still stacked correctly, to pick from a different player's hand, or even for a new set of cards to be obtained from a Narrator or another player before continuing with a test.

Players may also request that a Storyteller or Narrator be the one to provide cards or even make a critical draw on behalf of either side if ensuring an impartial outcome is absolutely essential. Storyteller or Narrator involvement should be limited to only the most extreme instances, however, such as resolving a test that would result in one character's death or decide the outcome of a major plotline.

Remember that an opponent asking you to display your cards, perform a shuffle or otherwise make a draw request is *not* accusing you of cheating. Quite the opposite, these are simply quick ways of ensuring that both parties are relaxed and confident that the test is honest, so no one has to worry about second-guessing the outcome. Should the worst happen and a player suspect that another is cheating, he should not be confronted directly, but be brought to the Storyteller's attention, who in turn takes any appropriate disciplinary measures.

Players who attempt to abuse any of these guidelines for their own benefit may face disciplinary action by the Storyteller.

Note: It is a fact of life that a small but potentially significant number of players are skilled at card tricks, either from training in sleight of hand and stage magic, or simply many nights spent playing cards. While the vast majority of such players are honest, players with such skills are advised to alert the Storytelling staff and other players before play begins to avoid unfounded suspicions if their talents are discovered. These individuals should not take it personally if other players are strict with them regarding card etiquette and hand checks. In return, opponents should remember that knowing card tricks does not automatically mean every draw a player makes is suspect, and to make any hand requests politely and reasonably.

ALTERNATIVES TO CARDS

Situations may arise when using cards will be too clumsy, either because of elaborate costumes or because players simply can't get their hands on a deck. In such cases, all involved players should first agree on the alternate system they want to use. Sometimes players may also find that an alternate system is faster or more convenient for them. Creative players can come up with various alternate methods. Some may simply place a ten-sided die in a clear plastic box, carrying it around with them, shaking it, then setting it down in plain sight if a challenge occurs. For players who don't want to use any props, a system of hand signals is the best alternative.

Hand Signals

To randomize a number, both players hide their hands behind their backs, display a number of fingers between one and ten, and then simultaneously reveal their hands to each other. The number of fingers is added up: If the number exceeds ten, ten is subtracted from it, so a total of thirteen fingers is actually a three. Attempting a high number is thus risky because matched with your opponent's number you can easily exceed a ten and start all over from the bottom again. The same of course applies to always trying a low number if your opponent does the same, or always tries a ten. Those concerned about other players spotting their displayed fingers early and changing their own mid-reveal can ask a Storyteller or another player to look at their fingers while they're behind their back and add them up without a reveal. Alternative hand signals are easy to devise, for instance if only one hand can be used. Showing the index finger would be a one, the index and middle finger a two, and so on. To form numbers above five, touch your thumb and index finger together to form a circle (the "OK" sign) for a six, your thumb and ring finger for a seven etc., with just the fist (no fingers) representing a ten. Then add up your number and your opponent's number in the same fashion as the two-handed signals. If players are more comfortable with cards but don't want to shuffle and draw, they can also simply simultaneously display a card of their choice from their deck to each other. The total values are added up and the final number calculated in the same way as hand signals.

TRAITS

Characters possess a variety of traits that describe their innate capabilities, trained skills and even how many wounds they can suffer before dying. These traits are fully described in subsequent chapters. Two types of traits are especially important: Attributes and Skills.

Each of these traits is rated in dots (•), ranging from 1 to 5, much like the "five-star" system many critics use to rate movies. For example, a character might have a Dexterity Attribute of • • • (3) and a Firearms Skill of • • (2).

Whenever your character performs an action that calls for a card draw, you most often determine your test pool by adding the most appropriate Attribute dots to the most appropriate Skill dots. When your character shoots a gun, you add his Dexterity • • • to his Firearms • • for a total of five.

MODIFIERS

Various conditions and circumstances can greatly improve or hinder your character's efforts, represented by bonuses and/or penalties to your test pool (not your hand size). Quality tools might give him a bonus to repair a car, or a Stradivarius violin might give him a bonus to play a symphony. Or a thunderstorm might impose hazardous driving conditions, levying a penalty on any driving tests, or a distant target is hard to hit with a gun, represented by range penalties. For example, when shooting a target at medium range with his pistol, your character suffers a –2 penalty. That gives you a modified test pool of three (5 – 2).

The Storyteller determines whether or not any circumstance imposes test-pool modifiers and how great those modifiers are.

TEST POOL

So, we can say that a test pool is determined like so:

Attribute + Skill + equipment modifier
+/– Storyteller-determined modifiers (if any)

In general, bonuses to your test pools are always added before penalties are applied (before points are taken away).

There are a few other complications, but you'll read about those in detail in the chapters to come.

DRAWING CARDS

Now that you know what your draw will be based on, let's see how to read the results. Draw one card, and add the value of that card to your test pool. So, if you draw a 6, you add six to your test pool. The result of this calculation is known as a draw total, and determines whether or not you were successful, and just well you did. The standard difficulty you want to equal or exceed is 10, which means you want your draw total to equal or exceed 10. (This target may occasionally be adjusted if the Storyteller desires.)

For every interval of five that your draw total equals or exceeds a total of 10, you earn one success. So if your draw total is 10, 11, 12, 13 or 14 (the first interval of five), you earn one success. If your draw total is 15, 16, 17, 18 or 19, you earn two successes. Multiple successes generally mean your character does better than she hoped, perhaps completing a task early or coaxing a bit more performance out of a piece of hardware. Storytelling doesn't just tell you whether your character succeeds or fails, it shows you how well he does.

If your total does not exceed the standard difficulty, or you draw an Ace on your initial draw, your draw fails automatically. This is rarely fatal. It's most often simply a setback, and your character can usually try the action again (or again and again in the case of combat). If an action using mental or social traits against another character fails, you usually have to wait for a scene (by default an hour) to attempt the same action against the same character again.

Obviously, the more dots and bonuses you have in your test pool, the better your character's chances of success and the greater your odds of gaining multiple successes. It's often easy to get a single basic success (a draw total of 10, 11, 12, 13 or 14) so long as your character isn't under extreme pressure or facing heavy odds, but getting multiple successes is another matter entirely.

In addition, there is a special rule called "10 Again." Whenever you draw a 10, you may draw an additional card and add that value to the draw total as well. So, if you have a test pool of 7 and you draw a 10, you shuffle your remaining hand again and draw once more. If the result in an 8, your draw total is an amazing 25! Even drawing an Ace for the second card isn't so bad under these special circumstances — it just counts as zero, not an automatic failure. If you draw a second 10, you do not keep drawing. Only one extra card is pulled on a 10 Again.

TURNS

By default, all actions happen within a turn – approximately three seconds of play time. The order in which characters act in a turn is determined by their initiative, but unless the characters are involved in combat there is no need to invoke initiative: actions happen as characters perform them. If a character takes a non-combat action that results in combat, the involved players check for initiative in the turn immediately following the action that caused the combat.

Example: Joshua and his friends have foolishly stumbled into an underground hive where Orlando is enacting a dark ceremony. Orlando is about to use a supernatural power on Joshua; once that action has been completed, Joshua's friends may enter combat, test for initiative and perform reflexive actions.

DURATION OF ACTIONS

Different tasks demand different times to accomplish them. It takes longer to rebuild a car engine than it does to stab someone with a knife. There are three types of action durations: instant, reflexive and extended.

An instant action is resolved with a single draw. Only one success (a draw total of 10, 11, 12, 13 or 14) is required to complete an instant action, although extra successes might improve the results. Instant actions include anything that can be accomplished in the span between one and three seconds: throwing a punch, jumping a fence or sneaking past a security guard. Instant actions are always invoked and take effect on a character's initiative if performed during combat turns. Otherwise they are presumed to last for the entirety of a three-second turn. A character may only take one instant action per turn.

An extended action is resolved with a series of draws. Successes from each draw are tallied until they equal or exceed the target number of successes to complete the task. The Storyteller determined both the required number of successes and how much time each draw represents within the story (anywhere from five minutes to a whole day).

For example, fixing a car takes about 30 minutes per draw. A simple tune-up might require only four accumulated successes, while a transmission rebuild might require 10 or more. Extended actions don't usually take place during live-action play time although some powers may modify the duration of extended actions to denote the need for multiple successes. Some supernatural powers require extended actions to that take place over the span of at least several turns: when the last necessary success is achieved, the power takes effect.

Reflexive Actions normally take no time at all: they are usually a response to another action or event and require no thought or time to enact. Performing a reflexive action does not prevent a character from performing another *action* within a *turn* – they are an addition to your normal action and are resolved immediately after the instigating action or attack (when the poison is injected, when the threat is leveled or when your character decides to go for broke). Outside of combat, a reflexive action can never pre-empt a character's action: reflexive actions are activated in response to another character's instant or extended action. Some reflexive actions may even be performed outside of a character's initiative ranking. Reflexive actions usually indicate in their description if they are reactive to another event, normally an environmental stimulus or another character's action. Those reflexive actions take place before that stimulus, for instance an aggressive action, is resolved. If a reflexive action isn't described as being reactive to such a stimulus or situation, it takes place on your character's initiative.

TYPES OF ACTIONS

Reflexive, instant and extended actions represent the amount of time needed to finish a task or a series of related tasks. One type of action that can either happen quickly, in the space of time of an instant action, or over a prolonged period during an extended action, is called a contested action. In a contested action, two or more opposing characters seek to accomplish a feat first or better than each other. Compare the number of successes yielded on the draw or draws. In cases that represent aggressive actions (such as the use of a supernatural power against a victim), each success gained by the "defender" reduces the "attacker's" successes by one. If the attacker gets five successes and the defender gets four successes, then the overall outcome is a single success for the attacker. In many other cases (such as a duel of wits or competing musical performances), you will simply subtract the lesser number of successes from the greater. He who gets the most successes (or the required total first in the case of an extended task) is the winner. Arm wrestling is an example of an instant and contested action. Two characters competing to be first to win a long-distance race is an example of an extended and contested action.

The final type of action is never performed during a live-action game session - a downtime action. It can be considered what a character does "off camera," taking place between game sessions. Most of the time, characters spend their downtime actions learning new traits, improving existing ones, researching critical information, maintaining their gear, going to work or school, repairing broken equipment, and performing other feats that are vital to existence but aren't usually dramatic enough to warrant actual roleplaying time. Certain traits or Merits allow characters to take special downtime actions, which in turn have results that are described with those traits. As a general rule, downtime actions are used to flesh out characters or to explain absences in play, and do not usually allow characters to battle or otherwise seriously endanger each other. Storytellers may allow characters to attempt to harm or kill each other during downtime actions, but doing so should be rare and always requires Storyteller supervision.

COMBAT

Fighting is usually a series of instant actions, lasting however long it takes for someone to surrender or be rendered unable to fight. Each turn of combat involves a series of instant actions, one per combatant.

Combat involves a single draw per attack. The result determines whether or not your character hits, and if so how much damage he inflicts. The test pool is determined as above, but the equipment modifier depends on the weapon used. A knife is more deadly than a fist, and a gun is more deadly than a knife.

Each success gained on your attack draw represents a point of damage inflicted against a target's Health trait. When the target has no more Health left, he is unconscious or dead (depending on the type of damage done).

There are three types of damage: bashing (caused by blunt weapons such as fists or clubs; these wounds heal quickly), lethal (caused by sharp weapons such as knives or bullets; these wounds heal slowly) and aggravated (caused by devastating supernatural attacks; these wounds take a very long time to heal).

There are a number of complications involved in combat, such as a target's Defense trait (which is subtracted from any close-combat attack test pools targeted against him), penalties for armor and for hiding behind cover. Details are described in the following chapters, but the basics are simple. Draw to hit and apply any successes as damage.

Important: Unless stated otherwise in their descriptions, all supernatural powers (such as vampiric Disciplines, werewolf Gifts, etc.) have a range of line of sight and activate on their user's initiative. This applies to natural sight; supernatural, mechanical or electronic means of sight enhancement or displacement don't establish line of sight for the purpose of using supernatural powers with very few exceptions, such as vision enhancement in a dark room. Similarly, unless a supernatural power states that if affects another plane of existence, it usually only affects characters or the environment on the user's current plane of existence. This doesn't apply to powers that affect the user directly – a supernatural means of invisibility doesn't fail because someone is observing the user from another plane of existence, for instance.

MASS COMBAT

As part of large combat scenes, multiple attackers are often going to converge on a single defender. A character can normally be only subjected to a total of four attacks per turn, whether they are physical or purely supernatural. The first four attackers by Initiative rank who choose the same target may act normally, but those acting later must choose a different target for their attention. You could therefore be struck by a sorcerer's fireball, have your mind scrambled by an insidious vampire, be shot by a sniper and hit by an axe-wielding maniac in a single turn, but that would be it. Since a turn is merely three seconds long, it is exceedingly difficult to succeed in harming an individual who is already under multiple attacks - shots go astray or hit the wrong target, blades clatter harmlessly against other attackers' weapons and so on. Even the mind can only be overcome by so many stimuli at a given time. Only attacks that seek to genuinely harm an individual count towards this limit: if your ally's high initiative allows him to act first, his action to lightly prod you in the arm does not matter.

Effects that target an area or a group of individuals, especially supernatural attacks that aren't directed at a single target, are exempt from this limitation. Similarly, testing against defensive capabilities such as supernatural deterrents to attack or invisibility isn't considered an attack for the purposes of mass combat limitations. The same applies to carefully contrived circumstances at Storytellers discretion, such as firing squads and similar situations.

In terms of physical positioning of attacks, it is assumed that four close-combat attackers would each strike from the front, the back, the left and the right. The same applies to ranged attacks - getting a clear shot is vitally important, especially for moving targets. If a defender has a protective ally on his side, an attacker first has to somehow displace that guard before he can strike at his intended target. Such defenders may declare their action in combat to be purely defensive, staying in their exact position to bar any attackers. They may act as normal but it is assumed that whomever they defend can't be reached by an attacker until they've been displaced. This is particularly bothersome if defenders have a very high Initiative rank, of course. Unless the defenders somehow conceal their protégé entirely from sight, line of sight to and from him can still be established. A target enclosed by four defenders is also unable to strike out at any targets that are separated from him by his defenders.

EXAMPLE

Let's see how it looks in action.

Your character tries to shoot at a thug who just killed her friend. Your character's Dexterity is • • •, her Firearms is • •, and she's using a Glock 9mm pistol, which provides a modifier of +2. Your test pool is therefore 7.

The thug is already a couple of houses away down the block — that's generally considered medium range. A –2 penalty is applied to attacks at medium range. So, your test pool to reduced to five.

But that's not all. It's raining cats and dogs. The Storyteller decides that there's an additional –1 penalty for poor visibility. That leaves you a test pool of four.

Your draw yields a 6, for a draw total of 10 — one success. The thug is hit. He suffers one point of lethal damage to his Health. It hurts, but it's not enough to stop him and he staggers away. Your character needs to decide whether to give chase and close the distance, or try to fire again at a rapidly receding target.

One important thing to keep in mind for Storytellers is that modifiers for range and environmental causes often slow down scenes, especially with many players involved. Establish any modifiers before starting the scene; in many situations it's perfectly reasonable to omit them entirely.

THE CHANCE DRAW

One final rule: If your test pool is ever reduced to zero or lower, you can still make a "chance draw." Your character makes a wild or blind attempt to accomplish a feat where he might normally be outclassed or have little chance. Draw a single card, but you get a success only if you draw a 10. Keep redrawing: every additional ten results in an additional success, allowing you to draw again.

Note that you can't back out of a draw once you know what your opponent's defense is. This applies to all types of actions, including chance draws and any supernatural action. You may choose not to pursue your course of action in a subsequent round, but you won't know how capably your opponent may defend himself until you test him.

SUCCESSES

It's not always obvious if something you've done has been a success or a failure or whether an action attempted against you has failed. Even though you are aware that another player's character just tried to use something against your character but drew an Ace and failed, your character isn't automatically aware that this happened unless that action was utterly blatant. Common sense is the guiding principle in establishing if someone is aware they were just the subject of an action, or if their own action somehow failed. For particularly obvious methods, Storytellers may allow the defender to perform a contested challenge using his Intelligence + Investigation against the test pool used by the attacker in the failed challenge.

Example: Orlando has followed Joshua home and is using a supernatural power of deception to subtly persuade Joshua to return to Orlando's lair. Orlando's player fails his draw and Joshua is merely unconvinced of Orlando's persuasive ability – he doesn't automatically recognize that he is being influenced. Growing increasingly irritated since he didn't realize that he had failed in swaying Joshua's mind, Orlando resorts to a brutal and very obvious supernatural power to brainwash Joshua on the spot, but fails yet again. The Storyteller allows Joshua's player to make a test: his Intelligence is • • • and his Investigation is • • • • for a total of seven. Orlando's pool was 10 - his Persuasion is • • •, his Wits is • • • • and his supernatural power added another • • •. Joshua draws a nine for a total of sixteen or two successes. Orlando draws a four, for a total of fifteen or one success. Since it's a contested challenge, Orlando's single success is subtracted from Joshua's two successes, leaving Joshua with aware that something unusual is going on.

GETTING STARTED

Now that you know the basics of the Storytelling System, you can proceed to create your own character. You can judge what kinds of traits you want based on their titles (they're mostly self-explanatory), and you know that the more dots you have in a trait the better your character is when accomplishing tasks with it.

Character Creation Summary

Creating characters in Mind's Eye Theatre is a simple seven-step process. Just make a copy of the character sheet, get a pencil and begin.

1. Choose background. First, create your character's concept. To help get a handle on your character's identity and motivations, come up with a short, two- or three-word description of him/her. This usually, but not always includes some idea of a career: "nightstalking journalist," "stoic mechanic," "lost waif," "petulant yuppie" or "angry young man."

Second, choose your character's faction. If you're playing a mortal, this is relatively unimportant. He could be a cop, a private investigator or a convenience-store clerk, but he is not defined by his factional alliances. A supernatural being, however, is drawn into a world of ancient legacies in which he is judged by even his involuntary affiliations. His faction is both his strength and his curse. For details on supernatural factions, see **Requiem, Forsaken, Awakening** or other **Mind's Eye Theatre** games.

Option: Preludes. An intense Storytelling method is to roleplay mortal characters *before* they become initiated into the supernatural world. That way, their introduction to the terrible truths hiding in the shadows has more meaning and can be especially traumatic, tragic or even triumphant. If you're creating a prelude character, wait to choose his faction based on how gameplay events transform him.

2. Select Attributes, your character's innate capabilities: Prioritize the three categories (5/4/3). Your character begins with one dot in each Attribute automatically, already filled in on the character sheet. Dots spent now are in additional to these starting ones. The fifth dot in any Attribute costs two of the dots that you have to allocate.

Example: Jeff wants his character to have a Dexterity of 5. This costs him five dots. His first dot is free and his fifth one costs two.

Mental Attributes: Intelligence, Resolve, Wits
Physical Attributes: Dexterity, Stamina, Strength
Social Attributes: Composure, Manipulation, Presence
For more information, see Chapter 2: Attributes.

3. Select Skills, your character's learned capabilities: Prioritize the three categories (11/7/4). The fifth dot in any Skill costs two of the dots that you have to allocate. For more information, see Chapter 3: Skills.

Mental Skills: Academics, Computer, Crafts, Investigation, Medicine, Occult, Politics, Science
Physical Skills: Athletics, Brawl, Drive, Firearms, Larceny, Stealth, Survival, Weaponry
Social Skills: Animal Ken, Empathy, Expression, Intimidation, Persuasion, Socialize, Streetwise, Subterfuge

4. Select Skill Specialties, your character's focused areas of expertise: Take three Skill Specialties of your choice. You can assign each as you like, whether each to a separate Skill or all three to a single Skill. There is no limit to how many Specialties can be assigned to a single Skill. For more information, see Chapter 3: Skills. Specialties improve your chances of making a successful draw in your character's area of expertise.

5. Add supernatural template, based on the transformation your character undergoes: The Embrace, the First Change, the Awakening or some other supernatural

Mind's Eye Theatre

Name: _____

Player: _____

Virtue: _____

Vice: _____

Faction: _____

ATTRIBUTES

Intelligence   ●○○○○
Wits   ●○○○○
Resolve   ●○○○○

Strength   ●○○○○
Dexterity   ●○○○○
Stamina   ●○○○○

Presence   ●○○○○
Manipulation   ●○○○○
Composure   ●○○○○

MERITS

_____ ○○○○○
_____ ○○○○○
_____ ○○○○○
_____ ○○○○○
_____ ○○○○○

FLAWS

_____
_____

EQUIPMENT

_____
_____
_____
_____

Size: _____

Speed (acting/running): _____ / _____

Initiative Mod: _____

Defense: _____ Armor: _____

MENTAL SKILLS
(-3 unskilled)

Academics _____ ○○○○○
Computer _____ ○○○○○
Crafts _____ ○○○○○
Investigation _____ ○○○○○
Medicine _____ ○○○○○
Occult _____ ○○○○○
Politics _____ ○○○○○
Science _____ ○○○○○

SOCIAL SKILLS
(-1 unskilled)

Animal Ken _____ ○○○○○
Empathy _____ ○○○○○
Expression _____ ○○○○○
Intimidation _____ ○○○○○
Persuasion _____ ○○○○○
Socialize _____ ○○○○○
Streetwise _____ ○○○○○
Subterfuge _____ ○○○○○

PHYSICAL SKILLS
(-1 unskilled)

Athletics _____ ○○○○○
Brawl _____ ○○○○○
Drive _____ ○○○○○
Firearms _____ ○○○○○
Larceny _____ ○○○○○
Stealth _____ ○○○○○
Survival _____ ○○○○○
Weaponry _____ ○○○○○

HEALTH

○ ○ ○ ○ ○ ○ ○ ○ ○ ○ ○
□ □ □ □ □ □ □ □ □ □ □

WILLPOWER

○ ○ ○ ○ ○ ○ ○ ○ ○ ○ ○
□ □ □ □ □ □ □ □ □ □ □

MORALITY

○ ○ ○ ○ ○ ○ ○ ○ ○ ○ ○

Derangements: _____
_____

metamorphosis. See **Requiem, Forsaken, Awakening** or other **Mind's Eye Theatre** games for more details on these changes. (If creating a prelude character, wait to choose template based on how gameplay events transform your character.) If not playing a supernatural character, skip this step.

6. Determine advantages, traits derived from your character's Attributes: Defense (the lowest of Dexterity or Wits), Health (Stamina + Size), Initiative (Dexterity + Composure), Morality (7 for starting characters), Size (5 for most humans), Speed (Acting Speed 5, Running Speed = Strength + Dexterity +5), Willpower (Resolve + Composure), and Virtue/Vice (choose one of each; see sidebar). For more information, see Chapter 4: Advantages.

Note: Most advantages cannot be raised directly through experience points. You must instead raise the traits from which they are derived. (Morality is the exception.)

1.1 – VIRTUES AND VICES

Choose one of each. For more information, see p. 118.

Virtues
Charity, Faith, Fortitude, Hope, Justice, Prudence, Temperance

Vices
Envy, Gluttony, Greed, Lust, Pride, Sloth, Wrath

7. Select Merits, representing character enhancements and background elements: Spend 7 dots on Merits. The fifth dot in any Merit costs two of the dots that you have to allocate. Note that many Merits have prerequisites. For more information, see the sidebar and Chapter 5: Merits. You may also select Flaws at this time (see Chapter 5) or spend experience points to reflect more seasoned starting characters than normal, assuming the Storyteller is using either or both of these last two, optional rules.

1.2 – MERITS

MENTAL MERITS
Common Sense (•), Danger Sense (••), Eidetic Memory (••), Encyclopedic Knowledge (••••), Holistic Awareness (•••), Language (•), Meditative Mind (•), Unseen Sense (•••)

PHYSICAL MERITS
Ambidextrous (•••), Brawling Dodge (•), Direction Sense (•), Disarm (••), Fast Reflexes (• or ••), Fighting Finesse (••), Fighting Style: Boxing (• to •••••), Fighting Style: Kung Fu (• to •••••), Fighting Style: Two Weapons (• to •••••), Fleet of Foot (• to •••), Giant (•••••), Gunslinger (•••), Iron Stamina (• to •••), Iron Stomach (••), Natural Immunity (•), Quick Draw (•), Quick Healer (•••••), Strong Back (•), Strong Lungs (•••), Stunt Driver (•••), Toxin Resistance (••), Weaponry Dodge (•)

SOCIAL MERITS
Allies (• to •••••), Barfly (•), Contacts (• to •••••), Fame (• to •••), Inspiring (••••), Mentor (• to •••••), Resources (• to •••••), Retainer (• to •••••), Status (• to •••••), Striking Looks (•• or ••••)

SPARK OF LIFE

To round out details on your character sheet, fill in the name of the chronicle in which your character will participate (provided by the Storyteller), and the name of her group of companions (if any). List any equipment she carries, taking care to secure approval from the Storyteller for all weapons, armor or specialized gear. It is also recommended that you at least take a look at some of the questions below to help further flesh out your concept and background. Once that's finished, your character is ready to confront whatever fate awaits in the World of Darkness.

In the end, remember that characters who have absolutely everything they want, and no fear of losing it can be dull, one-dimensional and static. Need creates action, action creates conflict and conflict creates drama. Entertaining characters should always *need* something, even if it's just to hold onto what they have in the face of some (perceived) threat.

Important Questions

While not strictly necessary to the character-creation process in a mechanical sense, taking time to look over these questions can help you flesh out your character in ways that dots alone cannot. It's not necessary to address each and every one of these. Just think of them as free-associative tools to spark ideas for character development. Note that the Storyteller may have some things he wishes to add/remove regarding your character history for the sake of the chronicle, particularly regarding the supernatural section, so it's best to consult with him before answering all of these questions conclusively.

• **Coming of Age** — Where and when was your character born? What was her family like? Did she fight for attention with her siblings, or was she an only child who couldn't avoid the spotlight? How well does she get along with her family now? Who were her friends and how did she meet them? Does she still see them or have they grown apart? Does she have any rivals or lasting enemies? Did she enjoy school, and if so what did she like best? Least? What were her dreams growing up and does she still hold on to them, or have they soured with time? Did she attend college? Did she have any important mentors or role models? What were the most defining moments of her youth, for better or worse?

• **Everyday Concerns** — Where does your character live now? Does she like it there or does she wish she was somewhere else? What does she do for a living? If she doesn't have a steady job, how does she make ends meet? Does she like her job? Is she content with her current position in life or is she still climbing ambitiously? Is she married, divorced, widowed, have a steady significant other or is she still single (and does she like it or not)? Does she have kids? Who does she go to when she needs to talk about something serious? How does she get around? Does she have a tight schedule or does she have a lot of free time on her hands? What are her hobbies? Has she had any particularly memorable successes, failures, trips, romances, adventures, friendships or business ventures in the past? What were they?

• **Ethics and Ideals** — What does your character believe in more than anything? What does she utterly reject? What acts are justified by her beliefs? What acts aren't? What line will she never cross (or so she tells herself)? Are there any commonly held beliefs to which she objects? That she wishes more people would accept? Is she devout, lapsed, agnostic or atheist? What thoughts give her the most comfort when she's hurt or scared? What is she most afraid of? Why? Does she have a strict code of ethics or does she judge things on a flexible, case-by-case basis? Has she ever crossed her own lines in the past? When? Why?

• **The Supernatural** — Is your character a skeptic? A believer? Is she superstitious, and if so what superstitions does she observe? Does she (secretly) believe in any "wild" theories: aliens, bizarre JFK conspiracies, Atlantis, Bigfoot? Has she ever actually encountered the supernatural, or at least thinks she has? If so, was she awed, frightened, angry, curious, overjoyed or something else entirely? If she is truly aware of the existence of the supernatural, does she still try to lead some semblance of a normal life, or has she given it up entirely to pursue forbidden knowledge (or the destruction of the unnatural)? Does she feel blessed to know the "truth" or is her knowledge considered a curse? Where does she think these uncanny beings and their powers come from — divine grace, demonic pacts, evolutionary advantages, alien experimentation or something else? Does the thought of somehow being turned into a supernatural being disgust and horrify her, or does she secretly find it somewhat intriguing (or maybe even appealing)?

OPTIONAL RULE: ADVANCED CHARACTERS

For experienced characters, the Storyteller might choose to award experience points that may be spent before play begins. Although the Storyteller can award any amount of experience points he desires with this option, the following standards give an idea of the power levels that can be achieved. Additional experience points don't apply to anything marked as available only during creation: although they are added during character creation, they denote experience gained during a character's life-span.

Seasoned characters: 35 points

Expert characters: 75 points

Heroic characters: 100 experience points

Note that when you spend experience points and want to go up more than one dot in a trait, you need to pay for all the intervening levels. That is, if you go from • • • to • • • • • in an Attribute, it costs you 45 experience points (20 to go from 3 to 4, plus 25 to go from 4 to 5).

Merits are a special case. The cost of a Merit depends on whether it is a graduated Merit or a simple Merit. Graduated Merits, like Fighting Style: Boxing, must be purchased one dot at a time, since each dot confers individual benefits. So for example if you want to purchase a • • • • Fighting Style: Boxing Merit from scratch, it costs you a total of 20 experience points (2 for the first point, 4 to go from 1 to 2, 6 to go from 2 to 3, and 8 to go from 3 to 4).

On the other hand, simple Merits like Inspiring are purchased all at once, since they only confer one benefit at their full value, and cannot be purchased one dot at a time. So if you want to purchase Inspiring (a • • • • Merit), you must spend a total of 8 experience points (4 x 2 = 8). This means that a • • • • Inspiring Merit is significantly less expensive than a • • • • Fighting Style: Boxing Merit, but that's because the Fighting Style: Boxing Merit confers increasing benefits (, while the Inspiring Merit only confers one benefit and cannot be purchased at lower levels. If multiple variants of the same Merit exist, for instance a two-dot and a four-dot version of Striking Looks, they are bought at simple Merit cost. Getting the more expensive version of the Merit after buying the cheaper version first requires you to buy the four-dot version from scratch.

1.3 – EXPERIENCE POINT COSTS	
Trait	**Experience Point Cost**
Attribute	New dots x 5
Skill	New dots x 3
Skill Specialty	3 points
Merit	New dots x 2
Morality	New dots x 3

Example of Character Creation

Meg plans to participate in Ben's **Mind's Eye Theatre** game. Ben tells her that the chronicle will focus on the revelation of several powerful supernatural beings in the midst of a sleepy college town, and what some ordinary people do when they learn about this dire threat. The mood will primarily be one of quiet horror, as opposed to more of an over-the-top splatter feel. Characters will have to contend with supernatural threats, but also face many mundane concerns and challenges as well. Ben therefore suggests that Meg develop a character who is mostly an ordinary person, but who is either open to the possibility of the supernatural or has had an actual brush with the unusual in her past, so that she will be predisposed to investigate strange occurrences rather than simply dismiss them.

Ben hands Meg a copy of the character sheet, and Meg spends a few minutes brainstorming some ideas before she starts turning them into a fully formed character concept.

STEP ONE: CONCEPT

Meg's first responsibility is to come up with a concept for her character. She decides that she wants to a young, idealistic medical student from a prominent family, who is generally very rational and scientific but who is also deeply religious, and has a very private love of fantasy and science fiction that keeps her imagination strong and open-minded.

Not wanting to name her character after herself, Meg thinks for a while and then settles on the name Rebecca Dunn. It sounds very proper and respectable to her, which makes her happy as it reinforces the character's wealthy past. At the last minute, Meg decides that Rebecca often goes by the nickname Becca, which is a nice balance to her very formal name.

STEP TWO: ATTRIBUTES

Meg must now prioritize and assign Becca's Attributes. Based on her concept, Meg decides that Mental Attributes are Becca's strong suit, so she sets them as primary. She wants Becca to be likeable and have a decent bedside manner, so Meg selects Social Attributes as her secondary category. This leaves Physical Attributes as tertiary, which suits Meg just fine. She sees Becca as a classic bookworm, not lacking in any physical category but not particularly good at any of them, either. Now it's time to paint a more precise picture of what makes Becca the way she is.

As her primary category, Meg has five dots to allocate among Becca's Mental Attributes. As befits a medical student, she decides that Becca is extremely smart, so allocates three dots to Intelligence, raising the total to 4. She also sees Becca as having rather a good grasp of her surroundings and fairly quick reaction time, so she puts her last two dots in Wits, raising it to 3. That leaves her with nothing to put in Resolve, giving her a rating of 1 in that Attribute, which doesn't make Meg too happy. She wants Becca to be rather timid, but this is a little low for her tastes. She makes a note to improve Resolve during play and moves on to the next Attribute category.

With four dots to assign to Social Attributes, Meg decides that Becca has a good Presence. Although she has a fairly average appearance, she has a bright, cheerful personality that allows her to make friends easily and to relate to other people naturally. She puts two dots in Presence, raising it to a 3. Given her medical training and her natural sense of calm, Becca gets a good Composure rating as well, putting two dots there as well. That gives her a 3. Becca has seen a lot of gruesome stuff and doesn't lose her cool easily. That leaves her with nothing to put in Manipulation, which Meg thinks is just fine. Becca is very nice and makes a good impression on others, but she never developed the finer social skills necessary to really get her way with other people.

Finally, Meg turns her attention to the Physical category to finish off her Attributes. She decides that Becca keeps herself in respectable shape, but with her studies and her other obligations she never seems to have time to do as much working out as she'd like. She therefore decides to allocate one dot to each Physical Attribute, making Becca thoroughly average across the board, with a total of 2 in each of Strength, Dexterity and Stamina.

STEP THREE: SKILLS

Like Attributes, Skills must also be prioritized and chosen. Meg decides to stay with the same prioritization as she used for Attributes, placing Mental as primary, Social as secondary and Physical as tertiary. Becca has stuck with her strengths as she goes through life, developing those Skills that come most easily to her and neglecting those with which she has little natural aptitude.

With 11 dots to assign in Mental Skills, Meg tries to imagine what Becca would have learned in her life so far. The most obvious choices are Medicine and Science, reflecting Becca's scholarly inclination. Meg puts three dots each in Medicine and Science. While not a real authority yet, Becca is still a well-educated young woman, as well as a very promising doctor-in-training. She puts two dots in Academics to reflect liberal arts courses taken along the way. Although primarily a medical student, Becca enjoys reading in a wide range of fields, and Meg decides that she has a particular soft spot for poetry and the classics. Another two dots go into Computer. Always a bit shy, Becca has been into computers since an early age and knows her way around a lot of online resources. Her last dot goes to Investigation, reflecting Becca's natural curiosity and analytical mind more than any real formal training.

Looking at the list of Social Skills, Meg decides how to spend her seven dots. Three dots go into Empathy. Becca is a genuinely kind and caring person, and has an excellent rapport with her patients. Another two dots go into Persuasion, reflecting that while Becca isn't naturally skilled at manipulating others, she can make a convincing argument when she has logic on her side. A dot goes into Animal Ken, reflecting Becca's minor affinity with animals as well as people. While no veterinarian, she used to ride when she was young and still likes animals. After some thought, Meg puts Becca's last dot in Expression. When Ben asks how the shy Becca expresses herself, Meg explains that she has had a diary for years, and maintains a blog as well, where she keeps her own private poetry and other thoughts. She'd never stand up in front of a crowd and do a reading, but she's not bad with the written word.

Finally, Meg needs to assign four dots to the Physical group. She decides that Becca takes weekly self-defense classes at college and still goes running when she can find the time. She decides the former would equate to about two dots in Brawl. Though no combat powerhouse, Becca takes her classes seriously, which make her a bit more formidable than her small stature might suggest. Her irregular running schedule and general fitness regimen gives her one dot in Athletics, which Meg decides is a suitable level of aptitude. Last, Meg decides that Becca used to go camping with her family on vacation every year when she was growing up. She therefore puts her last point in Survival. Becca should be able to find her way out of the woods if she must, provided nothing chases her....

STEP FOUR: SKILL SPECIALTIES

Now that Meg has assigned Becca's Skill dots, she needs to decide where to place her three Skill Specialties. Glancing over the Skills she's chosen, she tries to imagine which would be the most refined and singles out Medicine, Science and Academics. Focusing on Medicine first, Meg decides that Becca has done a lot of work with first aid and is more than qualified in it, so she writes that down as "Medicine (First Aid)." Naturally, she favors biology out of all the scientific fields, so writes that down as "Science (Biology)." Last, Meg decides that Becca really does have a deep love for poetry — while she hasn't studied the subject as formally as she'd like, she has good memory for it and dives into it eagerly. She notes this as "Academics (Poetry)." While it might not come up a whole lot during play, she thinks it expresses her character well, and Ben agrees.

Had she chosen to do so, Meg could have assigned more than one specialty to a single Skill. For example, if Becca was also a physics prodigy, she could have chosen the Specialties "Science (Biology and Physics)" to represent her aptitude for both disciplines.

STEP FIVE: SUPERNATURAL TEMPLATE

Since Ben is running a game focused on mortals and not supernatural beings, he informs Meg that she can skip this step. Becca might very well suffer some sort of supernatural transformation later, but for the purposes of character creation it's not necessary, so they move on.

STEP SIX: MERITS

Meg must next spend seven dots on Merits. Looking over the list of possibilities, she tries to find those that reflect Becca's life and talents. While she cannot access her full trust fund yet (she's not 25), Meg decides that coming from a wealthy family, Becca's parents gave her money to invest at an early age and she has managed it very sensibly. She puts three dots into Resources. She also informs Ben that she may purchase more dots of this Merit later when Becca comes of age, reflecting her gaining full access to her fund. Since that will make her very wealthy, she asks Ben if it's all right, and after talking to her about what form her finances take, how long it will be before she gets her trust fund in game, and how she plans on using her Resources, he approves the plan.

Meg next looks to see if she can find any other Merits that stand out to her, and decides that Eidetic Memory is a good choice. Becca has trained herself to absorb and retain information with near-perfect clarity, a talent that's bound to come in handy as the chronicle progresses. That Merit costs two dots, leaving her with two more dots to spend. Meg selects Language: Spanish at one dot. Becca volunteers at a free clinic from time to time and has picked up some Spanish from the patients there. She'd like to be more proficient at the language, but has another idea and need her last dot to fulfill it. Meg decides to purchase Meditative Mind for Becca, only she tells Ben that Becca doesn't quite meditate in the conventional sense, but relaxes by writing in her diary, which clears her mind and lets her focus.

Looking back, Meg sees where to use those four remaining experience points. On raising Becca's Language: Spanish Merit from one dot to two, making her fluent. Meg envisioned a quick study like Becca would be fully conversant after working at the free clinic for a while. A Merit costs the new dots times two, so that neatly accounts for her last four experience points (2 x 2 = 4).

Meg hands her sheet to Ben and explains the purchases she's made, and he approves them, feeling they all contribute to Becca's emerging personality.

Optional Step: Starting Experience Points

Ben does, however, inform Meg that he has chosen to use the optional rule allowing players to begin the game with a certain amount of experience points, to reflect that their characters are slightly more capable than usual starting characters. Ben tells her that she has 20 experience points to spend on improving Becca's traits, and shows her the cost chart on p. 32 so she can figure out how to spend her experience points properly. Those experience points are not considered part of normal character creation and thus can't be spent on Merits marked as creation only, for instance.

After a few moments, Meg announces that she would like to raise Becca's Resolve from one to two dots; she had wanted to have a higher Resolve for Becca, anyway. Since raising an Attribute costs the new dots times five, this change costs her 10 experience points (2 x 5 = 10). She then purchases two more Skill Specialties to represent more of Becca's natural aptitudes, buying "Medicine (Emergency Surgery)" — Becca is studying to be a trauma surgeon — and "Expression (Diary)" — she is very comfortable writing in her diary or her private blog. Each new Specialty costs three experience points, so those cost her another six, for a total of 16 spent so far.

Unsure of what to do with her last four experience points, Meg holds onto them for now.

STEP SEVEN: ADVANTAGES

Once Becca's dots have been assigned, Meg must now determine her character's advantages. Adding her Resolve and Composure, she records a Willpower score of 5 on her character sheet. Her Morality score starts at the standard 7. Meg chooses Faith as Becca's Virtue (given her deep belief in the goodness of all people) and Envy as her Vice (deeply shy, she sometimes feels ignored by others and is occasionally jealous of their accomplishments).

Adding her Size factor of 5 to her Stamina, Meg determines that Becca has seven dots of Health, and draws a dark vertical line to the right of the seventh box on the Health Chart. Combining her Dexterity with her Composure, she determines Initiative to be 5, and notes her Defense of 2, the lower of her Dexterity and Wits scores. Finally, she notes the standard Acting Speed of 5, and then adds her Strength + Dexterity + 5 to find her Running Speed, which she records as 9.

If those four remaining experience points alter any of Becca's traits, Meg will come back to refigure any advantages that are influenced.

SPARK OF LIFE

Meg has a pretty good grasp of her character at this point, at least conceptually, but the specific details of appearance and relationships are still a bit hazy. She decides that Becca comes from an upper-middle-class family, but grew up in an inner-city environment. Her parents were both surgeons and drove Becca to succeed in school. Despite their wealth and talent, they chose to work in local clinics and had Becca attend school in the neighborhood, making sure she never pitied or looked down on her less fortunate neighbors or classmates. Though she never quite got over her shyness from being the outsider in the neighborhood, Becca flourished academically and was eventually accepted by a top college, where she's been studying for the past three years. She also learned to find the good in life's challenges, and developed an abiding faith reinforced by weekly church services, which she still attends even while at school.

As the chronicle begins, Meg decides that Becca has fallen into something of a rut. Although she's doing well in college, between her classes, her studies and her volunteer hours at the clinic, she seldom has time to get out and do anything else. If even the slightest hint of a suitably mysterious occurrence presents itself, Becca is likely to investigate enthusiastically. (Of course, given what Ben plans to unleash on the unsuspecting town, things are likely to become a bit more complicated than that, but Meg knows that's half the fun....) Meg also decides to make Ben's job easier by declaring that Becca is a member of several different study groups as well as a few campus organizations, which means she will likely be able sit down with other players and work out a few relationships before play begins.

Meg decides that costumes will involve relatively upscale clothes, always in subdued colors. Despite Becca's sunny personality, she doesn't like being the center of attention, so tends to choose styles and colors that allow her to blend in. Meg also makes a note to find a white lab coat at a uniform store or costume shop, because sooner or later she'll want to portray Becca coming off a shift at the clinic or heading into the lab. For minor touches, Meg decides to pull her hair back in a loose bun and find a delicate pair of reading glasses, to help suggest Becca's studious nature. As for props, Meg finds a shoulder bag to carry Becca's ever-present textbooks, pens and notepads, as well a suitably worn-looking journal to act as Becca's beloved diary. Thinking about body language and voice patterns, Meg decides Becca talks softly, generally keeps her head down slightly, takes soft steps and keeps her arms close to her body — classic wallflower habits. That is, unless she talks to someone one on one, in which case she smiles a lot and opens up her posture to be noticeably more friendly.

Now that Meg has a better idea of who Becca is and how she will approach the characters, Ben hands her a survey to find out what she looks forward to in the chronicle. (See the Storytelling chapter, p. 264, for more on surveys.) Meg looks it over and eventually assigns 10 to mysteries and suspense, 7 to politics and intrigue, 3 to action/adventure, 6 to personal subplots, and 5 to supernatural elements. This tells Ben that as a player, Meg really enjoys solving puzzles and unraveling mysteries, is very interested in intrigue, likes personal subplots, is looking for an even balance between the supernatural and the mundane, and isn't really looking for a lot of combat or other physical action. Ben files this information away for later, so he can write suitable subplots and story hooks that will grab Meg's attention and keep her immersed in the game.

Becca is ready to delve into the shadowy mysteries of the ominous World of Darkness.

Glossary

The following is a summary of general Storytelling System terms used throughout this book. These explanations help you understand the rules that follow. It does not include entries for all traits (the qualifiers used to help define your character) used in the game. For any of those, refer to the index, p. 344.

Italics denote a word with a separate glossary entry. Refer to the index for page references for complete descriptions in the text.

10 Again: A draw of a 10 is re-drawn in an attempt to achieve more *successes*. Add the result of the second card to the first, unless it is an ace, which counts as zero. Do not draw again if the second card is also a 10.

action: A task that takes all of a character's time and attention. Storytelling measures *instant actions* (one to three seconds, taking place within a single *turn*) and *extended actions*, taking longer (duration determined by the Storyteller). Also, there are *reflexive actions*, which take no time and do not prevent a character from performing another action within a turn, and *contested actions*, in which two or more characters compete in a task or for a single goal.

advantage: A character trait such as *Health* or Willpower that usually represents abilities derived from other traits. Advantages are measured in *dots* and sometimes in *points*.

aggravated (damage): A *damage* point that inflicts a grievous or supernatural *wound*. Vampires suffer aggravated damage from fire; werewolves suffer it from silver. Mortals might suffer aggravated damage from a dire supernatural power such as a lightning bolt summoned from the sky by a witch. Aggravated wounds normally heal at a rate of one point per week.

Attribute: A character trait representing innate capabilities, Mental, Physical and Social. An Attribute is added to a *Skill* (or another Attribute in certain cases) to determine your basic *test pool* for a task.

bashing (damage): A *damage* point that inflicts a blunt or bruising *wound*, such as from a fist or a baseball bat. Bashing wounds normally heal at a rate of one point per 15 minutes.

chance draw: Whenever *modifiers* reduce your *test pool* to zero, you must make a chance draw of a single card. Unlike a normal draw, a chance draw succeeds only on a result of 10. Worse, a result of 1 (ace) causes a *dramatic failure*.

close combat: Attacks that involve hand-to-hand or weapon fighting. Such attacks use the Strength *Attribute* for their test pools. Characters apply their *Defense* against close-combat attacks.

contested action: Two or more characters compete in a task or for a single goal. The one who gets the most successes wins. Contested actions can be *instant* or *extended actions*.

damage: The points inflicted against a character's *Health* or an object's *Structure*, rated as *bashing*, *lethal* or *aggravated*. One point of damage inflicts one *wound*.

Defense: An *advantage* trait determined by the lowest of Dexterity or Wits. Characters can penalize a *close-combat* opponent's attack by subtracting their Defense from his *test pool*.

degeneration: Characters who violate their ethics lose dots of *Morality*. Degeneration can cause a character to acquire a *derangement*.

derangement: Characters whose *Morality* dots are lost through *degeneration* or who suffer horrible psychological trauma can acquire a derangement. Some derangements are classified as "mild," meaning they hinder the character mainly by plaguing his conscience. Others are "severe," often cases of clinical insanity. Derangements caused by degeneration can be healed by restoring lost Morality dots.

dot: The incremental measurement of a permanent trait. Most traits range from 1 to 5 dots, but some (such as Willpower) range from 1 to 10, and others (*Health*) can go higher.

draw: The act of a drawing a single card to determine the success or failure of an action, by adding the value of that card to the character's *test pool* and comparing it against *standard difficulty*.

draw total: The total value generated by adding a character's *test pool* + the value of a single card, which is compared to *standard difficulty* in order to determine how successful an action is.

Durability: A trait representing an object's hardness, based on the material from which it is made (wood has less Durability than metal, for example). Durability is measured in *dots*. An attack's *damage* must exceed Durability before the object is harmed.

equipment: Characters can improve their chances of succeeding in a task by using the right equipment. This benefit is represented by *modifiers* to a *test pool*, depending on the equipment used and its quality.

experience points: Points awarded by the Storyteller at the end of a game session and story, used to purchase new traits or to boost the dots of existing ones. See p. 32 for costs.

extended action: A task that takes time to accomplish. Players draw to accumulate *successes* during phases of the task, succeeding once they have acquired the total needed.

failure: Drawing an ace or failing to meet the standard difficulty is a failure — the character does not succeed at his task.

hand: The Storytelling System uses a hand of 10 cards to represent the element of chance. Use cards 2 to 10, with an ace representing a 1, meaning a failure on the initial draw or simply nothing if drawn on a Ten Again.

Health: An *advantage* trait, determined by adding Stamina + Size. Health is measured in *dots* and *points*. (See also *wound*.)

Initiative: An *advantage* trait representing the character's ability to respond to sudden surprise, determined by adding Dexterity + Composure. A character's Initiative helps him get a high standing in the *Initiative roster*.

Initiative roster: The list that determines when each character can perform an action within a turn. For each character that is not surprised, a player draws a card and adds his character's *Initiative* to the result. Whoever gets the highest number acts first, followed by the character with the next highest, and so on until everyone who can has acted that turn. Initiative is usually drawn once per scene.

instant action: A task that takes place within a single *turn*. A character can perform only one *action* per turn, unless he has a *Merit* or power that lets him do otherwise.

lethal (damage): A *damage* point that inflicts a sharp, slashing or piercing *wound*, such as from a sword or bullet. Lethal wounds normally heal at a rate of one point per two days.

Merit: A character trait representing enhancements or elements of a character's background, such as his allies or influence. Merits are measured in *dots*, but are not always used to determine test pools. Instead, they represent increasing degrees of quality or quantity concerning their subject.

modifiers: *Test pools* are often modified by a number of factors, from bonuses (adding points) for *equipment* or ideal conditions to penalties (subtracting points) for poor conditions.

Morality: An *advantage* trait representing a character's moral, ethical and even psychological standing and wellbeing. Morality is measured in *dots*, which can be lost to *degeneration* by performing unethical or criminal acts.

Narrator: A member of the *Storytelling staff* who assists the *Storyteller* in running a game. Narrators are generally limited to rules adjudication and do not have the authority to make broad decisions regarding ongoing plotlines, although this may depend on the Narrator in question.

point: A trait expended to gain certain effects, such as a Willpower point or a measurement of *damage* or *Health*. The amount of points available to spend is equal to the parent trait's *dots*. Spent points are regained over time or through certain actions.

reflexive action: An instinctual task that takes no appreciable time, such as reacting to surprise or noticing something out of the corner of your eye. Performing a reflexive action does not prevent a character from performing another *action* within a *turn*. Some reflexive actions can be performed even if a character hasn't reached her Initiative rank yet and are usually marked as such.

ranged combat: An attack that sends a projectile of some sort at a target, whether it's a bullet fired or a knife thrown. Such attacks use the Dexterity *Attribute* for their test pools. Characters' *Defense* cannot normally be used against firearm attacks, although targets can penalize an opponent's accuracy by going prone or taking cover.

Resistance: Characters can resist others' attempts to socially sway them, physically grapple them or even mentally dominate them. Whenever applying such resistance requires a character's full attention, it's performed as a *contested action*, but more often it's a *reflexive action*, allowing the target to also perform an action that turn.

scene: A division of time based on drama, such as the end of one plot point and the beginning of another. Whenever a character leaves a location where a dramatic event has occurred, or when a combat has ended, the current scene usually ends and the next one begins.

Skill: A character trait representing learned ability or knowledge. Added to an *Attribute* to determine a character's basic *test pool* for a task.

Specialty: An area of *Skill* expertise in which a character excels. Whenever a Specialty applies to a character's task, one point is added to his player's *test pool*. There's no limit to the number of Specialties that you can assign to a single Skill.

standard difficulty: The number that your *draw total* must equal or exceed in order to be successful. It is generally assumed to be 10, though special circumstances or Storyteller discretion may adjust the number.

Storyteller: The "director" or "editor" of the interactive story told by the players. The Storyteller creates the plot and with the help of *Narrators* often portrays many of the supporting characters, allies and villains, with which players' characters interact. In large games, there may be multiple Storytellers, in which case individual ones may be responsible for only certain storylines or specific aspects of the game.

Storytelling staff: The collective group of Storytellers and Narrators who are responsible for running a game.

Structure: A trait representing an object's integrity, determined by adding *Durability* and *Size*. Structure is measured in *dots*, which can be lost due to *damage*. Unlike the wounds of a living creature, an object does not heal damaged Structure; it must be repaired.

success: Every interval of five by which your *draw total* equals or exceeds the *standard difficulty* of 10 equals one success. (Exception: A *chance draw* must draw a 10 to succeed.) In an *instant action*, a player must draw at least one success for his character to accomplish a task. In an *extended action*, the number of successes required — accumulated over a series of draws — depends on the task. In an attack draw, each success indicates one point of *damage*.

test pool: The number to which a draw is added to determine failure or success (and degree of success) for a character's action. Test pools are usually determined by adding an *Attribute* to a *Skill*, plus any relevant *equipment* and/or *modifiers*.

troupe: Your gaming group of friends.

turn: A three-second period of time. *Instant actions* are observed in turns. Combat (a series of instant actions) is observed in consecutive turns as each combatant tries to overcome opponents.

wound: A marked *Health* point, denoting an injury from *damage*. *Bashing* wounds are marked with a "/", *lethal* wounds with an "X" and *aggravated* wounds with a "*." (See *Health*.)

Chapter 2: Attributes

People have the inherent capacity to act, behave and think. We can perform actions and have intuitive talents such as running, theorizing and persuading others. So does your character. His basic, fundamental capabilities are represented with Attributes, which are the foundation of all the acts that he performs. These traits are classified into three categories — Mental, Physical and Social — and are drawn to determine how well your character accomplishes efforts in the game.

Mental Attributes suggest how insightful, clever and determined your character is. They are Intelligence, Wits and Resolve.

Physical Attributes indicate how strong, graceful and enduring your character is. They are Strength, Dexterity and Stamina.

Social Attributes determine how imposing, magnetic and dignified your character is. They are Presence, Manipulation and Composure.

The Attributes of ordinary people are rated from 1 to 5. It's possible for someone to have more dots, but these individuals are typically beyond the human ken, partially or fully a part of the mysterious supernatural world. Perhaps they're touched by spirits or born to a legacy of service to unseen beings.

Your character, even as a mortal human, automatically starts with one dot in each Attribute. These dots are already filled in on your character sheet.

When your character performs an action, the Attribute most appropriate to the effort is referenced. If he tries to remember what he read during library research last week, you look to his Intelligence dots. If he tries to jump a chasm, you check his Strength. If he tries to make a good first impression on a group of people, you apply his Presence score.

Your character's dots are usually tallied as part of a test pool. Attributes are sometimes combined for a draw to see if an action can be accomplished, but they are more often combined with Skills. The Storyteller will tell you what Attributes are applicable to your character's actions, and what draws you can make. In general, the three classes of Attributes are used based on the circumstances. One of each of the Mental, Physical and Social traits has bearing on a different kind of action, as outlined in the boxed text.

What can we know? What are we all? Poor silly half-brained things peering out at the infinite, with the aspirations of angels and the instincts of beasts.

— Sir Arthur Conan Doyle, The Stark Munro Letters

2.1 – ATTRIBUTE CATEGORIES

Use	Mental	Physical	Social
Power	Intelligence	Strength	Presence
Finesse	Wits	Dexterity	Manipulation
Resistance	Resolve	Stamina	Composure

Power is the degree of effect that your character has on others and his surroundings. The higher his score, the smarter, more potent or more imposing he is. Intelligence, Strength and Presence therefore apply when your character seeks to force himself on his environment.

Finesse is a measure of your character's capacity to interact with the world and influence others. The higher his score, the craftier, more delicate and more influential he is. Wits, Dexterity and Manipulation have bearing when your character tries to anticipate and react to his environment, and to coordinate others.

Resistance indicates how well your character copes with influences from both without and within that might affect him adversely. The higher his score the more staunch, sturdy or dignified he is. Resolve, Stamina and Composure apply when your character responds to coercion, injury and influence. Resolve tests his ability to resist efforts to direct his mind, Stamina helps him shrug off physical trauma, and Composure helps him recover from horrifying experiences or social tension and still maintain control.

2.2 – ATTRIBUTE DOTS

Attributes are rated 1 to 5 for ordinary people, and each score suggests the degree of your character s raw capability in that area.

Dots	Talent
•	Poor. Unexercised, unpracticed or inept.
••	Average. The result of occasional effort or application.
•••	Good. Regular practice or effort, or naturally talented.
••••	Exceptional. Frequently applied, tested and honed, or naturally gifted.
•••••	Outstanding. The peak of normal human capability. Continuously exercised or naturally blessed.

Normally, it's not possible for a character to have zero dots in an Attribute as that suggests the absolute vacancy of any capability in the trait in question. A person could be physically, mentally or socially disabled or crippled, but those conditions are reflected with Flaws (see p. 311), not zero-rated Attributes.

Just about the only instance in which an Attribute can be reduced to zero (and usually temporarily) is by supernatural means. A spell, curse or affliction is imposed on your character that eliminates all of the dots in his trait. In these cases, no draw can be made at all whenever the Attribute in question would normally be called for. So, if your character is afflicted with total loss of bodily control (zero Dexterity), you make no draws for any situation that calls for Dexterity in a test pool, even if he has dots in a pertinent Skill or have access to tools that would be helpful. Your character can't even hope to aim a gun or direct his movements. In essence, the action fails outright.

Thus, you don't usually check Strength when your character is challenged in a social situation, because brute force doesn't apply where Composure (social recovery) is concerned. Similarly, Dexterity doesn't typically have bearing when interpreting a foreign language. That act calls upon the power of the mind and is the purview of Intelligence.

When creating your character, you must prioritize his capability with the Attribute categories. His Mental, Physical and Social traits must be given primary, secondary and tertiary emphasis. If you want your character to be active and hardy, Physical traits might be primary. If his ability to react to and deal with people is nearly but not quite as important, Social Attributes could be secondary. That leaves Mental traits as tertiary. He's not the sharpest tack in the box, or life just hasn't demanded that he exercise his cognitive potential.

You get to allocate five dots among your character's primary Attributes, four dots among his secondary Attributes, and three dots among his tertiary Attributes. The dots available to each category can be distributed among its three Attributes as evenly or unevenly as you like. So, you might decide to apply three dots to your character's Strength, one to his Dexterity and one to his Stamina. That's all five of his primary class allocated. Two of your four Social dots might go to each of Manipulation and Composure. And, you might assign one of each of your three Mental dots to Intelligence, Wits and Resolve.

Remember that the fifth dot in any Attribute costs two of the dots you have to spend at character creation. Each Attribute also gets one free dot automatically before you start assigning anything.

Attribute Descriptions

The following is a breakdown of what each Attribute entails and how it may be applied. Some tasks rely on your character's Attribute dots alone and these traits are drawn or even combined to determine how well he performs certain tasks. Such feats are typically ones any unimpaired person can perform, such as holding one's breath or lifting objects, and don't require any special training or expertise. The Attribute tasks detailed here are comprehensive. They're activities that rely exclusively on inherent talent (Attributes) alone, rather than on the learned capabilities of Skills (see p. 57). It's therefore not recommended that you invent other Attribute tasks during play; almost all other actions that characters can perform involve a combination of an Attribute and Skill.

Mental

INTELLIGENCE

Everyone else had long since quit due to eyestrain or fatigue, but Rebecca carried on, tracing and erasing patterns in her diary, trying to figure out exactly what the strange symbols on the parchment meant. A jumble of scattered papers on the desk in front of her displayed everything from historical data to occult carvings to last week's weather report.

Tony picked one up, frowning. "Becca, what is all this? It looks like you just circled stuff at random."

With a triumphant sigh, Rebecca leaned back in her chair, gesturing for the others to approach. "Not random," she said, taking the papers and laying them out in a precise array that transformed seemingly haphazard scribbles into a detailed map. It looked like the layout of the town, but from a very long time ago. "I knew they had to go together. I just hadn't found the right order." She squinted down at the lines, new possibilities clearly forming in her mind.

"Now the question is, why would a vagrant have been carrying a parchment map of town from two centuries ago?"

The raw power of the mind. Cognitive capacity. The inherent capability to digest, comprehend and remember information — and to learn more. Intelligence is a direct measure of how smart your character is. She may be dull-minded or have narrow-vision. She may be book-smart, or she may simply be able to grasp concepts, interpret situations and solve problems quickly. Intelligence is valued by planners, theorists, scholars, white-collar employees and leaders.

MEMORIZING AND REMEMBERING

Test Pool: Intelligence + Composure

Action: Reflexive

Committing something such as a name or a facial feature to memory can require an Intelligence + Composure draw, as can recalling that information later. The more calm your characters is the more likely it is that she retains the knowledge. If the information is familiar to your character or referenced often, no draw is required unless she's nervous or under pressure (Storyteller's discretion). If the information is brief or simple, such as a license-plate number, no modifiers may apply. The Storyteller may impose bonuses or penalties under various circumstances. Memorizing or recalling something at one's leisure offers a +1 to +3 bonus. A common name such as "Tim" is easy to memorize (+3). Extensive information, details studied quickly or distractedly, or unusual or strange facts such as foreign names are harder to remember (-1 to -5). Features witnessed hours ago are easy to recall (+1), while those observed days, weeks or years ago are harder to conjure up (-1 to -5).

Storytellers can make memory draws on players' behalf so the veracity of information called forth is never certain. Another option is to forego draws if a *player* remembers (or does not remember) the details.

Draw Results

Failure: In one ear and out the other, or your character draws a blank.

Success: The details are at your character's disposal.

WITS

Sean stopped short. His companions kept walking, apparently unaware of the dark flicker that had followed them from window to window as they walked by the old house. Not too long ago, he might have kept walking too, but that was before his world had been turned upside-down by those things. A keen observer, Sean had started paying more attention to the sights at the edge of his vision, to the sounds just below the noises of everyday life. What he learned frightened him more and more, but he never turned away. He had to do something.

Sean looked straight up at the old house. Had a pale face ducked back into the shadows? He was sure it had, and what's more, that glinting eyes still peered back at him from the darkness. "I see you," Sean said softly.

As he walked away, the curtain flurried as something moved from the window.

The ability to think on one's feet, under pressure or duress, without letting them see you sweat. Wits also encompasses an eye for detail, the ability to absorb what's going on in the environment, and to react to events. It might mean recognizing that the temperature in a room slowly drops, that a landscape painting incorporates a disguised human face, or that a trap is about to be sprung. Wits involves the powers of perception and response. Your character may be oblivious, dumbfounded, quick-eyed or wary. The trait is useful for entrepreneurs, charlatans, athletes, tacticians, lawyers and criminals.

DEFENSE

Derived Traits: Wits or Dexterity
Action: Reflexive

The lowest of your character's Wits or Dexterity is used to determine his Defense trait, which is subtracted from incoming Brawl, Weaponry and throwing attacks. See p. 215 for more information

PERCEPTION

Test Pool: Wits + Composure or a relevant Skill in place of Composure (see the "Skill-Based Perception" sidebar)
Action: Reflexive

Sometimes subtle or instantaneous actions occur around your character, testing his powers of observation. A shape races by. Someone hides behind nearby bushes. Maybe your character recognizes these events. Maybe he goes oblivious to them. Alternatively, a single unusual phenomenon is in his presence, and he may (or may not) recognize it without trying. Maybe a piece of furniture is out of place in a room or a door is unlocked when it should be locked.

The Storyteller typically knows when something unusual or out of place occurs in your character's vicinity, and may call for a reflexive Wits + Composure draw for your character to recognize it. Such observation almost always occurs without your character intentionally searching or looking (that's the province of "Investigation," p. 64). Perception draws simply check to see if your character instinctually notices what's going on. In many cases, the Storyteller may make perception draws for you, so that you remain as aware or unaware of what's going on as your character. Other times, he may leave perception cards at a scene or on an object. Making a successful draw allows you to flip over the card and read the information on the other side.

Draw Results

Failure: Your character notices nothing amiss or out of place.

Success: Your character recognizes that something has happened. If he wants to learn more, Investigation draws are called for. See "Investigation," p. 64.

Skill-Based Perception

During the course of play, you might be called upon draw to see if your character notices something in her vicinity, or that some detail is unusual. The Storyteller can always ask for a Wits + Composure draw to see if your character is aware of her surroundings, but there are other options. Perhaps more indicative of your character s life experience and training is combining Wits + a relevant Skill to determine if your character spots something amiss. It could be Wits + Survival to realize that a predatory animal lurks nearby in the woods. Or it might be Wits + Academics to notice that the books on a shelf aren t arranged alphabetically, but by date of publication. Sure, Wits + Composure might accomplish the same result, but if your character has some capability with a Skill that s more reliable than her Composure alone, the Storyteller might allow you to draw Wits plus that Skill, instead.

As a general rule of thumb, the highest of Composure or the Skill is used for the draw, along with Wits. While the stalked character in the example above might be a novice woodsman (Survival 1), he could still have decent Composure (say, 3). The latter of the two is drawn, because the character s inherent senses and alertness compensate for his green status in the wilds.

Bear in mind that dots in some Skills or under some circumstances simply don t matter, and Wits + Composure always applies. For example, if a gun lies in the corner of a room, having the Firearms Skill doesn t help spot it. Anyone who gets a successful Wits + Composure draw can see it.

The Storyteller always has final say on whether a Skill can be combined with Wits to make a perception draw, or if Composure applies.

REACTION TO SURPRISE

Test Pool: Wits + Composure
Action: Reflexive

An ambush is about to be launched, a trap is about to be sprung or your character is about to run into her enemy. She may recognize the threat in time or may walk right into it. Draw Wits + Composure for your character to determine if she's prepared for the worst. Even one success indicates that she is and you can draw Initiative (see p. 100) for a fight as usual. If your Wits + Composure draw fails, your character is caught off guard and can do nothing for the first turn of combat except stand and gape or get hurt. Her Defense is not applied against incoming attacks in that first turn. For more information, see "Surprise" on p. 205.

Draw Results

Failure: Your character notices nothing amiss and is caught off guard.

Success: Initiative may be drawn normally and your character can attack or defend herself without hindrance.

RESOLVE

Rae had no idea how long the monster had locked her in the dingy room. Her efforts to guess where she was faded early on, followed quickly by her sense of time, and later by her hope of avoiding injury as the creature began punctuating its "sessions" with angry backhands. All that remained was one thought: She had to survive to see her friends again. She would not die here. She could not die here.

"You will break sooner or later, mortal," the pale thing whispered, pulling her chin up and trying to catch her with his hypnotic eyes. She felt them tugging at her mind, trying to coax her into submission. Once again she imagined herself becoming a conduit of pure will, until she felt herself returning his invasive stare with raw defiance. A heartbeat, then another, and the creature pulled back with an angry hiss, slapping her hard before retreating from the room.

Feeling fresh heat and pain rising in her cheek, Rae added another goal to her core of dedication: Vengeance. She would live to see this thing pay.

The focus and determination to see your character's will done. The capacity to stay on target, ignore distractions and to resist coercion or browbeating. Resolve is your character's mental fortitude. Her personal conviction. Her clarity of vision or spirit. Your character

may be easily distracted, unable to concentrate, resolute or single-minded. The trait is pivotal to resisting supernatural forms of mental control; it acts as a veritable defense of the mind. Resolve is valuable to leaders, motivators, soldiers, athletes, police and organizers.

(Note: Resolve is not to be confused with Willpower. Resolve is your character's ongoing focus. Think of it as her *long-term* purpose, like a career plan. Willpower reflects your character's *short-term* highs and lows, her ability to dedicate herself in brief efforts to overcome challenges. Resolve does contribute to your character's Willpower dots, though — see p. 108.)

RESISTING COERCION

Test Pool: Resolve + Wits or Resolve + Stamina

Action: Reflexive

Another person seeks to turn your character's mind to her way of thinking, or tries to get him do something for her, possibly through debate, intimidation or threats. The action is probably a contested effort against someone else's Wits-, Intelligence-, Presence- or Manipulation-based draw. Whoever gets the most successes wins. Convincing evidence might impose a –1 to –3 penalty to your character's determination. Especially pointed or compelling threats or applications of torture impose a similar penalty, at the Storyteller's discretion.

A prolonged interrogation or torture session may require extended draws between parties, made every few minutes, hours or days, as appropriate. See the Interrogation Skill task on p. 88 for more details.

If successes drawn in a contested coercion attempt tie, the subject maintains his own will and does not break down.

Draw Results

Failure: The request or idea seems perfectly reasonable.

Success: "No way."

Physical

STRENGTH

It burst through the door and was almost twice the size of a normal person. Maybe if they could get a stake in its heart, that should incapacitate the thing. But how could they take down something so big? Then the creature swung a clawed hand, slashing Rae across the shoulder and throwing her against the wall. Tony let out a fierce shout and surged forward, hitting the monster low, lifting it off its feet and slamming it to the ground. He did his best to pin it as the thing thrashed wildly.

Moments later, after the creature had been dealt with, the others looked on with newfound respect as Tony got up slowly and tried to get the feeling back into his strained limbs.

"How did you do that?" Jack asked, shaking his head. "That thing was huge!"

Even with blood all around, Tony looked almost sheepish. "I was captain of the football team, you know." He glanced down at the monster's still form, then across the room to where Rebecca tended to Rae's injuries. "And it made me mad."

Physical might. Sheer bodily power. The capacity to lift objects, move items, hit things and people, and do damage. Strength is a measure of muscle. Your character could be 98-pound weakling, he could carry a spare tire, or he could be lean and cut or bulky and brawny. Your character's Strength score is used in hand-to-hand combat. This trait is instrumental to laborers, thugs, athletes, brawlers and law-enforcement agents.

Strength, along with Dexterity, is a factor in determining your character's Speed. (See p. 107.) Strength is also added to Brawl or Weaponry attack draws to determine the amount of harm your character inflicts in combat. (See p. 76.)

BREAKING DOWN A BARRIER

See "Breaking down a door" on p. 190 in Chapter 6.

LIFTING/MOVING OBJECTS

Test Pool: Strength (+ Stamina)

Action: Instant

Lifting and moving objects involves brute force; might over matter. In some cases, however, Stamina plays a part. Power alone doesn't have immediate effects, but power combined with the endurance to apply it does.

All people can accomplish feats of strength in momentary efforts, depending on their muscle mass. Working together, people can combine their might to accomplish tasks. Add all participants' Strength scores and refer to the chart below to gauge what can be moved just by spending an action (no Strength draw is necessary). To exceed this limit, a Strength + Stamina draw is required, with successes achieved adding one or two (see below) to your character's Strength score to determine what kind of task he can accomplish in that action. In a group effort to move something really heavy, a Strength + Stamina draw is made for each supporting participant. Successes drawn are added to a primary actor's draw as bonus points. (See "Teamwork," p. 180, for full rules on cooperating this way.)

If your character's modified Strength total exceeds that required to lift an object, it can be relocated as desired. If his Strength total matches that required to lift an object, it can be moved about a step.

The chart indicates how much a character can lift, but that amount represents a focused, one-time act. That weight isn't what he can walk around holding and wearing, day to day. Your character can realistically carry/tote 25 pounds per dot of Strength without

Strength	Feat	Lift
1	Lift a chair	40 lbs.
2	Lift a large dog	100 lbs.
3	Lift a public mailbox	250 lbs.
4	Lift a wooden crate	400 lbs.
5	Lift a coffin	650 lbs.
6	Lift a refrigerator	800 lbs.
7	Overturn a small car	900 lbs.
8	Lift a motorcycle	1000 lbs.
9	Overturn a mid-sized car	1200 lbs.
10	Lift a large tree trunk	1500 lbs.
11	Overturn a full-sized car	2000 lbs.
12	Lift a wrecking ball	3000 lbs.
13	Overturn a station wagon	4000 lbs.
14	Overturn a van	5000 lbs.
15	Overturn a truck	6000 lbs.

penalty. If he attempts to carry more, every action involving physical exertion incurs an automatic –1 penalty for every 25 pounds of excess gear that he has. Furthermore, every 25 pounds he piles on beyond what he can carry reduces his Speed by one. Perhaps he can actually lift everything he's wearing and holding, but he can't go anywhere with it. The Storyteller makes the final call on what your character may realistically carry.

Draw Results

Failure: Nothing is added to Strength.

Success: Add one to the character's Strength to determine how much the character may lift.

DEXTERITY

Jimmy had a head-start on the creatures chasing him, but not enough of one, and it sounded like they were closing quickly. A desperate hope came to mind, and Jimmy turned down an alley, hoping the neighborhood was still as rundown as he remembered. Sure enough, a tall chain-link fence stood at the end of the alley, topped with a few flimsy strands of barbed wire. He put on a final burst of speed and leapt at the fence, scrambling up the links with practiced hands, narrowly avoiding a slip as one of the things slammed into the fence below him.

Scrambling over the top and dropping to the concrete with a catlike move, Jimmy looked back at all the gaping maws and filthy nails of the creatures and said a silent prayer, appreciating the hours he spent as a kid getting into places he shouldn't have been. One big question remained, however. Where would he go now?

Quickness. Response time. A delicate touch. Dexterity indicates how quickly and with how much finesse your character responds to his physical world. While high Wits dots helps your character spot trouble, high Dexterity dots help him react to it, whether with a counteraction or to simply get the hell out of the way. Dexterity also helps with hand-eye coordination, be it to fire an accurate shot, to juggle objects or to perform delicate jobs such as handle explosives. Your character might be sluggish, clumsy, slight, quick or nimble. Dexterity is invaluable to criminals, sports stars, surgeons and dancers.

Dexterity, along with Strength, is a factor in determining your character's Speed. (See p. 107.) Dexterity is also combined with Composure to determine your character's Initiative in a fight. (See p. 100.)

DEFENSE

Derived Traits: Dexterity or Wits

Action: Reflexive

The lowest of a character's Dexterity or Wits is used to determine his Defense trait, which is subtracted from incoming Brawl, Weaponry and throwing attacks. See p. 99 for more information

STAMINA

"Where are you?" The voice sounded like it was miles away, and Dietrich fought to bring it closer, to stay conscious for just a few minutes longer. Aware of the unnatural source of the crowd's hysteria, he'd tried to drive them back without violence, but they kept coming, and there were too many pale faces mixed in with the healthy ones. He remembered firing until his gun was empty, and then a few swings of the rifle butt, but then everything went black.

Summoning a last reserve he didn't know he had, Dietrich raised his head and managed a hoarse, "Here," through the shooting pain. A minute later, shapes moved above him, one of them slowly resolving into the relieved face of Father Sheridan.

"Thank God!" he said. "We thought that infernal mob got you, son."

Ignoring the blood in his eyes and the noises of disbelief from his team as they examined his wounds, Dietrich clasped his friend's hand and managed a weak smile. "Oh, you know me, Father. I'm damn near riot proof."

Sturdiness. Steadfastness. Sheer physical resilience. Stamina is a measure of how tough your character is. It indicates how far he can push his body, and how much physical abuse he can endure. Your character might be sickly and frail, or hardy and unstoppable. Bouncers, brawlers, triathletes, survivalists, heavy lifters and workaholics thrive on Stamina.

Stamina, along with Size, is a factor in determining your character's Health dots. (See p. 235.)

HOLDING BREATH

Test Pool: Stamina

Action: Reflexive

A character can hold her breath for a number of turns based on her Stamina dots, as follows:

Stamina	Time*
•	30 seconds
••	One minute
•••	Two minutes
••••	Four minutes
•••••	Eight minutes
••••• •	15 minutes
••••• ••	30 minutes

* If your character is in combat while underwater or otherwise deprived of breath, she can hold her breath for one *turn* per Stamina dot.

When she has reached her normal limit, a Stamina draw is made to continue. Each success grants 30 extra seconds (or one extra turn per success in combat).

When she can no longer hold her breath, she begins suffocating/drowning. She suffers one lethal Health wound per turn. (Werewolves and other living supernatural creatures cannot regenerate this damage until they can breathe again. Since vampires and the walking dead don't breathe, they cannot suffocate or drown.)

RESISTING POISON OR DISEASE

Test Pool: Stamina + Resolve

Action: Reflexive (potentially extended)

Toxins or ailments affect people only as far as these afflictions can overcome bodily resistance, and often the personal imperative to remain healthy. The human body can fight back against foreign substances and illness, but determination to resist goes a long way toward recovery, too.

Mere exposure to an illness or poison might call for a reflexive Stamina + Resolve draw to determine if your character falls victim. If the draw is successful, he remains healthy or immune. If the draw fails, the symptoms kick in.

If an affliction has long-term effects, efforts to fight back might call for extended and reflexive Stamina + Resolve draws. They might be made every turn or hour for a poison, or every hour, day or week for a disease. The total number of successes needed to overcome might be 10 for a weak poison or 30 for a virulent disease. The victim suffers from any effects of the illness while it is being fought. The Storyteller might impose a limit on the number of draws that can be made before a severe condition proves fatal. If required successes aren't accumulated by then, your character dies.

Draw Results

Failure: The intruding effect takes or continues to take its course.

Success: In a simple reflexive draw, the condition is resisted. In an extended draw, some progress is made in resisting the condition, but symptoms persist until the illness is defeated completely (when the required successes are accumulated).

Social

PRESENCE

Sam wasn't the strongest member of the team, or the best trained. Hell, he was savvy enough to realize he wasn't the smartest of the group either, but they still looked to him for leadership. Because when it came down to it, Sam could take command of the room with little more than an offhand comment and a wave of his hand. When he entered the room, people noticed; when he talked, people listened. It was as simple and powerful as that.

It was also exactly what they were counting on tonight. Always a smooth operator, Sam entered the club in grand style, his clothes fashionably immaculate, his poise impeccable. He timed his arrival precisely at the moment when the music died down and the house lights came up. Dozens of pairs of eyes turned in his direction, most lighting up with interest and approval, but Sam feigned indifference, letting his eyes roam until he saw their target. Pale and beautiful in equal measure, she sat in a distant corner booth, surrounded by admirers... but she had noticed him too. His eyes met hers, and he let the gaze linger for a just a moment. She smiled, and he turned the corners of his mouth up just slightly in response before breaking eye contact, not wanting to appear too obviously interested yet.

"Think she's taken the bait," he muttered into the microphone concealed in his lapel as he walked to the bar and casually ordered a drink, as though he hadn't just caught the eye of every lady in the room. Sure enough, a few minutes later one of her friends approached and asked if he'd like to come over for a drink and some conversation. He'd made the impression he was after — now it was time to see if his charm and his story could back it up.

Bearing. Stature. Assertiveness. Presence suggests the power of your character's very identity. Physical attractiveness is only part of the trait. Your character may be jaw-dropping handsome, average-Joe or downright ugly, but his Presence means much more. It reflects his sheer command over the attention of others. It's his capacity to impose his will on others by being socially aggressive or powerful — a veritable bull in a china shop or someone who simply doesn't accept no for an answer. This trait is essential to leaders, enforcers, interrogators, models, politicians and salespeople.

Note that raw physical attractiveness alone is represented by the Striking Looks Merit (p. 149), which grants bonus points to certain Presence draws.

MANIPULATION

Sometimes, Victor hated how easy it was to get inside their defenses, to say all the right things that made the others accept him, trust him. They were so paranoid about the dangers that lurked out there, yet they were so quick to take in another "lost soul" who'd seen what waited in the shadows.

All he had to do was cry a little and make up some stories about the creatures that haunted him, about the horrible things he'd been forced to see and do, and they were ready to trust him with their lives. He might even have been their friend, if the Voices hadn't gotten to him first.

The Voices had broken him long before. A phantom chorus that told him horrible truths until he wept and begged them to stop. He swore he'd do anything to know peace again. They told him about the others, the ones who jeopardized what the Voices wanted. They commanded him to join this group so he could break it from within. The Voices even told him what lies to tell, and whenever he felt a stab of guilt over how easily they worked, Victor consoled himself with the knowledge that the charade would be over soon.

Charm. Persuasiveness. Charisma. The capacity to play upon the desires, hopes and needs of others to influence them. Manipulation reflects your character's finesse in social situations. How well he can appeal to, gain the favor of and generally coerce others. Manipulation is applied to win smiles, to put people at ease and to gain favors. Where Presence deals in social force, Manipulation focuses on social subtlety. It's the tool and trade of businesspeople, politicians, salesfolk and publicists. Your character may be a wallflower, he could frequently make off-color statements, he might have a winning smile and a hardy handshake, or he may be able to sell sand in the desert.

COMPOSURE

"Do you really think I'll let you have him back? He's mine now! Mine!"

Dr. Mitchell felt the spirit's unholy presence flare like heat from a fire, willing him to cower before it in fear. He reminded himself of the possessed child and managed to hold his ground, keeping his expression calm. The thing glared with seemingly infinite hatred from behind those innocent eyes. Yet he saw a flicker of uncertainty when he didn't collapse, and he knew he'd made some progress.

"I don't know who you are, but my name is Dr. Phillip Mitchell. You can call me Phil if that makes you more comfortable." It still took an effort to not give in to the gnawing fear emanating from the possessed child, but he found that reciting his standard professional introduction gave him stability. "I'd like to help if you'll let me."

The child's features shifted, showing uncertainty, and Dr. Mitchell felt control of the situation shifting in his favor. After all, this was still a troubled child, and even if he didn't understand exactly what had happened to the boy, he was willing to bet some things stayed the same. If he could keep the spirit from noticing the sweat building on his forehead, he — and the child — just might make it through alive.

Poise. Dignity. The capacity to remain calm and appear — and actually be — unfazed in social and threatening situations, usually harrowing ones. Your character might lose his temper at the slightest perceived insult, collapse emotionally under a mere pretense, weather a storm of verbal (or literal) slings and arrows, or have the nerve to look unspeakable horror in the eye. This trait is a measure of emotional fortitude, restraint and calm. It's ideal among leaders, soldiers, moderators and anyone whose movements are public consumption. Composure is vital to resisting social influence and pressure — overt, covert or otherworldly.

Composure is pivotal to resisting supernatural forms of emotional control; it acts as a veritable emotional defense. The trait is also vital to efforts among supernatural beings such as vampires and werewolves to restrain themselves when their blood is raised and frenzy threatens.

Composure, along with Resolve, is a factor in determining your character's Willpower. (See p. 108.) Composure is also added to Dexterity to determine your character's Initiative at the beginning of a fight. (See p. 100.)

MEDITATION

Test Pool: Composure + Wits + equipment

Action: Extended (4 successes; one draw represents 30 minutes)

Meditation is a means of relaxation and reflection that is useful to counterbalance daily stresses and to restore one's emotional center. It helps to filter out extraneous influences and allows a person to re-dedicate herself to personal beliefs, values and aspirations. For game purposes, this practice has a powerful effect on maintaining emotional balance and bolstering one's moral resolve in the face of potential degeneration (the decline of one's Morality, as explained on p. 101).

Performing a successful meditation session requires at least 30 minutes of actual, uninterrupted in-game time during which your character turns her attention inward and tunes out the world. Each draw represents one 30-minute segment, and meditation sessions can potentially run for several hours as the practitioner struggles with life's distractions and seeks her focus. Situational modifiers such as the character's mental and physical condition and environmental distractions can apply. Four successes are required for a rewarding effort. If successful, your character gains a +1 bonus on her next degeneration draw. This bonus lasts until that degeneration draw is made or until the character sleeps, whichever comes first. Once she awakens, she has to meditate again in order to reclaim the bonus. Once the degeneration draw has been made, she can meditate again for a bonus on her next draw, even if she hasn't slept yet.

Chapter 3: Skills

Chapter 3:
Skills

Chapter 3
Skills

A character's Attributes measure his innate physical, mental and social qualities — how strong he is, how quick he thinks on his feet, and how well he interacts with other people. The different ways in which a character can apply these Attributes are determined by his Skills. A character's Skills reflect the education and training he's acquired over the course of his life, and are a reflection of his origins and interests. Skills can be acquired in any number of ways, from institutionalized learning to hard, hands-on experience. A young recruit at the police academy is trained to use a handgun, while a gangbanger learns to shoot as a matter of survival.

Like Attributes, Skills are broken down into three general categories: Mental, Physical and Social. A character's initial Skills are purchased during character creation and are prioritized in the same manner as Attributes, with 11 points to allocate among primary Skills, seven points to allocate among secondary Skills, and four points to allocate among tertiary Skills. Skill dots can then be increased further using experience points (both at the conclusion of character creation if the Storyteller allows it, and later during play). Or new Skills can be purchased during a chronicle at the player's discretion. For more information on selecting Skills for starting characters, see p. 28.

The devil can cite Scripture for his purpose.

— Shakespeare, The Merchant of Venice

Skill Dots

Skills are rated from 1 to 5, with each score suggesting your character s relative level of proficiency and knowledge in that area.

Dots Proficiency Level

• Novice. Basic knowledge and/or techniques.

•• Practitioner. Solid working knowledge and/or techniques.

••• Professional. Broad, detailed knowledge and/or techniques.

•••• Expert. Exceptional depth of knowledge and/or techniques.

Master. Unsurpassed depth of knowledge and/or techniques. A leader in the field.

Skill Specialties

Skills represent broad bases of knowledge and physical training in a given subject. An auto mechanic doesn't just know about fixing engines, for example, but is versed in repairing tires, replacing windows and painting the body. In addition to this broad foundation of knowledge, characters can specialize in a particular aspect of a Skill, giving them an edge in a particular application due to their increased focus. There's no limit to the number of Specialties that your character can have in a single Skill. You choose three Specialties at character creation. Any more must be purchased during play with experience points. Draws involving a Skill Specialty gain a +1 modifier over and above any other situation modifiers. Therefore, if your character has Crafts, but also has a Specialty in Automobiles, you gain a +1 bonus when he works on cars.

You are limited only by your imagination when devising your character's Skill Specialties, although their focus should be fairly specific. A character possessing the Drive Skill might focus on sports cars, trucks, off-road or high-speed driving. Each Skill listed in this chapter has a number of suggested Specialties to give you an idea of the possibilities, while the Storyteller has final approval over which she will permit in her chronicle and when they apply.

Only one Specialty applies per draw — thus if you have a Firearms Specialty in "quick draws" and another one in "revolvers," and you quick-draw a revolver in combat, you still receive only a +1 bonus to your test pool. Having multiple Specialties in a Skill is a way to illustrate an even more in-depth knowledge of the field than your Skill dots might otherwise suggest, not a means to create a hyper-focused, unbeatable character.

Specialties can apply to esoteric or even supernatural powers, but in those cases they have to be narrowly specialized, usually only applying to a single ability.

Skill Roleplaying

Most Skills and Skill tasks are assumed to be instant — they are performed in a single combat action or perhaps in a minute outside of combat. If a Skill has a specific time listed with it, however, you are required to roleplay carrying out that action for the requisite amount of time. So, if a character hacks a computer system and the Skill task specifies that each draw represents five minutes of work, and it requires two draws for the action to succeed, roleplay sitting at the computer and altering code for 10 minutes of real time. While this roleplaying need not be absolutely realistic and convincing (this is a *game*, after all), neither can you simply sit across the room, sipping coffee and periodically announcing, "By the way, my character is actually at that computer hacking away right now."

If a player cannot actually perform the action in question (a non-musical person whose character writes a symphony, for example), or it would be unsafe for you to depict the action (such as assembling a gun in a public location), simply mime the action as best you can and/or verbally describe what your character does for other players in the area to hear, repeating the description every few minutes until the action is finished. Failing that, you should sit in an out-of-game area for the requisite amount of time, though this option should be reserved for times when no other alternative suffices; it doesn't add much to the roleplaying environment.

Skill Tasks

If a Skill represents a particular body of knowledge or training, a Skill task describes a specific application of the Skill in question. "Healing Wounds," for example, is a task describing an application of the Medicine Skill. Skill tasks combine an applicable

Attribute with a Skill, plus any relevant equipment modifiers to form a test pool, minus any situational modifiers. Climbing a steep cliff, for example, is a Skill task combining Strength + Athletics + equipment such as rope, pitons and cleats. Many Skills in this chapter have one or more tasks associated with them that suggest different ways in which the traits can be applied in various situations. Use these as guidelines for determining other Skill tasks that arise in your stories.

THE RIGHT TOOLS FOR THE JOB

Having the proper equipment for a task can often mean the difference between success and failure. In addition to situational modifiers and Specialties, Skill draws gain bonuses if your character uses high-quality or specialized equipment when performing a feat. For example, a driver with a high-performance sports car has an edge in a race over someone in an old pickup. See "Equipment," p. 192, in Chapter 6 for more information on the gear available to your character. Each task presented in this chapter lists a variety of tools that could provide bonus points to your Skill draw.

These lists are by no means exhaustive. You're encouraged to employ other types of tools or equipment to assist in performing a task, but the Storyteller is the final arbiter on what bonus, if any, gear provides. Using poor-quality tools might even make a task more difficult to perform, so choose wisely. Also note that equipment is sometimes a basic necessity to perform a task in the first place. It's unlikely that you can overhaul an engine with your bare hands alone. In these cases, equipment may offer a bonus only if it's of exceptional quality or is particularly well suited to the task.

SKILL MODIFIERS

Applying bonuses to Skill usage during game-play tends to slow down the flow of play. Nonetheless, it's only natural that some tasks would be significantly more difficult to accomplish than others. Researching a fairly basic academic theory should be reasonably effortless, whereas delving deep into research that requires advanced knowledge of the subject field ought to be much more difficult. Storytellers are encouraged to apply modifiers from +5 to -5 in difficulty to Skill test pools depending on the difficulty of a task and the character's knowledge and ability. As an example, having a slow computer might penalize a Hacking test pool by -2. Having a slow internet connection would raise it to -3. Outdated software would add another penalty, making it -4. Having access to classified hardware and software and possibly to a database of as-yet-unreleased security exploits might change the modifier to a +3 instead.

In some situations, characters may fail utterly at performing a Skill. Storytellers are encouraged to come up with creative ways of narrating such dismal failures. An apparently successful car repair job turns out to be shoddy at a crucial point in time. A character's research succeeds spectacularly until she realizes that she's fallen for a hoax. In contrast, five or more successes can be narrated as fantastic triumphs: a character not only finds that trap door she's been looking for but also notices the hidden level behind the bookcase and spots the unusual smell coming from the liquid on the door handle.

Skill Times During Play and Downtime

Astute readers will no doubt notice that many Skills have two different temporal measurements, depending on whether an action is being attempted during play or during downtime. This is no accident. Quite simply, the time an action takes to accomplish during play is often compressed for the sake of drama, much like in a movie or television show. Sure, we all know it would actually take hours to locate the right volume in a massive library or to perform an autopsy, but nobody wants to watch that time drag by, much less act it out. It s not exciting, and more importantly it slows down the story. So, many action times are greatly reduced in order to speed play and help maintain dramatic tension. It may still take a computer hacker 15 minutes of real-time roleplaying to hack a system during a game, but that s a whole lot better than having that player sit for an hour-and-a-half just for the sake of realism.

Storytellers should feel free to adjust times as they see fit to make a scene dramatic. For example, you could allow a player to make a draw every combat turn if she tries to get crucial data from a system while her companions hold off an enemy s goons. Sure, that action normally requires five minutes per draw, but the Storyteller likes the idea of the hacker trying desperately to download the information in the midst of a raging firefight, so he adjusts the time accordingly. Likewise, the Storyteller could increase the amount of time it takes to perform a Skill task if he feels it would be accomplished too quickly otherwise. If you increase task times, just make sure players don t feel they ve wasted an entire chapter accomplishing a single action.

It also bears noting that just because an action can be performed during downtime doesn t mean a character has an infinite amount of time or number of attempts to get it right. Players may see that a Skill requires a half-hour per draw, look at the month of downtime they have, and ask why they have to bother making draws when they have so much time on their hands. Other factors often limit the number of attempts that can be made during downtime. For example, a character attempting to work the black market might get only a certain number of attempts before she s caught in a police raid. Another character trying to decipher a strange enigma might have a limited number of tests before the Storyteller rules she has exhausted all her leads and hit a dead end. Indeed, imposing such limiting factors is crucial to ensuring that players do not perceive downtime as a guarantee of resolving their problems. Chapter 6 addresses the limits of attempted actions further under Rule of Thumb: Extended Actions, p. 167.

Mental Skills

Mental Skills are applications of a character's insight, acumen and focus, such as examining a crime scene for clues, unraveling an enigma or diagnosing an illness. These Skills are almost entirely gained from a period of formal education, and most characters with high Mental Skills can claim a degree or even a doctorate in their field of study. These traits are generally associated with your character's Mental Attributes, but can also be paired with Physical Attributes for hands-on applications such as performing surgery (Dexterity + Medicine) or computer repair (Dexterity + Crafts).

Untrained Skill Use: If your character doesn't have the necessary Mental Skill required for an action, she can still make the attempt. Draw her Attribute alone, but at a –3 penalty. At the Storyteller's discretion, some particularly complicated or delicate

Mental Skill tasks may be impossible to attempt untrained. While it's possible that someone might be able to try basic first aid without formal instruction, there's just no chance for someone to perform neurosurgery without proper training.

ACADEMICS

Illuminated by the sickly silver light of the monitor, the group read the online journal entries posted by the missing professor, detailing her investigation into the mysterious tablets that had been recovered at the archaeological dig outside of town. The entries got stranger and stranger as they went on, describing the professor's increasingly obsessive search for the origins of the tablets and their bizarre inscriptions.

"She's dead," Becca said slowly, pointing to the cryptic last entry on the screen. The others looked at her, not understanding. "Professor Kincaid is dead. That's what this entry means. Somehow, she knew she was about to die."

"How do you know that?" Tony asked. "All it says is, 'He kindly stopped for me.' She might just have been expecting a visitor that night."

"No, it's a quote from a Dickinson poem," Becca said. "The complete line is: 'Because I could not stop for Death, he kindly stopped for me.' She must have known what was going to happen. Now we have to figure out exactly what happened to her... and why the danger didn't stop her research."

Academics is a broad-based Skill that represents a character's degree of higher education and general knowledge in the Arts and Humanities — everything from English to history, economics to law. Dots in this Skill do not always directly correlate to a given level of education. Your character could have entered a doctorate program, but spent more time partying than studying, resulting in low dots. Conversely, a self-taught individual who read voraciously and studied intensively could have high dots without ever earning a diploma.

Possessed by: College graduates, executives, lawyers, librarians, scholars, students

Specialties: Anthropology, Art, English, History, Law, Religion, Research

Draw Results

Failure: Your character is unable to summon the necessary information. It's on the tip of his tongue, but the name, date or reference eludes him.

Success: Your character is able to summon the necessary knowledge to serve his needs.

RESEARCH

Test Pool: Intelligence + Academics + equipment

Action: Extended (3–10+ successes; each draw represents five minutes of research during play, or one hour during downtime)

Researching information is a straightforward task that involves querying libraries and databases. Draw Intelligence + Academics + equipment. The number of successes required depends on the complexity and/or obscurity of the desired information. A simple set of facts might demand three successes to obtain, while a little known or difficult-to-find reference might demand 10 or more successes to uncover. Depending on the quality of the libraries or databases available, the Storyteller may grant a +1 or higher modifier to task draws.

During a game session, the Storyteller may change the time needed for research to help game flow, rather than require 30 minutes per draw. A character may quickly glean a snippet of information needed by skimming the appropriate material, for instance.

Draw Results

Failure: Your character makes no progress in locating the information he's after.

Success: Your character makes progress in his search for information.

COMPUTER

Judging from the security measures in place, it looked like the Asher Institute had spent a great deal of money for the latest encryption software and online safeguards. Odd for a group that claimed to be a small charitable foundation. The work had clearly been done by one of the city's well-known, widely advertised corporate online security firms. Given a little more time to examine the code, Connor probably could've narrowed it down to a few programmers. She'd been on the other end of their work often enough.

Fortunately, one advantage to dealing with corporate security like this was that it was also a big target. Dozens of other hackers were already probing the systems for weaknesses. Connor smiled as she keyed herself in through the latest backdoor to be discovered, only a day or two old and still not patched. Now it was time to find out where this quiet little charity got all its money.

Characters possessing this Skill have the necessary training or experience to operate a computer. At high levels (3 or more), a character can create his own computer programs. People with high levels in this Skill are also familiar with a variety of programming languages and operating systems.

Note that dots in Computer do not apply to manually fixing or building machines, only to operating them. Construction and repair is the province of the Crafts Skill (see below).

Possessed by: Businesspeople, professors, programmers, students, sysadmins

Specialties: Artificial Intelligence, Data Retrieval, Graphics, Hacking, Internet

Draw Results

Failure: The task your character attempts does not go off properly or the database query he makes returns no useful information.

Success: Your character's function executes properly or his queries come back with the desired information.

HACKING

Test Pool: Intelligence + Computer + equipment versus Intelligence + Computer + equipment

Action: Extended and contested (5–10+ successes; each draw represents five minutes of programming during play, or 30 minutes in downtime)

Gaining root access to a network requires talent, creativity and patience, and often results in a battle of wits with the system's administrator(s). Before the hacking attempt begins, the Storyteller determines the network's level of security. If there is a system administrator on duty, the hacking attempt is an extended and contested action. If the network is protected by basic security software alone, the task is simply an extended action.

In a contested and extended action between hacker and sysadmin, draw Intelligence + Computer + any equipment modifiers for both participants. The winner is the first to accumulate the required number of successes. The hacker needs to accumulate a number of successes equal to the network's basic security setup. This can be anywhere from five to 10 based on the sophistication of the network. The sysadmin needs to accumulate a number of successes equal to the hacker's Intelligence + Computer. If the hacker wins, he gains unfettered access to the network. If the sysadmin wins, he kicks the hacker out of the network and blocks any further attempts from that invader that day.

If a character attempts hacking during a game session, the Storyteller may change the time needed for each challenge to help game flow, rather than the usual 30 minutes per draw.

Example: *Connor hacks into the network of a local financial group, which is protected by an on-duty sysadmin. Connor's Intelligence is 4, her Computer is 3 and she's using an average computer*

setup (no bonuses). The sysadmin's Intelligence is 3, his Computer is 3 and he's using a decent system that gives him a +1 modifier. The network's basic security software requires seven successes to be overcome. The sysadmin also needs to accumulate seven successes (the total of Connor's Intelligence + Computer). The first draws net three successes for Connor and two successes for the sysadmin. Connor needs to gain four more successes to make it past the sysadmin and gain access, while the sysadmin needs to accumulate five more successes to kick the intruder out of his network.

If the network is protected by basic security software alone, the hacker needs to accumulate a number of successes equal to the network's basic security setup, as above.

Example: Later, Connor tries to hack into the network of the city's Department of Motor Vehicles. The DMV network doesn't have a sysadmin on duty, so the task is an extended draw. The network's basic security software requires six successes to be overcome, so Connor simply needs to keep hacking at the system (and not suffer any failures) to get in.

Draw Results

Failure: Your character does not succeed in making any headway in his effort.

Success: Your character makes progress in his effort.

CRAFTS

They'd come to its lair, the arrogant mortals, thinking themselves brave and carrying their pathetic armaments. Theirs were little better than tools fashioned into weapons by frightened hands and uncertain hearts. The creature, meanwhile, hammered its hate out on the hot steel, smashing and reshaping it, letting anger temper the emerging blade with an edge beyond mortal capability. The damnable mortals had managed to hurt the creature, but if they thought it would run from the likes of them, they were in for a cruel surprise.

The foul being paused in its work, ignoring the searing heat of the ancient forge and holding the weapon to the light, examining it with a critical eye. The blade was an unnatural black, as though thirsty for light, the edge curved and keen. Still, it was not quite ready. Not quite prepared to hold the terrifying enchantments the inhuman smith had in mind. It bent and hammered again, thinking of nothing but hate and flame and steel.

Crafts represents a character's training or experience in creating works of physical art or construction by hand, from paintings to car engines to classical sculpture. Characters possessing this Skill typically have the knowledge, but not necessarily the tools or facilities to make use of their capabilities. A character might be an exceptional mechanic, for example, but still needs to sweet-talk his boss into opening the garage after-hours to work on his friend's car. Crafting a piece of art or creating an object is almost always an extended action, with the length of time and number of successes required determined by the complexity of the piece. The Storyteller has final say on the time required and the number of successes needed for a particular item.

During a game session, the Storyteller may change the time needed for the quick creation of art — say, for sketching or impromptu creations — to facilitate game flow. The difference between such art and that created using the proper amount of time is easily noticeable, however — you're not going to sketch the Mona Lisa and pass it off as a legitimate da Vinci.

Possessed by: Contractors, mechanics, plumbers, sculptors, welders

Specialties: Automobiles, Aircraft, Forging, Jury-Rigging, Sculpting, Sewing

Draw Results

Failure: Your character makes no progress in creating the item in question.

Success: Your character makes progress in crafting the piece (apply successes drawn toward the total needed).

CREATE ART

Test Pool: Intelligence + Crafts + equipment

Action: Extended (4-15+ successes; one draw equals 10 minutes of work during play, or one hour during downtime)

Your character sets out to create a piece of art, whether it's a painting, drawing or sculpture. It's quicker and easier to create a bowl or doodle than a life-size replica or mural. The former may call for only four successes while the latter may call for 15 or more, and hours of effort.

Creating poems, songs, novels or speeches calls for the Expression Skill (see p. 87).

Draw Results

Failure: Your character makes no headway in his project.

Success: Your character makes progress in his project.

REPAIR ITEM

Test Pool: Dexterity + Crafts + equipment

Action: Extended (4-10 successes; one draw equals five minutes of work during play, or 30 minutes during downtime)

Repairing a damaged item is an extended action, requiring a number of successes depending on the extent of the repairs and the overall difficulty of the job. Changing a spark plug in a car might require only four successes, while rebuilding the entire engine might demand 15 or more. Generally, one success is required on an extended draw to repair one point of damage to a broken object's Structure. (See "Objects," p. 178.)

Many repairs require specific tools and/or facilities. If your character does not have all the necessary equipment available, a –1 modifier applies. If he does not have any of the necessary tools to fix the item, the Storyteller may declare that the task is impossible.

At a Storyteller's discretion, quick attempts at fixing an item may not require the usual 30 minutes per draw during the course of a game. Such hastily repaired items will almost always fail soon afterward, however — say, for a single shot with a pistol or a brief travel distance in a car.

Example: Scott is asked by a friend to fix a damaged computer. Scott's Dexterity is 3 and his Crafts (with a Computer Specialty) is 2. This is a downtime action. That is, it does not place during a chapter. He has all the proper electronics and tools to make the repair, so there is no negative modifier to the draws, but his equipment is of average quality and doesn't give a bonus. His test pool is therefore six. Repairing the computer is a complicated task, so the Storyteller determines that it requires seven successes to complete. Five draws (and two-and-a-half hours) later, the necessary successes are accumulated and the computer is fixed.

Draw Results

Failure: Your character fails to make any headway in repairing the item.

Success: Your character makes progress in completing the repair.

INVESTIGATION

"We shouldn't be cooped up in here in this damn library," Leeds groused for the third time. "We should be out there trying to find out who killed those people!"

Mariah returned with another armload of books. "Trust me, this is going to be a lot more productive," she said, sitting down and opening several volumes. A little over an hour later, Mariah had managed to find a connection the police had missed. The murders took place where Native American settlements had once stood. And the same sites, if records were to be believed, bore witness to the wholesale slaughter of natives by invaders' hands.

Two hundred years later, it was the descendents of those colonists who had turned up dead.

Investigation is the art and science of solving mysteries, examining seemingly disparate evidence to find a connection, answering riddles and overcoming paradoxes. It not only allows your character to get into the head of a killer to grasp his motives or plans, it allows her to look beyond the mundane world to guess at answers to mysterious problems, or to have a "eureka" moment that offers insight into baffling circumstances. Your character might realize that all murder victims have the same digits jumbled in their phone numbers. She might interpret a dream that has striking similarities to events in the real world. Or she could recognize why an intruder took the time to paint a room red. Certain individuals such as law-enforcement officers, forensic specialists, scientists and investigators are trained in the art of examination, while others simply develop the knack through years of practice.

Note that Investigation is different from the perception Attribute task detailed on p. 47. Perception (Wits + Composure or Wits + another Skill) is typically checked when a character could spot something unusual or amiss when she isn't actually looking for it. Investigation-based draws are typically made when a character *actively* studies a situation. Dots in Investigation don't give a character sudden insight or capability in the realms of other Skills, however. She can't miraculously identify changing brushstrokes in a painting. That would be the realm of Academics or Crafts. Nevertheless, she might identify how the placement of paintings throughout a house creates a pattern and conveys a message.

Possessed by: Criminals, doctors, forensic examiners, police officers, scientists, scholars, soldiers

Specialties: Artifacts, Body Language, Crime Scenes, Cryptography, Dreams, Autopsy Diagnoses, Puzzles, Riddles, Scientific Experiments

Draw Results

Failure: Your character fails to notice the details or information for which she searches. It might be right under her nose but she overlooks it.

Success: Your character studies the situation or problem and finds useful details that answer her questions. A single success might be sufficient to solve a simple puzzle, but more successes may be required to gather extensive clues. The Storyteller may offer small insights with each success in an examination, starting with the obvious and ending with the obscure.

EXAMINING A CRIME SCENE

Test Pool: Wits + Investigation + equipment

Action: Extended (3–10+ successes; one draw represents five minutes of activity during play, or one hour during downtime)

Examining a crime scene involves studying evidence and clues to piece together useful facts about events, perpetrators or a mystery. Draw Wits + Investigation. During a chapter, each draw represents five minutes of nothing but observation and interpretation, and possibly referencing databases and calling expert witnesses. Depending on the size of the crime scene and the complexity and obscurity of details, the task could demand anywhere from three to 10 successes (or more) for your character to make sense of things.

Unlike many tasks, this isn't an all-or-nothing effort. If your character has to abandon the project before it's completed, he may still come away with some useful information depending on the number of successes earned. The Storyteller should share information each time a draw yields a success, starting with the most obvious facts and revealing increasingly obscure bits as the investigation continues. At no time should the player know how many successes are needed to complete the analysis — he should always wonder whether his character should invest a little more time and dig deeper. Storytellers may choose to make these draws for players in secret to add uncertainty and suspense.

Example: *Tracy is called to the scene of a murder at a local park. Taking stock of the situation, she studies the area around the body to piece together what happened. The Storyteller decides that it takes eight successes to gather all the clues available. Tracy's Wits is 3 and her Investigation is 4. Her first draw total is 15. With two successes, Tracy has gathered a quarter of the information available. The Storyteller reveals that the victim died due to massive blood loss, but there are no bloodstains around the corpse. At this point, Tracy can continue to investigate or decide that she's seen enough and move on.*

Draw Results

Failure: Your character uncovers no useful information.

Success: Your character uncovers useful information, but is that all there is to learn?

SOLVING ENIGMAS

Test Pool: Intelligence + Investigation + equipment

Action: Instant or extended (3–10+ successes; one draw represents five minutes of activity during play, or 30 minutes during downtime)

A man scrawls a bizarre message before he dies. A ghost utters some cryptic, haunting words that are the clues to freeing it from this world. A killer leaves a hint to his next crime. Your character is posed with a perplexing mystery, riddle, puzzle, code or series of clues to contemplate. Sometimes these brainteasers can be solved quickly, such as a short riddle meant to lead him to his next destination. Such conundrums might be solved with a simple success and an instant action. Other stumpers demand consideration, research, interpretation and/or legwork — an extended action. For your character to understand what "Blue Heron" written in blood means, he needs to look into the murder victim's past and do research into what that term meant to her.

Often times, such an enigma goes unsolved until the required successes are gained. Partial insights along the way aren't forthcoming, because the elements of the answer don't make sense until they're all gathered. When they are, eureka! Other conundrums are so complicated or elusive that they can almost never be solved. See "Rule of Thumb: Extended Actions" on p. 167.

Draw Results

Failure: Your character does not solve the puzzle or gains no headway toward the answer.

Success: Your character finds a simple answer, or gathers some information or insight toward complete comprehension.

MEDICINE

"Corey, open up! We need your help! Steve's been hurt bad! Open up!"

When Corey opened his door, he saw the sight he'd come to dread. Colin and Jeff stood under the porch light, the two of them supporting a pale, semi-conscious Steve. A telltale circular black burn was centered on Steve's right thigh, the leg of his jeans ominously dark. Corey's practiced eye also noted that Colin and Jeff had several cuts and bruises that would require his attention.

Gesturing for them to take Steve downstairs to the makeshift operating theatre he'd built, Corey raced to grab his bag. As a paramedic, he was able to keep extra supplies with him, and it looked like he was going to need everything he had. He'd worry about explaining where those supplies went later. For now he prayed he would be able patch his friends up after their latest "encounter."

The Medicine Skill reflects a character's training and expertise in human physiology and how to treat injuries and illness. The trait represents knowledge of human anatomy and basic medical treatment. Characters with a low level in this Skill (1 to 2) often possess only rudimentary first-aid training, while characters with high levels (3+) are the equivalent of experienced paramedics, physicians or surgeons.

Possessed by: Medical students, paramedics, physicians, psychologists, surgeons

Specialties: Emergency Care, Pathology, Pharmaceuticals, Physical Therapy, Surgery

Draw Results

Failure: Your character's diagnosis or treatment has no effect on the patient's condition.

Success: Your character's diagnosis and treatment improves the patient's condition.

HEALING WOUNDS

Test Pool: Dexterity or Intelligence + Medicine + equipment

Action: Extended (one success is required per Health point of damage suffered; each draw represents one minute of work during play [first aid] or one hour of work during downtime [long-term hospital treatment])

Application of the healing arts can help restore a patient's lost Health points. Treatment can occur in the field through first aid or in a doctor's clinic or ER. While medical treatment can stabilize a patient or alleviate his pain, it isn't usually capable of miraculous cures or recoveries. That requires time and rest on the patient's part, and prolonged care.

Dexterity + Medicine may be drawn in the field or ER, while Intelligence + Medicine may be drawn in a lab or operating room, where science and technology does much of the work of healing injuries. Typically, Dexterity + Medicine is drawn when a patient is dying while being cared for. Intelligence + Medicine is drawn once a patient has been stabilized and can undergo long-term care.

Achieving sufficient successes (equal to the total Health points lost by the patient) restores one Health point lost to bashing damage, in addition to any healing that the character already does under his own power. A patient may regain no more than one "extra" Health point by this means per day. Alternatively, a patient who's bleeding to death or in a coma is stabilized if one success is achieved on the draw. (The loss of Health points to aggravated damage each minute is stopped; see "Incapacitation," p. 239.)

Round-the-clock, intensive care diminishes a patient's injuries, downgrading the nature of wounds by one degree. Thus, a lethal wound can be downgraded to bashing, and an aggravated wound can be downgraded to lethal. Such treatment can occur only in a hospital or other intensive-care facility. An extended Intelligence + Medicine draw is made. The number of successes required is five for a lethal wound and 10 for an aggravated one. Each draw requires an hour, although this time may be changed to one day during downtime to reflect longer hospital stays.

This kind of treatment always focuses on the worst of the patient's injuries first. Thus, an aggravated wound is downgraded to lethal before a lethal wound is downgraded to bashing. No more than one wound can be downgraded per day of treatment.

Note that this treatment does not eliminate wounds. It simply minimizes them. A patient must heal downgraded injuries completely by himself or receive other treatment to eliminate them.

Example: *Someone has beaten the crap out of Drew. He has lost all of his 7 Health points to lethal damage and is now bleeding to death (acquiring an aggravated wound per minute). Corey discovers Drew and performs first aid. Corey's Dexterity is 3 and Medicine is 4. He must accumulate seven successes to stop the flow of blood and save Drew's life. Until Corey accumulates the number of successes required to stop the bleeding, Drew continues to gain one aggravated wound per minute as he keeps bleeding (see "Incapacitation," p. 239). Three draws (and minutes) pass before Corey accumulates the required successes, at which point Drew stops incurring aggravated* injuries. That leaves him with three aggravated and four lethal wounds. If Corey's draws were repeatedly unsuccessful, Drew could have died while being treated.

Later, in the hospital, the attending physician puts Drew in intensive care to alleviate the worst of his injuries. The doctor has 4 Intelligence and 4 Medicine, and gains a +4 bonus for tools and facilities. In three hours, 10 successes are drawn for him and he reduces one of Drew's aggravated wounds to lethal damage. At least two more days of such successful treatment must pass before Drew's remaining two aggravated wounds are reduced to lethal, one per day. After that, Drew is allowed to recover on his own with rest. It takes two days before he heals one of his lethal injuries and his right-most Health box is emptied (see "Healing," p. 240). Before any more time is lost, however, a staggering Drew escapes from the hospital to avoid explanations, to hole up and to plot his revenge.

Draw Results

Failure: Your character makes no progress in alleviating the patient's injuries. If the subject is bleeding to death, a wound turns from lethal to aggravated over the course of the wasted minute.

Success: Your character makes progress in alleviating the patient's injuries. Until you acquire the total number of successes required to stop a patient from bleeding to death, one more of his wounds turns from lethal to aggravated per minute.

OCCULT

"What do you suppose those symbols mean?" Pete pointed to the strange marks on the ground. There were dozens of the glyphs all around the abandoned warehouse, all done in garish red spray paint, some several feet across. He stooped down, examining them more closely. "Lots of anti-Christian stuff here – do you think we're dealing with some sort of Satanic cult?"

Sean shook his head, not bothering to look any closer. "Hardly. It's a distraction. All of this is mainstream symbolism, the kind of stuff you'd find on the backpack of a kid who wants to upset Mommy and Daddy. It doesn't match the highly ritualistic stuff we've seen so far."

Something caught Sean's eye and he walked over to the far wall. "Here." He pointed to a much smaller, more precisely drawn symbol done in a much darker red. "This is the real deal. Late 16th century alchemical notation. Looks Italian by the design. Not exactly something you'd find in the New Age section at the mall." He tapped the wall absently, thinking. "But who drew it in rural New Jersey?"

The Occult Skill reflects a character's knowledge and experience with the world's various legends and lore about the supernatural. A character with this Skill not only knows the theories, myths and legends of the occult, but can generally discern "fact" from fiction. Characters may come by this Skill in a variety of ways, from oddball college courses to hearing legends and myths from the lips of superstitious family members.

Possessed by: Anthropologists, authors, neo-pagans, occult scholars, parapsychologists

Specialties: Cultural Beliefs, Ghosts, Magic, Monsters, Superstitions, Witchcraft

Draw Results

Failure: Your character is unable to identify or remember any useful facts about the situation at hand.

Success: Your character properly identifies or remembers facts about an example of occult phenomena.

POLITICS

"You can't be serious! I can't order this! It's criminal! It could ruin my career!"

Savastano leaned back in his chair, enjoying the sound of the man's panic. When he at last replied, his voice was smooth and measured, almost pleasant, but there was also no mistaking the conviction of his words. "Only a brief scandal at most, and with my help, you'll make it through just fine. You always do. That was our agreement, remember?" Silence. "Good. Now, can I count on you to ensure that absolutely all police patrols will be diverted from that neighborhood?"

Silence again, but only for a moment. "Yes, master. It shall be done."

Savastano allowed himself a private smile, edged with razor-sharp teeth. "Good."

Characters possessing this Skill are not only familiar with the way the political process works, they're experienced with bureaucracies and know exactly who to call in a given situation to get something done. Your character keeps track of who's in power and how she got there, along with her potential rivals. He has a grasp of the issues of the moment and how they affect the political process, and knows whose palms to grease. It's possible that your character acquired this Skill by running for political office at some point, or by working on a campaign or as a public servant. Alternatively, he could simply be someone who follows the news and understands the money trail.

Possessed by: Bureaucrats, civil servants, journalists, lawyers, lobbyists, politicians

Specialties: Bribery, Elections, Federal, Local, State, Scandals

Draw Results

Failure: Your character makes no headway in his efforts in the political arena. Perhaps he can't get the right politician to return his calls or a recent shakeup in an office means he has to work harder to find the right "in."

Success: Your character achieves his objective.

SCIENCE

This was the third time Tracy had run the test, and she still couldn't believe the results. She had stayed on even after the rest of the technicians left, saying that she was going to try to make

a dent in some of her backlog. In truth, she was still working on one case. At first she thought the sample was merely polluted, or that someone had slipped her a red herring as a joke, but later tests confirmed that it was no mistake. It was simply the strangest blood sample she'd ever examined. And that meant one question remained: How could a human being have animal blood flowing through his veins?

This Skill represents your character's understanding of the physical and natural sciences: biology, chemistry, geology, meteorology, physics. Science is useful not only for understanding how the world works, but for making the most of the resources at hand to achieve goals. A character with a strong Science background could describe the chemical process for plating metals, for example, allowing another character with Crafts to make a silver-edged sword.

Possessed by: Engineers, scientists, students, teachers, technicians

Specialties: Biology, Chemistry, Geology, Metallurgy, Physics

Draw Results

Failure: Your character is unable to summon the necessary information from memory. It's on the tip of his tongue, but the formula, chemical or equation eludes him.

Success: Your character is able to summon the necessary knowledge to serve his needs.

Too Many Tasks!

Some players may be a little confused or overwhelmed by the number of possible Skill tasks presented in this chapter, while others may wonder why some are included at all   animal training, foraging for food   since they are generally fairly unlikely to come up during live-action play. There are a number of reasons for the various Skill tasks presented.

First, remember that while some Skills or tasks may be used in downtime more often than in regular play, that doesn t mean they re necessarily any less critical for a character to possess! A character lost in the woods during a downtime period finds the foraging task of Survival essential. The same is true for downtime uses of Academics to research a creature s weaknesses, or Crafts to make a batch of wooden stakes.

Second, the tasks provided represent some of the most common applications of Skills that players may attempt. It s important to present rules for those activities to ensure that they re handled consistently throughout **Mind s Eye Theatre**.

Third, showing how different Skills might be used in specific situations gives Storytellers a foundation for adjudicating actions not covered here.

Of course, if the Storyteller likes he can also wing it and call for a simple Attribute + Skill draw that determines the success or failure of an action. Quick and easy. It s not always trivial to remember the exact test pool for everything that can be attempted: if players want to make sure the test pool is used that they expect, make sure to note it down before attempting that action. You shouldn t gripe because your Storyteller used a pool slightly different from what you expected, only for you to figure out the correct pool after the game when you look at the books.

Physical Skills

Physical Skills are applications of a character's might, endurance and coordination, such as climbing a mountain, driving a car or shooting a gun. They are most often paired with a character's Physical Attributes in various combinations, but can also be paired with Mental Attributes when the character tries to draw on his Skill to identify an object or answer a question. Intelligence + Firearms is required to identify a particular rifle, for example, or Intelligence + Survival to read a map. Physical Skill scores represent a combination of personal experience and/or formal training rather than extensive schooling. You can't earn a degree in fist fighting, but you can graduate at the top of your class in the school of hard knocks.

Untrained Skill Use: If your character doesn't have the necessary Physical Skill required for a draw, he can still attempt the action. Draw his Attribute alone with a -1 penalty.

ATHLETICS

Yards flew by in a moonlit blur as Tony raced through the graveyard, weaving and sidestepping inbetween the crumbling monuments with unthinking expertise born of many years of football practice. He didn't look down, trusting his feet to find the way safely. Nor did he look back. "Always assume they're less than two steps behind you and just run like hell," his old coach had often said, and though Tony knew he'd meant pursuing linebackers, it was still good advice when faced with the... things that had crawled out of the earth.

No, Tony kept his eyes on the car ahead and didn't think about the hideous growling noises behind him. Forty yards... thirty... twenty. He fished his keys out of his hip pocket, losing only a step in the process, and poured on the last of his speed. Ten yards – and then he was there, throwing open the car door and starting it just as the growls caught up and shadows moved outside the car window. Tony hit the gas and the car roared out of the cemetery, heading for the halfway house where his friends would be waiting.

He was winded – but alive.

Athletics encompasses a broad category of physical training, from rock climbing to kayaking to professional sports such as football or hockey. The Athletics Skill can be applied to any action that requires prolonged physical exertion or that demands considerable agility or hand-eye coordination. Examples include climbing a high wall, marching long distances and leaping between rooftops. In combat, the Skill is combined with Dexterity to determine the accuracy of thrown weapons.

Possessed by: Professional athletes, police officers, soldiers, survivalists, physical trainers

Specialties: Acrobatics, Climbing, Kayaking, Long-Distance Running, Sprinting, Swimming, Throwing

Draw Results

Failure: Your character fails to accomplish the attempted action. His throw misses the mark. He doesn't make it to the far rooftop. In the case of an extended physical action such as climbing or long-distance running, he doesn't lose ground but doesn't make any real headway, either.

Success: Your character accomplishes the action as planned. His throw hits the mark. He gains on the fleeing, shadowy figure. He catches the falling baby.

CLIMBING

Test Pool: Strength + Athletics + equipment

Action: Instant or extended (one success is required per floor or 10 feet of height; in an extended task each draw represents one minute of climbing)

Climbing an object requires a number of successes in an instant or extended action. Your character can climb 10 feet with each success drawn. Objects that are 10 feet or less in height can be climbed as an instant action. Draws may be modified based on the availability of hand- and footholds, sheerness or slipperiness of the slope, and wind conditions, all at the Storyteller's discretion. Similarly, if the character chooses to take his time and pick his way carefully up the incline, each minute added to the draw provides a +1 modifier, to a maximum of +3. Thus, if a character takes his time and each draw represents three minutes of effort instead of one, a +2 modifier is added to each draw.

Example: Your character attempts to climb a tree to get his bearings while lost in a forest. He finds a suitable tree with lots of accessible branches and starts to climb. The Storyteller determines that the tree is 60 feet tall, and that it has been raining so the branches are slick. Your character's Strength is 3 and his Athletics is 2. He has no tools other than his hands and feet, so he takes his time; three minutes pass on each draw for a +2 bonus. The Storyteller imposes a −1 modifier due to the slippery conditions. Climbing to the top of the tree requires a total of six successes (one success per 10 feet) over the course of an extended action. If it takes four draws to accumulate the required six successes, your character reaches the top of the tree after 12 minutes.

Draw Results

Failure: Your character doesn't make any headway on his attempted climb. He doesn't lose altitude, but he doesn't gain any, either.

Success: Your character reaches the top of the object he wishes to climb (if performed as an instant action), or makes continued headway to the top (in an extended action).

OPTIONAL TASK: FOOT CHASE

This is an optional task because it might not always apply to every situation, particularly combat, due to the existence of the Fair Escape rule (see p. 207). It is therefore recommended for use only in scenes specifically designed to showcase foot chases for maximum dramatic effect, in which it should replace the simplified chase rules of Fair Escape.

Test Pool: Stamina + Athletics + equipment versus Stamina + Athletics + equipment

Action: Extended and contested (each draw represents one turn of running)

It's inevitable that your character will chase someone (or more likely be chased) in his burgeoning experiences with the supernatural. He may interrupt a creature preying upon a hapless victim and race after the thing, or he may stumble upon a scene not meant for his eyes and suddenly he's the hunted.

A chase is a matter of endurance, reflexes and fleetness of foot. Draw Stamina + Athletics for each participant. This is not quite the conventional extended and contested task, however. Draws are made for each participant in each stage (in each turn), but the quarry has a different goal than the pursuer. The number of successes that must be acquired for the quarry equals the pursuer's Running Speed. Therefore, if the pursuer has a Running Speed of 12, successes accumulated for the quarry must reach 12 for him to get away.

The pursuer, however, does not seek to get away. His goal is much more specific: to stop the quarry from escaping. The number of successes that the pursuer needs is therefore different. He seeks to tally a number that equals or exceeds the quarry's current total of successes at any point in the chase. If the pursuer gets that number, he catches up.

The Running Speed trait of quarry and pursuer is also a factor in determining who is likely to get away or be caught. A human adult isn't likely to catch a cheetah, for example, but a cheetah can probably catch a human adult. For every three points of difference between competitors' Running Speed traits, the faster one gets a +1 bonus on chase draws. Remainders are rounded down. Therefore, if a pursuer has a Running Speed of 11 and a quarry has a Running Speed of 8, draws made for the pursuer get a +1 bonus. If a pursuer has a Running Speed of 10 and a quarry has a Running Speed of 11, neither party gets a bonus (the difference between Running Speed traits is less than three and is rounded down).

Example: Jack runs from a would-be attacker. He has 2 Stamina, 2 Athletics, athletic shoes and a Running Speed of 10. The attacker has 3 Stamina, 1 Athletics and a Running Speed of 9. The difference between their Running Speed traits is not sufficient to give either a bonus (it's less than three, so is rounded down to zero). Five points are collected for Jack's test pool, and a total of 10 successes must be accumulated for him to get away. Four points are collected for the attacker's pool, but she only needs to accumulate a number of successes that equals or exceeds what Jack has in any turn. Thus, if Jack gets one success in the first turn and the pursuer gets one or more, she catches Jack right away. If by the fifth turn Jack has eight successes and she has four, and her total successes from turn to turn has never equaled or exceeded his total, Jack has always maintained the lead. If by seventh turn Jack has nine successes and his pursuer has eight, he gets away. His pursuer runs out of steam or stumbles.

If the quarry of a chase has a head start, she gets a number of automatic successes at the beginning of the chase. Any successes drawn for her throughout the extended and contested task are added to that number from turn to turn, giving the quarry an advantage throughout. As a rule of thumb, when calculating a head start, each turn of combat or five steps outside of combat that the fleeing character has been running without pursuit is worth one automatic success. So, if Jack had already been running for three turns when the chase broke out, he would have a foundation of three successes on which to add his own throughout the chase. That bonus would make it all the harder for his pursuer to accumulate an equal or greater number than he has in any given turn.

Negative modifiers to draws due to hazardous terrain or dangerous conditions apply equally to opposing participants. A desperate escapee can even intentionally incur a negative modifier (leaping a hurdle or navigating a construction site) to force her pursuer to cope with the same conditions.

All of a participant's actions must be dedicated to running in a chase. If someone performs a different action in any turn, such as firing a gun, his Stamina + Athletics draw for that turn is forfeit. The character might even perform another action and travel his Acting Speed instead of his Running Speed, but he loses momentum in the race; he adds no successes to his total. Only a character who possesses a supernatural power or a special Merit might maintain a chase *and* be able to perform a separate action in a turn.

The actual distance between quarry and pursuer at any point in a chase is based on the difference of total successes between them. Each success is worth about 10 steps. So, if Jack has six successes and his pursuer has two, he is 40 steps ahead. Of course, the Storyteller can compress this scale or set another standard for what the difference measures. If opponents race over broken, uneven ground, each success between them could represent only five steps. Or, if the chase occurs in wide-open spaces, each success between subjects could represent 20 steps.

If a pursuer's total successes ever equal or exceed a quarry's in any given turn, the pursuer catches up. The race ends. The pursuer is allowed one free action against the quarry, such as a charge maneuver. See "Charging," p. 225. The quarry is fully aware of the threat, is not surprised and is entitled to her Defense. Initiative is drawn thereafter for both participants if combat breaks out.

Note that a simple foot race in which competitors seek to be the first to cross a finish line is handled like a conventional extended and contested task. Successes for each participant are accumulated and all seek the same total number of successes. The first one to get that total is the winner.

Draw Results

Failure: The participant gains no ground in the pursuit.

Success: The participant gains some ground in the chase, whether fleeing or in pursuit.

JUMPING

Test Pool: Strength + Athletics + equipment

Action: Instant

A character can jump one foot vertically for each success gained on a jumping draw. In a standing broad jump, a character can cross one step per success drawn. In a running jump, a character can cross a number of steps equal to her Size + four steps per success drawn. So, if a person who's Size 5 gets three successes in a running jump, she travels 17 steps. In order to make a running jump, a character must be able to run a distance of at least 10 steps. If space is limited, every two steps (rounding up) short of 10 impose a –1 penalty on the Strength + Athletics draw. So, if a character who wants to make jump needs at least 10 steps in which to get a running start, but she has only five steps with which to work, the draw suffers a –3 penalty.

Before jumping, a character may attempt to gauge the distance and her chances of success before committing. Draw Intelligence + Composure or Athletics, at the Storyteller's discretion. If the draw is successful, you learn the number of successes needed to make the jump and decide if it's worth the risk. You may also learn what penalties are imposed by having insufficient space to get a proper running start.

Example: Nick finds himself trapped on the roof of his apartment building with the vampire's blood slaves charging up the stairs after him. His only hope is to jump to the roof of the adjacent building and hope that the thugs won't have the nerve to follow. The Narrator rules that the distance between buildings is 20 steps. Nick is Size 5. A jumping draw must generate at least four successes (for a total of 21 steps) and he needs at least 10 steps to get a running start, which the Narrator says is available. His Strength is 3 and his Athletics is 3. Nick gets lucky and draws a 10, then a 3, for a draw total of 19 – four successes. Leaping from the stone parapet, Nick crosses the intervening distance and lands on the far roof with his usual stylish flair.

It was a dangerous feat, though. Under less stressful circumstances, Nick might have gauged his chances before risking his life. The Storyteller could have allowed his player an Intelligence + Composure or Athletics draw to determine that four successes were required. Or if the Storyteller decided that only eight steps were available to get a running start, a successful gauging draw would have told Nick's player that four successes were required, and that a –1 penalty would have applied.

Draw Results

Failure: Your character doesn't achieve any significant distance at all — he jumps too early, has a false start or loses his nerve. He gains a few inches vertically or about a foot horizontally, which could also mean a fall.

Success: Your character leaps a number of feet based on the successes drawn.

THROWING

Test Pool: Dexterity + Athletics + equipment

Action: Instant

Characters can throw all manner of objects at each other, from weapons like knives and spears to mundane objects like footballs and baseballs, or even items that aren't normally intended to be thrown at all, such as laptops, tiles or briefcases. Note that throwing distance is somewhat simplified in **Mind's Eye Theatre**. Barring supernatural Strength or other mystical enhancements, a character is limited to medium range when throwing items, unless the object is designed to be aerodynamic (like a football or a spear), in which case it may be thrown to long range normally. For an explanation of range categories, see "Range" in Chapter 7: Combat, p. 221.

Damage for thrown weapons is listed with the weapon's description. Items not intended to be used as thrown weapons such as laptops or chairs typically confer a +1 bonus to the draw and inflict bashing damage, unless the Storyteller specifically rules otherwise. Even though it might seem odd to give a small object like a bookend the same bonus as a chair, that bonus reflects the fact that neither item is designed or weighted for throwing, and so their difference in size and mass doesn't matter much in the end.

See the "Catching Thrown Objects" sidebar.

Draw Results

Failure: The object misses its mark or simply does not make it as far as intended.

Success: Your character hits his intended target. In the case of a thrown weapon, each success inflicts one point of damage.

Catching Thrown Objects

An object thrown to or at a target could be caught by him. Obviously, the distance between thrower and target cannot be greater than the range to which the object can be thrown. The thrower s accuracy is also a factor in whether an intended receiver can successfully catch the item.

If an object is thrown *to* a receiver with the intent to be caught, Dexterity + Athletics is drawn for the receiver. The receiver s draw gets a number of bonus points equal to the number of successes achieved in the thrower s draw. Thus, if Tony throws a football to Justin and three successes are drawn for Tony, Justin s Dexterity + Athletics draw to catch the ball gets a +3 bonus. If the thrower s draw fails to earn any successes, the target is missed. The intended receiver cannot catch the item at all.

If an object is thrown *at* a target (probably with the intent to hit and hurt him), and the target is unaware of the object s approach, the object can t be caught. Indeed, the target gets no Defense. He is essentially surprised (see p. 205). Successes achieved in the throw inflict points of damage to the target. (Damage might also be done to an intended receiver of an object if the draw for his catch suffers a particularly dismal failure. Points of damage equal the successes achieved in the throw.)

The Storyteller may allow an unaware target to recognize an incoming object before he s hit. The target s player makes a reflexive perception draw (see p. 47). If it fails, the attack proceeds as discussed above. If the Wits + Composure draw succeeds, the target can try to get out of the way (his Defense applies normally), or he can try to catch the object.

If he tries to catch it, he loses his Defense against the attack (after all, he tries to put himself in the object s path). A contested Dexterity + Athletics draw is then made against the thrower s draw. If the thrower gets more successes, the target is still hit and those successes are inflicted as damage. If the target gets more successes, he catches the item. In the case of a tie, the would-be catcher is hit and the thrower s successes are inflicted as damage. The Storyteller may rule that catching a blunt object such as a rock might be done completely without harm, but catching a sharp object such as a knife might still inflict a point of lethal damage. The receiver cuts open his hand. Perhaps five or more successes achieved on a catching draw negate damage from even a sharp item.

Of course, ranged attacks made from guns or bows cannot normally be caught unless the target has some kind of supernatural power that allows him to see and react to such fast-moving objects.

BRAWL

"Want some advice? You should get out of my way, little lady." The unkempt thug, easily a foot taller than Stein and probably with a hundred pounds on her, sneered. Stein was unimpressed. A professional wouldn't have bothered with small talk. He would have simply taken her down. When the man moved forward and Stein held her ground, he got close, wagging a thick finger as warning. "That's it, princess. I'm giving you to the count of—"

Stein grabbed his wrist with one hand and tugged it quickly toward her, pulling him completely off-balance, then jerked down hard, bringing the thug to his knees. As he fell, she brought her elbow up under his chin in a hard strike. The force snapped his jaw shut violently enough to knock out two teeth and cause his eyes to roll back into his head. Just to be sure, Stein held on to his wrist and followed him to the ground, locking him in a nerve hold.

"Next time, less talking." Stein said to the unconscious thug, reaching into her pocket for her cell phone to call the police.

Brawl defines your character's prowess at unarmed combat, whether she's a black belt in karate, a hard-bitten street tough or a college student who's taken a few self-defense courses. Characters with this Skill know how to hit an opponent, where to hit for maximum effect and how to defend themselves from attack. It can mean using fists, but also elbows, knees, shoulders, head butts wrestling, joint locks and choke holds. Characters with a several dots could be familiar with multiple techniques of unarmed combat. Expertise in such techniques is reflected in the Fighting Style Merits (see pp. 134-135), which are based on Brawl.

Brawl is added to your character's Strength to battle people in unarmed combat.

Possessed by: Bikers, boxers, gangsters, police officers, soldiers

Specialties: Blocking, Boxing, Dirty Tricks, Grappling, Kung Fu, Throws

Draw Results

Failure: Your character's attack misses its target.

Success: Your character scores a hit against her opponent. See Chapter 7 for details on combat and inflicting damage.

DRIVE

One thing Marcus hated about watching car chases in movies was that they always took too long. In his experience, barring massive police involvement, a real car chase was over in two minutes or less. It boiled down to who was willing to take bigger risks, and perhaps more importantly who pulled them off. Fortunately, as a professional driver used to pulling a getaway in just about any vehicle, Marcus had mastered most of those risks.

Which made it all the more disturbing that the black sedan was still behind him, even after eight minutes of evasive city driving. Whoever was behind the wheel easily matched him trick for trick, risk for risk, as if his opponent had already seen how this chase would turn out. Marcus tried to quell his rising anxiety even as he searched for another escape route. He didn't even know who they were. The Feds? The Family?

Marcus turned a tight corner and immediately cursed, seeing the road ahead blocked by two more identical cars. It was time to take another crazy risk... or to pick up the gun on the seat next to him.

Drive Skill allows your character to operate a vehicle under difficult or dangerous conditions. Characters don't need this Skill to simply drive a car. It's safe to assume in modern society that most individuals are familiar with automobiles and the rules of the road. Rather, this trait covers the training or experience necessary to operate at high speeds, to tackle hazardous road conditions and to push a vehicle to the limits of its performance. Drive is the difference between a typical suburban parent with a minivan and a police officer, car thief or racecar driver.

The Skill also applies to piloting and controlling boats; your character's Drive dots are applied equally to handling boats. In order for your character to be able to pilot a plane, he needs a Pilot Specialty in the Skill. With that, efforts to control a plane call for a Drive-based draw, plus one point for your character's Pilot Specialty. A character with the Drive Skill who does not possess a Pilot Specialty cannot effectively operate a plane. His efforts to fly are based on Attribute alone, at a –1 untrained penalty.

Note that dots in Drive do not apply to manually fixing or building vehicles, only to operating them. Construction and repair is the province of the Crafts Skill (see p. 63).

Possessed by: Car thieves, couriers, delivery drivers, emergency responders, police officers, racecar drivers

Specialties: High-Performance Cars, Motorcycles, Off-Road, Pursuit, Shaking Tails, Stunts

Draw Results

Failure: Your character doesn't complete his intended maneuver. The direction the vehicle travels (if it goes anywhere at all) is determined by the Storyteller rather than by your character.

Success: Your character completes his intended maneuver.

FIREARMS

None of the goons had their guns out. From his hiding place in the bushes, Dwayne recognized that they weren't expecting a fight. The strangers obviously didn't know how folks out this way lived. In these parts, you took to trespassers about as kindly as you did the tax man. Dwayne sighted down his rifle and waited until they were at his front door, their phony bank papers in hand, thinking they would just swagger in and take his land like he was some hick. He'd show them.

Dwayne had been a Marine in the first Gulf war, and had hunted all of his life. He couldn't have asked for sweeter shots than his own land allowed. When the intruders knocked, he opened fire.

His first two were free. The others were amateurs and froze up as their leader and his second collapsed. Finally, they ran and pointed to where the shots had come from, but Dwayne had already moved to his second position, where he got three more of them. It was over in moments. "Bring as many guys as you want," Dwayne muttered as he emerged from cover, carefully covering the motionless bodies. "I got all the bullets in the world."

Firearms allows your character to identify, operate and maintain most types of guns, from pistols to rifles to military weapons such as submachine guns, assault rifles and machine guns. This Skill can represent the kind of formal training provided to police and the military, or the basic, hands-on experience common to hunters, criminals and gun enthusiasts. Firearms also applies to using bows. Your character can use guns and bows equally.

Note that dots in Firearms do not apply to manually fixing or building guns, only to wielding them. Construction and repair is the province of the Crafts Skill (see p. 63).

Possessed by: Criminals, gun dealers, hunters, police officers, soldiers, survivalists

Specialties: Autofire, Bow, Pistol, Rifle, Shotgun, Sniping, Trick Shot

Draw Results

Failure: Your character misses his intended target. The Storyteller determines what, if anything, the bullet actually hits.

Success: Your character hits his intended target. See Chapter 7 for details on inflicting damage with firearms.

LARCENY

Nick stared at the lock, perplexed. So far this job had been by the numbers, almost boring, but suddenly it was a lot more interesting. The locks on the back and basement doors had been high quality, but nothing he hadn't seen before. He'd been able to run a standard bypass on the electronic security system. It was high-end gear for a charity, that was for sure, but nothing outside his experience.

Until now, anyway. It looked to Nick like this door was fitted with a standard lock set, but it also had a strange black box right above the knob, which didn't look like anything he knew. At first he thought it must be some electronic security measure, but it didn't seem to have any juice in it, nor did it appear to be able to broadcast any signal. As he looked more closely, Nick could make out strange symbols etched into the surface. He didn't know what they meant, but they gave him a chill.

Still, he had a job to do. Bypassing the ordinary locks, Nick took one last look at the box and pushed the door open. Alarms sounded, but unfortunately for Nick, they weren't meant to alert mortal authorities. In the darkness beneath the building, something wicked stirred, smelling warm flesh.

Larceny is a broad Skill that covers everything from picking locks to concealing stolen goods. Most characters obtain this Skill the hard way, by committing crimes and often paying the price for their mistakes. Some individuals such as government agents and members of the military receive formal training in bypassing security systems and stealing valuable assets.

Possessed by: Burglars, commandos, government agents, private eyes

Specialties: Concealing Stolen Goods, Lockpicking, Pickpocketing, Security Systems, Safecracking

Draw Results

Failure: Your character doesn't complete his intended action. His attempt at picking a mark's pocket comes up empty, or the lock he works on refuses to cooperate.

Success: Your character completes his action without arousing any notice or suspicion. He pockets the stolen wallet, slips inside the dark building or plucks the diamond from the nest of laser beams without anyone the wiser.

BYPASS SECURITY SYSTEM

Test Pool: Dexterity + Larceny + equipment

Action: Extended (5–15 successes, depending on the complexity of the system; each draw represents a turn — three seconds — of work)

Bypassing a security system can be as simple as shorting out two contacts on a window frame, or as complex as opening a junction box and making major modifications to a sophisticated circuit board, all in a matter of seconds. The task is an extended action, with the required number of successes depending on the complexity of the system in question. A basic alarm might demand 4, while a standard home-security system might require as many as 8. Sophisticated corporate or government security systems might require 15 or more successes to disarm, at the Storyteller's discretion. Using specialized tools can add modifiers to the draw.

If a character attempts this during a game, the Storyteller may rule for game flow purposes that the intruder only has to make a single draw, with the difficulty set by the complexity of the system he is trying to bypass. If an alarm is triggered by a failure, the Storyteller may give the intruder a chance to disable it, using a single draw with the complexity of the alarm system setting as the difficulty. Storytellers, be careful with this fast-and-dirty system. Characters who have taken pains to ensure security should have some reasonable degree of expectation of that security's effectiveness, and letting a neonate sneak past an elder's significant defenses "in the interests of game flow" does a disservice both to the elder's player and the setting.

Most home and corporate alarm systems have a warning period of 30 or 45 seconds to allow for an authorized user to disarm the system before triggering an alarm. Thus, a would-be burglar has only 10 or 15 turns to locate and disarm the system before the alarm goes off.

Example: *Nick picks the lock on the councilman's back door and slips inside. The house's security system beeps a warning and Nick heads for the main junction box in the basement. It takes three turns to dash down the stairs and find the box, leaving only seven turns before the alarm activates. Nick's Dexterity is 4 and his Larceny is 4, and he has a set of electronics tools that give him a +1 modifier. A standard home-security system requires 8 successes to disarm, and the first draw is a 5, for a draw total of 14 – one success earned, nine to go. The second draw earns no successes. The third draw total is 16 – two more successes that bring his total to three. The fourth draw total is 15 – two successes. With time running out, the fifth draw total is 20 – three successes and enough to disarm the system, six seconds (two turns) before the alarm activates.*

Draw Results

Failure: Your character fails to make any headway in disarming the security system. Is it the red wire or the yellow one?

Success: Your character makes progress in disarming the system (apply successes drawn toward the total needed).

LOCKPICKING

Test Pool: Dexterity + Larceny + equipment

Action: Extended (2–12+ successes required, depending on the sophistication of the lock; one draw represents one turn – three seconds – of work)

Picking a lock is one of the most common applications of Larceny, and requires nothing more than a basic set of tools, a steady hand and a few moments' concentration. The task is an extended action, requiring a number of successes based on the toughness and sophistication of the lock. A suitcase or diary lock might require two or three successes, while a padlock or a house lock might demand anywhere from four to seven. Combination locks could require anywhere from eight to 12. Using specialized lockpicking tools (as opposed to improvised picks) can add a bonus to the draw.

Example: *Once inside the house, Nick finds the mayor's study and locates his wall safe. The safe has a basic combination lock requiring eight successes to pick. Nick's Dexterity is 4 and his*

Larceny is 4, and he has a set of safecracking tools that add a +1 modifier. The first draw total is 19 – he is halfway there with four successes. The second draw total is 20, for another four successes. The last tumbler clicks into place and the small door swings open after only two turns (six seconds).

Draw Results

Failure: Your character makes no headway against the lock.

Success: Your character makes progress toward picking the lock (apply successes toward the total needed).

SLEIGHT OF HAND

Test Pool: Dexterity + Larceny + equipment versus Wits + Composure or Wits + Larceny

Action: Contested

Your character picks a pocket. Palms an item. Slips something inside his clothing or bag – all without being noticed, or so he hopes. Your character could develop this talent for unscrupulous reasons, or because he's a magician or performer. Or maybe he runs an "honest" shell game on the street. Regardless of the rationale, your character can take things or move things without attracting attention. They typically need to be Size 1 or less – he can't make a piano disappear with a flick of the wrist. However, he might make an artifact disappear from a museum showing with the right timing and a convenient distraction.

Draw your character's Dexterity + Larceny + equipment versus a victim or possible observer's Wits + Composure or Wits + Larceny (whichever makes for the larger pool). The Storyteller decides how many people could be possible observers, or just makes a single collective draw for a crowd. If you get the most successes, your character grabs, produces or hides something. If the victim or observer gets as many or more successes, she's wise to your character's efforts. She could call foul, call for the police or call your character out privately and insist on a cut of whatever scheme he's running.

Draw Results

Failure: The effort to grab, move or hide something goes incomplete. The item remains where it was or is still exposed in your character's hands. The Storyteller could allow one or more successive attempts (see p. 176) before your character draws attention to himself.

Success: Your character steals, palms or moves an item as planned, without notice.

STEALTH

Victor knew from experience that only seasoned veterans or raw amateurs tried to avoid being seen altogether when infiltrating a location. Modern security devices were so small and sophisticated that it was generally best to assume that you would be seen. Going unnoticed was the key, blending in with the regular traffic whenever possible.

So, when Victor tailed a creature back to its midtown apartment, he didn't don black from head to toe and attach suction cups to his hands and knees. He got a delivery-service outfit from a uniform store, fabricated a "package" to deliver, and dug up enough information on his target's next-door neighbor to make it past the doorman. Beyond the front desk, Victor drew his weapons from the package and was ready to hit the creature's apartment.

The Stealth Skill represents a character's experience or training in avoiding notice, whether by moving silently, making use of cover or blending into a crowd. When attempting to sneak silently through an area or to use the local terrain as concealment, draw Dexterity + Stealth + equipment. When trying to remain unseen in a crowd, Wits + Stealth is appropriate. The Storyteller may make Stealth draws secretly on your behalf, since your character usually has no way of knowing he's been noticed until it's too late. If your character attempts to avoid notice by a group of alert observers, a contested draw versus the observers' Wits + Composure + equipment is required.

Possessed by: Criminals, hunters, police officers, private investigators
Specialties: Camouflage, Crowds, Moving in Darkness, Moving in Woods

Draw Results

Failure: Your character fails to move or act in a stealthy fashion. If potential observers get at least one success on a Wits + Composure draw, your character is busted.

Success: Your character avoids notice if his successes exceed his opponents'.

SURVIVAL

It had been five days since the last of Dietrich's supplies had run out, but he still made his way across the desolate landscape. The thought of finally confronting the creature in its lair and putting an end to it kept him going. That, and the rigorous training he'd put himself through before the hunt began. The others had mocked him as he struggled to pitch a tent, start a fire or curse as he failed his own tests to locate fresh drinking water. But without that intensive practice, he knew he would have fallen three days ago.

Of course, keeping himself alive and keeping himself in fighting shape were two different things, and Dietrich was well aware that if his trip took much longer, he'd be in no condition to take the thing on. So he conserved his strength as much as possible, and focused on the end of the line. If all went well, he'd still have to make this trek back... but with one less burden.

Survival represents your character's experience or training in "living off the land." He knows where to find food and shelter, and how to endure harsh environmental conditions. The more capable your character is, the fewer resources he needs in order to prevail. A master survivalist can walk into a forest, desert or mountainous region with little more than a pocketknife and the clothes on his back and survive for weeks if necessary.

Note that Survival is not synonymous with Animal Ken (see p. 85). The former helps your character stay alive in the wilderness, living off the land with whatever supplies he has brought with him. The latter involves understanding animal behavior and interacting directly with animals. Your character could be knowledgeable in creating shelter and gathering plants to eat (Survival), but might know nothing about anticipating the actions of a bear in his camp (Animal Ken).

Possessed by: Explorers, hunters, soldiers, survivalists

Specialties: Foraging, Navigation, Meteorology, Shelter

Draw Results

Failure: Your character fails to find the proper resources to fulfill his needs. All the available firewood is wet and the trout line he strings doesn't catch anything.

Success: Your character finds enough resources to fulfill his needs for the day.

FORAGING

Test Pool: Wits + Survival + equipment

Action: Extended (five successes required; one draw covers 10 minutes during play or represents one hour of searching during downtime)

Foraging for food and water is an extended action. Each draw represents an hour of diligent work during downtime. Five successes are required to gather enough food and water to sustain one person for a single day. One success still provides some amount of food and water, but fewer than five means that your character becomes progressively malnourished and vulnerable to deprivation (p. 241) and disease (p. 242).

Draw Results

Failure: Your character does not locate any sources of food or water, despite careful searching.

Success: Your character is on his way to gathering sufficient food to fulfill his needs for the day (apply successes to the total needed).

WEAPONRY

"What are you going to do with that little thing, mortal?" The creature laughed as Drew threw down his gun, drew his knife and adopted a ready stance. "Shoot me. Stab me. I do not die."

The monster lunged forward with a massive swipe of a claw, aiming to take Drew's head off his shoulders. Drew ducked under the swing and buried his blade in the creature's upper arm, slashing muscle and tendon with a single expert cut. The beast howled in pain and fell back, its now-useless arm flopping limply, its eyes full of pain, hate... and fear.

"You may be hard to kill, but your body still works like everyone else's," Drew said, ready for another pass. "Ready to spend eternity in little pieces?"

As the name implies, the Weaponry Skill represents your character's experience or training in fighting with everything from beer bottles to pipes, knives to swords. While formal instruction in Weaponry is uncommon (restricted to military and law-enforcement training and a few martial arts), any character who has grown up on the street or spent a lot of time in seedy bars has had ample opportunity to learn this Skill.

A character's Weaponry is added to his Strength to stage armed attacks. For more information, see Chapter 7: Combat, which also provides sample weapons and their Damage ratings, which are added to Weaponry draws as equipment bonuses.

Note that dots in Weaponry do not apply to manually fixing or creating weapons, only to wielding them. Construction and repair is the province of the Crafts Skill (see p. 63).

Possessed by: Bikers, criminals, martial artists, medieval re-enactors, police officers, soldiers

Specialties: Improvised Weapons, Knives, Swords
Draw Results
    Failure: Your character's attack misses its target.
    Success: Your character scores a hit against his opponent. See Chapter 7 for details on combat and inflicting damage.

Social Skills and Players' Characters

Use of Social Skills on Narrator characters and incidental roles played by the Storytelling staff is straightforward. There can be some confusion, however, on just how influential such Skills should be when they re used on other players characters. This section discusses three possible interpretations of results, based on how influential the Storyteller wants Social Skills to be.

Default Ruling: Influence, Don't Adjudicate

Mind's EyeTheatre assumes that successful use of a Social Skill on another players' character has the same effect as a strong influence or recommendation on the subject. Social Skills don't automatically force a target to do what the Skill user wants in hypnotic fashion. Unless the subject is absolutely dead-set against a suggested course of action, however, she should shift her roleplaying to a significant degree. The shift need not be overtly dramatic, but should be noticeable, especially to those that know the character.

As a rule of thumb, when it comes to determining how much of an effect Social Skills should have, achieving a single success should be the equivalent of giving a target a suggestion from a minor authority figure, a request from a friendly personal acquaintance, or a threat from a rival of equal standing. A success implies a suggestion from a powerful authority figure, a request from a close friend, or a threat from a rival of greater standing. Conversely, failure means the target is unmoved. Note this all means by default that players' characters should ignore the normal results described for each Skill in favor of this simplified system. Those results should, however, be used as written when dealing with Narrator characters, provided a player's roleplaying backs up his character's Skill use. Just beware those same Narrator characters using their own talents on you!

Optional Variant #1: By the Book

This approach subjects players' characters to the same rules as Narrator characters. The results of Social tests apply as written, without modification. For example, if another character gets several successes against you on a Persuasion test, you should adjust your roleplaying to not only believe what you've been told, but to accept further implications without question. This system gives characters with Social Skills a great potential to alter the behavior of others, and Storytellers should be careful to make sure players perform an appropriate amount of roleplaying before making tests, and not simply using them as a shortcut or substitute for roleplaying. This approach does avoid a great deal of debate, though. It gives players a clear standard on how they should react when Social Skills are used against them.

Optional Variant #2: No Effect

This variant goes to the other end of the spectrum and holds roleplaying freedom as essentially inviolate. (That us, unless supernatural powers are involved, in which case their rules prevail.) Social Skills have a definite game effect only on Narrator characters, and may not even be effective against certain powerful Narrator characters such as main villains or influential mentors, who are treated the same as players' characters. Players may use Social Skills against each other and make tests normally, but a target is not under any compunction to heed the results beyond his own discretion and how much the user's roleplaying influences him to do so.

This approach avoids the need to quibble over whether players respond properly to use of Social Skills. And yet, Storytellers should take care to ensure that there are plenty of opportunities for players with personable characters (who spent their points on a lot of Social Skills) to use their talents or they'll feel cheated.

Social Skills

Social Skills are applications of your character's bearing, charm and poise, such as negotiating with a bank robber, wooing a crowd or telling a faultless lie. These Skills most commonly represent innate capabilities honed by years of experience rather than by any formal training. You can teach someone the basic principles of Persuasion, but true leaders are born rather than made. These Skills are generally paired with your character's Social Attributes, but can also be used with Physical or Mental Attributes in cases such as bodily threats (Strength + Intimidation) or orchestrating a complex deal (Wits + Persuasion).

While they should *never* replace roleplaying, and Narrators are encouraged to heavily penalize or even prohibit tests if a player attempts to use a Social Skill with little to no actual roleplaying to back it up, players should remember that **Mind's Eye Theatre** is a roleplaying game. You assume roles that may be very different from your real-world personality. Just as a skinny teenager can play a champion wrestler with powerful Physical traits, a shy loner can play a smooth social chameleon. Other players should respect both choices equally. That means ignoring another player's use of a Social Skill just because he isn't very suave or persuasive out-of-character is essentially the same as ignoring an attack test because you figure you could actually beat up the opposing player.

As in real life, most Social Skills take time and attention to be truly effective. You can't just walk up to another player, talk to them for five minutes, win a single test and demand that another character leaps in the sack with yours, or spills a lifetime's secrets. Such dramatic and immediate results are the province of supernatural powers (or truly exceptional roleplaying), not Skill use.

Social Skills are just like any other type of Skill. They help adjudicate the outcome of uncertain or contested situations, but they do not automatically create their own circumstances out of thin air. In other words, no matter how talented a character is at Persuasion, a single Skill draw can't spontaneously force another character to enter contract negotiation with him. But if both are in a negotiation already, the result of his draw may influence the results in his favor.

Unless it specifically states otherwise in a Skill description, a player may only have his character use a particular Social Skill against a given target only once each scene. There is no necessary limit to how many characters he may target with a particular Skill in a scene, but he cannot use it more than once against a single target in the same scene.

If you rely on game mechanics alone to achieve the social changes you desire, you must modify a target's behavior slowly over the course of a chapter. (This statement does *not* apply to supernatural powers that involve a Social Skill as part of their test pool, unless stated otherwise. Those changes are made instantly and completely.) You cannot attempt a Social Skill test against a target over and over again in the span of several minutes until you get a favorable result. If you've tried and failed to persuade another character to see your way of thinking four times already tonight, it's bound to be more and more difficult to impress her as the night goes on.

Untrained Skill Use: If your character doesn't have the necessary Social Skill required for a feat, he can still make the attempt. Draw his Attribute alone at a -1 penalty.

ANIMAL KEN

It was the biggest wolf Leeds had ever seen.

It moved slowly out of the underbrush and approached him, ears laid back and teeth bared in a threatening display, a rumbling growl issuing from its throat. Leeds resisted the urge to run, remembering what his father had taught him: If he ever found himself face to face with a predator, he couldn't run or it would see him as prey and chase him. Likewise, he couldn't look it directly in the eyes, or it would perceive him as a challenger and attack.

Fighting the instinctual voices that told him to escape, Leeds crouched low, looking at the wolf indirectly, imitating the behavior of a friendly subordinate as best he could, and waited. The wolf stopped in its tracks, growl dying in its throat, its tail coming up in a sign of curiosity. It sniffed several times, loudly, then turned and vanished back into the forest. Almost unable to believe his luck, Leeds continued down the trail, choosing not to look back for fear of what he might see.

Somewhere far behind, he heard a chorus of wolves howling.

Anticipating and understanding human emotions is one thing, but being able to interpret and recognize the behavior of animals is something else entirely. Your character intuitively grasps or has been trained to read animals to know how they react to situations. The Skill also involves innately understanding how the animal mind operates, and what may appease or enrage beasts. The knack often coincides with a respect for animals, but it could derive from the analytical observation of a lab scientist or from years of abuse inflicted by a callous animal handler.

Animal Ken could be applied to grasp the thoughts or intentions of supernatural animals, if the Storyteller allows. Sometimes these beings have human or greater intelligence and cannot be read by this Skill alone.

Possessed by: Animal rescue workers, hunters, longtime pet owners, park rangers, ranchers, trainers, veterinarians

Specialties: Animal Needs, Imminent Attack, Specific Kind of Animal, Training

Draw Results

Failure: Your character is unable to gauge the animal's true state.

Success: Your character has a good read on the animal's true emotional state.

ANIMAL TRAINING

Dice Pool: Composure + Animal Ken + equipment (trainer) versus Stamina + Resolve (animal)

Action: Extended and contested (the task demands a number of successes equal to the opponent's Willpower; each draw represents one day of training; if a need exists to train an animal during a session, assume each session requires roughly 10 minutes of roleplaying per draw, but tricks learned in this fashion are not permanent and must be reinforced by more extended draws later)

Training an animal involves communicating a need, encouraging a type of behavior and/or discouraging unwanted behavior. It's an extended and contested process. Make Composure + Animal Ken + equipment draws for the trainer. Draw Stamina + Resolve for the animal. The number of successes that each participant seeks is equal to the other's Willpower dots. Thus, if a trainer has 5 Willpower and the animal has 3, the interrogator wins if he accumulates three successes first. The animal wins if it accumulates five successes first. The winner breaks the opponent's will to continue training or to resist the desired behavior. The trainer's draw can be modified by equipment such as rewards (food) offered and punishments inflicted. Draws made for the animal might receive a bonus based on how feral it is. A cat brought in from the wild might get a +3 bonus, for example. Likewise, non-mammals (lizards, birds) can be harder to train than mammals, imposing a penalty on a trainer's draw (say, –1 to –3). Some animals such as wolverines are so fierce that they simply can't be trained.

Only one trick or type of behavior (house breaking, "attack," or retrieving a certain item whenever it's thrown) can be taught per extended and contested series of draws. Alternatively, a few minor tricks such as "sit," "shake" and "stay" can be combined in a single series of draws.

Should an extended and contested training session end in a tie, neither side applies its will over the other. The process must start again from scratch if the trick is to be learned.

If training for a type of behavior is interrupted for a number of consecutive days in excess of the animal's Intelligence, all successes gained thus far are lost. Training for that trick must start again from scratch. Animals with zero Intelligence cannot be trained at all.

An animal can be taught a number of tricks (can undergo a separate number of training sessions) equal to its Wits.

Example: *Kathy has a pet dog that she seeks to train to attack on command, which the Storyteller agrees is one trick. Kathy has 4 Composure, 3 Animal Ken and 8 Willpower. The dog has 3 Stamina, 4 Resolve and 7 Willpower. Kathy needs to get seven successes before eight are obtained for the dog. The process begins, but is interrupted for two days in which no training occurs at all. Those two days exceed the dog's 1 Intelligence, so the training process has to begin again from scratch.*

For animals' traits, see p. 323.

Even after an animal has been trained in a behavior or trick, it does not necessarily perform the action automatically on command. You need to make a successful Manipulation + Animal Ken draw for the animal to respond as intended. You also get a bonus on the draw equal to the animal's Wits.

Draw Results

Failure: Your character fails to make any progress on the current trick.

Success: Your character makes progress in conditioning the animal's behavior.

EMPATHY

"All I ever wanted was a family," wailed the ghostly child, rubbing its spectral hands across its eyes as tears sparkled down its cheeks. Its shoulders heaved with sobs, and Jack could see even his most hard-hearted companions were moved. His own his heart went out to the poor thing, and he was about to step forward to offer it what comfort he could when he noticed it was actually peeking out from behind its hands. What he saw made him shudder: a sinister red light. What had been grief just moments before had twisted into a look of pure hatred.

"Don't believe him! He's lying!" Jack yelled. The ghost's sobbing changed to manic, high-pitched laughter, and objects around the room rose into the air and flew at the living.

This Skill represents your character's intuition for reading people's emotions. For some, it's a matter of observing body language and non-verbal cues. Others employ an extraordinary sense that helps them divine a person's true mood. As the name implies, Empathy also involves the capacity to understand other people's views and perspectives, whether your character agrees with those positions or not. This Skill is useful in everything from negotiations and crisis counseling to reading faces in a crowd and looking for potential trouble. If a subject actively conceals his emotions or motives, make a contested draw versus the person's Wits + Subterfuge + equipment.

Possessed by: Counselors, diplomats, entertainers, profilers, psychiatrists, police officers

Specialties: Emotion, Lies, Motives, Personalities

Draw Results

Failure: Your character is unable to gauge a subject's true emotional state.

Success: Your character has a good read on a person's true emotional state, regardless of whatever front the subject puts up. You may ask one of these questions: "What emotion are you feeling most strongly right now?" or "Was the last statement you made a deliberate lie?"

EXPRESSION

"Hey man, I just wanted to tell you that was a great set," came a soft female voice. Jimmy turned from breaking down his gear and saw a slight young woman dressed in punk clothes. She looked on with obvious admiration. "I mean, your lyrics are kind of out there, but they're really good. I feel like I really understand them, you know?"

"Thanks," Jimmy replied. He was used to such feedback. After all, he poured as much truth into his music as he could, at least without putting his friends in the band in danger. Most of the time it got them dismissed as a "gimmick band" obsessed with conspiracy theories, but it was the only outlet he had for what he'd experienced. "I'm glad you liked the set."

Jimmy turned back to continue packing up his equipment, but she put a firm hand on his arm. He saw something in her eyes he'd missed before – a hint of fear, sure, but also relief.

"I don't know how to say this, but when you were singing that song about the secrets stories of the world — I think I really *know* what you *mean*." She looked around. "Is there any place we can go to talk? I've been dying to talk to someone about it."

Expression reflects your character's training or experience in the art of communication, to both entertain and inform. This Skill covers the written and spoken word and other forms of entertainment, from journalism to poetry, creative writing to acting, music to dance. Characters can use it to compose written works or to put the right words together at the spur of the moment to deliver a rousing speech or a memorable toast. Used well, Expression can sway others' opinions or even hold an audience captive.

When *composing* a poem or writing a novel, draw Wits or Intelligence (depending on whether the work is poetic or factual) + Expression. When *reciting* to an audience, draw Presence + Expression. Playing an instrument involves Intelligence + Expression for a known piece, and Wits + Expression for an improvised one. Dance calls for Dexterity + Expression.

You're encouraged to actually compose or perform artistic pieces when using this Skill during play, but given that **Mind's Eye Theatre** is about make-believe, you're not required to do so. If you desire, you may simply narrate what kind of performance your character gives, followed by the number of successes you earn (to give other players a gauge of how impressive the effort is). In the case of written works, you must at least compose a summary of what the work is about and state the number of successes achieved for it, for similar reasons.

Possessed by: Actors, ballet dancers, journalists, musicians, poets, rock stars, writers

Specialties: Classical Dance, Drama, Exposés, Musical Instrument, Newspaper Articles, Speeches

Draw Results

Failure: Your character's performance fails to capture the audience's interest or attention.

Success: Your character's performance gets its point across in the manner intended, capturing the audience's interest.

INTIMIDATION

"You're wasting your time." The suspected snitch spit at Jules through a mouth of bloody teeth. She'd hoped he wouldn't be so roughed up when she arrived, but it looked like her father's goons had been a little too... enthusiastic about detaining him. "If the Don himself couldn't break me, what the hell makes you think I'm going to talk to his bitch of a daughter?"

Jules leaned forward until she was almost nose to nose with the man, allowing herself a predatory smile. She heard him breathe in sharply, a dead giveaway that his tough façade was collapsing. "Because I'm the one my father sends in when all else fails. Because he knows I enjoy my work. Because he knows I'm a cold 'bitch' who gets what she wants. When he calls me in, he gives you up for dead."

Jules watched the man fold like a house of cards.

Intimidation is the art and technique of persuading others through the use of fear. Your character can intimidate someone with a show of brute force (Strength + Intimidation), through more subtle means such as verbal threats (Manipulation + Intimidation), or simply through menacing body language (Presence + Intimidation). It can be used to get other people to cooperate (even against their better judgment), back down from a confrontation, or reveal information that they'd rather not share.

Possessed by: Bodyguards, bouncers, gangsters, executives, police officers, soldiers

Specialties: Bluster, Physical Threats, Stare-Downs, Torture, Veiled Threats

Draw Results

Failure: The victim isn't impressed and does not cooperate. Your character cannot attempt to intimidate the target for the rest of the scene.

Success: Your character overpowers his victim with threats and compels cooperation for the moment.

INTERROGATION

Test Pool: Wits + Intimidation + equipment (interrogator) versus Stamina + Resolve (subject)

Action: Extended and contested (the task demands a number of successes equal to the subject's Willpower; each draw represents 10 minutes during play or one hour of interrogation during downtime)

Interrogation involves wearing down a subject's resistance until he or she is incapable of concealing information. It's an extended and contested process. Make Wits + Intimidation + equipment draws for the interrogator. Draw Stamina + Resolve for the subject. The number of successes that each participant seeks is equal to his opponent's Willpower dots. Thus, if an interrogator has 5 Willpower and his subject has 3, the interrogator wins if he accumulates three successes first, and the subject wins if he accumulates five successes first. The winner breaks the opponent's will to continue asking questions or to resist any longer. The interrogator's draw can be modified by equipment such as torture instruments. If the subject is allowed sleep between interview sessions, draws are made for him normally. If he's denied normal sleep, he suffers a cumulative –1 penalty for each night of sleep that he misses. Thus, he's at –1 after the first night, –2 after the second, and so on.

Example: *Jules leans on a reticent "cousin" to learn exactly what he meant when he made that cryptic comment about her father being allergic to daylight. Jules' Wits is 3, her Intimidation is 4, and she has her subject tied up in an isolated and empty warehouse, which provides a +1 modifier. Jules' Willpower is 6. The cousin's Stamina + Resolve test pool is five, and he has a 5 Willpower. Jules' first draw total is 15 (two successes), while the cousin's draw total is 10 (one success). Ten minutes have gone by, and Jules needs only three more successes to break her cousin, but can she get them before the rest of his crew tracks their friend down?*

If participants' accumulated successes meet the target's simultaneously, the interrogator fails to learn what he wants and the process must start over again from scratch.

Draw Results

Failure: Your character fails to make any headway against his opponent, either as interrogator or subject.

Success: Your character makes progress against his opponent.

PERSUASION

"You really don't want to do this," Doctor Mitchell said calmly, seemingly oblivious to the knife that Tyler held to Lonnie's throat. Behind him, Mitchell could feel the others tensing to rush Tyler, but he knew that could only go badly. No, if this was going to end without anyone getting hurt, it was up to him to help Tyler see reason.

"Why shouldn't I?" the boy snarled, cutting Lonnie slightly. "What's the point in staying here? I'm just going to wind up in jail anyway."

"Well, that depends," Doctor Mitchell said. "If you do this now, you're right, you will wind up in jail. Not only that, you'll have Lonnie's death on your conscience for the rest of your life. I know you're not a bad young man at heart, Tyler. Otherwise, you wouldn't be here at a halfway house to begin with." Seeing Tyler's grip loosen, Doctor Mitchell pressed on. "I know other people have given up on you before, but you're here with us now. We've never given up on anyone in this house, and I'm not about to start now." He held out his hand. "If you put the knife down and let Lonnie go, I'll make sure you don't go to jail and we can talk about what to do next."

There was a pause, and then the knife clattered to the floor as Tyler burst out crying. Another crisis averted. Doctor Mitchell breathed a sigh of relief even as he reached out and gathered Tyler into a comforting hug.

Persuasion is the art of inspiring or changing minds through logic, charm or sheer, glib fast-talking. Though it can be taught to varying degrees of success, most characters with the Skill possess a natural talent and have honed it over years through trial and error, practicing their delivery until it rolls effortlessly off the tongue. Persuasion is the Skill of convincing others by force of personality alone, making one's point through carefully chosen words, body language and emotion.

Possessed by: Con artists, executives, generals, lawyers, politicians, salesmen, sexual predators

Specialties: Fast-Talking, Inspiring Troops, Motivational Speeches, Sales Pitches, Seduction

Draw Results

Failure: Your character does not convince her subject.

Success: Your character convinces the subject to accept her assertions.

CUTTING A DEAL

Test Pool: Manipulation + Persuasion + equipment versus Manipulation + Persuasion + equipment

Action: Extended and contested (3–10+ successes required; each draw represents as much as 10 minutes during play or an hour of negotiation during downtime)

Negotiating terms for legally binding arrangements such as contracts, settlements or treaties is a long and complex process, with both parties fighting hard to gain every possible advantage. The Storyteller must assign a required number of successes for negotiations as a whole, relative to the complexity of the terms under discussion. An entertainment contract might require only three successes, while a class-action lawsuit might require six. Major negotiations, such as cease-fires between nations or the drawing of national borders, could demand as many as 10 or more successes to resolve.

Once the success value has been determined, both parties lay out their positions and the drawing begins. Make a contested Manipulation + Persuasion + equipment (if any) draw between the leaders of the two parties. Successes earned are added to their respective totals. Discussions end when one party hits the success value set. That participant is the winner, but must make some concessions to the competitor based on the difference between the two parties' success totals. If the winner has three times the competitor's successes, no concessions are required. If the winner has double the competitor's successes, the winner must concede to a quarter of the competitor's demands. If the winner has only a simple majority of successes, he must concede to half of the competitor's demands. The winner of negotiations gets to choose which concessions to make, but the Storyteller is the final arbiter over every aspect of the process.

At a Storyteller's discretion, the hour of negotiation time constraint may be compressed to enable faster game play during a session. In such cases, success at a single contested action between the characters would result in a minor concession in favor of the victor. Major negotiations using Cutting a Deal should be undertaken outside of normal game play, or roleplayed during a game session.

Example: *Sam negotiates a new job with his "employers," who asks him to assemble a rather large team for a break-in at the Asher Institute. Sam is suspicious about why they want so much talent for one job, so he asks for twice the going rate and more details about the job. Who owns the place, what security they can expect and what's the interest in a charity organization? Naturally, his employer isn't interested in paying extra, much less giving out more information about the heist, and replies that Sam should stick with the usual rate and not get too curious.*

The Storyteller determines that the negotiation requires five successes to settle, with each draw corresponding to two minutes of haggling. Sam's Manipulation is 4 and his Persuasion is 4. He has no pertinent equipment to help him, but he mentions that his contact sounds rushed, which means he might be able to use that urgency to help seal the deal. The Storyteller agrees and awards him a +1 bonus.

The employer's Manipulation is 3 and his Persuasion is 2. He has no equipment or leverage, either. He's talks a good game, but he doesn't really know anyone else that can put together the team he needs, so the Storyteller imposes a –1 penalty for the weakness of his position.

Five draws and 10 minutes later, Sam wins the negotiation with five successes to his employer's two. Since Sam's total is more than double his opponent's, he has to concede to a quarter of the client's demands. Since his contact doesn't want him to have anything extra, a concession in this case means giving up one of his four objectives. After some consideration, Sam concedes that he is probably better off not knowing why his employer wants a charity ripped off. He settles for practical information about who runs the target and what kind of security he can expect to face, and gets the extra money.

If opponents achieve their required number of successes simultaneously, they remain at loggerheads. Both must concede at least one point of contention to the other if talks are to continue. The process then begins again from scratch.

Draw Results

Failure: Your character makes no headway against her competitor. Time to try a different tack.

Success: Your character stakes out a significant position against the competition that may be difficult to overcome.

FAST-TALK

Test Pool: Manipulation + Persuasion + equipment (talker) versus Composure + Empathy or Subterfuge (subject)

Action: Contested

Your character needs to convince another person to perform a service, to look the other way or to simply be distracted for a few moments' time. Or maybe he just wants to convince some thugs to let him go. Rather than cook up an elaborate lie or ruse, he hurls explanations, excuses, pleas and/or trivia at his target in hopes of bewildering her. The intent is to achieve his intended result in the confusion.

Fast-talk is a contested action. Draw Manipulation + Persuasion + equipment for your character, against the target's Composure + Empathy or Subterfuge. (Empathy if your character preys upon the subject's feelings, Subterfuge if he preys upon her intellect.) If your character wins, the subject performs the intended minor chore, or is otherwise tricked into doing what your character wants. If the target wins, she sees through the bluster and refuses to comply or needs further convincing (see "Cutting a Deal," above, at this point). If the two tie, the subject is in a daze, not convinced to do anything, yet too confused not to listen. In the case of a failed or tied effort, your character can make a successive attempt (see p. 176) if the Storyteller agrees that the subject can or will still listen.

Fast-talk can be used to achieve only harmless favors or results, such as gaining entrance to a club, allowing your character to "take a closer look" at the diamonds that should be kept under glass, or distracting a guard while partners sneak by. It cannot be used to convince subjects to perform actions that are patently dangerous or harmful. The target still retains her common sense.

Draw Results

Failure: Your character has no success in getting the subject to listen to him.

Success: Your character's blather lulls the target into a daze of compliance.

ORATORY

Test Pool: Presence + Persuasion + equipment versus highest Resolve + Composure of audience

Action: Contested

Sometimes your character is called on to convince a crowd of people to accept his assertions, calling for a rousing, compelling speech. This is a contested action. Draw Presence + Persuasion + equipment versus the highest Resolve + Composure present in the audience. If the orator wins, he convinces the crowd. If he fails, one or two people believe, but the group on the whole is unconvinced. A tie indicates that the group is willing to listen, but remains unconvinced. In the case of a failed or tied effort, your character can make a successive attempt (see p. 176) if the Storyteller agrees that the crowd is willing to listen.

Note that oratory conducted to convince a crowd to do what your character wants is different from a performance. The former is based on Persuasion, because your character tries to sway listeners, while the latter is based on Expression, because your character simply seeks to entertain or inform an audience.

A character must actually deliver some sort of speech to his audience, however perfunctory, to attempt to use this Skill. Players without much knack for public speaking — but with characters who are convincing speakers — may borrow from classic speeches or other inspirational sources. At the end of the speech, the number of successes achieved (if any) should be announced in order to give an idea of how persuasive the speech is in-character.

Draw Results

Failure: Your character has no success in getting the crowd to listen to him.

Success: Your character's speech convinces the crowd to accept his assertions.

SEDUCTION

Test Pool: Presence + Persuasion + equipment or Manipulation + Persuasion + equipment (seducer) versus Wits + Composure + equipment (subject)

Action: Contested and/or extended (the extended and contested part of the task requires a number of successes equal to double the seducer's Presence or double the subject's Resolve; one draw covers a half-hour of banter)

Your character seeks to ply his allure, charm and sheer magnetism to make someone else compliant to his will, typically to agree to a sexual tryst. Or your character's aim might be some goal short of a physical encounter, such as getting a person's phone number, learning his or her address, or convincing a subject to do a favor with the implicit reward of romance. The same forms of coercion might also be applied on your character by inhuman beings, to make him agreeable to a private rendezvous that could mean his life.

The act of seduction has two basic elements, physical and social, and those elements tend to indicate stages of the overall process. The first stage is based largely on physical attraction. Your character plies his appearance and demeanor to win the subject's attention and interest. This phase is typically non-verbal. Presence + Persuasion + equipment is drawn in a contested action against the subject's Wits + Composure + equipment. Appearances are important, so possessing the Striking Looks Merit (p. 149) offers a bonus to the draw for the seducer. If the seducer gets more successes, he gains the subject's interest. If successes tie or the seducer gets fewer, the subject is disinterested or needs further convincing (see below).

"Equipment" in the contested draw might include alluring clothing (+1), an appealing perfume or cologne (+1) or an offered drink (+1) for the seducer. The subject might have an existing significant other (+1 to +3), a headache (+1) or be in a really bad mood (+1) for his or her draw.

The social aspect of the seduction begins after the initial contested action is complete. The social aspect involves dialogue and interaction between participants. In this stage, the seducer's Manipulation + Persuasion + equipment is drawn against the subject's Wits + Composure + equipment in an extended and contested task. A draw is made about every half-hour of game time, which means your character probably has to talk to his subject for quite a while. The winner of the previous contested draw also gains a bonus equal to the successes drawn before. So, if your character seeks to seduce a woman at a bar and you win the initial contested draw with three successes to her two, you add three points to your Manipulation + Persuasion draws in the social part of the process. "Equipment" bonuses at this stage might include a good pick-up line (+1), an excellent line (+2), a mutual acquaintance (+1) or suggestive physical contact (+2) for the seducer. Those listed above can be applied again for the subject.

The required number of successes for the seducer equals twice the subject's Resolve. The required number of successes for the subject equals twice the aggressor's Presence. While the process has become much more interactive, the relative attractiveness of the aggressor is still encouraging or discouraging. Whoever accumulates the required number of successes first gets their way, either convincing the other to cooperate or refusing the proposal. Once a would-be seducer is rebuked, no other attempts can be made to entrance the same subject in the same scene.

If the seducer loses the initial contested draw to determine physical interest, he can still try to engage in social interaction to sway the subject's opinion. He's on thin ice, though. The subject gains the number of successes drawn for her in the contested action as a bonus to her draws in the extended and contested process. So, if in the previous example the seducer had acquired two successes and the subject had acquired three, she would have gone unimpressed with his looks. If he had still tried to engage her socially, her Wits + Composure draws would have received a +3 bonus to resist his charm.

Example: *Though a complete social dud in life, now that Eric is dead, he has discovered that he possesses an unearthly air that attracts almost anyone he desires. Little do they know that he really desires their life's breath. Hungry for more, Eric turns his allure on a woman in a mall. Eric has 5 Presence and 3 Persuasion. He uses no particular props beyond his own bearing to get her attention. The woman has 2 Wits and 2 Composure and is happily married (which the Storyteller decides is worth a +3 bonus). Eric's draw nets four successes. The woman's draw gets two. Despite herself, the woman is physically interested in Eric.*

Eric's four successes on the first draw give him a +4 bonus in the social stage of the seduction. He also has 1 Manipulation and 3 Persuasion, but the Storyteller decrees that his days spent without washing and his narcissitic habits impose a –2 penalty, for a total of six in his pool. Once again, the woman has a Wits + Composure of four, with a +3 bonus for being happily married. The woman's Resolve is 3. Eric therefore needs a total of six successes to win (twice the woman's Resolve), and the woman needs 10 (twice Eric' Presence).

After four draws, the woman accumulates 10 successes while Eric has only five. She soon wonders what she saw in him. Suffering pangs of guilt for even considering an indiscretion, she quickly leaves. Eric must seek prey elsewhere.

Example: *A rival investigator wants to learn what Mariah has discovered thus far on a case. He decides to seduce her for whatever information he can get, but has no intention of actually participating in a physical encounter. Not exactly interested in men as a rule, Mariah is disinterested in the rival physically. She gets one success to his none in the initial contested draw. He doesn't let that stop him, though. He becomes more aggressive and tries to tease Mariah into confessing what she knows in return for "favors."*

Both parties arrive at their required number of successes simultaneously in the extended and contested part of the process. The Storyteller rules that Mariah sees through the ruse, confesses nothing and expects nothing, and sends her rival packing. Had Mariah lost the extended and contested task, the Storyteller was prepared for her to reveal one piece of information for every point that she was short of her required successes. Therefore, if she had lost the competition and still needed three more successes, she would have revealed three pieces of information. The fact that she would have gotten nothing in return would have been learned too late.

For most human interaction, seduction involves both verbal and non-verbal interaction. (Thus, both Presence + Persuasion and Manipulation + Persuasion draws for the aggressor.) More instinct-driven seduction, such as that between animalistic or bestial beings, can be based on physical attraction alone. In those cases, the Storyteller may rule that Presence + Persuasion versus Wits + Composure draws are made in an extended and contested action. There is no two-step process. There is still a contest of attraction and will, but it's based purely on demeanor rather than dialogue. In this case, each participant still seeks a number of successes equal to double the opponent's Resolve or Presence.

Draw Results

Failure: Your character kills time with the object of his attention, but gains little ground. She is not yet encouraged or discouraged in him.

Success: Your character gathers some interest in his subject.

Socialize

Pete knew from the moment the man walked into the that there was something deeply wrong with him. Not just the everyday problems like job, school and wife, either, but something really wrong. The kind of deep unease that he knew all too well himself these days. He'd bet the guy knew about things that weren't supposed to exist, things that nevertheless stalked people from the shadows.

Pete served the man a few drinks, keeping the small talk to a minimum, until closing time rolled around. When the man stood up to leave, Pete gestured for him to keep his seat, poured him another drink and let his staff lock up. "So, tell me what's really bothering you," he said once the staff was safely out the door.

The man looked at him with haunted, skeptical eyes, but also with a faint glimmer of hope. "You wouldn't believe me if I told you."

"Oh, I don't know about that," Pete said. "You'd be amazed at what bartenders believe – or have seen."

Socialize reflects your character's ability to interact with others in a variety of situations, from talking people up at bars to comporting himself with dignity at state dinners. This Skill represents equal parts gregariousness, sensitivity, etiquette and custom. Knowing how to make friends is no less important than understanding how to treat guests in formal situations. Characters with low dots might be naturally entertaining or approachable, but unschooled in the finer arts of social interaction. Or they could be punctilious with their manners but difficult to approach. Conversely, characters with high dots could have the social graces of a practiced diplomat or raconteur, knowing just what to say and when to say it in any given situation.

Possessed by: Diplomats, entertainers, executives, politicians, salesmen

Specialties: Bar Hopping, Dress Balls, Formal Events, Frat Parties, State Dinners

Draw Results

Failure: Your character doesn't succeed in winning friends, but he doesn't embarrass himself, either.

Success: Your character blends effortlessly with the crowd and is accepted by his immediate companions.

CAROUSING

Test Pool: Manipulation + Socialize + equipment (carouser) versus Composure + Empathy (subject)

Action: Extended and contested (the task requires a number of successes equal to double the highest Stamina among the character's acquaintances; one draw equals 10 minutes during play, or one hour of carrying on during downtime) .

Sometimes the best way to uncover someone's secrets or to secure their help is to show them a good time on the town — provided your character can keep up with his intended victim. Carousing is an extended and contested action. Draw Manipulation + Socialize + equipment for your character. The subject's Composure + Empathy is drawn in competition (or draw the highest test pool in a group of companions). The side that accumulates a number of successes equal to double the opponent's Stamina wins the contest. If your character wins, the victim is at his mercy and agrees to any reasonable request your character makes. If your character loses, he's left in the dust by his hard-drinking buddies and can't try again until the following night — provided he doesn't wind up in jail first.

Example: Pete is eager to uncover the secret behind Steve's recent erratic behavior, and takes him out for a night on the town, hoping that a few beers will loosen Steve's tongue. Pete's Manipulation is 2 and Socialize is 4, but he has no special equipment to aid him in his endeavor. Steve's Composure is 2 and Empathy is 2. Pete's Stamina is 3 and Steve's Stamina is 3, so they begin on an even footing, each requiring six successes to win. On the first draw, Pete gets three successes and Steve gets one. On the next draw, Pete gets one success while Steve gets two. On the third draw, Pete gets three successes and Steve gets only two — Pete wins with seven successes to Steve's five. Steve tells Pete everything about why he's been acting so strangely, revealing a plan that Pete never even suspected. Steve will regret it the next day — if he remembers at all.

If both sides achieve the required number of success simultaneously, no advantages are gained and the carouser's efforts go for naught — this time. Another night on the town starts the process all over again.

Draw Results

Failure: Your character keeps up with his partying companions but doesn't gain the upper hand over them.

Success: Your character hangs tough and dares his companions to keep up.

STREETWISE

"Rae? That you?" Rae winced inwardly but managed a big smile as Rodney swept her up in a bearlike hug. The other kids on line to enter the club shot her evil glances as the bouncer pulled her out and straight to the door, her friends trailing slightly behind. "Damn, girl, where you been at?"

"You didn't hear? I got popped six months ago for possession, but my folks' lawyer managed to get it dropped to probation and rehab. Like that'll work." Rae rolled her eyes, relieved by Rodney's outraged reaction. "Anyway, I'm looking to get my crew hooked up, you know?" She slipped a bill in his back pocket and let her hand linger just slightly on his hip as she did, whispering, "You're still my boy, right?"

She could see Rodney's natural suspicion war with his greed and desire, and she knew which side would win out. He smiled devilishly. "Hell, yeah! There's a new girl running things, tho'. She's kinda touchy about dealing wit' strangers, knowumsayin'?" Rodney swung the club doors wide.

Characters possessing this Skill know how life on the streets works and are adept at surviving by its harsh rules. Streetwise characters can gather information, make contacts, buy and sell on the black market, and otherwise make use of the street's unique resources. The Skill is also important for navigating urban dangers, avoiding the law, and staying on the right side of the wrong people.

Possessed by: Criminals, gangsters, homeless people, private investigators, police officers

Specialties: Black Market, Gangs, Rumors, Undercover Operations

Draw Results

Failure: Your character has no luck hooking up with any of his street associates, or of convincing the locals that he's legit.

Success: Your character hooks up with someone who can provide what he needs.

Working the Black Market

Test Pool: Manipulation + Streetwise + equipment

Action: Extended (2–10 successes; each draw represents 10 minutes of searching the street during a game, or one hour doing the same during downtime)

Black markets thrive in every city across the globe, making money from illegal property such as weapons and stolen merchandise. Practically anything can be had on the black market if a buyer has enough money and time to find the right contacts and to secure a deal.

When your character wants to turn to the black market to buy illegal items (or unload stolen goods), the Storyteller first determines how many successes are necessary to complete the task. That number depends on the size or value of the items sought. Buying or selling handguns might require only three successes, while dealing in stolen cars might demand six. Highly illegal, hard-to-find items such as military hardware might require eight or more successes. A successful series of draws means your character finds someone able to trade, and a meeting is arranged. All your character has to do is show up with the money (or items to sell) and the deal is done.

Example: Victor is on the run and needs a weapon, fast. He knows a few people on the street who deal in hot guns, so hits the corners. Victor's Manipulation is 4 and his Streetwise is 3. He has some stolen property he can offer as gifts, to sweeten the deal, which the Storyteller decides is a +1 modifier. Fortunately, the first draw nets Victor three successes. He connects with an old friend who sets him up with a piece, no questions asked. Now the only question is, will that be enough to keep him alive?

Draw Results

Failure: Your character has no luck finding an associate who can lead him to the goods.

Success: Your character locates a potential seller or buyer and a meeting is arranged.

Subterfuge

"This is where she said we were supposed to meet?" The creature threw Sam a suspicious look, gesturing toward the decrepit warehouse with one clawed hand. Sam couldn't help but notice that its eyes reflected the light from a nearby streetlight, like those of an animal. "This doesn't look like any of the places she normally uses."

Sam made a show of swallowing deeply (but not too deeply), hunched his shoulders slightly, and put what he hoped was the right mixture of nervousness and eagerness to please in his voice. Knowing these creatures and their arrogant dismissal of human beings, he knew taking the tone of a frightened servant would massage the creature's ego and put it at ease. They might have supernatural powers, but they were still as vulnerable to a flattering lie as any mark. "Trust me," Sam said. "Can we get going? I don't want to be late. She'll be... angry."

The creature snorted contemptuously and led the way. Behind it, Sam readied himself, hoping his friends had taken their appointed positions. If they had, this would be quick.

Subterfuge is the art of deception. Characters possessing this Skill know how to lie convincingly, and they recognize when they're being lied to. Subterfuge is used when telling a convincing falsehood, hiding one's emotions or reactions, or trying to notice the same in others. The Skill is most often used to trick other people, but characters also learn it to avoid being tricked themselves.

Possessed by: Actors, con artists, grifters, lawyers, politicians, teenagers

Specialties: Con Jobs, Hiding Emotions, Lying, Misdirection, Spotting Lies

Draw Results

Failure: Your character's deception fails to convince his subject. If the Storyteller agrees, he can still try to lie his way out of the situation through successive attempts (see p. 176).

Success: Your character pulls off the deception without a hitch.

DISGUISE

Test Pool: Wits + Subterfuge + equipment (impersonator) versus Wits + Subterfuge (subject)

Action: Contested

If your character attempts to pass himself off as someone else, draw Wits + Subterfuge in a contested action against the individual whom he tries to deceive. The subject gets the same draw. If your character has supporting documents (passport, driver's license) that help reinforce the disguise, apply a +1 to +3 modifier depending on the quality of the documentation (see below). If the subject knows or is familiar with the person being impersonated, apply a –2 to –5 modifier to your draw (–2 if familiarity is passing, –5 if it's intimate).

If draws achieve the same number of successes, re-draw.

Example: *Sam attempts to bluff his way into a corporate office by posing as a police officer. Sam's Wits is 4 and Subterfuge is 4. He has a fake badge and ID that looks good enough to pass a cursory inspection, adding a +2 modifier to the draw. The secretary at the front desk has a Wits of 3 and a Subterfuge of 1. Sam wins the draw handily with three successes to her one, and the secretary hurriedly ushers the "detective" into the vice president's office.*

Draw Results

Failure: Your character does not pass himself off as someone else.

Success: Your character manages to pass himself off as someone else.

Chapter 4: Advantages

Advantages are aspects of your character that set him apart from her peers, for good or ill. A strong will, an unshakable moral conviction or a simple talent for ducking are all possible benefits in a rough and uncertain world. As your character develops over time, her advantages can increase to exceptional levels.

Most advantages are derived traits determined by adding two or more Attributes together. Others, such as Morality and Size, have a base value with which all characters begin play. As your character's Attributes increase through the expenditure of experience points, her advantages increase as well. Likewise, as Attributes are temporarily decreased through supernatural curses or other strange events, their linked advantages are similarly reduced.

DEFENSE

Traits: Your character's Defense is equal to his Dexterity or Wits, whichever is lower.

The object of any fight is to knock the other guy out without letting him do the same to you. At the same time that your character throws punches and looks for a chance to land a knockout blow, he bobs, weaves and ducks, making himself as difficult a target as possible for his opponent's counterblows. Your character's Defense trait is applied as a negative modifier to his opponent's draws for Brawl, Weaponry and thrown-weapon (Dexterity + Athletics) attacks. Your character's Defense cannot normally be used against Firearms (gun and bow-based) attacks, unless they're conducted within close-combat range; one to two steps (see "Firearms and Close Combat," p. 209). Defense does not apply if your character is taken by surprise or is immobilized by some means.

Example: *Pete finds himself in a barroom brawl with three bikers. His Dexterity is 4 and his Wits is 2. Taking the lower of the two Attributes, his Defense trait is 2. As the bikers wade in Pete does his best to avoid their swings. All bikers suffer a –2 modifier to their attack draw – Pete's Defense.*

Defense is not affected by any wound penalties (p. 239) that your character may have incurred.

For more details on how Defense is used in combat, see Chapter 7, p. 215.

As your character's Dexterity and Wits increase through the application of experience points (or through temporary enhancement during the course of a story), his Defense may change as well. If you increase your character's Dexterity or Wits don't forget to adjust his Defense accordingly.

As a universal rule, a character may lose her Defense only once per turn. You'll notice that throughout the rules, several situations or abilities can cause a character to lose Defense. This doesn't happen cumulatively, nor do Defense losses roll forward beyond the normal cycle of turns.

HEALTH

Traits: Stamina + Size

A character's Health trait reflects his body's capacity to cope with injury and remain functional. As your character suffers damage, whether accidentally or in combat (see Chapter 7 for details), each point of damage inflicted lowers his Health by one. When your character's Health points are reduced to three, he suffers a negative modifier to his test pools. As his Health points continue to decrease, this negative modifier increases as he is slowly overcome by shock and physical trauma. When all of your character's Health points are marked off as aggravated damage, he is dead. See Chapter 7, p. 210, for more details on types of damage and how they affect a character's Health. Obviously, the larger and more robust a character is, the more damage he can withstand before dying.

Health is marked on your character sheet and has both a permanent and a temporary rating. Your character's permanent rating is filled in on the dots of your character sheet. His temporary points are recorded in the corresponding boxes. Every time your character loses a Health point to damage, mark off the kind of injury inflicted from left to right. When dots and filled boxes are equal, your character is badly hurt or dying.

Your character regains lost Health points at different rates based on the type of damage inflicted. See Chapter 7, p. 240 for details on recovering Health and healing times for bashing, lethal and aggravated harm. When points are recovered, the Health boxes on your character sheet are emptied from right to left.

As your character's Stamina increases with experience points (or through supernatural enhancements), his Health increases as well. Don't forget to adjust your character's Health dots when his Stamina changes.

INITIATIVE

Traits: Dexterity + Composure

Your character's Initiative trait reflects her reaction time and ability to think on her feet in a crisis, be it a barroom brawl, a firefight or a desperate lunge to stop a child from wandering into a busy street. When the Storyteller calls for an Initiative draw, you draw one card and add the result to your character's Initiative trait. The total determines the order in which your character interacts with all other participants of the scene. Once you draw, your character's Initiative number does not usually change through the course of the scene. She always acts after characters with a higher total, and before those with a lower total. Possible exceptions occur by delaying your character's action (see p. 205). In the event of a tie between two characters, the one with the highest actual Initiative trait (including any Merits or supernatural bonuses) goes first. If both Initiative traits are the same, draw a card for each player with the highest draw going first.

Example: *Greg's character has a Dexterity of 3 and a Composure of 2. Adding the two produces an Initiative trait of 5. During play, Greg's character is approached by a mugger and a fight breaks out. Greg draws and adds the result to his character's Initiative trait. The draw is*

7, so his character's Initiative total is 12. The Storyteller draws for the mugger and gets a 4. The mugger's Initiative trait is 4. Adding the two together produces an Initiative total of 8. Greg's character gets the first action, and continues to do so in subsequent turns until the fight is over or the mugger somehow alters his place in the roster.

For more information on Initiative and how it applies to combat, see Chapter 7, p. 204.

As your character's Attributes change through the use of experience points (or through temporary enhancement during the course of a story), her Initiative changes as well. If your character's Dexterity or Composure increases during play, don't forget to adjust her Initiative, too.

MORALITY

Base Value: 7

Morality reflects a character's sense of compassion for his fellow human being and basic respect for the rule of law. This isn't an absolute value. As people grow and change over time their perspectives on society and morality often shift. Some individuals strive to become more compassionate and virtuous, while others, driven by desperation or embittered by dire circumstances, reject their old convictions and adopt a more callous and selfish approach to existence.

Your character's Morality is not fixed. Depending on his actions it can increase or decrease during play. A starting character has a Morality of 7 – a basic respect for the law and a realistic sense of compassion for other people. He believes in the need to uphold the law, and treats others as he would expect to be treated himself. He has the potential to become more selfless and virtuous, or has a long way to fall into the depths of human barbarity. The course he follows depends entirely on the choices he makes during the course of the chronicle. If you choose to play a character whose beliefs and actions prior to the chronicle haven't been average, either the Storyteller or the player ought to adjust them accordingly. A common gangbanger, for instance, should have a Morality rating closer to 4 than 7, for instance.

Each Morality rating has a threshold of sinful behavior from which your character must refrain in order to avoid degeneration to a lower moral state. The aforementioned gangbanger with Morality 4, for instance, would have to test if he committed a Morality 4 sin to avoid falling to Morality 3. Intentional mass property damage leaves him cold, but he's still affected by manslaughter.

Morality	Sin
10	Selfish thoughts. (Draw five times.)
9	Minor selfish act (withholding charity). (Draw five times.)
8	Injury to another (accidental or otherwise). (Draw four times.)
7	Petty theft (shoplifting). (Draw four times.)
6	Grand theft (burglary). (Draw three times.)
5	Intentional, mass property damage (arson). (Draw three times.)
4	Impassioned crime (manslaughter). (Draw three times.)
3	Planned crime (murder). (Draw two times.)
2	Casual/callous crime (serial murder). (Draw two times.)
1	Utter perversion, heinous act (mass murder). (Draw two times.)

LOSING MORALITY DOTS — DEGENERATION DRAWS

If a character commits a sin equal to or worse than the threshold of his current Morality trait, make a number of draws equal to the value assigned to that level of sin on the chart. These are not normal draws, in which a test pool is formed and added to the result of a draw, but just a simple draw (i.e., picking one card out of the hand each time). Additionally, a player may not spend a Willpower point on any of these draws. If an 8, 9 or 10 is pulled, the draw is considered a success. Each Ace drawn represents a failure, which is subtracted from the number of successes. Before each draw, all cards are returned to your deck and shuffled. Tens may be redrawn once, with an 8, 9 or 10 representing an additional success.

If even one success is left at the end of the entire draw sequence, the character's overall sense of compassion remains intact, and his Morality does not change. If the degeneration draws result in a failure (no net successes), your character's sense of right and wrong is altered by his experience and he loses a point of Morality. His soul hardens to the needs of others and he becomes inured to greater acts of selfishness or violence.

Note that these draws are merely the rules mechanic that reflects the deterioration of your character's spirit due to immoral activity. They should not replace roleplaying such ethical crises. They merely indicate how it can be roleplayed. Indeed, success on a degeneration draw does not mean that your character can laugh about how she dodged an ethical bullet, but that she feels sufficient guilt and remorse for her action that her overall moral structure remains intact. While you need not be melodramatic about such a turbulent emotional state, don't mistake passing a degeneration test as a sign that your characters is perfectly happy about it, either.

Example: *Victor has a Morality of 7. Referring to the chart, he does not risk degeneration unless he commits a deliberate act of petty theft or worse. During play, he is confronted with a need to purchase hunting supplies in order to carry out the commands of his mysterious masters, but he doesn't have any money. Desperate, he is walking downtown and notices that someone has left their wallet in their open car. Hesitating only a second, he reaches through the car window and steals the wallet. This crime (petty theft) is equal to the threshold of his current Morality, so a degeneration draw must be made to determine if Victor loses a Morality dot. Petty theft allows for four draws. Victor's player Dan performs four different draws, and gets the following cards: 8, 10, ace and 4. He re-draws the 10, as described, but it comes up a 5, so he does not gain an additional success from the re-draw. In the end, the 8 and the 10 each count as a success, but the ace subtracts one success, while the 4 does not add or subtract anything, so Dan has a net total of one success. Victor's Morality doesn't change; he doesn't feel too great about what he did, but his sense of self remains intact.*

If Victor had committed an impassioned crime such as manslaughter to get some money (a sin more severe than what Victor's 7 Morality can tolerate), Dan would have drawn three times to see if Victor suffered degeneration, since that is the number of draws assigned to a crime of that magnitude.

Optional Rule:
Alternative Morality Systems

While the Morality system is intended to be universal and not intricately tied to a specific set of real-world beliefs, the fact remains that it does tend to lean toward a Judeo-Christian conception of morality. This is not done out of disrespect for any other religions, cultures or beliefs, but simply because that is the belief system with which most White Wolf players and Storytellers are most familiar (whether they practice it or not). That said, troupes are free to devise alternative systems to represent the moral standards of other cultures or religions, which in turn can help craft a unique roleplaying experience for players portraying characters of diverse origins.

Storytellers should ensure that any new Morality systems enhance the roleplaying experience of the game, and not simply allow players to devise a code of ethics that allows them to do what they like without penalty. Completely inhuman, self-serving or otherwise utterly antisocial paths should *never* be allowed as the basis for actual Morality systems. Similarly, Morality systems ought to be suited for live-action play: paths that define destroying your fellow players' characters as ultimately desirable don't contribute much to the game environment. Moralities that value quiet study at home and shun interaction with other individuals or groups are similarly counter-productive to live-action play.

OPTIONAL RULE: MORALITY DERANGEMENTS

Characters' development of mental ailments as a result of performing offensive acts is an optional rule in **Mind's Eye Theatre**. While it's very appropriate to maintaining a mood of horror and creeping paranoia, keeping track of derangements in a large group of characters is overwhelming, not to mention making characters a challenge to roleplay. Manifesting such conditions is recommended for small games and on a limited basis for large games, such as when a character commits an act far below her Morality (say, three or more). A character with Morality 8 committing manslaughter (a Morality 4 crime), for example.

As a character's Morality slips ever lower, she becomes more deranged and perhaps more of a monster, capable of virtually any depraved act. When a Morality dot is lost because of a sin perpetrated, make a test draw against standard difficulty using your character's *new* Morality trait as a test pool. If the draw succeeds, she finds some kind of balance or existence at her new state of spiritual and ethical standing. If the draw fails, she manifests a derangement.

Derangements are mental and emotional ailments or conditions, in this case brought on by your character's stress, grief or even remorselessness over acts performed. Derangements are detailed at length later in this chapter.

If your character develops a condition, you and the Storyteller can decide what is appropriate based on the circumstances. An avoidance condition might set in whenever your character enters a situation that reminds her of the sin she committed. If she decided to harm a child and paid the emotional price, being around children thereafter might cause her to escape. Note that the conditions detailed later each have a mild and severe form. Your character probably starts with a mild ailment in any new derangement, unless something horribly traumatic occurs and you feel that she should descend directly into a severe problem.

On your character sheet, write the derangement gained on the line associated with the Morality trait to which she has fallen. If your character manifests a fixation when she drops from 6 to 5 Morality, write "Fixation" on the line associated with 5 Morality.

Example: Let's say that the degeneration draw made for Victor's theft fails. The four draws turn up no net successes. That means his Morality drops from 7 to 6. At the Storyteller's discretion, a check may be made to see if he suffers mental or emotional damage for his sin. His player has a test pool of 6 (his new Morality). Dan draws a 3, for a total of 9 – failure. That means Victor does indeed manifest a derangement. Dan and the Storyteller decide that Victor exhibits depression over his inability to stand up to his supernatural masters, and that's entered on the line next to 6 Morality on his character sheet.

Repeated degeneration and Morality draws that fail cause your character to incur more and more or worse and worse conditions. If you want to minimize the diversity of ailments that he manifests, focus on increasingly intense ones, acquiring the mild form of any condition first and then assigning the severe one the next time your character incurs another problem.

If a character descends so far that his Morality drops to zero, he can no longer be played in any meaningful way. He becomes a true monster, inflicting pain and suffering on everyone around him without the slightest hint of remorse and with no hope of redemption. At that point, control of the character passes to the Storyteller.

VIRTUES AND DEGENERATION

It's important to note that Virtues (explored later in this chapter) are not extensions of a character's Morality. Rather, they are ideals that inform his actions and provide a framework by which he interacts with society. Thus, it's possible for a character to commit ostensibly immoral acts in the pursuit of his Virtue. This doesn't excuse the immorality of a particular act, but the character may be able to rationalize the deed as a necessary one in pursuit of a higher purpose, and thus avoid compromising his ethics.

If your character commits an immoral act in pursuit of his defining Virtue, the Storyteller may allow you to add a single extra draw to your degeneration draw series. Higher modifiers are possible if the Storyteller feels that your character is compelled to sin in order to uphold his Virtue, but should never rise higher than three additional draws. These extra draws need be performed only if no successes are achieved so far on the regular number of tests, in order to avoid them turning out to be more hindrance than help by potentially drawing an ace. It's important to remember that individuals perform actions out of their own free will: their vices may contribute to it, but no Storyteller ought to accept the explanation that 'my vice made me do it.' Vices represent the demons that lurk in the darker corners of the human psyche; they are not external mechanisms of control that force somebody's hand. If you choose to follow your Vice, you only have yourself to blame. A character who kills someone and blames his Vice – Wrath – should be reminded that this inherent part of his character's personality merely contributed to the act: your Vice didn't commit the murder. You shouldn't rely on your Vice to explain or justify behavior gnawing away at your Morality.

Degeneration and Morality draws also have to be made for involuntary acts, although the Storyteller may allow for an extra draw to represent the loss of free will. Being forced to kill others or doing so in an involuntary murderous rage doesn't remove the dehumanizing effect of the act, but it may reduce its impact on an individual's psyche. Forcing another character to perform an act that would cause you to make a Morality check should result in such a test for you, as well. Ordering a murder is not that dissimilar from murdering yourself.

Example: *Jimmy is putting equipment in the back of his car after a gig when he hears what sounds like a drunken fight down the street. The nightclub is in a pretty seedy neighborhood, but he doesn't hesitate to grab a baseball bat from his trunk and run to investigate. He sees two men viciously shoving another man, yelling obscenities, and he calls out for them to stop, hoping the sight of his weapon will send them packing. One of the attackers laughs and draws a knife, callously stabbing his victim in the gut. Reacting with pure outrage, Jimmy swings the bat and hits the man squarely in the temple, nearly smashing his head in. The attacker dies not long afterward, and no matter what the courts might call the act, Jimmy's knows he has taken a life.*

Jimmy's Morality is 7. His defining Virtue is Justice. The act of manslaughter demands a degeneration draw, but the act was mandated by Jimmy's Virtue, so the Storyteller decides an extra draw can made if necessary.

Regaining Morality

It's possible to reverse your character's slide into damnation and insanity through concerted effort and contrition. The road is long and difficult, though.

A character's Morality trait can be increased primarily by spending experience points, but Morality can be increased by only one point at any given time. See p. 32 for the experience points required to achieve each Morality rating. Storytellers are encouraged to require that characters demonstrate the desire to redeem themselves with concrete acts of contrition before a Morality increase is warranted. A good rule of thumb is to encourage character actions that aspire to the *highest* level of Morality that the player wants his character to attain. A moral existence is much more about the journey than the destination, after all. Typically, the best time to allow experience points to be spent on increasing Morality is at the end of a story, but exceptions can always be made for significant character actions between chapters or even scenes.

When a derangement is assigned to a Morality point, that ailment is overcome when the next, higher point is gained. The experience spent to gain a Morality dot represents your character's efforts to come to terms with her sin and thus free herself of her condition. She might also undergo treatment or simply forgive herself.

Example: *Victor's life has spiraled into a bleak existence of theft, violence and deceit. He hates himself even as he routinely manipulates and victimizes others to serve his vicious supernatural masters. His Morality trait has sunk to 4, although he has acquired only one derangement: depression. He's willing to lie, cheat and use violence to achieve his goals, but at the same time part of him loathes what he's become and wants to fight his way back to his normal life, before the sinister Voices made him their puppet. The player decides that a Morality of 7 is Victor's target. Over the course of the next story, Victor tries to break from his supernatural masters, avoid manipulating others, and makes a concerted effort to stop the cycle of violence that entraps him. At the end of the story, the Storyteller determines if Victor's actions were sufficient to allow buying an increase in Morality with any experience points earned.*

Upon eventually rising to 7 Morality once again, the "Depression" entry ascribed to 6 Morality on Victor's character sheet is erased. He comes to terms with the crimes he's committed, having paid penance and done good deeds to alleviate his guilt. He returns to being a normal, functioning individual.

Derangement Evolution

When a derangement is overcome by rising to a higher Morality, that ailment can be erased from your character sheet or ignored for the time being. Say, Tim's character has a phobia assigned to 5 Morality and his character's Morality rises to 6. That phobia is overcome. Tim could erase "Phobia" from his sheet or just leave it there. If in the future a degeneration draw fails, his character falls back to 5 Morality. If a Morality draw also fails, a new derangement can be chosen for him or his old phobia may resurface. The first occurs if "Phobia" is erased from his character sheet. The second occurs if the condition is left there but is ignored — until now.

Erasing old derangements and acquiring new ones to replace them can signify dramatic changes in your character's life. He moves on from old experiences without looking back, and evolves as a result. Keeping but ignoring old derangements (reactivating them when Morality falls again) suggests that your character is set in his ways. He has a pattern of behavior or some consistent issues with which he wrestles or that he revisits.

Of course, if your character's life is diverse — he defeats some problems for good and struggles with others that just won't go away — you can erase some derangements and keep but ignore others as his Morality rises and falls.

The Storyteller also has the option of awarding a Morality dot at the end of a story if your character performs a particularly redeeming, generous or self-effacing act. The deed can't have been performed with the intent to regain Morality, to alleviate a derangement or to gain any personal reward. In fact, the character probably suffers repercussions for the deed, but gains some solace in having done the right thing. A character who commits a theft or murder might turn herself in, for example. Or someone who steals may not keep the rewards, distributing them among the needy.

Such a roleplaying-based award should be reserved for the end of a story, not the end of a scene or chapter. Only one Morality dot should ever be gained by a character at a time. (If experience points are spent to regain Morality, an extra play-based award should not be doled out at the same time.) A free Morality award can eliminate a derangement if the sickness corresponds to your character's former rating. So, if your character suffers narcissism at 5 Morality, he loses it upon rising to 6 Morality when a free point is gained. A free Morality award can also exceed any previous height that a character's trait has reached. If he's currently at 7 and has never gone any higher, an appropriate act of charity or purity could take him to 8.

Roleplaying-inspired awards are increasingly hard to come by. They not only become more demanding the higher one's Morality — saintly acts are necessary at high scores (8 and higher) — but new and different acts are required. Donating everything one owns over and over again doesn't keep netting free Morality dots. It does so only once and then the character needs to top even that.

If a character ever loses any Morality dots in the course of a story, he probably invalidates himself from the prospect of gaining a free dot through sacrifice or benediction. The exception might be if the character's sacrifice or penance far exceeds the weight of any sin that he performs. For example, he might have resorted to theft earlier, but before the story's end he risks death by taking a bullet for an innocent bystander.

Draw Results

When making degeneration draws, use only the number of draws associated with the level of the sin committed. Likewise, when drawing Morality to check for a derangement, do not add other Attributes, traits or bonuses and do not apply any penalties. You may *not* spend Willpower to gain a modifier on either kind of draw.

Failure: On a degeneration draw, your character loses the struggle to maintain his standards of behavior when faced with the reality of his sin. He loses one dot of Morality. On a failed Morality draw, he gains a derangement.

Success: Your character emerges from his crisis of conscience with his sense of right and wrong intact. His Morality is unchanged and he remains as sane as before.

Derangement Immunity

The threat of manifesting derangements because of falling Morality looms for most ordinary people. That is, it applies to people with everyday standards of behavior. More charitable, pious or peaceful individuals gain some protection against derangements. Their behavior is generally altruistic or compassionate such that they're not as likely to suffer excessive guilt or shame. When a character achieves a Morality of 8 to 10, no derangements are incurred if he ever drops from that rating. His degeneration draw can fail and he can lose a dot of Morality, but no Morality draw is made to see if he manifests a derangement. Such Morality draws and the threat of mental ailments apply only when a character falls from 7 Morality or lower.

SIZE

Base Value: 5 (adult human)

A character's Size is relative to his species (human) and age. The average adult human's Size is 5. A child's is 3. Size is one of the two component values used to determine your character's Health dots (see above), reflecting her overall capacity to withstand damage. Generally, your character's Size does not change unless she undergoes some strange supernatural transformation.

Here are some sample Sizes for various creatures.

Size	Creature
1	Human infant (up to 1 year old)
3	Human child (5 to 7 years old)
4	Wolf
5	Human
6	Gorilla
7	Grizzly bear

SPEED

Traits: Acting Speed = Species factor (5 for adult humans, 3 for human children; see below for other examples). Running Speed = Species factor + Strength + Dexterity (no other actions usually allowed that turn). Unless noted otherwise, references to Speed are assumed to refer to Acting Speed, not Running Speed.

Your character's Speed ratings are the number of steps — not *paces*, just *steps* — she can travel in a single turn under different circumstances. For simplicity's sake, this trait is broken down to two categories: Acting Speed and Running Speed. Acting Speed is a simple base number that is always constant for a species, and represents the number of steps a character can take and still act normally in combat. Running Speed represents how fast a character is when forsaking all other considerations to cover as much distance as possible, and is a combination of her Strength (lean muscle mass), Dexterity (coordination and agility) and a species factor that reflects her age, physical configuration, Size and other considerations. Other species such as horses and cheetahs have physical configurations that lend themselves to high travel rates.

Factor	Species
1	Turtle
3	Human toddler
5	Human adult
8	Wolf
10	Caribou
12	Horse
15	Cheetah

So, Acting Speed is determined directly by the number listed above, while a being's Strength and Dexterity are added to that number to determine Running Speed.

Your character's Acting Speed represents the number of steps she can move in a turn and still perform an action. Note that unless she has a special Merit or other trait that says otherwise, all steps in a turn must be taken at one time. She can move and perform an action in a turn, or perform an action and move, but she cannot move, perform an action and move again all in the same turn.

Alternatively, she can use her Running Speed to move a great distance in a single turn, but can usually take no other action. See Chapter 7, p. 199, for details. In addition, when your character suffers an injury modifier based on her current Health, both types of Speed are reduced. A character's Speed cannot be reduced below one step per turn, unless an attack or other power specifically limits movement as part of its effect.

Example: Jeff's character has a Strength of 2 and a Dexterity of 2. The character is a human adult, so his Acting Speed is 5, and his Running Speed is 9 (2+2+5). He can walk or jog five steps per turn and act, or run nine steps per turn if he forsakes all other actions. If the character is injured and has only three Health points remaining, he incurs a –1 modifier to test pools and to both types of Speed, reducing his Acting Speed to 4 and his Running Speed to 8.

If your character's Strength or Dexterity changes through the use of experience points (or through temporary enhancement during the course of a story), his Running Speed changes as well. If you change your character's Strength or Dexterity, don't forget to adjust his Running Speed.

Acting Speed does not normally change unless a character's species factor changes somehow, such as using magic to transform into an animal. Furthermore, unless specifically noted in the trait's description or explicitly permitted by the Storyteller, Acting Speed is *not* affected by spells or powers that increase a character's rate of travel. Only Running Speed is increased by such effects. This approach to movement is a bit simplistic, but it keeps Acting Speed easy to remember, levels the combat playing field somewhat and discourages potential abuse, while still allowing powers that increase Running Speed to make a difference when it comes to chases or escapes, for which they are best suited.

WILLPOWER

Traits: Resolve + Composure

Willpower measures your character's self-confidence, determination and emotional resilience. A character with a high Willpower is focused, driven to achieve his goals, and capable of resisting his dark impulses. It would be tempting to call such a character virtuous, but Willpower doesn't equate to altruism. A criminal mastermind or a serial killer could possess an iron will just as easily as could a saint. The first two are ruthless in their ambitions, and determined to see them through.

Willpower is rated on a scale from 1 to 10 and has both permanent dots and temporary points. Your character's permanent score is filled in on the dots on your character sheet. His temporary points are recorded in the corresponding boxes. When a temporary point is spent, just check off a box. When dots and checked boxes are equal, your character is out of Willpower. When your character regains a Willpower point (see below), a check is erased from one of the boxes on your sheet.

Willpower is not drawn. Points are spent for various effects, mostly representing sheer determination in overcoming obstacles in your character's path. They can also be spent to gain bonuses to resist forces applied against your character.

Characters with no Willpower points left are exhausted, physically, mentally and emotionally. They've used up their reserves of determination and tend to be listless and depressed. Characters can regain Willpower in various ways, but it isn't easy, so consider spending Willpower points carefully.

Uses of Willpower are explained more fully in the Dramatic Systems Chapter, under "Heroic Effort," p. 177.

•	Spineless
••	Weak
•••	Timid
••••	Certain
•••••	Confident
••••••	Resolute
•••••••	Driven
••••••••	Determined
•••••••••	Iron-willed
••••••••••	Implacable

Note: Willpower is not to be confused with Resolve. Resolve is your character's ongoing focus. Think of it as his *long-term* purpose, like a career plan. Willpower reflects your character's *short-term* highs and lows, his ability to dedicate himself in brief efforts to overcome challenges. Resolve does contribute to your character's overall Willpower dots, though.

SPENDING WILLPOWER POINTS

Willpower represents the ability to succeed through sheer determination. It's useful for a number of things. Only one Willpower point can be spent per turn to achieve any one of the following effects. This expenditure is reflexive and can be made even if you haven't reached your Initiative ranking.

• You can spend a point of Willpower to gain a +3 modifier on a draw during a turn. Only one test pool can be affected per turn, and the Storyteller may determine that some draws cannot be modified in this way. For example, you cannot spend a point of Willpower to gain a bonus on a degeneration or Morality draw (see above). Your character cannot steel his will against spiritual degradation in this fashion. You can never get such a modifier to offensive actions in combat or to use a Skill or supernatural ability to attempt to incapacitate an enemy: it is assumed that you're already trying as hard as you possibly can to harm someone, or to take them out entirely. Defensive Willpower expenditures are entirely acceptable, however – your desperate attempt to confuse your opponent or to scramble out of the way of an attack can be enhanced this way.

• A Willpower point can be spent to add three to your character's Stamina, Resolve, Composure or Defense to resist mental or social/emotional pressures asserted on him, or to make a concerted effort to avoid being harmed. See "Resistance," p. 179.

REGAINING WILLPOWER POINTS

Your character can recover lost Willpower through any one of four ways, detailed below. Willpower points can never exceed your character's Willpower dots. The only way to increase her Willpower dots is by increasing her Resolve and/or Composure (see Chapter 8, p. 308 for more details).

Recovering Willpower is usually a matter of reaffirming your character's sense of confidence and wellbeing, so certain actions and situations may allow her to recover Willpower. Ultimately, it's up to the Storyteller to decide when characters recover Willpower during a story. Storytellers should tailor recovery to suit the story, keeping in mind that it's a powerful and useful trait. Characters shouldn't be allowed to regain it too quickly, or players may abuse its effects.

• Your character may regain one Willpower point per scene if her actions play out in a manner appropriate to her Vice (see below). Your character may regain *all* spent Willpower if her actions play out in a manner appropriate to her Virtue (see below). No more than one Willpower point may be regained per scene by fulfilling a Vice. Willpower can be regained by fulfilling a Virtue no more than once per chapter (game session). The Storyteller is the final arbiter as to whether your character's actions are shaped by a Virtue or Vice, and can refuse to award Willpower if your character acts purely for the rules gain and against concept.

• Your character regains a point of Willpower for every week of downtime that passes. If your chronicle does not occur in real time — say, the Storyteller rules that only a day or two passes

between games instead of the weeks of real time that elapse — one Willpower point is regained for each night of rest and recuperation.

• If your character achieves a significant goal or performs a particularly impressive act that affirms her sense of confidence, the Storyteller may choose to award a Willpower point.

• Your character regains all spent Willpower points at the end of a *story*. Not at the end of a game session, but at the conclusion of an overall story. The Storyteller may require all characters to achieve some particular goal or objective or otherwise feel like they succeed (even just a little) in order to regain Willpower. If characters are frustrated or events result in a stalemate, a partial recovery of Willpower may be appropriate.

Storytellers may choose to determine the length of a local LARP story or use the default of 30 days, letting players regain all Willpower points at the end of a month.

Storytellers can choose other occasions on which to allow Willpower recovery to suit the needs of the story. Characters may be able to recover Willpower if they find themselves in dire straits and have to push on in order to succeed, for example, or if they refuse to give up despite the odds. Awarding extra Willpower recovery makes things a little easier on the players, while withholding Willpower makes things more challenging.

If for some reason your character's Resolve and/or Composure temporarily increases during a game, perhaps as a result of a mystical spell, he gains one Willpower point per dot increase. Essentially, he has access to one or more free Willpower dot for the duration of the effect. When his Attributes return to normal, your character loses any extra Willpower dots. If they were never spent, he no longer has access to them.

Derangements

Derangements are behaviors that occur when the mind is forced to confront intolerable or conflicting feelings, such as overwhelming terror or profound guilt. When your character is faced with impressions or emotions that he cannot reconcile, his mind attempts to ease the inner turmoil by stimulating behavior such as megalomania, schizophrenia or hysteria as an outlet. People in the World of Darkness, unwittingly tormented, persecuted and preyed upon by incomprehensible beings, often develop these ailments by the mere fact of existing. Alternatively, regret, guilt or remorselessness for inflicting abuses eats away at mind and soul. The night's creatures are not immune to such pressures, either. Existence as an unnatural thing overwhelms what little humanity these beings might have left, driving them mad.

The primary means by which your character may develop derangements is by performing heinous acts and suffering the mental or emotional repercussions. See "Morality," earlier in this chapter, for more details.

Otherwise, the Storyteller may decide that a scene or circumstance to which your character is exposed is too much for him to bear and he breaks under the pressure. A bad drug trip might reveal too much of the monstrous reality of the world for a person's mind to bear. A drug overdose could imbalance a character mentally. Alternatively, witnessing a creature in all its horrific glory might make an onlooker snap.

Ailments caused by fallen Morality can be healed through your character's own efforts toward treatment or contrition (by spending experience points). The Storyteller decides if a more spontaneously inspired condition is temporary or permanent. A spontaneous ailment might be temporary, lasting until the character resolves the situation that triggered the condition. It might become permanent if reconciliation is refused, the condition goes untreated or the trigger that caused it is insurmountable. With Storyteller approval, a starting character might have a spontaneously inspired derangement as a Flaw (see p. 311), gaining experience in stories in which the condition or problem is prominent. Spontaneous ailments developed during play might be represented in-game as evolutionary Flaws, not ones established at character creation.

It must be noted that people who are "crazy" are neither funny nor arbitrary in their actions. Insanity is frightening to onlookers who witness someone rage against an unseen presence or hoard rotten meat "to feed to the monsters." Even something as harmless-sounding as constantly talking to empty air can be disturbing to observers. Players must portray their characters' insanity within the bounds of **Mind's Eye Theatre** safety and decorum. This means that derangements should not be taken as a license to scream wildly, touch other players, run through the play area or otherwise violate public codes of conduct or the Only Rules That Matter. While insanity may lead a character to perform all manner of strange or unsettling deeds, the portrayal of these actions should never be so extreme or grotesque that it prompts non-players to call the authorities, or even makes other players genuinely uncomfortable out-of-game. If a player believes his deranged character would perform an action that is likely to have these results, it is generally best to simply narrate it instead, or find some other way to convey it that is less likely to result in ejection from the play area or the disquiet of fellow players. At the other end of the spectrum, players who routinely

"forget" their characters' insanity when it's convenient should be chastised or forced to spend experience points gained on raising Morality and overcoming a derangement, since their characters are obviously getting better. A derangement may contribute to actions that would lead to Morality checks: this shouldn't be overlooked – even if a character's madness caused her to commit an atrocity, her already tenuous grasp on Morality may slip even more.

The insane respond to a pattern only they grasp, to stimuli that they perceive in their own minds. To their skewed perceptions, what happens to them is perfectly normal. A character's derangement is there for a reason, whether she committed a crime or saw her own children devoured. What stimuli does her insanity inflict upon her, and how does she react to what happens? Work with the Storyteller to create a pattern of provocation for your character's derangement, and then decide how she reacts.

Each of the following ailments is defined in terms of mild and severe. The first might apply to your character if an action or experience imbalances him, but he remains functional. The second can apply if a previously mild condition intensifies with more irreconcilable behavior or spectacles, or if a single act or scene is so mind numbing that only full-blown insanity and dysfunction can result. If treatment or reconciliation occurs and ailments are alleviated, a severe case of a condition must be addressed and overcome before a mild case of the same derangement.

Mild	Severe
Depression	Melancholia
Phobia	Hysteria
Narcissism	Megalomania
Fixation	Obsessive Compulsion
Suspicion	Paranoia
Inferiority Complex	Anxiety
Vocalization	Schizophrenia*
Irrationality	Multiple Personality*
Avoidance	Fugue*

* Your character must experience a life-altering trauma or supernatural tragedy to acquire one of these extreme derangements. They cannot normally be acquired by failing a Morality draw unless the sin performed is truly gut wrenching or horrific, such as murdering one's own children.

Depression (mild): If your character fails to achieve a goal (not just fails a draw, but fails to accomplish some personal, desired end such as getting a job or saving a friend's life), he might go into a bout of depression for the remainder of the scene. A failure that occurs in any activity might also bring on a bout of depression. Regardless of the circumstances, make a reflexive Resolve + Composure draw.

Effect: If the draw fails, your character loses one Willpower point and cannot spend any Willpower points for the remainder of the scene.

Melancholia (severe): Severe depression. In addition to the above effects of a failed Resolve + Composure draw, all test pools suffer a –2 penalty for the remainder of the scene.

Phobia (mild): Your character is scared of a particular type of person, place or thing such as lawyers, heights or spiders. When that trigger is encountered, a reflexive Resolve + Composure draw must be made successfully or your character suffers a bout of fear.

Effect: Your character moves away from the object of her phobia. If she must be near it, she can tolerate being no closer than her Running Speed. If it approaches her, she must move away at least her Acting Speed in distance in her next action. She cannot easily target the trigger with close combat or ranged attacks. Such attacks suffer a –5 penalty as your character shakes just looking at it. If space or circumstances don't allow her to maintain her distance, she freezes like a deer in headlights until she finds an opening by which to escape. (Her Defense still applies if attacked and she can choose to dodge and can take cover from Firearms attacks, but she can take no other actions while "frozen.")

Hysteria (severe): This condition operates as a phobia, but on a failed Resolve + Composure draw your character cannot be in the same room with the object of her fear. She must run away from it immediately, and cannot tolerate being within sensory range (sight, sound, smell) of it. If the trigger comes within sensory range, she must run away at full Running Speed as soon as she can take an action. She cannot target it for an attack under any circumstance. If it touches her, make another Resolve + Composure draw for her to not freak out and run as far away as she can, thinking of nothing else until she's left the subject far behind. (Even if this draw succeeds, your character must still leave the room or area.) If your character is unable to escape, she faints and loses consciousness for the remainder of the scene. If your character is unaware of the object's proximity until it touches her, your Resolve + Composure draw suffers a –3 penalty. If it touches her where she can't see it but she can feel it — a spider dropping on her neck or in her hair — the penalty is –5.

Narcissism (mild): Whenever your character *succeeds* at a goal (not simply succeeds in a draw, but achieves a desired end such as knocking a challenging opponent unconscious or hacking into a well-protected computer), it might go to his head and pump up his overweening ego. Draw Resolve + Composure to avoid a bout of vanity.

Effect: On a failed draw, your character does not work and play well with others — even if the victory that brings on a bout of narcissism was partly won with their aid. For the remainder of the scene, when called upon to aid in a task your character does so only half-heartedly, unless it's a task focused on him or his own needs or wants. He suffers a –3 penalty when participating in teamwork efforts (see p. 180). And he's such a self-obsessed bore that Social draws all suffer a –1 penalty.

Megalomania (severe): The effects of Narcissism apply, except that the penalties intensify by one. Your character is also highly competitive. He cannot allow himself to fail a contest (even a contested draw). If he does, he obsesses about it and works to arrange a rematch when it's most beneficial for him. If, for example, he fails to pick a lock while an ally succeeds, he doesn't let it go. He constantly insists that he did the job and that his successor took the glory, and demands that similar efforts be tried again, even under inappropriate circumstances such as at an office or restaurant.

If your character ever loses a contest to someone he feels is socially inferior, he loses one point of Willpower due to shame and self-loathing (which is at the heart of his megalomania; he secretly fears that he's a fraud).

Fixation (mild): If your character fails or succeeds at an important action such as leaping between buildings or making a getaway in a sports car, he might fixate on his loss or victory. Draw Resolve + Composure after such an event for him to avoid this unhealthy obsession.

Effect: If your Resolve + Composure draw fails, draw a single card. The result is the number of scenes in which your character is focused on the offending or inspiring event or task, to the possible exclusion of more important goals. He fixates on what he believes caused him to lose or win his goal, whether it's an opponent, a broken shoelace or the model of car driven. In the case of a defeat, he cannot help but simmer in anger, cursing a circumstance or trying to devise a method of circumventing it in the future. In the case of a victory, he becomes a fanatic, spending much of his time researching, observing or acclaiming an activity or factor that allowed him to succeed.

The Storyteller rules on how this derangement affects your character's test pools and behavior. It might cause him a –1 on any task not related to his fixation, or he might refuse to engage in an activity if it doesn't somehow tie into his obsession. Since this derangement is potentially active for many scenes, rather than one, its effects should be mild but persistent.

Obsessive Compulsion (severe): The trauma, guilt or inner conflict that causes this derangement forces your character to focus nearly all of his attention and energy on a single repetitive behavior or action. Obsession relates to an individual's desire to control his environment — keeping clean, keeping an area quiet and peaceful, or keeping undesirable individuals out. A compulsion is an action or set of actions that an individual is driven to perform to soothe his anxieties — placing objects in an exact order, constantly checking to make sure a weapon is loaded, praying every few hours to give thanks for surviving that long.

Effect: Determine a set of specific actions or behaviors that your character follows to the exclusion of all else (even if doing so interferes with his current agenda or endangers his life or others'). The effects of obsessive compulsion can be negated for the course of one scene by making a successful Resolve + Composure draw at a –2 penalty. If your character is forcibly prevented from adhering to his derangement, he may lose control among enemies or allies and attack either (or both) indiscriminately.

Suspicion (mild): Anytime your character suffers intentional misfortune at the hands of another, he might become extremely suspicious of *everyone's* motives toward him. He might crash as a result of being cut off in traffic or receive little help from assistants in a teamwork effort (see p. 180). Draw Resolve + Composure for your character to resist the suspicion compulsion.

"Misfortune" is characterized as failing an important task due to the intentional intervention of another person — even if it's a friend or ally. Those people whom your character already mistrusts for good reason can still trigger his suspicious nature if they successfully foil his task — everyone then becomes a suspect, plotting to do him wrong. Combat does not necessarily trigger this derangement. A Resolve + Composure draw is made only if combat is the means by which someone intentionally prevents your character from achieving a goal. (Note: A draw for a task might fail and your character chooses to blame someone else, but that doesn't necessarily trigger this derangement's effect. Only if someone *directly* causes him to fail is a draw made to avoid triggering his suspicious nature.)

Effect: Your character's trust is undermined for the remainder of the scene, regardless of whether or not the person or persons who did him wrong meant any harm. He questions everyone's sincerity and doubts that anyone tries to help him, even if someone saves his life. He suffers a –1 penalty on all Social draws. Note that, although your character is suspicious, he can still be taken in by con men and hucksters. He gets no special bonus to resist their attempts to sway him even though he suspects them of being as bad as everyone else.

Paranoia (severe): Your character believes that her misery and insecurity stem from external persecution and hostility. (That would be an accurate assumption in the World of Darkness, if people actually knew of monsters' existence.) Paranoids obsess over their persecution complexes, often creating vast and intricate conspiracy theories to explain who torments them and why. Anyone or anything perceived to be "one of them" might be subjected to violence.

Effect: A character who suffers from paranoia automatically suffers a –2 penalty on Social draws. The character is distrustful and wary of everyone, even close friends and family. The slightest hint of suspicious behavior is enough to provoke a Resolve + Composure draw to retain control (made at a –2 penalty). A failed draw indicates that your character flees or attacks an offender.

Inferiority Complex (mild): Whenever your character is subjected to a stressful situation in which the result of a single choice or draw can determine success or failure, she might be overcome with such self-doubt that she threatens the outcome. She might need to tell a convincing lie to get out of a dangerous situation, or cut a wire to disable a bomb. Draw your character's Resolve + Composure for her to remain composed.

Effect: If your draw fails, the weight of the momentous choice is too much for your character and she is flustered, doubting her ability to choose correctly or to perform adequately. Once in this state, any draws made for the remainder of the scene – including the momentous act itself – suffer a –1 penalty. In addition, a Willpower point cannot be spent on the singular draw that inspires her bout of inferiority.

Anxiety (severe): As Inferiority Complex, but your character's general anxiety plagues things so badly that she suffers a –2 penalty on all draws for the remainder of the scene, and Willpower points cannot be spent to bolster *any* draws in that period.

Vocalization (mild): Whenever your character is stymied by a quandary and must make an important decision about a course of action, or is under extreme stress, she might talk to herself without realizing it. Draw Resolve + Composure to avoid this discomforting habit.

Examples of important decisions include:

Trying to figure out which fork in the road to take so that the guerrillas don't get to the village first. The wrong choice means arriving precious minutes late and finding innocents killed or kidnapped.

When your character has one bullet but two foes, both of whom prepare to strike lethal blows against two separate friends. Which should be shot?

When the attorney slides a piece of paper with his final offer across the table. Your character has minutes to say "yes" or "no."

Effect: On a failed draw, your character vocalizes her internal monologue but only realizes she's doing so if it's pointed out by others, at which point she can stop for one turn per dot of Wits that she has. After that period, she forgets herself and starts doing it all over again. This behavior persists for the remainder of the scene.

Your character vocalizes even if opponents or rivals can hear. It's hard to keep her thoughts and feelings secret when she speaks them aloud. For example, a rival might demand that she reveal the location of a hidden heirloom. She smirks and thinks to herself (and unwittingly speaks aloud), "You'll never find it in my hidden wall safe."

Schizophrenia (severe; extreme): Conflicting sets of feelings and impulses that cannot be resolved can cause your character to develop schizophrenia, which manifests as a withdrawal from reality, violent changes in behavior and hallucinations. This derangement is the classic sort, causing victims to talk to walls, imagine themselves to be the King of Siam, or to receive murderous instructions from their pets.

Roleplaying this derangement requires careful thought. The Storyteller must determine a general set of behaviors relevant to the trauma that causes the condition. Hallucinations, bizarre behavior and disembodied voices stem from a terrible inner conflict that the individual cannot resolve. Establish a firm idea of what that conflict is and then rationalize what kind of behavior it causes.

Effect: A character with this derangement is unpredictable and dangerous. He automatically suffers a –2 penalty on all Social draws and may be aggressive or violent toward people who confront him with trauma such as accusations, disturbing truths or heated arguments. Make a Resolve + Composure draw for your character to avoid escaping or attacking the source of trauma.

Irrationality (mild): Whenever your character is threatened with violence or suffers extreme tension by being persecuted, challenged or accused, she might react without logic or reason. Draw her Resolve + Composure to keep her cool.

The persecution, challenge or accusation needs to bear some realistic threat to your character's wellbeing, whether related to finances, emotional security or social standing. A hobo threatening to sue is no real threat, but a rich executive who says he's going to ruin your character qualifies as a threat. Likewise, a society-page gossipmonger who threatens to expose your character's faults is a threat *if* your character relies on that crowd for social acceptance, but not if he is a bicycle messenger who's never been inside a penthouse.

Effect: On a failed draw, your character's only way to comfortably deal with confrontation is to act crazy or over the top, in wild hopes that she will scare away her oppressor or at least mitigate her own fears. This behavior persists for the remainder of the scene. Ironically, she takes dangerous risks that might harm her worse than the actual threat posed. If a bouncer demands to know what your character is doing in an off-limits part of a club, she might overreact and get in his face. Make a Wits + Composure draw for her to be able to take any action that removes her from the scene or that directly diffuses the situation (such as accepting a hand offered in a conciliatory handshake). The truly ironic part about this behavior is that during such a bout, your character cannot initiate violence, only respond to it if it occurs. She can threaten or cajole challengers, but can't take the first swing. (That, in fact, is what her crazed behavior tries to avoid.)

Multiple Personality (severe; extreme): The trauma that spawns this derangement fractures your character's personality into one or more additional personas, allowing her to deny her trauma or any actions the trauma causes by placing the blame on "someone else." Each personality is created to respond to certain emotional stimuli, and it is extremely rare for a personality to spontaneously appear outside of those circumstances. An abused person might develop a tough-as-nails survivor personality, create a "protector," or even become a murderer to deny the abuse she suffers. In most cases, none of these personalities is aware of the others, and they come and go through your character's mind in response to specific situations or conditions. They may not be aware of anything that happens while the others are active, or may be aware of those events but somehow rationalize them as their own, depending on the nature of the syndrome.

You must work with the Storyteller to detail each personality, what causes it to surface and what it believes it is capable of, as well as what triggers if any might cause it to submerge once again. As a rule, each personality believes it is the dominant or "true" one. If somehow made aware of the others, each personality resists being put back under in favor of another personality. Indeed, some personalities that become aware of the original psyche seek to replace it, feeling that it must have been too weak to deserve life if it needed to create them in the first place, and they are better suited or more deserving to run the character's life.

Effect: A character with multiple personalities can manifest different Skills or perhaps increased or diminished Social Attributes for each identity (the number of dots allocated to your character's Social Attributes are rearranged by anywhere from one to three). Note that all Skills and other traits must still be purchased normally if you actually want another personality to display real proficiency in these areas. Otherwise the personality simply *believes* it is talented, but doesn't actually know what it's doing (though it always finds a way to rationalize its lack of ability). It's also possible for a character to manifest lower than normal traits, particularly for personalities that are victimized or helpless. For example, a character with Firearms 4 who's separate personality is a younger, abused version of himself might "forget" all of his Firearms dots while that persona is dominant. Such dots are simply lost for the duration of the bout and cannot be reallocated to other traits.

Avoidance (mild): When confronted with a situation or person associated with a previous, significant failure or trauma (a long-term rival, an ex-wife, the house in which one suffered a painful childhood), your character prefers not to face the situation and might do everything he can to avoid it. Draw Resolve + Composure for him to master his nervousness.

Effect: On a failed draw, your character does everything in his power to avoid the situation, short of harming himself or others. He might escape the scene or disguise himself as a bystander to sidle away. If he must confront (or can't escape) the situation, any draws made suffer a –1 penalty.

Fugue (severe; extreme): Victims suffering from fugue experience "blackouts" and loss of memory. When subjected to a particular variety of stress, your character performs a specific, rigid set of behaviors to remove the stressful symptoms. This syndrome differs from multiple personalities in that an individual in the grip of a fugue has no separate personality. Instead, he is on a form of "autopilot" similar to sleepwalking. Decide on the kind of circumstance or exposure that triggers this state, be it the death of a defenseless person by his hand, a confrontation with a specific sort of creature or confinement in a small, dark room.

Effect: Make a Resolve + Composure draw when your character is subjected to his trigger. If the draw fails, roleplay your character's trance-like state by performing a sequence of behaviors that he performs almost robotically. He might repetitively untie and tie his shoes, walk to the corner of the room and refuse to come out, or curl into the fetal position. If the Storyteller is not satisfied by your character's reaction, he give you a mechanical behavior to perform for the duration of the bout. The spell lasts for the remainder of the scene. At the end of the fugue, your character "regains consciousness" with no memory of his actions. If outsiders (including friends and enemies) interfere with or try to prevent your character's mechanical activities, he may attack them for as long as it takes to get them to go away so he can carry on with his actions.

Virtues and Vices

All characters have strengths and weaknesses, noble aspects and dark sides to their personalities. While most people try to cultivate virtues and eschew vices, both are intrinsic elements of identity and both equally reinforce a sense of self, whether we like to admit it or not.

Every character starts play with one defining Virtue and one defining Vice, chosen during character creation. Virtue and Vice may clearly reflect your character's background and concept, or they can be used to contrast his outward nature to create sources of conflict that make for excellent roleplaying. A character that is a priest might have the defining Virtue of Faith and the defining Vice of Pride. He's a man of great conviction and belief in his fellow man, but there are times when his beliefs lend themselves to self-righteousness. This is a complementary application of Virtues and Vices based on character concept, as they both stem from the character's background.

A contrasting approach might be to give the character the Virtue of Faith and the Vice of Wrath. He believes in the path of righteousness and the intrinsic worth of mankind, but sometimes the state of the world is such that it fills him with a violent rage to punish those who ignore the tenets of his religion. The result is a source of conflict within the character as he tries to reconcile an essential part of his nature with his dedication to the church.

When a character's actions in difficult situations reflect his particular Virtue *or* Vice, he reinforces his fundamental sense of self. If the Storyteller judges that your character's actions during a *scene* reflect his Vice, he regains one Willpower point that has been spent. If the Storyteller judges that your character's actions during a *chapter* (a game session) reflect his Virtue, he regains all spent Willpower points.

Note that these actions must be made in situations that pose some risk to your character, whereby he stands to pay a price for acting according to his Virtue or Vice. Everyday expressions of, say, Faith or Pride are not enough to reaffirm a character's determination or sense of self. For example, sleeping with someone does not qualify your character to earn spent Willpower simply because he has the Vice of Lust. He has to have risked a lot or sacrificed something significant in order to satisfy that desire.

Example: *Stein is a juvenile corrections officer with the defining Virtue of Justice and the Vice of Wrath. She checks on her kids one night and stumbles across Akers, another guard, terrorizing the kids. Apparently this abuse has gone on for a while, but the kids have been too scared to tell anyone. Akers tells her that if she turns him in, he'll make sure the administrators learn about the extracurricular trips that she and some of the kids have taken to the old cemetery after hours. He doesn't know the real reason they've gone out, but it's still enough to get her in a lot of trouble. If Stein reports Akers' actions to her supervisor, she risks losing her job. If she does so anyway despite the risk, she acts in accordance with her Virtue and regains all spent Willpower. Or if she gives in to her outrage and simply beats Akers until he agrees to never harass the kids again, she risks going to jail, not to mention potentially taking a beating of her own. Resorting to violence is in accordance with her Vice and allows the character to regain a single Willpower point.*

Fulfilling a Virtue is more rewarding than fulfilling a Vice for two reasons. One, it is inherently challenging to accomplish a surpassing act of goodness in a world that's rife with selfishness and aggression. Doing so demands sacrifice and perseverance. Two, the temptation to indulge base inclinations and desires is constant and often means taking the path of least resistance, which precludes doing the greater good. Fulfilling Vices therefore offers small rewards that are somewhat easy to come by.

Your character does not gain extra Virtues or Vices during play. The fundamental qualities that define him do not change. Nor are they compounded by more such traits. At the Storyteller's discretion, *truly* exceptional circumstances in a character's life — the death of a child or spouse, the realization of a deeply held personal dream, the gain or loss of a great deal of Morality — may justify a change of Virtue and/or Vice. These cases should be extremely rare, however, the result of genuinely heartfelt roleplaying.

As with Morality itself, the seven Virtues and Vices detailed below are ostensibly drawn from Western, Judeo-Christian beliefs (the Seven Heavenly Virtues and Seven Deadly Sins), but it's important to note that nearly all cultures value these ethics and revile these sins.

VIRTUES

When creating your character, choose one of the seven Virtues detailed here as your character's defining quality. This is not to say that she may not have other worthwhile or altruistic qualities, but her defining Virtue is the one that most clearly evokes her basic beliefs.

CHARITY

True Charity comes from sharing gifts with others, be it money or possessions, or simply giving time to help another in need. A charitable character is guided by her compassion to share what she has in order to improve the plight of those around her. Charitable individuals are guided by the principle of treating others as they would be treated themselves. By sharing gifts and taking on the role of the Samaritan, they hope to cultivate goodwill in others, and the gifts they give will eventually return to them in their hour of need.

Your character regains all spent Willpower points whenever she helps another at the risk of loss or harm to herself. It isn't enough to share what your character has in abundance. She must make a real sacrifice in terms of time, possessions or energy, or she must risk life and limb to help another.

Example: Rae could feel the others looking at her, not sure what to say. It had just been decided at the end of an hour-long debate that she and the other kids would go in "undercover" at the new club across town, where those teens had last been seen and those strange new drugs were rumored to originate. The others looked to her; none of them had ever gone clubbing before. Only she knew how to go unnoticed, to sort truth from rumor, and to track down the real dealers. It had been her scene, after all. She knew it like the back of her hand.

Problem was, it was that same scene that had turned her into a drunk and a junkie.

She'd been at the halfway house for less than a year, and was still pale and drawn. She still suffered from occasional fits of withdrawal that shook her body so hard she could barely move. She still had moments when she wanted a fix more than life itself. Going back into a place like that, where all her old connections would be hanging out, where there'd be booze and drugs for the taking.... She could already feel the cravings rise, and wanted to refuse any part in the plan.

But without her, the others would be made in moments. Nobody would learn anything. More poison would be peddled and more kids would die. With a long, shuddering breath, Rae looked around the room, "I'll do it. I know who to see to score this stuff."

Rae gains all spent Willpower for her act of charity. Her willingness to risk herself and her recovery for others validates her defining Virtue.

Other Names: Compassion, mercy

Possessed by: Philanthropists, saints, soup-kitchen workers

FAITH

Those with Faith know that the universe is not random, meaningless chaos, but ordered by a higher power. No matter how horrifying the world might be, everything has its place in the Plan and ultimately serves that Purpose. This Virtue does not necessarily involve belief in a personified deity. It might involve belief in a Grand Unified Theory whereby the seeming randomness of the universe is ultimately an expression of mathematical precision. Or it might be a view that everything is One and that even evil is indistinguishable from good when all discriminating illusions are overcome.

Your character regains all spent Willpower points whenever he is able to forge meaning from chaos and tragedy.

Example: "Why? Why did this have to happen?" The ghost repeated the phrase over and over, sobbing inconsolably. For weeks, it had appeared every night at the same time in the old house, weeping for several minutes over some unseen horror before turning to vanish. It was a pathetic existence, and for a moment Becca wondered if this was really what God had in mind, to create a place like this where so many souls lingered in suffering.

She took a deep breath, reaffirming her faith with the thought that most ghosts were trapped in prisons of their own making, not God's design. Shaking spirits out of their routine could be

difficult, not to mention dangerous, but if helping them to their final reward wasn't right, what else could be?

"Excuse me," she said, calmly but firmly, stepping forward to where the ghost could not help but see her. It took a moment, but the ghost actually turned to acknowledge her, staring with a tear-streaked face. Becca smiled at the apparition, holding out her hand. "Do you want to talk?"

The ghost wavered a moment, then reached for her hand, eyes grateful.

By helping a lost soul find its final peace, knowing that there must be a way to bring such troubled spirits rest, Becca regains any spent Willpower points.

Other Names: Belief, conviction, humility, loyalty

Possessed by: Detectives, philosophers, priests, scientists, true believers

FORTITUDE

A person's ideals are meaningless unless they're tested. When it seems as though the entire world is arrayed against him because of his beliefs, a person possessing Fortitude weathers the storm and emerges with his convictions intact. Fortitude is about standing up for one's beliefs and holding the course no matter how tempting it may be to relent or give up. By staying the course — regardless of the cost — he proves the worth of his ideals.

Your character regains all spent Willpower points whenever he withstands overwhelming or tempting pressure to alter his goals. This does not include temporary distractions from his course of action, only pressure that might cause him to abandon or change his goals altogether.

Example: "You don't have to do this, Tony." The creature advanced slowly, but there was no mistaking its predatory posture, nor the long claws that it absently clicked together as it approached. "You know I'm not after you."

"I made them a promise," Tony replied, putting his back to the door of the halfway house and bringing up his heavy flashlight in a defensive stance. "Nobody else gets hurt while I'm here. Not again."

"So you promised to protect them. So what?" The creature revealed a crooked grin of broken, rotting teeth. "The whole white knight business is old and done, my friend. Nobody cares about protecting damsels in distress anymore. Those times are long past. So just let me by, and I won't kill you, too."

Tony found his nervous tremors easing, his strength returning along with his conviction. Whatever the creature had hoped to accomplish with its little feint, it had achieved the exact opposite. "Go to Hell," Tony spat at the creature, meaning every word. "Nobody threatens my friends."

Stopping a few feet away, the creature regarded the man with obvious contempt. "You'd really die for them? A bunch of whores and junkies? What can that possibly accomplish?"

"The end of things like you," Tony said, smiling and swinging with all his might.

By refusing to break his promise and let others suffer, Tony behaves in a way that validates his defining Virtue and he regains any spent Willpower points.

Other Names: Courage, integrity, mettle, stoicism

Possessed by: Dictators, fanatic cultists, gumshoes

HOPE

Being hopeful means believing that evil and misfortune cannot prevail in the end, no matter how grim things become. Not only do the hopeful believe in the ultimate triumph of morality and decency over malevolence, they maintain steadfast belief in a greater sense of cosmic justice — whether it's Karma or the idea of an all-knowing, all-seeing God who waits to punish the wicked. All will turn out right in the end, and the hopeful mean to be around when it happens.

Your character regains all spent Willpower points whenever she refuses to let others give in to despair, even though doing so risks harming her own goals or wellbeing. This is similar to Fortitude, above, except that your character tries to prevent *others* from losing hope in their goals. She need not share those goals herself or even be successful in upholding them, but there must be a risk involved.

Example: "I'm not your enemy," Jack said soothingly. In the corner of the cave, a deep growl arose, and slitted animal eyes glared back at him in the dim light. Jack inched a little closer, palms up and open, eyes sympathetic. "You have to trust me when I say that. I want to help you."

Jack heard strange noises and then a rough voice spoke. It was deep and harsh, mixed with growls and animal breathing, but there was no mistaking the words it managed, or its cautious tone. "You... not hurt... me?"

"No, I'm not going to hurt you. There's been enough hurting in your life." Jack reached slowly into his pack, brought out a sandwich, unwrapped it and held it out. "Here, you must be hungry. It's okay. Come on out."

A furred hand with thick claws reached out of the darkness and took the meal. Jack sat down opposite the dark shape, listening as it ate ravenously. When it was finished, he let the silence settle, then spoke. "How can I help you?"

There was another moment of silence, more strange noises, and then a young woman covered in bramble cuts and tattered clothes stumbled out of the darkness and into Jack's arms, crying. He held her for a long time, not speaking.

By believing in its innate goodness and reaching out to a tormented creature at his own personal risk, Jack regains any spent Willpower.

Other Names: Dreamer, optimist, utopian

Possessed by: Anti-globalization activists, entrepreneurs, martyrs, visionaries

JUSTICE

Wrongs cannot go unpunished. This is the central tenet of the just, who believe that protecting the innocent and confronting inequity is the responsibility of every decent person, even in the face of great personal danger. The just believe that evil cannot prosper so long as one good person strives to do what is right, regardless of the consequences.

Your character regains all spent Willpower points whenever he does the right thing at risk of personal loss or setback. The "right thing" can be defined by the letter or spirit of a particular code of conduct, whether it be the United States penal code or a biblical Commandment.

Example: *Everyone else in the room was arguing. They'd finally managed to uncover the real truth about the old inn on the hill, and its sinister connection to the strange incidents at the abandoned workshop outside of town. The evidence was all there. Incredible, but all there. There were ghosts in town, spirits that had possessed civic leaders in pursuit of a horrific agenda that defied belief. Several people had already died, and others would soon follow if they didn't act.*

Knowledge of a common threat should have brought everyone together, Pete thought to himself as he looked around the room, but it had done the opposite. There was some agreement that the ghosts had to be stopped and the buildings closed up before their corrupting influence could spread, but nobody could agree on anything else. They argued about why the ghosts were there and what could be done to help them. Everything but what was really important: What they had to do to stop the supernatural reign of terror.

To Pete, it was simple. "I'll do it," he said quietly, repeating himself until everyone in the room fell silent and looked at him. "I'll burn the damn buildings to the ground." He looked around and saw the questions in their eyes. "I don't care about going to jail. It's just the right thing to do."

If Pete takes the law into his own hands and runs the risk of making himself a criminal as a result, he acts in a way that validates his defining Virtue and he regains any spent Willpower.

Other Names: Condemnatory, righteous

Possessed by: Critics, judges, parents, role models

PRUDENCE

The Virtue of Prudence places wisdom and restraint above rash action and thoughtless behavior. One maintains integrity and principles by moderating actions and avoiding unnecessary risks. While that means a prudent person might never take big gambles that bring huge rewards, neither is his life ruined by a single bad hand of cards. By choosing wisely and avoiding the easy road he prospers slowly but surely.

Your character regains all spent Willpower points whenever he refuses a tempting course of action by which he could gain significantly. The "temptation" must involve some reward that, by refusing it, might cost him later on.

Example: *"Come on! Let's finish it off now!" Pete pointed down the hallway, where the faint white light was rapidly receding into the depths of the house. The group had split up to search the dilapidated mansion, but he and Sean had been the first to run into the malevolent spirit that was haunting the place. It had manifested right in front of them, a young man with a frightening, decayed countenance, but they had responded by brandishing crosses and beginning to pray aloud. That seemed to wound the apparition, and it had begun to slowly back away, its inner light fading, until it finally turned and fled at a high rate of speed.*

"Wait!" Sean said, grabbing Pete by the arm and holding him back. "We should get the others before we go any farther. For all we know, this could be a ploy."

"Sean, you saw what I saw – the prayers were really hurting it! If we go after it now, we can finish the damn thing off, but if we don't, it might vanish before we get another shot at it!" Pete's tone was exasperated. "We don't have time!"

Sean understood his friend's concerns. The mansion was huge and maze-like, with a lot of strange dead ends and interconnecting hallways; it was all too possible they wouldn't get another shot at this. Besides, the thing had hurt too many people in the past, and it certainly had looked like the prayers were weakening it considerably... but there were still too many uncertain factors to go charging off. "We're waiting," Sean declared flatly, fishing out his walkie-talkie. "Let's do this right."

If Sean passes on the possibility of immediately destroying the ghost to wait for his team to catch up, he acts in a way that validates his defining Virtue and regains any spent Willpower.

Other Names: Patience, vigilance

Possessed by: Businessmen, doctors, priests, scientists

TEMPERANCE

Moderation in all things is the secret to happiness, so says the doctrine of Temperance. It's all about balance. Everything has its place in a person's life, from anger to forgiveness, lust to chastity. The temperate do not believe in denying their urges, as none of it is unnatural or unholy. The trouble comes when things are taken to excess, whether it's a noble or base impulse. Too much righteousness can be just as bad as too much wickedness.

Your character regains all spent Willpower when he resists a temptation to indulge in an excess of any behavior, whether good or bad, despite the obvious rewards it might offer.

Example: Doctor Mitchell had seen how much damage the creature had caused, had heard what the kids at his halfway house had told him about the drugs and worse things going on at the club. He had even helped track the creature down, despite his nagging doubts about what the rest of the group intended to do with the information. When they at last suggested violence, he knew he had to make his move before they did something rash.

Now he found himself outside the creature's door, ready for the meeting he'd arranged through one of her servants. When the door opened, he swallowed involuntary. The kids had told him she was stunning, but their words didn't do her justice. Her hair fell in shining golden waves, framing a perfectly shaped face, luscious lips and eyes the perfect blue of a tropical sea. A slinky red dress, a slightly raised eyebrow and a sultry pout completed her air of absolute sensuality.

For a moment, Doctor Mitchell forgot everything he'd come there for, thinking only of how perfect it would be to lose himself in her presence. He'd lived a solitary life for too long, and he felt all of that loneliness catch up to him. It would be so easy... and so wrong. He felt his resolve return, straightened his tie and saw the creature look slightly startled at his sudden recovery.

"Hello, I'm Doctor Phillip Mitchell. I'm here to talk to you about a problem."

By remaining centered and refusing to give in to extreme and compelling impulses, Doctor Mitchell acts in a way that validates his defining Virtue and he regains any spent Willpower.

Other Names: Chastity, even-temperament, frugality

Possessed by: Clergy, police officers, social workers

VICES

When creating your character, choose one of the seven Vices detailed below as her defining one. This is not to say that your character may not have other weaknesses or base impulses, but her defining Vice is the one that most clearly evokes her basic behavior.

ENVY

An envious person is never satisfied with what she has. No matter her wealth, status or accomplishments, there is always someone else who seems to have more, and it's coveted. Envious characters are never secure or content with their place in life. They always measure themselves against their rivals and look for ways to get what they deserve. They might be considered paranoid or just consumed by a self-loathing that they project onto others.

Your character regains one Willpower point whenever she gains something important from a rival or has a hand in harming that rival's wellbeing.

Example: *Victor sat off to the side, only half-listening to the rest of the group as they talked about things like classes, jobs and family. They'd spent most of the night furtively planning what to do about the latest supernatural "threat" they'd uncovered. Now the others were relaxing, enjoying a few drinks and letting off steam, trying to convince themselves that when it was all over, they could go back to the lives from before.*

Victor knew it was all a lie. There would be no going back, not for people like them. At war with enemies and forces they could barely comprehend, he knew they would simply stumble blindly from one crisis to the next until they finally wound up in jail, an asylum or a grave. It was inevitable.

Yet still he found himself hating the others, because they at least could delude themselves with thoughts of a normal life. His constant contact with the strange beings he knew only as the Voices and their barrage of inhuman demands had denied him even that small mercy. He'd been forced to drop out of school, quit his job and even leave his house. He lived at the mercy of the others, hating them for their pity even as he was forced to scrape to survive.

That had all changed two nights ago, however, when the Voices offered a deal. Lead the others to a trap and the creatures would accept the lives as payment for Victor's own. No more nightmares. No more fear. Just a normal life. He hated himself for his weakness, but in the end he just couldn't resist. After all, he'd suffered more than anyone. Why should they be the only ones with happiness, with hope for the future?

Victor took a long drink. His plan had been a big success tonight.

By selling out his "friends" for a shot at the happiness they enjoy, Victor indulges his defining Vice and regains one point of spent Willpower.

Other Names: Covetousness, jealousy, paranoia

Possessed by: Celebrities, executives, politicians

GLUTTONY

Gluttony is about indulging appetites to the exclusion of everything else. It's about dedicating oneself to sensual pleasures or chasing the next high. A glutton makes any sacrifice to feed his insatiable appetite for pleasure, regardless of the cost to himself or those around him. He might be considered a lush, a junky or even a kleptomaniac (he steals things he doesn't need just for the thrill of it).

Your character regains one spent Willpower point whenever he indulges in his addiction or appetites at some risk to himself or a loved one.

Example: *By all rights, he should've "retired" years ago, but Nick just couldn't stay out of the game. In fact, he kept up with the ins and outs of the trade better than most of the kids half his age, reading everything from electronics catalogs to security trade magazines to keep up with the latest developments, and occasionally ordering a piece of hardware just to take it apart and learn what made it tick. He even frequented a number of police bars — incognito, naturally — to see the new faces and perhaps pick up on a few bad habits that he might exploit in a pinch.*

He'd already made his name on the street years before by being a reliable man and a stand-up guy when the heat was on. He even enjoyed status as a good luck charm of sorts, having never been convicted in all the years he worked. He had more money than he'd ever needed, a nice townhouse, and luck with the ladies that was second only to the fortune he enjoyed on the job. Realistically, he had little to gain and a lot to lose by pulling jobs, but he just couldn't help himself. Even tonight, when he'd agreed to lift some files from that charity institute, it wasn't really about the money, though the money was good.

It was just too much damned fun.

By stealing just for the thrill of it, Nick indulges in his defining Vice and regains a point of spent Willpower.

Other Names: Addictive personality, conspicuous consumer, Epicurean

Possessed by: Celebrities, junkies, thieves

GREED

Like the envious, the greedy are never satisfied with what they have. They want more — more money, a bigger house, more status or influence — no matter that they may already have more than they can possibly handle. Everything is taken to excess. To the greedy, there is no such thing as having too much. If that means snatching someone else's hard-earned reward just to feather one's own nest, well, that's the way it goes.

Your character regains one Willpower point whenever he acquires something at the expense of another. Gaining it must come at some potential risk (of assault, arrest or simple loss of peer respect).

Example: Dwayne moved carefully down the neat rows of shelving, all handmade and installed personally into his basement walls. He held his clipboard and made tiny notations as he passed each shelf, inspecting its contents and making sure they matched if not exceeded the records from last month. Not normally a methodical man, he took his time and double-checked himself.

Several hours later, he sat back on the basement steps and allowed himself a beer, drinking it slowly and taking in his stock with pride. Six months worth of rather luxurious rations, plus another eight months worth of dehydrated materials. Survival gear, communications equipment, body armor and first-aid kits. Enough to outfit a full platoon. Three dozen assault rifles, two dozen shotguns, an equal number of rifles, over a hundred handguns, and enough knives of different lengths to supply a small town. Fifteen thousand rounds of ammunition, all kept in safety cases to keep out the environment.

Nobody was going to put him off his land now, not with this much gear. But he still needed more, especially now that he knew he'd hadn't been far off when he'd called those suits at the bank "bloodsuckers" in past. Just thinking about them made him break into a cold sweat. He consoled himself the thought that he'd be able to hit another truck soon, and that would bring in even more supplies for his stockpile. After all, being prepared wasn't cheap.

By robbing others in order to stockpile weapons and equipment, Dwayne indulges his defining Vice and regains a point of spent Willpower.

Other Names: Avarice, parsimony

Possessed by: CEOs, lawyers, stock brokers

LUST

The Vice of Lust is the sin of uncontrolled desire. A lusty individual is driven by a passion for something (usually sex, but it can be a craving for virtually any experience or activity) that he acts upon without consideration for the needs or feelings of others. A lusty individual uses any means at his disposal to indulge his desires, from deception to manipulation to acts of violence.

Your character is consumed by a passion for something. He regains one Willpower point whenever he satisfies his lust or compulsion in a way that victimizes others.

Example: There was nothing Sam could do about it. He was attracted to Rachel, and even though he and the rest of his group suspected (knew) that she was one of those bloodsucking creatures, he couldn't help but want her. She was so smart, so sexy, so dangerous.... He couldn't stop thinking about her. By day he reviewed the information they'd gathered. By night he followed her, first in his car, later in his dreams.

Finally, one night while he was supposed to be shadowing her, he got out of his car and followed her into the club. When she said, "What's been keeping you?" and winked, he knew she had to be his, no matter what the cost. So he took the drink she offered, and then another. By the time she started questions about the others, he had no problem answering truthfully and in complete detail.

She was his tonight.

By giving in to his urges despite his better judgment and so betraying his friends, Sam indulges his defining Vice and regains a point of spent Willpower.

Other Names: Lasciviousness, impatience, impetuousness

Possessed by: Movie producers, politicians, rock stars

PRIDE

Pride is the Vice of self-confidence run amok. It's the belief that one's every action is inherently right, even when it should be obvious that it's anything but. A prideful person refuses to back down when his decision or reputation is called into question, even when the evidence is clear that he's in the wrong. His ego does not accept any outcome that suggests fallibility, and he's willing to see others suffer rather than admit that he's wrong.

Your character regains one Willpower point whenever he exerts his own wants (not needs) over others at some potential risk to himself. This is most commonly the desire for adulation, but it could be the desire to make others do as he commands.

Example: Dietrich looked at the rough tunnel descending into the earth before him. The others had made a big deal about how the walls were covered in "ominous symbols" and "disturbing markings." True enough, there were a fairly large number of glyphs etched into the earth. Indeed, the more he looked, the more they seemed to draw him in, telling tales of murder, madness and dark sorcery, dragging his mind back to a dark era full of blood and pain.

Dietrich shook his head sharply, clearing it. If a bunch of occult scribbles were supposed to deter investigators, their creators were sorely mistaken. He drew himself up to his full height, turned back and faced the rest of the group, who looked uneasy. "I don't know about the rest of you, but I think this tunnel has to be explored. Who knows what might be down there, coming out at night and feeding on the town like those other things did?"

"We have to do this. If none of you are strong enough to see that, I guess I'm going down alone." He started into the tunnel, and allowed himself a grim smile as he heard the others move to follow. One way or another, he knew they'd follow his lead.

By refusing to back down to the challenge, and reveling in his own self-assurance, Dietrich indulges his defining Vice and regains a point of spent Willpower.

Other Names: Arrogance, ego complex, vanity

Possessed by: Corporate executives, movie stars, street thugs

SLOTH

The Vice of Sloth is about avoiding work until someone else has to step in to get the job done. Rather than put in the effort — and possibly risk failure — in a difficult situation, the slothful person simply refuses to do anything, knowing that someone else will fix the problem eventually. The fact that people might needlessly suffer while the slothful person sits on his hands doesn't matter one bit.

Your character regains one Willpower point whenever he successfully avoids a difficult task but achieves the same goal nonetheless.

Example: Leeds sat on his front porch, drinking straight from the bottle and wondering what he was going to do next. He couldn't deny that what he'd seen over the past couple of weeks had

been pretty strange. First there were the tracks, far too big for any coyote. Then the stories about the lost hiking groups, who'd disappeared not too far from his house. And finally, the thing he'd run into in the woods the other night. He still had nightmares about being chased.

His instincts screamed that something was dreadfully wrong, that he was in great danger. Every morning he came close to packing up and just leaving everything behind. Or better yet, going in search of what he was now sure was lurking in the woods. But then he'd find a bottle for a bit of courage and the threat would go away.

After all, his family had lived there for eight generations. He wasn't about to let some damn animal scare him off his land. It had been a close call, but he'd had plenty of those while hunting in the past, so this was nothing new.

It was probably just some escaped zoo animal, rabid thing or some crap like that. The sheriff would take care of it soon enough. Leeds took another swig from the bottle and leaned back. That was it, he'd let the sheriff handle it.

By avoiding action despite the repercussions, Leeds indulges his defining Vice and regains a point of spent Willpower.

Other Names: Apathy, cowardice, ignorance

Possessed by: Couch potatoes, trust-fund heirs, welfare cheats

WRATH

The Vice of Wrath is the sin of uncontrolled anger. The wrathful look for ways to vent their anger and frustration on people or objects at the slightest provocation. In most cases the reaction is far out of proportion to the perceived slight. A wrathful person cut off on the freeway might try to force another driver off the road, or a wrathful cop might delight in beating each and every person he arrests, regardless of the offense.

Your character regains one spent Willpower point whenever he unleashes his anger in a situation where doing so is dangerous. If the fight has already begun, no Willpower points are regained. It must take place in a situation where anger is unwarranted or inappropriate.

Example: "Wait! Don't you see that it's only trying to protect its home?"

Jimmy whirled around and glared at Greg. "I don't care what that thing wants! It doesn't belong here! And it had better tell us what's going on in this neighborhood," he turned and tore an ornate portrait off the dusty walls, "Or I'm going to make it talk the hard way!"

The ghost's face, only seconds ago a study of piteous confusion, warped into a mask of demented rage at the sight of Jimmy lifting the portrait, an eerie wail issuing from its spectral throat. Greg reached for Jimmy's arm, trying to calm him down. "You don't have to do this! It might talk to us!"

"To hell with talking!" Jimmy yelled in response, heaving the portrait and smashing it against the granite fireplace. "It's done nothing but bring people pain! I say it gets the hell out of this house right now!"

The newly enraged ghost gave an inhuman howl and unleashed the full might of its supernatural strength against the intruders.

By giving in to his anger and resorting to destruction when it causes rather than sidesteps danger, Jimmy indulges his defining Vice and regains a point of spent Willpower.

Other Names: Antisocial tendencies, hot-headedness, poor anger management, sadism

Possessed by: Bullies, drill sergeants, street thugs

Chapter 5: Merits

Merits are special capabilities or knacks that add individuality to your character. They're purchased during character creation or with experience points over the course of your chronicle.

The Merits in this chapter are organized alphabetically into three broad categories: Physical, Mental and Social. Some apply to your character's basic traits to enhance them in particular situations. Some have prerequisites that must be met before they can be purchased. For example, a character with the Gunslinger Merit must have a Dexterity of 3 and Firearms of 3 or higher to be able to accurately fire two weapons at the same time. Similarly, some Merits apply drawbacks that balance out their inherent advantages. A character with the Fame Merit, for example, is treated like a star wherever he goes, but has a hard time blending into the crowd when he wants to.

Each Merit has a number of dots (•) associated with it. These dots represent the number of points that must be spent to purchase the Merit. Some Merits allow for a range of dots (say, • to • • •). These allow you to purchase a low rating if it's appropriate to your character concept, or you can start with a low level and increase it over time with experience points.

Some Merits are such that a character must either be born with them or develop them very early in life, while others can be acquired through trial and error, training, and effort later in life. The first kind can be acquired at character creation only and are labeled as such. The second kind can be acquired during play with experience points.

> We make our own fortunes, and call them fate.
>
> — Benjamin Disraeli

"But I Worked So Hard On It!"

Some players inevitably make a case for purchasing particular "character creation only" Merits once the chronicle is underway. Perhaps they argue that a character has started spending four hours a day in the gym, six days a week, where he's deliberately building up his off-hand to be equal to his dominant one, so he should be allowed to purchase the Ambidexterity Merit. As always, Storytellers are free to make allowances if they like, but be extremely careful when allowing players to take Merits late when they are normally limited to character creation. It might cause trouble with other players who wanted to take Merits during character creation and didn't, and who will now come to you looking for the same consideration. Before you know it, everyone in the game will have what was supposed to be a rather limited trait, and the game may be thrown out of balance as a result.

Mental Merits

COMMON SENSE (•)

Effect: Your character is exceptionally grounded and pragmatic, and can usually be depended on to make sound, straightforward decisions after a few moments' thought.

A Storyteller or Narrator can make a reflexive Wits + Composure draw once per chapter for your character if he's about to embark on a disastrous course of action, or if you find yourself at a point in the story where you're completely stumped for ideas. If the draw succeeds, the Storyteller may point out the risks of a particular course, or suggest possible actions that your character can take that might get events back on track. Note: While you're free to ask the Storyteller for a Common Sense draw when you're out of ideas, he is under no obligation to comply. It's an aid, not a crutch. Available at character creation only.

Storytellers may choose to temporarily award this Merit for free to new players unfamiliar with the World of Darkness, removing it from their character sheet once they've familiarized themselves with the nature of the game. Storytellers, use this option sparingly. The intention is to free a *character* from the inexperience of the *player*. For characters who are supposed to be naïve or inexperienced, as many starting characters should be, awarding this Merit would be counterproductive.

DANGER SENSE (• •)

Effect: You gain a +2 modifier on reflexive Wits + Composure draws for your character to detect an impending ambush. This kind of draw is typically made prior to the first turn of a surprise attack.

Your character has a well-developed survival instinct that warns him of impending danger. He might be adept at reading subtle clues in his environment, or perhaps spent time under fire as a soldier or an inner-city cop, or maybe he just possesses an uncanny "sixth sense" when it comes to avoiding trouble.

EIDETIC MEMORY (• •)

Effect: Your character has a near-photographic memory, being able to recall vast amounts of observed detail with astonishing accuracy. You do not normally need to make a draw for your character to remember an obscure fact or past experience, unless he is under stress (such as in combat). Under stress, he gains is a +2 modifier on any Intelligence + Composure or other Skill-based draw (say, Academics, to remember a fact) representing memory recall. Note, however, that this does *not* apply to any draws related to analysis or interpretation of data, only raw feats of recollection.

Recalling an obscure fact, distant memory or fleeting impression may also require a turn or more of concentration, at the Storyteller's discretion. This pause also covers any time that might be required to dig up the necessary facts out-of-game, if the player doesn't actually recall them. It is highly recommended that the player work with the Storyteller to keep a record of particularly useful or important memories as a "cheat sheet" to ensure that valuable information that a character should remember is not actually forgotten out-of-game, especially in long-running chronicles. Eidetic memory doesn't normally allow a character to sit down and recall an entire lifetime of events, and some traumatic events may very well weaken the character's memory even further. Available at character creation only.

Encyclopedic Knowledge (• • • •)

Effect: Your character is a veritable font of trivial (but sometimes surprisingly useful) information on a variety of topics. Chances are he can come up with an anecdote pertaining to any situation based on something he's read, witnessed or seen on TV.

Once per topic, you can make an Intelligence + Wits draw when your character is confronted with a situation or phenomenon outside his normal realm of experience. If the draw is successful, he may recall a "factoid" that he's heard at some point that may shed light on matters. This may be a small bit of information that the player knows, or it may come directly from a Narrator. Remember that this is supposed to reflect a relatively trivial, often quirky sort of knowledge. These facts don't typically mean much on their own, but when plugged into a mystery or situation that a character faces, they might shed some light or offer an interesting solution. Players who attempt to abuse this Merit to bring in inappropriate amounts of out-of-game knowledge or as a way of bypassing the need to acquire Skills should be disciplined by the Storyteller, and could possibly lose this Merit.

Available at character creation only. Either your character has been soaking up trivia all his life or he hasn't.

Failure: Your character wracks his brain but comes up empty.

Success: Your character remembers a detail or fact that sheds some light on the situation. "You said there was an almond odor? Seems to me I read somewhere that's a sign of cyanide poisoning."

Holistic Awareness (• • •)

Effect: Your character is skilled in the arts of whole-body healing, promoting health and recovery by keeping a person's entire physiology balanced and strong. The result is that he is able to treat sickness and some injuries (those not requiring surgery, and ones suffered to bashing or lethal but not aggravated damage) with a collection of natural remedies rather than resorting to a doctor or hospital.

Make an Intelligence + Medicine draw once per day when your character spends an hour treating a patient. If the draw is successful, the patient's healing times that day are halved. The worst of a patient's injuries must be treated first. So, if he has suffered a lethal wound and a successful draw is made, the wound heals that day rather than in two days. If the patient has suffered nothing but bashing damage, all wounds are healed in mere minutes (about eight each). See Chapter 7, p. 240, for healing times.

Failure: The treatment has no effect and normal healing times apply to any bashing wounds or to a single lethal wound. If the Storyteller allows, your character can make a successive attempt to try again that day (see p. 176). If still no successes are gained to heal a single lethal wound or one or more bashing wounds, those must be allowed to heal naturally before another effort can be made. Thus, if no successes are drawn to heal one of a patient's lethal wounds, that wound must heal naturally over two days before your character can try to heal another lethal wound.

Success: Your character's treatment is rewarding and the patient's healing time that day is halved.

Suggested Equipment: Holistic medicines (+1), healing-touch manuals (+1), body-purifying foods and liquids (+1)

Possible Penalties: Lack of remedies (-1 to -4), noisy environment (-1), imminent danger (-3), improvised facilities (-1)

LANGUAGE (•)

Effect: Your character knows an additional language besides his own, one that he can read, write and speak with fluency. If he wishes to convince others that he is a native speaker, however, the Storyteller might call for an Intelligence + Expression draw, contested by a reflexive Intelligence + Academics draw by anyone who is suspicious.

You must specify which language your character is familiar with when purchasing this Merit. There is no limit to the number of languages that a character may learn, though each language must be purchased as a separate Merit. To signify to other players that your character is speaking in a different language, either hold up one hand with the thumb and forefinger making an "L" sign while conversing, or clearly announce "Speaking [language]" at the beginning of each exchange.

MEDITATIVE MIND (•)

Effect: Your character can effortlessly enter a meditative state when she chooses, and can remain in it for as long as she wishes. All environmental penalties imposed to Wits + Composure draws to meditate are ignored. Not even wound penalties apply to your character's efforts to focus. See the Meditation Attribute task in Chapter 2, p. 55.

UNSEEN SENSE (• • •)

Prerequisite: Mortal (non-supernatural); Wits • •

Effect: Your character has a "sixth sense" when it comes to the supernatural. Perhaps his hair stands on end, goose bumps race along his arms, or a shiver runs up his spine. Regardless of the manner, his body reacts to the presence of unseen forces. He can't see or hear anything, and in fact he might not know at first what causes this reaction. It might be a response to a specific type of supernatural phenomenon such as ghosts or vampires, or it might be a general sense that something isn't right. Over time and with a little trial and error, he might be able to qualify what his body tries to tell him.

The specific type of supernatural phenomenon to which your character is sensitive must be determined when this Merit is purchased. It can be something as vague as a creepy feeling when in the presence of ghosts, or something as specific as a sudden chill when a vampire is nearby. The Storyteller has final say on the exact nature and trigger of your character's sixth sense, and can keep its nature secret if desired, leaving you to figure it out during play.

Only mortal, mundane characters can possess this Merit. The pivotal moment of becoming or being changed into a being with supernatural capabilities eliminates it, though kindly Storytellers may allow you to convert it into experience points for purchasing supernatural sensory powers and the like, at their discretion.

Physical Merits

Unless stated otherwise, Merits that give combat bonuses may not be combined with other such Merits in a single turn.

AMBIDEXTROUS (• • •)

Effect: Your character does not suffer the −2 penalty for using his off-hand in combat or to perform other actions. This Merit can usually be combined with Fighting Styles or other Merits. Available at character creation only.

BRAWLING DODGE (•)

Prerequisite: Strength • • and Brawl •

Effect: Whenever your character performs a Dodge (see "Dodge," p. 216), you can choose to add his Brawl Skill dots to his Defense *instead* of doubling his Defense. He essentially draws on his training in blocking and evading attacks rather than relying on his raw ability alone. While this might provide little benefit to a brawling novice, it can give the advanced fighter an edge.

Your character can choose to use a Brawling Dodge in any situation that allows for a Dodge. Brawling Dodge applies against incoming Brawl- and Weaponry-based attacks, against thrown-weapon attacks, and against Firearms attacks made within close-combat range. Your character can move up to his Acting Speed and perform a Brawling Dodge maneuver in a turn but may not attack. A character can't use any Fighting Styles in a turn in which he uses a Brawling Dodge.

DIRECTION SENSE (•)

Effect: Your character has an innate sense of direction that instinctively allows him to remain oriented. He can enter unfamiliar territory and always retrace his steps back to his starting point, and can orient himself to any of the compass points (i.e., face north, face south) without references. He may ask a Narrator out-of-game which way he came, and retrace his steps without fail.

DISARM (• •)

Prerequisite: Dexterity • • • and Weaponry • •

Effect: Your character has refined his Weaponry Skill to the extent that he can use a melee weapon to disarm opponents in close combat. When making a normal attack, compare your successes to the opponent's Dexterity. If you get a number of successes equal to or greater than the opponent's Dexterity, you can choose to have your character disarm him instead of doing damage. A weapon lands a number of steps away from the opponent equal to the successes drawn on the attack, in a direction of your choosing.

Disarming is a different activity than specifically attacking or breaking weapons or items carried by opponents. See "Equipment" (p. 192) for rules on doing that.

FAST REFLEXES (• OR • •)

Prerequisites: Dexterity • • •

Effect: +1 Initiative per dot

Your character's mix of sharp reflexes and steady nerves helps him get the drop on adversaries.

FIGHTING FINESSE (• •)

Prerequisite: Dexterity • • • and Weaponry • •

Effect: Your character prefers to fight with a chosen melee weapon in a manner that favors agility over power. With that one weapon (a rapier or katana, for example), you may substitute your character's Dexterity for Strength when making attack draws. Supernatural means of enhancing strength do not help with attacks made with Fighting Finesse: your blows are swift and precise incisions rather than hammering blows. Natural or supernatural body modifications such as claws can't be used with Fighting Finesse.

This Merit may be purchased multiple times to gain agility with more weapons, one for each purchase.

Using Fighting Styles and Combat Maneuvers

A character cannot employ more than one Fighting Style at a time in a turn. Nor can he combine any of the Fighting Styles with the Gunslinger Merit. Sometimes this is fairly self-evident (it's hard to justify using Boxing when your character wields two knives), but some players go to ridiculous lengths to justify unlikely combat combinations in order to gain every possible advantage. Likewise, no more than a single Fighting Style can be used per turn.

Nothing prevents a character with access to several of these Merits from switching between them from one turn to another if he desires. For example, a character can use Boxing one turn, then draw a pair of knives to use Two-Weapon style in the next turn, and then pull a pair of pistols in the third turn and use the Gunslinger Merit (not to mention the Quick Draw Merit). Unless the rules or the Storyteller specifically states otherwise, however, a character cannot use the maneuvers of or otherwise benefit from more than one Fighting Style in a single turn. They are powerful enough on their own. Combining them makes for an extremely unbalanced play situation.

Note that with the exception of inherent enhancements to speed and strength, these fighting styles preclude the use of special powers or abilities that aren't inherent and natural to the creature using them. A vampire could not for instance combine Kung Fu with a claw attack and a supernatural being taking any alternate shape could not resort to using a Fighting Style.

FIGHTING STYLE: BOXING (• TO • • • • •)

Prerequisites: Strength • • •, Stamina • • and Brawl • •

Effect: Your character is trained in the art of boxing, able to deliver swift, powerful punches, and to duck and weave away from opponents' attacks. He might have participated in the sport in high school or college, or made a go of it professionally. Alternatively, he might have taken some classes at the local health club as a form of exercise, and decided to take his training to the next level when he discovered what lurks in the night.

Note that while boxing instructors can be found a bit more readily than those of exotic fighting styles, this Merit typically requires more intense training than simply hitting the gym once or twice a week, especially at high levels. A general effort can be reflected by regular Brawl itself. Serious adherents of boxing devote extensive amounts of time training, and the Storyteller may require a character to spend a large amount of time maintaining his expertise. At high dots of this Merit (3+), practice might demand a downtime action every month or so. Failure to do so may temporarily reduce a character's dots by one until he can get back on his training regimen.

If a character decides to use a brawling attack, every dot of the Boxing Merit increases his Defense rating by one against incoming brawling attacks during that turn. The character is highly trained to spot attacks coming and to avoid them, bobbing and weaving away as he sees muscles tensing and other tell-tale signs of an impending assault.

A character may use neither mundane nor supernatural weapons (such as claws) while employing the Boxing Fighting Style. This cannot be combined with the Brawling Dodge Merit and it may only be used in a turn in which a character isn't performing a full dodge.

FIGHTING STYLE: KUNG FU (• TO • • • • •)

Prerequisites: Strength • •, Dexterity • •, Stamina • • and Brawl • •

Effect: Your character is trained in one of the many forms of Kung Fu, conditioning his mind and body for the purposes of focus and self-defense. He may have begun his training at an early age, following in the footsteps of family or friends, or he may have joined a school as an adult for the purposes of exercise or protection.

Note that this Merit requires a lot more training than simply hitting the dojo once or twice a week. That kind of casual training can be reflected by regular Brawl itself. Serious adherents of Kung Fu must devote extensive time to training, and the Storyteller may require a character to spend considerable time keeping her training sharp. Practice might even demand a downtime action every month or so, particularly at high dots of this Merit. Failure to do so may temporarily reduce a character's dots by one until she can get back on her training regimen.

When performing a brawl attack to strike an unarmed opponent, declare the use of Kung Fu. Every dot of Kung Fu reduces your opponent's base Defense by one, including any additional Defense dots she may receive from the Boxing Merit. Kung Fu can never reduce an opponent's Defense below zero.

A character may use neither mundane nor supernatural weapons of any kind (such as claws) while employing the Kung Fu Fighting Style. Kung Fu may also not be used for additional damage on a Chance Draw attack.

FIGHTING STYLE: TWO WEAPONS (• TO • • • • •)

Prerequisites: Dexterity • • • and Weaponry • • •

Effect: Your character has trained to fight with a melee weapon in both hands, allowing him to attack and parry in the same turn . Your character suffers a –2 offhand penalty for making weaponry attacks when wielding two weapons (unless you have also purchased the Ambidextrous Merit, which can be combined with this Fighting Style).

Like the other Fighting Styles, this Merit typically requires more intense training than simply mugging folks or crossing foils once or twice a week, especially at high levels. That kind of relatively casual effort can be reflected by regular Weaponry itself. Learning to fight with two weapons at the level represented by this Merit takes a lot of training and effort to master, and the Storyteller may require your character to spend a lot of time maintaining his expertise. At high levels of this Merit (3+ dots), training may demand a downtime action every month or so. Failure to practice may temporarily reduce a character's dots by one until she can get back on her regimen.

When fighting with two melee weapons, every dot of this Fighting Style increases your Defense rating by one against incoming weaponry and thrown weapon attacks during that turn. The character's blades are a whirlwind of striking and parrying, easily able to deflect incoming blows. Characters must wield a mundane melee weapon in each hand to use this Fighting Style.

FLEET OF FOOT (• TO • • •)

Prerequisites: Strength • •

Effect: +1 Running Speed per dot

Regardless of your character's physical build, he can run exceptionally quickly when he chooses to.

GIANT (• • • •)

Effect: Your character is seven or more feet tall and over 250 pounds. He is +1 Size (and thus +1 Health). Available at character creation only.

Drawback: Your character needs to shop at big-and-tall clothing stores and get clothes custom tailored. He might also be required to purchase two seats for air travel, depending on the airline. Finally, he stands out in a crowd. You must wear a prominent description tag and/or costuming to indicate his large size.

GUNSLINGER (• • •)

Prerequisites: Dexterity • • • and Firearms • • •

Effect: Your character's capability and experience with firearms is such that he can accurately fire two pistols at the same time. Your character still suffers the –2 offhand penalty for shooting with his secondary hand (unless he also possesses the Ambidextrous Merit, above), but he can shoot both pistols as a single action during a turn.

Instead of making only one draw, reshuffle the first card after looking at it and make another draw. You can choose which one of the two draws applies to this challenge: the first bullet may have missed, but the second one will hopefully find the target. The second draw is made at a -2 penalty unless the character is ambidextrous. The Gunslinger Merit can't be used in conjunction with any firearm with a damage rating of 3 or higher.

Drawback: Your character cannot use his Defense against any attack in the same turn in which he intends to use this Merit . If he uses Defense against attacks that occur earlier in the Initiative roster, before he can perform this maneuver, he cannot perform the maneuver this turn. He is too busy ducking and evading incoming attacks.

IRON STAMINA (• TO • • •)

Prerequisites: Stamina • • • or Resolve • • •

Effect: Each dot eliminates a negative modifier (on a one-for-one basis) when resisting the effects of fatigue or injury. For example: A character with Iron Stamina • • is able to ignore up to a –2 modifier brought on by fatigue. See "Fatigue," p. 246. The Merit also counteracts the effects of wound penalties. Therefore, if all of your character's Health boxes are filled (which normally imposes a –3 penalty to his actions) and he has Iron Stamina •, those penalties are reduced to –2. This Merit cannot be used to gain positive modifiers for actions, only to cancel out negative ones. It also offers no benefit in resisting incapacitation or death. Once a character is that injured, not even his tolerance can keep him going.

Your character can push his body well past the limits of physical endurance when he has to, pressing on in the face of mounting exhaustion or pain. Perhaps he trained himself to go without sleep for days at a time in order to get through college, or a lifetime of sports has taught your character how to play through the pain no matter how bad it gets.

Drawback: When your character does finally rest, he sleeps like the dead. After staying awake for an extended period, your character is extremely difficult to wake until he's slept for a minimum of 12 hours, regardless of the situation.

IRON STOMACH (• •)
Prerequisites: Stamina • •

Effect: Your character can eat almost anything, under almost any conditions. Greasy bacon and runny eggs on a raging hangover? No problem. The green meat in the fridge? No problem. Milk two weeks past its expiration date? No problem. He could be dropped in the middle of the forest and could live off bugs and roots as long as necessary in order to survive — and with no ill effects. Add two to appropriate Survival draws. Add three to Stamina to resist deprivation (see p. 241), provided there is at least *some* sustenance be had, however horrid it might be.

NATURAL IMMUNITY (•)
Prerequisites: Stamina • •

Effect: Your character gains a +2 modifier on Stamina draws to resist infection, sickness and disease, and generally does not have to worry about most common conditions at all unless your character is already particularly injured or uncommonly unlucky. His immune system is exceptionally effective at resisting infections, viruses and bacteria. Your character can probably count on one hand the number of times he's been seriously ill.

QUICK DRAW (•)
Prerequisites: Dexterity • • •

Effect: Your character can draw a pistol and fire or pull a melee weapon and attack without penalty as a single action in a turn. If a weapon is hidden on your character's person (under a coat or in a purse), it can be drawn and used in the same turn without the normal loss of Defense. A separate Quick Draw Merit must be acquired for use with firearms and melee weapons. This can be combined with the Ambidextrous and Gunslinger Merits to draw (and fire) two weapons in a turn.

QUICK HEALER (• • • •)
Prerequisite: Stamina • • • •

Effect: Your character's healing abilities are remarkable, allowing him to bounce back quickly from injuries that would leave most people bedridden for months.

Your character recovers from injuries in half the time that others do. One point of bashing damage is healed in eight minutes. One point of lethal damage is healed in one day. One point of aggravated damage is healed in four days.

STRONG BACK (•)
Prerequisites: Strength • •

Effect: Your character gains a +1 modifier to her effective Strength for all actions involving lifting or carrying heavy weights. She can lift and carry much more weight than her build and body type suggests.

STRONG LUNGS (• • •)
Prerequisite: Athletics • • •

Effect: Your character is practiced at holding his breath for long periods. He might be a pearl diver or escape artist, capable of staying underwater without aid for longer than most people believe is possible.

When determining how long your character can hold his breath, add two to Stamina when referencing the Holding Breath chart on p. 52. For example, if your character's Stamina is 2, he can hold his breath for four minutes before you need to make a draw.

STUNT DRIVER (• • •)

Prerequisites: Dexterity • • •

Effects: Your character can drive a vehicle and perform an unrelated action (e.g., fire a gun, punch another passenger) in the same turn. Drive draws may still be necessary for dangerous maneuvers or situations.

TOXIN RESISTANCE (• •)

Prerequisite: Stamina • • •

Effect: Your character gains a +2 modifier to Stamina draws to resist the effects of drugs, poisons and toxins. His body is capable of withstanding high levels of chemicals without suffering any ill effects. He's probably never had a case of food poisoning, much less a hangover.

Drawbacks: Your character's body can't tell the difference between recreational toxins and intentional ones. It's very difficult for him to become intoxicated, whether from alcohol, nicotine or other drugs. Also, painkillers and anesthetics are only half as effective as normal, and offer half the normal bonus points, if any (round down).

WEAPONRY DODGE (•)

Prerequisite: Strength • • and Weaponry •

Effect: Whenever your character performs a dodge (see "Dodge," p. 216), you can choose to add his Weaponry Skill dots to his Defense *instead* of doubling his Defense. He essentially draws on his training in parrying and evading attacks rather than relying on his raw ability alone. While this might provide little benefit to a fencing novice, it can give the advanced fighter an edge.

Weaponry Dodge applies against incoming Brawl- and Weaponry-based attacks, against thrown-weapon attacks, and against Firearms attacks made within close-combat range. Your character can move up to his Acting Speed and perform a Weaponry Dodge maneuver in a turn.

A character can possess both the Brawling Dodge and Weaponry Dodge Merits, but only one can be used per turn. You can't use Weaponry Dodge and Two-Weapon Fighting in the same turn and you must wield a mundane melee weapon in your hand while performing a Weaponry Dodge.

Social Merits

ALLIES (• TO • • • • •)

Effect: Allies are people who are willing to help your character from time to time. They may be associates, friends of convenience or people who owe your character a favor. Each acquisition of this Merit is dedicated to one type of ally, whether in an organization, society or circle. Examples include the police, City Hall, criminals, unions, banks, university faculty and hospital staff. In order to have alliances in more than one venue, you need to purchase this Merit multiple times, each trait with its own dots. Thus, your character might have Allies (Police) • •, Allies (Criminals) • • • and Allies (City Hall) •, each acquired separately at character creation or during play.

Each dot that your character has indicates how deep his influence runs in that group. One dot might mean he can ask for minor favors, such as being spared a parking ticket if alliance is among police, or being allowed to see an article before it goes to press if alliance is among reporters. Three dots garner considerable favors, such as a building permit "going missing" at City Hall, or a strike resolution being wrapped up early among union leaders. Five dots allow for dangerous and even overtly criminal favors, such as a stock being sabotaged on Wall Street or the answers to an exam being shared by a university professor. In game terms, Allies have Status in their organization equivalent to their value as allies. (See "Status" p.146).

The kinds of requests made of people in an organization typically have to relate to their sphere of influence. Asking a criminal to slow the bureaucratic process at City Hall makes no sense, but asking him to pass along word of a drug buy does. Favors might be minor and within the bounds of a person's job or role, such as processing some paperwork more quickly than usual, or could be significant or dangerous and outside what's allowed or even legal, such as allowing a civilian access to the police evidence locker. Bear in mind that requests made of Allies can take longer to complete than orders given with Status, since your character has no direct say over how fast his connection can perform the task.

The Storyteller has final say over what is an acceptable request and what is not. If there's any doubt, the Storyteller could call for a Manipulation + Persuasion draw, with a bonus equal to your character's Allies dots. Penalties might also apply based on the importance or danger of the request. Asking someone to do something already within the bounds of her role imposes no modifier, while asking her to do something that could get her suspended imposes a –3 penalty, and asking for something that could get her jailed or killed is –5 (if it's deemed possible at all). Frequent favors asked of the same group also imposes a penalty as

group members grow tired of being called upon, especially if the character never does anything in return.

Similarly, a draw of Manipulation + Persuasion where Allies dots count as a bonus could determine how many police answer your character's call for help, or how many longshoremen turn up when your character needs a show of force (one per success drawn).

Allies doesn't have to be defined in terms of specific individuals over whom your character has sway. He could simply know a variety of people among city reporters and he can call upon them in general from time to time. You should, however, explain why your character has influence in a particular body. Maybe he worked there himself at one time and still has friends in the organization. Or he has done a group a favor and its members still owe him.

Allies can also help by performing downtime actions on your character's behalf, provided it's within their experience and it makes sense that they could do so. For example, an Ally could perform research or purchase unusual equipment on a character's behalf, but she couldn't do his training for him (though she might be able to help him find a suitable teacher). Downtime actions "handed off" in this fashion allow a character to perform more deeds during downtime, thanks to his extensive network of connections.

Drawback: Allies are not automatons, waiting for your character to ask for help. They have their own lives and needs. An alliance is a two-way relationship. Calling for favors makes your character indebted to his friends, and they are sure to call such favors in when they need help. The Storyteller can use such debts as inspiration for future stories, or she may simply rule that your Allies dots are gradually reduced until your character pays the debts he incurs. Particularly serious dismissals, such as refusing to honor a major debt or assist, may even result in the loss of this Merit.

Handing Off Downtime Actions

Normally, a character is allowed to take only one downtime action between games. And yet, several Merits specifically allow a character to "hand off" downtime actions as a means of allowing the character to use his connections to perform additional downtime actions. For example, a character can have a Retainer take care of maintaining his equipment, he can call his Allies in the police department to get some cases bumped to the top of the priority pile, he can use his Status (Corporate Executive) to order a junior executive to prepare the quarterly report for him, and then he can take care of managing his Resources expenditures personally. The character effectively performs four downtime actions, but because he's cultivated a large network of connections, associates and personal staff, he can delegate a lot of responsibility and manage his time efficiently.

Unless the Storyteller or a trait description says otherwise, only one action can be handed off to each of these Merits in a downtime period. For Merits that may be purchased multiple times, such as Allies, each separate trait can be used only once. Increasing dots in a single trait simply allow for more complicated, dangerous or difficult tasks to be handed off. Most ordinary downtime actions such as training or performing basic research require at least one dot (they're rated •) for these purposes.

At the Storyteller's discretion, players may also undertake a downtime action on behalf of another player's character, but a character may accept no more than one action from one other character per downtime, and the action must be performed personally. This does not otherwise affect the number of downtime actions the character can take herself. The performer cannot turn around and hand it off to one of her own support staff. She must also be capable of performing the action, which may be difficult to justify for particularly demanding activities, unless the character accepting responsibility possesses an appropriate amount of clout (she has a sufficiently high Merit trait of her own). This rule is designed to avoid having certain characters become "action farms" on whom other players dump their responsibilities.

The following Merits can be used to hand off downtime actions:

Allies may be given downtime actions related to their sphere of influence or ability; as a rule of thumb, the more complex, dangerous or demanding the task desired, the greater the number of dots a character must have in the relevant Ally. Asking too much of a low-level Ally may result in outright refusal, unintentional mistakes due to lack of ability, serious delays, a request for significant favors in return or even severing of ties if the favor is too heinous or extreme. A particular Ally may only be handed one action per downtime period, no matter what her rating might be.

Contacts may be handed a downtime action, but *only* for the purposes of gathering information related to their specific area of expertise. They will *not* perform any other actions for a character, even something as simple as arranging a meeting — that is for other traits like Allies and Mentors. A character may only use a given area of Contacts in this fashion once per downtime period, so unless he has selected a specific area of Contacts more than once he is limited to one information-gathering action in that area per downtime.

Mentors cannot normally be handed actions in a mechanical sense — they act as guides, teachers and benefactors, not errand boys. However, this does not mean that they cannot occasionally undertake actions on behalf of the character on their own or even at his specific request. It simply means that such benevolence is entirely within the Storyteller's discretion, and thus she has complete control over when such actions occur and how they are handled. Even if they do aid a character in this fashion, most Mentors will eventually expect something in return, which can be the hook for any number of interesting stories. In general, however, players should see downtime actions performed by Mentors as unexpected favors, not the regular course of business. Those who turn to their Mentors too often or insistently often find the relationship souring quickly.

Retainers may be given any downtime action they are capable of performing, as determined by the number of dots invested and the nature of the servant in question. As with Allies, asking too much of a low-level Retainer may result in refusal, mistakes, delays, loss of the Retainer, etc. Due to the nature of the relationship, Retainers are generally much less likely to refuse a character's request outright, and will typically do their utmost to attempt a task even if it is beyond their capability. (Of course, this may be little better in the end.) A particular Retainer may only be handed one action per downtime period, no matter what his rating might be.

BARFLY (•)

Effect: No matter what town or city your character is in, he can find his way into the best nightspots with a few quick words and a timely bribe. There isn't a velvet rope made that can keep him out of a restaurant or club. In game terms, the Narrator may grant your character a bonus to making a good first impression in a club or when talking to regulars, reflecting how naturally he fits in.

CONTACTS (• TO •••••)

Effect: Contacts provide your character information in a particular area of awareness. Each dot in this Merit represents one arena or circle in which your character has a web of connections and from which he may draw information. If he has Contacts •••, his dots might be assigned to computer hackers, couriers and big business, respectively. Contacts can include individuals whom you or the Storyteller defines, but more likely they comprise an array of people from whom your character can draw information with a phone call, email or face-to-face query. Contacts are strictly information-gathering resources. Contacts do not come perform services for your character, rush to his aid or perform downtime actions on his behalf. Those benefits are the purview of other Merits.

Gaining information from contacts during a chapter requires a successful Manipulation + Persuasion or Socialize draw, depending on the relationship between your character and the people in question. Penalties might apply if the information sought is little known (–1 to –3), confidential (–3), or if sharing it could get people in trouble or harmed (–3 to –5). Success doesn't guarantee exactly the information for which your character looks. Contacts aren't all-knowing, and the Storyteller is perfectly justified in saying that a particular contact simply doesn't know something.

Failure: The contact doesn't have the information your character needs.

Success: The contact is able to provide some information that's helpful to your character.

Suggested Equipment: Gift (+1), small bribe (+1), large bribe (+2), an outstanding favor (+1 to +3)

Possible Penalties: Lack of bribe (–1), frequent and recent requests (–1 to –2), information confidential (–1 to –3), information scarce (–2), information obscure (–3), information highly dangerous (–3 to –5)

Contacts may also be handed downtime actions between sessions, as detailed in the sidebar describing handing off downtime actions.

FAME (• TO •••)

Effect: Your character has a measure of recognition in today's media-saturated society, possibly as a performer, athlete, politician or other sort of public personality. He's frequently identified and can often get star treatment. On the other hand, it's difficult for your character to go places without being recognized, and the media watches him carefully.

If the player desires and the Storyteller agrees, a character might be able to apply Fame in regard to only a small set or subculture rather than the public at large. For example, the character might be a respected academic authority who's largely unknown outside his field, or a talented member of a local band that only local, devoted music fans recognize. While it might not seem to make sense to limit Fame in this regard, it offers the benefit of not being recognized as a celebrity nearly as often as a "general" celebrity, as well as the potential to reap slightly greater rewards from those who do recognize him.

Each dot in this trait adds a +1 modifier to your character's Socialize (or Persuasion, where applicable) draws among those who are impressed by his celebrity status. If a player limits his character's fame and the Storyteller feels the restriction is strong enough to warrant a commensurate bonus when this Merit actually applies, the player may receive an additional +1 bonus when dealing with the chosen subculture, though he still risks being recognized by members of the same when it's least desired (see the drawback, below). So, if your character has 2 Fame among fans of the local music scene, you get a +3 bonus when interacting with them.

In order for limitations imposed on this Merit to qualify, they must significantly reduce a character's ability to apply the trait. If a character is known only to local club-goers, and most game sessions takes place at a local club, then it's hardly a limitation. The Storyteller is the final arbiter on whether a set or subculture is rare enough for an additional bonus to apply.

Fame can be represented with a description tag or other indicator if necessary, although Storytellers may also simply weave the reputations of characters with this Merit into the game's backstory or into the introductions given to players.

Drawback: The more famous your character is, the more easily he is recognized by the public. The Storyteller should apply the same +1 modifier per dot to a general Wits + Composure draw to see if he is recognized by anyone on the street. If a character of limited renown qualifies for the additional bonus of that status, +1 is added to the rolls of his public to recognize him, but he is unknown outside that field.

INSPIRING (• • • •)

Prerequisite: Presence • • • •

Effect: Your character is able to rally others in times of great distress, renewing their courage and determination in the face of adversity.

Once per game session, your character can exhort those around him to redouble their efforts in the face of great stress or danger. You must have the crowd's attention and speak for at least a minute or so (preferably longer), and make a Presence + Persuasion draw. If the draw succeeds, any individuals who actively assist your character and who are within earshot regain one spent Willpower point (not to exceed their Willpower dots). Your character may not use this Merit on himself, and may not use it on the same subjects more than once a day. This Merit can't be used during downtimes.

MENTOR (• TO • • • • •)

Effect: This Merit gives your character a friend and teacher who provides her with advice and guidance. Your character's mentor acts on her behalf, although the Storyteller determines exactly how. A mentor usually offers advice, allowing the Storyteller to use him to help guide your character through tough situations. A mentor may also use his influence or abilities to help your character out, although he probably wants to see his charge do things for herself. A mentor is likely to give up in disgust on a pupil who constantly asks for aid, especially if that pupil never seems to be around when favors are called in or chores need to be done. Indeed, mentors may also ask for something in return for their assistance, which can lead your character into some interesting situations.

The number of dots purchased in this Merit determines the relative power, knowledge and experience of your character's teacher. One dot indicates a mentor with one or more specialized Skills and a small amount of experience in your character's field of interest. Two dots indicate a mentor with a wide range of capability and experience in your character's field of interest. Three dots indicate a mentor possessing a broad range of Skills, years of experience and significant influence in your character's field of interest. Four dots indicate a mentor who not only possesses a broad range of Skills and decades (or in some cases, *centuries*) of experience, he is also a preeminent figure with major influence in your character's field of interest. Five dots indicate a mentor with towering influence and power in your character's field of interest. A five-dot patron watches over your character and influences her life in ways both obvious and subtle, and likely has an agenda in which your character is pivotal.

Mentors cannot normally be handed downtime actions to perform on your character's behalf, although they may occasionally undertake independent actions to aid your character, at the Storyteller's discretion. The Storyteller may also gradually decrease the dots of this trait over time, reflecting that a mentor has less to teach your character, unless she builds a different sort of relationship with him.

RESOURCES (• TO • • • • •)

Effects: This Merit measures your character's material resources, both possessions and wealth. All characters are assumed to have a job or a source of income (trust fund, parents) that is sufficient to cover their basic needs: food, shelter and transportation. Dots in this Merit represent *disposable* income — wealth and assets that can be liquidated for more money in case of emergency. The number of dots indicates your character's general level of wealth. One dot suggests low disposable income: $500 a month and approximately $1,000 worth of assets. Two dots suggest moderate disposable income: $1,000 a month and approximately $5000 worth of assets. Three dots suggest significant disposable income: $2000 a month and maybe $10,000 worth of assets. Four dots suggest substantial disposable income: $10,000 a month and $500,000 worth of assets. Five dots suggest significant wealth: $50,000 a month and as much as $5,000,000 worth of assets. Note that moving around significant amounts of money is likely to attract the unwelcome attention of inland tax revenue services in many countries, and may even lead to confiscation and arrests should unwholesome activities be suspected.

Resources can be used to determine if your character can reasonably afford a purchase or expenditure. Equipment, weapons and items throughout these rules are assigned costs in dots. The Storyteller can assign cost dots to other items during play based on what's here. If your character has the same or more dots in Resources, he can afford the item on his disposable income. That doesn't mean he has a blank check with which to buy everything he sees. He might be able to afford one or two items with a cost equal to his Resources dots in a single month. Items with lower costs can be acquired more often. The Storyteller has final say on what's too much or what's too often.

Your character's Resources dots aren't spent and don't go away. They represent available cash at any given moment. The only means by which your character's Resource dots might decrease is if story events conspire against them. Perhaps your character's fortune is wiped out, he loses his job or his company is subjected to a hostile takeover. The Storyteller therefore influences how your character's dots might decrease, and whether they can be salvaged.

Note that while mundane assistants and the like can be employed through use of this Merit, Storytellers should beware of players who try to abuse this trait and the money it represents to emulate the benefits of other Merits such as Retainers, Contacts and Allies. While players may certainly use wealth as a justification for being allowed to purchase those Merits with experience points (since they have the capital to hire servants or grease palms), Resources should not *replace* the need for those other Merits.

RETAINER (• TO • • • • •)

Effects: Your character has an assistant, aide, indentured servant or fanatical follower on whom she can rely. You need to establish how this trusty companion was acquired. He may be paid exorbitant amounts of money that buy his unwavering loyalty. He might owe his life to your character (or to your character's predecessors). Your character might blackmail this person or threaten his family with harm if services are not rendered. Or your character might have a supernatural hold over this poor person. Regardless of the circumstances, this person is constantly loyal and follows almost any order without question.

A retainer can be called upon to perform many duties without fail. A bodyguard might be willing to hurt other people on a mere command. A dedicated street kid might hang on your character's every word and get her information or contacts without being asked. Unless your character has direct control over a retainer's mind, however, this person can't be *compelled* to perform any task. He might not risk his own life unduly or perform a task that violates his own morals. You or the Storyteller should detail your retainer with an identity, background and character sheet of his own. The Storyteller or a Narrator usually portrays your character's retainer.

Each acquisition of this Merit grants your character one follower. Dots spent in the trait indicate the training, capability or flexibility of the aide. One dot suggests a child, an automaton or a madman with limited capabilities and freedom of thought. Two dots indicate an ordinary person over whom your character has sway. The servant is completely mundane and has no particular training above the human norm (he has two dots in all of his Attributes and Skills). Three dots represent a capable employee with a range of training at his disposal (some of his traits have three dots). Four dots represent a valued and irreplaceable assistant (someone with a handful of traits with four dots each). Five dots indicate an extraordinary follower who is exceptional in many ways.

For larger-scale games, Storytellers may have to apply clearer regulations across the board. In those cases, create a one dot retainer like you would create a mortal character without any additional experience points. For every additional dot of retainer you buy, add ten experience points to that character. If you merely want to have a large number of fairly inexperienced followers, you can continue buying additional single-point Retainers, effectively buying a one-point Merit again and again at single-point cost. If you want to have more competent Retainers, you will have to buy additional Retainer dots for each of them at increasing Merit cost, at best having a single five-dot Retainer with forty experience points. Once you have purchased a five-dot Retainer, you may buy the Retainer Merit from scratch again and again to get additional highly competent followers.

Retainer is different from Allies in that no draw is ever made to get results from an aide. He performs the task requested, unless subjected to repeated abuse or an utterly intolerable assignment (as decided by the Storyteller based on the assistant's personality).

As with Allies, Retainers may be handed downtime actions to perform on your character's behalf, provided a task is within a servant's capabilities. Retainers can't normally have Merits that would allow them to bypass your character's own restrictions: they can't have Retainers themselves and although they may have access to Resources or similar Merits, they can't place them at the full disposal of your character. Storytellers should be watchful for players creating hordes of comparatively cheap one-point thuggish Retainers with Fighting Styles.

Drawback: If your retainer is ever hurt, he may be incapable of service while recovering. If he is killed, he's lost forever unless he's supernatural in origin. A retainer who possesses his own will and who is forced to perform a duty that offends his sensibilities or defies his morals may abandon your character, either temporarily or even permanently. Dots spent to acquire a retainer who is killed or driven off are lost.

STATUS (• TO • • • • •)

Prerequisites: Varies (see below)

Effects: Your character has standing, credentials, authority or respect within an organization, group, company or social body. He might have an official position or title, or might simply be revered and honored within the group and therefore accorded a degree of authority. Your character might be a company vice president, a police sergeant or lieutenant, an army corporal or a nurse at a hospital. Or he could be a lowly member of the group whom everyone likes or who has won some acclaim and is allowed more standing than he is officially entitled.

Each acquisition of this Merit is dedicated to one type of authority, whether in an organization, society or circle. Examples include police, City Hall, criminals, unions, banks, a university faculty and hospital staff. In order to have authority in more than one venue, you need to purchase this Merit multiple times, each trait with its own dots. Thus, your character might have Status (Police) • •, Status (Criminals) • • • and Status (City Hall) •, each acquired separately at character creation or during play. You would need to explain how he reconciles all this authority in the setting. The aforementioned character might be a dirty police sergeant who has paid his dues in civil elections and gained some recognition among city officials.

Status represents the privileges and liberties that your character is authorized to take *within the confines and definitions of his group*. Increasing dots reflect increasing clout or possibly even an actual official position. A cop with Status 1 can enter the suspect lockup and interrogation rooms, while a cop with Status 4 can enter the evidence locker without supervision or get involved in a crime-scene investigation without specifically being called in.

The phrase "within the confines and definitions of his group" is emphasized above because Status operates exclusively through official channels. A surgeon might have one patient seen or operated on before another, because that's within the official confines of his authority. Destroying records of a patient's treatment or having another doctor cover his absences is not, because exceeding the confines of legitimate authority or proper channels transcends the limits of the Status Merit. Going above and beyond — to ask for favors rather than give orders or to requisition an official request — enters the realm of the Allies or Mentor Merits. Therefore, a police detective who orders a lower-ranking officer to investigate a case may do so with Status. That request is conducted through proper channels. Meanwhile, a police detective who asks another officer to overlook some evidence or to delay an investigation does so by talking to an Ally or by using his own legwork. The favor is asked outside official channels.

While Status might allow your character to give orders to underlings, the Merit doesn't automatically get results immediately. Subordinates or co-workers might resent their assignments, dislike your character or have personal agendas that interfere with your character's needs. Efforts to get things done through official channels still call for Manipulation + Intimidation, Persuasion or Socialize draws, whichever Skill is appropriate to the request, circumstances and your character's standing within the organization. Bonus points equal your character's Status dots. Penalties might apply if your character browbeats someone (–1), uses threats (–2), skirts the limits of his authority (–2) or exceeds his authority (–3 to –5).

Your character may hand off a downtime action to someone under him in the chain of command, provided it is within the underling's capability and job description to perform the task. Regardless of your character's Status dots, only one downtime action may be handed off in this fashion per period. Increased Status dots simply allow for more complicated or demanding tasks to be delegated to subordinates.

Some sample organizations and the basic benefits, perks and privileges of standing in them are listed below.

Academic: Your character may have a position at an educational institution, but more than that he has a scholarly reputation commensurate to his dots in this Merit. A low number indicates an up-and-coming theorist or an authority in a little-known but respected field, while a high number (3+) tends to indicate a reputation in a much larger or well-known field. The greater his reputation, the more likely people are to take him seriously when he discusses matters related to his expertise, and the more forthcoming responses he can expect from fellow scholars. **Prerequisite:** Academics • •, with at least one Specialty in your character's field.

City Hall: Your character holds a local political office, with all the powers that accompany the title and its responsibilities. It could be an appointed post, in which case it's in her interest to see to it that the person who put her there stays in power, or it could be an elected position, which means she must campaign for office again from time to time. A low-ranking official might be in charge of one small department, while a character with high levels (3+) might be in charge of a large municipal system or even be the mayor of a small town. **Prerequisite:** Politics •

Clerical Standing: Your character is a licensed minister, gaining access to people and places such as accused criminals, hospital patients, crime and accident scenes, and restricted areas in religious institutions. **Prerequisite:** Academics Skill Specialty: Religion.

Corporate Executive: A low-level corporate executive has access to much of the company's resources, including corporate credit cards, vehicles, cell phones and computer equipment. Depending on the company, he can also access sources of information and influence not available to the public. Executives (3+) have larger salaries, expense accounts, and hiring and firing powers, not to mention social perks and access to connected political figures and/or celebrities.

Criminal: Your character holds a recognized position in an established criminal organization of some kind, whether it's a ragtag street gang or a full-blown Mafia crime syndicate. This clout is useful when threatening people or acquiring illegal services, though a high amount of this Status (3+) also makes your character a natural target of rival operations and law enforcement. **Prerequisites:** Streetwise • •, plus one of Brawl • •, Melee • • or Firearms •.

Diplomat: Your character is a registered diplomat for a sovereign country. If he works in a foreign country he has free lodging, access to his country's embassy and immunity from foreign criminal prosecution. **Prerequisites:** Politics • • and Persuasion • •.

Licensed Professional: Your character is licensed in a recognized profession that affords him privileges unavailable to most civilians. He might be a private investigator authorized to carry a concealed weapon and to have access to restricted databases and government files. He could be a lawyer capable of issuing subpoenas and initiating lawsuits. Or he could be a building contractor and be authorized to own and use explosives for professional applications. **Prerequisite:** Academics Skill Specialty: Law (private investigator), Academics Skill Specialty: Law • • • (attorney), Science Skill Specialty: Demolitions (building contractor).

Medical: Your character is licensed to practice medicine. He can write prescriptions, access medical records and gain access to restricted areas such as crime and accident scenes. **Prerequisite:** Medicine • •.

Occult: Whether your character is a true believer or not, membership in a secret society or occult circle grants limited access to the trappings of various mystical rites, as well as a number of adherents and perhaps a few juicy arcane secrets. Within the circle, discussion of topics such as monsters and the unknown may not raise suspicion or result in being considered a lunatic, at least not out of hand. **Prerequisites:** Occult • • or Persuasion • • •.

Police: A patrol officer has legal powers of search, seizure and arrest, is permitted to carry a firearm at all times and has access to a wide range of local databases. High-ranking officers (3+) can initiate investigations, coordinate with neighboring county or state police, and call in urban-assault teams. **Prerequisite:** Firearms •, Drive •.

Union/Rotary: A basic member in good standing has access to the local meeting hall and a network of members who can provide union-related information or perform club-related duties. A basic member can also benefit from the organization's emergency fund in times of need. High-ranking members (3+) have access to other unions or clubs around the country, and have sway over connected civic groups and political figures.

Drawback: Your character's standing in a given organization is dependent on the fulfillment of his duties and on abiding by the regulations required of members. While routine requests and actions don't necessarily raise any alarms, the more often a character uses his standing to gain special perks, access to restricted materials or equipment, or to otherwise exploit his position, the more likely it is to come back to haunt him, and the more closely the Storyteller should watch him to make sure he does everything his organization expects him to.

Striking Looks (•• or ••••)

Effect: Your character is exceptionally attractive by modern standards; heads turn and conversations stop when she enters a room. You are required to wear a prominent description tag or some other indicator to alert other players to your attractiveness.

For two dots, your character gets a +1 modifier to all Presence or Manipulation draws when she attempts to use her looks to entertain, persuade, distract or deceive others. This does apply to supernatural situations, but not for any genuinely offensive purposes: your looks entrance, they don't frighten.

For four dots, your character's looks are angelic; she gets a +2 modifier.

Drawback: The more attractive your character is, the harder it is for her to avoid notice in public. Witnesses to any criminal acts are much more likely to remember your character's appearance, and easily recognize her in a lineup. Your character is also likely to receive a great degree of unwanted attention in social situations. Your character's appearance modifier may therefore become a bonus on draws when others try to remember what she looks like, or whether she was present at an event.

Chapter 6: Dramatic Systems

A Storytelling game is primarily about people getting together with characters, and with a plot to be explored. Your troupe — your gaming group — is prepared to tell a story, and everyone involved works together to do it. But what happens when your character wants to do one thing and another character tries to accomplish something different — or directly opposed? Who wins? Who loses? Who gets his way? In a sense, Storytelling goes back to the games of Cops and Robbers that you played as a kid. Now, as then, you need some means to decide who shot whom. The major difference is, Storytelling games take such questions to complex degrees. Did my character crack the safe? Did she perform the incantation correctly? Can she stab that night-crawling creature in the heart with a stake?

That's where rules come in. All games need rules. They're the foundation that allows players to understand the events that happen. If the complexity of that safe, incantation or attack is true for one character, it's true for another. About the only factors that may help one character over another are talent and good fortune. The means of attempting the effort and the rules for resolving it remain the same.

All that said, rules can be as subtle or as overt as you like. Some troupes prefer to resolve as many matters as possible through roleplaying alone. If a character's act seems reasonable or convincing, the Storyteller or the other players involved allow him to do it. Even combat situations or other hotly contested actions can sometimes be played out without resorting to rules. That is, if the players involved are willing to be reasonable, creative and cooperative, the events of the story carry on without game mechanics getting in the way.

Other troupes prefer to resolve most actions through card draws and rules references. They ensure that the story unfolds "by the book," with all tasks performed according to regulation so that all possible factors are considered, from talent to chance. While **Mind's Eye Theatre** is designed to emphasize roleplaying over use of mechanics to settle disputes, this approach to Storytelling is just as valid. It simply defers to rules — the backbone of the game — to determine the legitimacy of story developments.

Ultimately, most troupes fall somewhere between these extremes. Events flow uninterrupted by rules checks when things happen fast and loose. When tensions run high, such as driving at 100 mph down a busy highway or deactivating a bomb, rules are referenced to see how characters fare and how the story unfolds.

TIME

Time flies when you're having fun, or so they say. In a Storytelling game, time not only flies, it slows, crawls, skips and warps. **Mind's Eye Theatre** is normally assumed to be played in real time. If five minutes pass in reality, then five minutes have passed in the game as well. During the course of your game, however, you'll find that time can do some strange things at times. How you control the passage of time affects the smoothness of play. While most events are handled in real time, certain actions such as combat need special attention as real time and game time may differ. When your characters enter combat, it may take several real time minutes to roleplay mere seconds of game time.

Alternately, you may wish to cover *weeks* of game time in just a few real time minutes, assuming nothing worthy of attention occurs in that period. As in a novel, the authors of the story — you and your players — can gloss over intervals between important events or slow the progression to a crawl when detailing critical moments.

Six basic units describe the passage of time. Like puzzle pieces, these small units combine to form larger images until you can see the big picture. These measurements are deliberately flexible in order to suit the needs of those involved in a scene. They should be viewed as guidelines rather than ironclad terms. They're a way to agree on reasonable durations without literally needing to break out stopwatches.

• Turn — The smallest increment, and often the most important, a turn is roughly three seconds. It's the amount of time it takes a character to perform an instant action (see p. 23). Turns are mainly observed in combat, when the action is fast and furious, with all characters doing something dramatic in a short timeframe.

Unless it is instantaneous or has a specific duration, any power or ability that lasts a number of turns in combat lasts roughly the same number of minutes outside of combat. This may seem like a large jump, and the Storyteller is free to adjust this avoid a particular trait becoming too powerful or unrealistic. In the real-time flow of **Mind's Eye Theatre**, however, this equivalency often works out quite neatly.

• Scene — A scene in a roleplaying game resembles a scene in a theatrical play. Your Storyteller sets the stage, and the players take their roles. The scene evolves in one location and usually encompasses a single, specific event. For example, the arrival of an important person and their entourage, the discovery of a murdered friend's body, or meeting with sources to learn about the recent rash of disappearances. Though it is assumed to be held in real time, the flow of time within a scene may actually vary in troupe-style play. It may be played out in turns, or run parallel to real time. Your Storyteller and fellow players may fast-forward through parts of it, so long as the location and general events do not change.

For example, a scene may begin with combat, which is measured in turns. It may then slip back into real time as your characters discuss what to do with the corpses they've created. After a fast-forward through the tedious scene of loading the bodies onto a truck, the scene may return to real time as your characters argue over who will drive. All events occur in the same scene and location, but time warps to focus on the most fun and important parts. A Storyteller or Narrator generally determines when one scene ends and when another begins. Changes of scene should be announced if they are not immediately obvious. This lets characters with powers that have a duration of one scene are aware of the shift.

Many live-action games take place in one location throughout most if not the entire session. This means that changing locations is not a viable means of determining when a scene ends. Therefore, a scene can be assumed to be about one hour of real time, so powers and effects that last for one scene last for one hour unless otherwise noted.

Note that some traits have a duration of "combat;" this is defined as the duration of one fight from start to finish. This may occasionally be the same as one scene, particularly if the combat was long, involved every character present at the chapter or was the sole purpose of a single scene.

• Chapter —A chapter represents one game session. (In fact, the term session is often used interchangeably.) From the moment you enter the playing area and assume your role to the moment you doff your costume and pack up your cards, you play out a chapter in the story. Your Storyteller has specific challenges and revelations planned for the night's episode. While they do not need to end in a pulp-style cliffhanger — that device can grow old quite quickly — the end of each chapter should leave you wanting more, asking questions, and with a sense of the session's relative completion.

• Story — A story tells one entire tale, whether it comprises several chapters or is completed in a single session. It has an introduction, a plot arc that involves rising conflict, and a climax that brings events to a conclusion.

• Chronicle — In the big picture, the term "chronicle" refers to a collection of stories. Your Storyteller has a goal in mind for the chronicle, a possible destination for your characters, or an overarching plot line that connects all chapters. As your game progresses, you and your fellow players write your chronicle, linking parts and pieces together and developing a full-blown epic.

• Downtime — In **Mind's Eye Theatre**, downtime refers to the time between chapters. This is often at least a week of real time and can stretch up to a number of months depending on how regularly the game is scheduled. During this time, characters are generally assumed to be handling mundane obligations. They could be going to work, attending school, performing research, maintaining equipment and otherwise performing the vital but less-than-glamorous tasks that make up their daily lives.

And yet, downtime can be active, particularly in games with long periods between chapters, Such activity involves what's called a downtime action. These actions help keep players interested in the game and their characters, they move along plots that aren't well suited to regular play sessions, and they give the game another dimension to explore.

Since many live-action games are played an average of once a month, downtime can be as important as chapters themselves. Players typically use this time to make subtle political moves, to ply their connections, to challenge other characters' assets, to perform research, and to otherwise set up the action for the next game session. Note that downtime actions may not always apply between chapters. If a session ends on a cliffhanger or is intended to pick up right where it left off at the next game, no time passes between episodes. If in doubt, ask the Storyteller if downtime actions can be used between chapters. More about downtime actions and how they work can be found later in this chapter.

Lastly, downtime can be used *during* a game session. When your Storyteller decides to fast-forward and skim over a period of time to get to the "good parts," he invokes downtime. You may summarize events that transpire during downtime, but you do not actually play them out. Your Storyteller may say something like, "Okay, you spend the night in the warehouse. At dawn, voices in the alley outside wake you." Nothing happens while your characters sleep, so there's no reason to play it out. Your Storyteller leaps ahead to the next interesting event. Downtime actions and other extended mechanics do not normally apply to in-session periods of downtime, only to long periods of inactivity between chapters.

Look for more on chapters, stories and chronicles in Chapter 8: Storytelling.

DISTANCE MEASUREMENTS

As with units of time, **Mind's Eye Theatre** is designed to use a flexible system of measurement for distance. If it were regimented, players would be required to carry yardsticks and measuring tapes, which would ruin the mood. The following list describes the basic terms used for measurements. Please note that these distances can be adjusted to suit the size of your play area, if necessary. A game in a large convention hall might allow them to be expanded to make full use of traits such as Speed. Meanwhile, a game in a small apartment might require that distances be reduced to a representational scale. The living room is one building and the kitchen is another, with a "street" between.

Step — One normal walking step. Roughly equivalent to one yard if a more precise measurement is absolutely required.

Pace — One stride to full (but not ridiculous) extension. Considered to be about twice the distance of one step.

Melee Range — Close enough for two characters to engage in unarmed or weaponry combat; within (possibly weapon-assisted) touching distance.

Conversational Distance — Close enough for two characters to speak normally without needing to raise their voices to be heard clearly. Use common sense in loud surroundings such as busy nightclubs and the like.

Line of Sight — As far as a character can see without artificial magnification. (An upper limit of about half a mile at most is assumed, unless otherwise noted.) Line of sight refers to in-game visual range. If a player can see a target but for some reason his character cannot, a line-of-sight-based capability cannot be used. Unless a trait itself states otherwise, viewing a target remotely through hidden cameras, clairvoyant powers, telescopic sights or similar means does not count to establish line of sight.

Immediate Area — One room of average size in a normal house.

One Floor — An entire floor of a normal house or half the play area, whichever is larger. In a truly huge environment such as a convention center, this can be used to describe one entire set of related rooms or a similar well-defined area.

Play Area — The entire in-game area. Effects on this scale can be massive and difficult to adjudicate at large events. Storytellers should take careful note of any powers in use when this measurement applies.

DRAWING CARDS

The Storytelling staff has two options when events need to be resolved in your story. It can simply decree that an action succeeds or does not, often based on your character's trait scores. Maybe Strength 2 is required to lift a tire and throw it, and your character has Strength 4, so the Storyteller doesn't even call for a draw. Your character is obviously strong enough to do it without much effort. This approach minimizes interruptions to the flow of the narrative, as previously discussed.

The other option in exploring how a story unfolds is to call for a card draw on your part. Your character seeks to accomplish a feat. There's an element of chance that he could succeed or fail, and a Narrator asks you to decide your character's fate. Draws are usually reserved for activities that involve an element of danger, loss or threat if things go badly. You don't have to draw to decide if your character can accomplish ordinary actions such as crossing the street safely. If he's trying to cross the street during a drive-by shooting, however, the ordinary becomes extraordinary — and dangerous.

Mind's Eye Theatre uses 10 ordinary playing cards, called a hand. The hand consists of the ace and the numbered cards of one suit, to help simulate the whims of fate. A card is drawn at random from this hand and combined with a representation of a character's aptitude, ability and other modifiers involved in the situation. This is called your test pool. Ideally, each player should bring at least one hand of 10 cards to the game — more sets if they have the pockets to ensure that there are always enough cards to go around. Bridge cards and travel-sized playing cards are also available, which should be small enough to fit somewhere on just about any costume.

INITIATING A TEST

Once they understand how tests work, players may wonder how to properly initiate one with a Narrator or another player during a game. Typically, this is best handled by announcing, "<Trait> test," where the most pertinent trait is used to describe the challenge. Experienced roleplayers can work the announcement of a test into an otherwise ordinary conversation, perhaps even continuing to roleplay while both parties get their cards out and draw.

Thus, the player of a character who throws a punch gets the attention of his target and announces "Brawl test," while the player of a character attempting to talk another out of taking a particular course of action might say "Persuasion test." This announcement applies even if the character has no dots in a Skill. He still attempts an action related to the trait, he just suffers a penalty due to his lack of expertise. If a supernatural power is used, its name is used to announce the test, even if its test pool is actually derived from Attributes and Skills. For example, the player of a ghost would announce "Possession test" to signify that he attempts to use a power take control of a character's body. In the case of Attribute tasks, use whichever Attribute is most relevant, or simply describe the action instead. For example, lifting heavy objects can requires both Strength and Stamina, so a player might simply say, "Lifting test," and name the traits involved if further explanation is required.

Note that this announcement is considered out-of-game; while many actions have obvious results, if a player is initiating a test with a trait or power that doesn't have any noticeable effects, an opponent may not realize anything has happened. Just because the player is aware of the challenge does not automatically mean the character is aware of the situation.

As a rule of thumb, a test announcement should be about as loud as the both the action and its results are obvious, within the limits set by the play area. Thus a Persuasion test may be announced at conversational volume, because that's exactly as noticeable as the action itself is likely to be. A Firearms test, however, should be announced loudly, because a character pulling a gun and firing draws a lot of attention (unless perhaps the attacker uses a silencer). Regardless of the action, the intended target(s) must be able to hear the announcement.

Not all Storytellers may like this method of action announcement. They may find it causes too many disputes, or they may simply want the game to keep a low profile if played in a public place. In this case simply announce the test to the target in a normal tone of voice and proceed from there.

Forming Test Pools

As described in the preceding chapters, your character's talents and capabilities are represented by traits and dots. These values help measure how effective your character is at different activities. Attributes and Skills are rated 1 to 5 for ordinary people. One Attribute and one Skill are typically combined when your character performs a feat. Sometimes two Attributes may be combined instead (see below). The total of the two traits is considered your "test pool." This is added to the value of the card drawn and used to help determine if your character succeeds or fails.

The Attribute and Skill combined for the test pool are the ones most appropriate to the task performed. The descriptions of all these traits in Chapters 2 and 3 help you decide which dots should be combined. If doubt or dispute arises, a Narrator or Storyteller may dictate which traits apply in a given situation. If your character climbs a cliff, you look to her Strength + Athletics scores. If she seeks to pressure someone to do a favor for her, you use Presence + Intimidation. If your character climbs a cliff and you compose a pool based on 3 Strength and 2 Athletics, you have a test pool of five.

Sometimes various Attributes or Skills could apply to an activity, and there's some gray area on just which two should be combined. If your character needs to climb a cliff quickly more so than safely, you might ask the Narrator (or he might decide) if you should use Dexterity rather than Strength. If your character seeks to convince rather than pressure someone to do a favor, you might use Persuasion or Socialize instead of Intimidation. *Use whichever trait is most appropriate to the manner in which your character seeks to accomplish her goal.*

Emphasis is put on these last words because you shouldn't try to get traits combined simply because your character has several dots in them. The Storyteller shouldn't allow you to draw Dexterity + Athletics to climb *every* cliff just because your character has a high Dexterity score. That might only apply when your character needs to climb quickly, or when it's more of a matter of agility than muscle power. Each situation should actually call for a specific combination of Attribute and Skill. If a satisfactory combination cannot be agreed upon by the players involved, consult a Narrator or an impartial third party.

Specialties

Chapter 3 also discusses Specialties that your character may possess in Skills. These are areas of expertise that give your character an edge. His Specialty in Athletics might be "Climbing." Having that Specialty adds one to your test pool in any tests for which it is relevant. Again, a Specialty must apply according to the action being performed. If you use Stamina + Athletics for your character to swim across a lake, his Climbing Specialty really doesn't apply, does it? If in doubt, reach an agreement with the other players in the scene or consult the Narrator to see if a Specialty applies.

Regardless of how many Specialties a character has that might apply to a particular test, only one ever counts for a specific draw. Consider a character that has Specialties in Science: Forensic Pathology, Science: Ballistics, and Investigation: Homicide. Even though he has multiple relevant Specialties, you still get only one bonus point when he conducts an autopsy and tries to deduce what kind of gun killed a person. His range of investigative Specialties makes it likely that he receives a Specialty bonus on many different criminal cases, but they are not cumulative in a single test for a considerable bonus.

Attribute Tasks

Sometimes actions require no special expertise to perform. They're activities that anyone can do, such as lifting or resisting poison. These efforts don't necessarily involve any Skills. Indeed, they're often based on your character's inherent capabilities alone. These efforts are called Attribute tasks, many of which are detailed in Chapter 2 under the appropriate traits. When your character performs one of these feats, two Attributes — a primary and secondary — are combined to determine your test pool. The primary is the one that contributes the most to the effort, such as Strength in lifting. A secondary Attribute plays a support role in the effort, such as Stamina when your character tries to lift something. In some cases, there is no secondary Attribute; only a primary determines success, as with Stamina in holding one's breath.

When your character performs an Attribute task, your test pool equals his dots in the traits involved. If your character lifts something and has 2 Strength and 2 Stamina, you have a test pool of four. If he holds his breath and has a Stamina of 3, you have a test pool of 3.

As a rule of thumb, if an act can be performed without any expertise it can be handled as an Attribute task.

QUALIFIERS

For simplicity and game balance, your Storyteller should not usually allow you to combine more than two traits in a single test pool. It's probably an Attribute (inherent talent) and a Skill (learned capability), or an Attribute plus an Attribute (raw talent alone). *Two Skills are never combined to form a single test pool.* Learned capabilities have to be based on some foundation of talent (i.e., on an Attribute).

If your character has no dots in an applicable Skill, the Storyteller may allow you to draw a test pool equal to your character's relevant Attribute alone. Say your character seeks to install a computer program. He has Intelligence dots, but no Computer dots. Your character's innate Attribute, in this case Intelligence, still offers him a chance to succeed, albeit a small one. If your character attempts an action for which he is not trained (he has no Skill dots), he may attempt the feat at a penalty. That penalty is –3 for actions based on Mental Skills, and –1 for actions based on Physical and Social Skills. Thus, if your character has no Medicine Skill but he attempts first aid, you still form a test pool based on his Dexterity and the draw is at –3. Likewise, if an effort calls for Strength + Athletics and your character doesn't have that Skill, your test pool is based on Strength alone and you suffer a –1 penalty.

Some traits such as Willpower are rated on a scale of 1 to 10 instead of the usual 1 to 5 rating. Your Storyteller should not usually combine these special traits with others to produce your test pools, unless such a combination is specifically called for in a relevant description. For the most part, these high-rated traits should stand alone, or if not, at least be pitted against another high-rated trait on the part of the defender. Most of the time, however, they're not even tested directly, but instead provide points that are spent to influence other draws.

Basic Test Resolution Steps

Step 1: Start with a core test pool. It's usually Attribute + Skill. For Attribute tasks, draw primary Attribute + secondary Attribute (if any).

Step 2: Apply any bonuses or penalties. That is, add appropriate bonus modifiers to your pool, then subtract any negative modifiers. Bonuses include a Specialty that your character might have in a Skill or equipment that he uses.

All bonuses to your pool should be added before any points are removed for penalties. Penalties include difficulty incurred by injuries, unforeseen setbacks or being forced to use inferior equipment. What remains is the final test pool. If no points remain, you're reduced to a chance draw (p. 164).

Step 3: Draw one card at random and add your test pool to it. Base your success on meeting or exceeding a target number of 10. (See p. 169.)

POOL MODIFIERS

If we always knew just how an action was going to turn out, how all factors would apply, and just what events might contribute, we'd never make mistakes. Everything we'd ever try would come out perfect every time.

The world's not like that, though. We don't always foresee the factors that will be involved in an event. Neither does your character. Sure, he can drive to work without undo threat. He might even be an alert driver and adept at avoiding accidents. However, when you add uncontrollable elements such as bad weather, faulty steering, and a violent, fanged passenger clawing at him from the backseat, emerging safe and sound becomes a challenge.

Sometimes the factors involved in an action work to your character's benefit, such as using specific tools that make a job easier or having plenty of time to do the job right. Other times, they work to his detriment. See the case of the atmospheric, car-maintenance and monstrous-passenger problems posed above. As in life, so in the World of Darkness. The conditions that work against your character often seem to outweigh those that work in his favor. When complications arise, they're not usually for the better — or at least not as often as we'd like.

In these rules, circumstances apply as points added to or subtracted from your test pool before a draw. These are called modifiers, whether bonuses or penalties. Modifiers typically represent the tools, weapons or gear that your character brings to bear in an effort. He might drive a high-performance car, wield a knife or carry a set of precise lock picks. The Storyteller or these rules assign a fixed rating to the equipment. That rating dictates the number of modifier points that you add to your test pool.

So, if your character enters combat with a knife and that weapon is rated +1, you add one point to your combat test pool.

Circumstances can involve more than just tools used, however. The Storyteller often decides what factors apply to your character's actions. Most times they're self-evident, based on the scene or on the events that have led up to the moment. Your character may be injured and has trouble acting. Weather plays its part. Your character's opponent may be concealed or trying to avoid incoming attacks. Some of these conditions help your character's effort and add to your pool. Other factors impede your character's effort and reduce in your pool.

Just as some factors may be known and obvious, others may be unknown to you and your character. Narrators may know that your character was drugged in the previous scene, for example, and the effects just kick in now. Her vision suddenly blurs and she feels dizzy. Or perhaps a supernatural benefactor has placed a mystic blessing on her without her knowledge, so that what should be a difficult task comes unusually easy for to her. Regardless of the circumstances, such modifiers are announced by Storytellers but not necessarily explained.

In general, each bonus from a tool or circumstantial factor adds one to your pool. Each penalty subtracts one from your pool. Say your character has 3 Dexterity and 3 Drive. He drives a high-performance car at high speeds at night and in bad weather. Your test pool starts at six (3 Dexterity + 3 Drive). His car is rated +3 for maneuverability, giving you a pool of nine. The Narrator decides that darkness and bad weather combine to impose a –4 penalty, however, so your pool is reduced to five.

Chapter 3 details many tools and their bonuses for Skills. This chapter and Chapter 7 list modifiers for weapons and other circumstances.

Adding and Subtracting

Be sure to add all the bonuses that apply to your test pool before penalties are applied. That is, take your starting test pool based on your character's traits, add bonuses and then subtract penalties. The number remaining, if any, is added to the card drawn to determine success. Yes, it's possible for extreme penalties to reduce your pool to one or zero. See "The Chance Draw."

APPLYING MODIFIERS

These rules, or a Storytelling, decides the value of modifiers applied to test pools. This book strives to detail and codify as many different possible situations and permutations as possible. These range from the quality of tools to environmental effects to character disabilities. All are factors that you can apply as bonuses or penalties during play. Not every contingency can be foreseen here, though. The Storyteller and her Narrators always have final say on what modifiers are added to or subtracted from a player's pool. That combination allows you to play a game that simulates the world as closely as possible, with all kinds of factors taken into account.

Another approach to card drawing is more freeform. Your troupe can play a fast-and-loose game that doesn't involve counting "official" modifiers to such a degree. The Narrator or even just the players involved in a challenge look at the overall circumstances and determine the challenge of it. This method essentially reviews the situation as a whole and makes a general call, potentially speeding up the pace of the game.

In general, players are quick to calculate all the bonus modifiers that add to their pools for, say, lock picks used. They may also propose others, like that a lock has been damaged and is weakened as a result (another +1 bonus). Assuming a Storyteller agrees to all these variables, this allows him to focus solely on what penalties might apply — say, the door has two deadbolts— a –3 penalty. Just be aware that while most players are honest, some may attempt to take advantage of this method to boost their bonuses and ignore possible penalties.

Alternately, say that two players are opposing each other in a Computer test — one wants to hack into a system, while the network administrator wants to keep the intruder out. They decide they can handle judging modifiers on their own, and candidly compare relevant equipment and situations out of game. The hacker has superior hardware and a head start, but is also racing to beat a particular deadline and is suffering from a lack of sleep. The players decide that this results in a +1 modifier for the hacker, since his advantages outweigh his disadvantages only slightly. The network administrator receives a +2, because while his equipment is outmatched, he is well-rested and has several assistants who can help him search for signs of intrusion and seal them.

By this intuitive approach, slight bonuses or hindrances are rated one. Moderate ones are rated three, and extreme situations are rated five. The first might apply to a Dexterity + Drive pool in the rain. The second might be for a draw in a flood. The third might kick in when your character is caught in a tornado.

As a rule, a single modifier never exceeds five, whether as a bonus or penalty. That means all tools and situational effects are each rated one to five. A knife may offer a combatant a bonus of one, while a halberd might give him five. A light rain might remove one while a monsoon might remove five. Troupes may look up official values so that modifiers for, say, tools, weather and character disabilities accumulate. That is, they're totalled.

Alternatively, your Storyteller may simply consider *all* the factors in terms of a one-to-five range and come up with one total modifier. He might allow players to calculate some bonuses, but he decides that weather and character disabilities make an effort difficult, and remove three from your pool.

Here are some general suggested modifiers.

Bonus	Degree of Challenge
+1	A helping hand
+2	A walk in the park
+3	Nothing to it
+4	Easy as pie
+5	You can do it in your sleep

Penalty	Degree of Challenge
−1	A minor obstacle
−2	A hard time
−3	A trying task
−4	It's demanding
−5	Sorely tested

Storyteller Caveat

Sometimes, the Storyteller wants to keep you as ignorant as your character is about the circumstances surrounding an effort. Maybe the effects of the aforementioned drug added to your character's drink are gradual and subtle. They kick in before your character even feels them. Maybe your character tries to do some research, but she doesn't know that the book she uses intentionally provides false information.

Under these circumstances, the Storyteller makes the draw for you. He assembles your test pool, applies all modifiers, and makes the draw without showing you the draw or the results. You don't know what factors apply or why, and your character is similarly none the wiser. All she knows is that her effort succeeds or fails, and you must abide by the Storyteller's draw. That way, you're as much in the dark about what's going on as your character, and you can enjoy the story just as she does.

As helpful as this device can be to creating suspense and mystery, a wise Storyteller avoids enforcing such authority too often. Players enjoy drawing cards because it gives them a feeling of control over their characters' fate. "Executive draws" are thus best reserved for situations in which characters and players must be kept out of the loop about unfolding events. A Storyteller should *never* use a draw like this to kill or permanently maim a character. All that does is breed resentment and possibly even allegations of unfair treatment. Remember, there's nothing more frustrating to players than having control of their characters' actions — and draws — taken away too often.

STANDARD DIFFICULTY

Okay, so you've figured out your test pool, so now it's time to deal with those 10 cards in your hand. How do you use them? Unless specified otherwise in a specific trait's description or by a Storyteller, all draws made in **Mind's Eye Theatre** have a target number of 10. What does that mean? It means that you want the combined total of the values of your test pool and the card you draw to equal or exceed 10.

A draw plus the test pool that equals or exceeds 10 grants one success. For every interval of five that your total meets or exceeds 10, your character achieves a success at the action he performs. 15-19 are two successes, 20-24 are three successes, 25-30 are three successes and so on. Most actions a character performs require only a single success. This not only makes the game flow quickly, but minimizes the amount of Storyteller involvement required to oversee events. Sometimes the number of successes determines the results, however, such as in combat. Other times, successes are tallied to represent lengthy efforts, such as cracking a security system over a number of minutes.

Note that the interval of five *always* applies for determining the number of successes achieved, regardless of any difficulty adjustment involved. For example, using the optional rule the Storyteller raises the standard difficulty of an action to 12. A draw total of 12 to 16 therefore equals one success. A draw total of 17 to 21 equals two successes, and so on. Likewise, if the standard difficulty is lowered to 6, a draw total of 6 to 10 equals one success, while a total of 11 to 15 equals two.

Example: Your character tries to identify the kind of vehicle from which a particular part comes. His Intelligence + Crafts equals 6, and he has a Specialty in engines, offering a +1 bonus. You form a test pool of 7. The Storyteller decides that the wear and tear on the part makes it difficult to recognize (he imposes a –1 penalty). You remove one point from your test pool and are left with six, plus the draw of one card, against a target number of 10.

You draw a 9, giving you a draw total of 15. Consulting the standard interval chart, that means your character achieves two successes. Since only one success is required to pull off the feat, your character recognizes the part as originating from a military truck.

6.1 – INTERVALS OF SUCCESS

Draw Total	# of Successes
10–14	1 success
15–19	2 successes
20–24	3 successes
25–29	4 successes
30–34	5 successes
35–39	6 successes
40–44	7 successes

FAILURE

Sometimes even the best characters have an off moment, when things just don't go their way. While exceptionally skilled characters may fall short only once in a while, it does happen. On any draw (except for a chance draw — see below), pulling an ace on your first draw means your character simply fails. It doesn't matter what your test pool is or what modifiers you might have.

What failure means depends on the test in question. In combat, it might mean that your character's punch misses its mark. In a social situation, it might mean another party is unimpressed by your character's efforts to win her over. In an extended action, it could indicate that your character doesn't make any progress in rebuilding that engine.

In the case that a social or mental action against another character fails, the character initiating the action has to wait until for the entirety of a scene (usually one hour) until attempting that action against the same character again.

Note that drawing the ace doesn't automatically mean your character suffers an actual setback, just that he fails to make any real progress. (Absolute disasters are covered by the chance-draw rules, below.) Of course, simple failure might be still be pretty terrible in a specific instance. For example, failing a test to rebuild an engine might just mean your character wastes an hour or two; the engine's condition doesn't actually get worse. By comparison, failing a test to defuse a bomb while the last seconds tick away is disastrous.

Example: *Your test pool, with modifiers, is an impressive 15. Success seems almost guaranteed, but you draw the ace. Something about your character's efforts just doesn't come together, and his action fails. Nobody's perfect, after all.*

Note that drawing an ace at any time after the first draw for an action doesn't normally result in automatic failure. The most common example of this situation is if you draw a 10. The "10 again" rule (explained fully below) allows you to make an additional draw to try to add more to your total. If your first draw is a 10, and you make an additional draw and get an ace, it simply counts as zero. It doesn't add to your total, but it doesn't automatically mean automatic failure, either.

Example: *Your test pool is 8 and you draw a 10. The "10 again" rule applies, so you re-shuffle and draw another card, hoping to add to your draw total. Your second card is an ace. It doesn't indicate failure, but it doesn't add anything, either. You're left with the original 10 and it's added to your test pool for a draw total of 18.*

FAILED SOCIAL AND MENTAL TESTS

Note that special circumstances apply to failing Social and Mental tests against other characters. If a Social or Mental test fails, it cannot be attempted against the same target again for the rest of the scene. If your character attempts to intimidate someone and fails, that person is unlikely to suddenly become afraid of your character 30 seconds later if you try again. Subsequent attempts in the same scene might be made only if a feat description in these rules — or a Storyteller — allows it. Note: Unless otherwise noted, this rule also applies to any supernatural powers based on Social or Mental traits.

It should be noted that this rule generally does *not* apply to tests against objects as opposed to other characters. For example, a character who attempts to decipher a code and fails the Intelligence + Enigmas test may make another test at the next available interlude (as noted in the Skill's description). He doesn't have to wait a scene before attempting this Mental action again.

When a Social or Mental feat can't be tried again, your options are limited. You could try another course of action that doesn't rely on the same action or draw. Or you could roleplay the event anyway and hope that you don't need mechanics to back your character's efforts.

The limitation on failed Mental and Social actions prevents players from badgering each other with Social Skills or mental powers until they get lucky or a subject submits simply to end the annoyance. This rule isn't intended to limit *roleplaying* such actions. Even if your Intimidation attempt fails, you may continue trying to pressure your subject. This rule simply limits the number of times a player may attempt to invoke game mechanics to back up a confrontation.

OPTIONAL RULE:
LIMITING FAILURE

The standard systems of this game incorporate some chance of failure for even capable characters by introducing the ace as an automatic failure in an action. If a character is extremely capable and has a high test pool, however, the Storyteller can implement one of the following optional rules to diminish the character's chance of failure from the standard one in 10. Use of these rules should be announced before play, so everyone knows the terms of the game.

Note: Neither of these variants applies to chance draws in any way. An ace produced on the first pull of a chance craw always indicates tragedy, regardless of how capable a character is. Likewise, the following optional systems should never apply in combat or under high-stress circumstances such as when diffusing a bomb. Some circumstances are just too uncertain for characters to ever have a chance to make them "safely."

Optional Variant #1:
Buying off the Risk

A player may sacrifice a portion of her test pool to "buy off" the chance of outright failure. Doing so reduces the number of successes that she can expect to achieve in return for a greatly reduced chance of failure. She must have a test

pool of 10 or higher (after all situational modifiers). She also announces that she is "buying off" the failure chance *before* the draw. Doing so imposes an immediate –3 penalty directly to her test pool. (Yes, this penalty might reduce the player's test pool to below 10, but that's the price paid for diminished chance of failure. It doesn't invalidate her use of this optional rule.)

If an ace is drawn, the player immediately re-shuffles and makes another draw. If she draws the ace a second time, she suffers an automatic failure. Otherwise, her draw is considered zero and adds nothing to her test pool, regardless of what card was actually pulled on her second draw.

For example, suppose that Nick is an incredibly skilled burglar, with a total test pool of 15 for picking locks. Using this rule, Nick could take a –3 penalty to his pool to buy off the risk of failure, lowering his pool to a 12 in the process. If he draws an ace, however, he does not automatically fail; he must draw two aces in a row to fail outright. By sacrificing a little bit of his expertise to make sure he does the job carefully, Nick reduces his overall result, but makes it much less likely he will simply fail.

Optional Variant #2: Standard Adjustment

This rule does not require that players actively declare that they reduce the risk of failure. It simply states that if a player's test pool equals or exceeds a certain number (either before or after modifiers are calculated, at the Storyteller's discretion), he suffers outright failure only if he draws two aces in a row. The standard minimum test pool is 15, although the Storyteller is free to adjust that number to reflect the test pools she sees in her chronicle. Players of supernatural creatures, for example, may routinely exceed test pools of 15 under certain circumstances, necessitating a higher minimum to keep this rule fair. Upon drawing an ace, a player simply announces "standard adjustment" and gets to draw again.

10 AGAIN

When you're hot, you're hot. Anytime you draw a 10, you add that value to your total and you get to re-shuffle and draw again. That's called "10 again." Add the second draw to the first and thus to your test pool. You get only one additional draw. If this second draw is another 10, you do not draw a third time. (Thus, the maximum value that you can add to your test pool is 20.) If you get an ace on your second draw, it does not indicate automatic failure. It simply counts as a zero.

The "10 again" rule allows for ordinary or outmatched characters to occasionally perform outstanding feats, or for one character in an even match to break ahead.

Example: *Your test pool is 7. You draw a 10, and get to draw again. Your second draw is a 6, so you add the two draws together, giving you a +16 draw value. Added to your test pool of 7, the total is 23 – five successes.*

The "10 again" rule applies to everything from gathering information to punching someone.

A draw of a 10 always calls for an additional draw, even on a chance draw (see below). Of course, a 10 is required to achieve any success on a chance draw. If you keep drawing 10's on a chance draw, you keep accumulating successes. This is the single exception to the rule that you get only one extra draw in a "10 again" situation.

THE CHANCE DRAW

Any time your test pool is reduced to zero or less, you may still make a chance draw. It's a "Hail Mary," desperate, last-ditch effort that your character would seem to have no right to achieve. Maybe he squeezes off what seems an impossible shot or he tries to win the favor of a mob determined to kill him. Be careful, though. A "Hail Mary" attempt can be a miracle or it can have tragic results.

Draw a card, called a chance draw. This card isn't added to your test pool in the regular fashion. Drawing a 10 nets you one success. You then reshuffle the whole deck and you draw again. If you get another 10, you accumulate successes and keep drawing. Anything other than a 10 ends the chance draw series. You're left with as many successes as you drawn 10's. Unlike the normal "10 again" rules, as long as you keep drawing 10's, you continue to draw.

Example: *Your character tries to fire a shot at a target that is almost completely concealed and at long range. The penalties for those circumstances reduce your test pool to zero. That leaves you with a chance draw if your character attempts the feat at all. He goes for it. You draw a card and need a 10 to get a success. You draw a 10 for one success. The chance draw rule allows you to draw again after a 10 to accumulate successes. Another 10 turns up, so you have two successes and get to keep drawing. Your third draw produces an 8, ending the chance draw with a total of two successes. Your character hits his target, against all odds, and does two points of damage.*

Note that a desperate action has to somehow be possible in order for even such a long shot as the chance draw to apply. The Storyteller has final say over exactly what circumstances merit a chance draw and what ones are beyond even that slim hope. Thus, while your character could hit that distant target with a lucky shot, you wouldn't get a chance draw to try to cut through a steel safe with a toothpick. That's not a long shot, it's flat out impossible.

ACTIONS

Like you, your character can try to do pretty much anything he sets his mind to. He can attempt to jump, read foreign languages or seduce someone. His relative success is based on his traits, any tools he brings to bear, the size of his test pool, and how well you draw. Various activities call for different kinds of draws. Some, like throwing a punch, have immediate results, while others, such as rebuilding an engine, can involve more long-term time and energy. Other activities have either immediate or extended effects, but involve direct competition with someone else. He who does the best job prevails. Examples of the last include arm wrestling (immediate) or trying to win a long-distance race (prolonged).

The following are the actions your character can perform, along with systems for deciding how well he does.

INSTANT ACTIONS

Many actions take almost no time. Shooting a gun is an obvious example. Karate chopping a piece of wood is another. These feats are performed and completed in the moment, usually with obvious results. The attempt fails or succeeds. Any activity that can be performed and completed in the space of one turn – three seconds – is considered an instant action. These efforts are resolved with a single draw added to a normal trait pool.

If you get no successes on the draw, your character fails at the activity. Most likely, no result occurs and he wastes his time. Instant actions usually require only one success to be performed. Sometimes the actual number of successes that you achieve is counted, as in combat to determine damage.

The Attribute and Skill tasks described in Chapters 2 and 3 suggest possible results when failure and success occur.

The possible results from any instant action:

Failure	No successes are achieved on the draw
Success	One or more successes are achieved on the draw

165

10 AGAIN | CHANCE DRAW | ACTIONS

By this system, the challenge of any feat is laid out before you. One success always indicates a positive result. Five or more successes suggest a great success, but one is always the benchmark. You always draw against a standard difficulty of 10. The likelihood of success is determined by the number of modifiers added to or subtracted from your test pool. The higher the number of your pool, the more likely it is that the draw results in success. The lower the number of your pool, the slimmer your character's chances. When your character performs an activity that takes a turn to accomplish, compose a test pool based on his traits, add or subtract numbers based on bonuses or penalties, and draw. If you get a total that equals or exceeds 10, your character succeeds in the moment.

Example: *A ghost holds a mirror that Jimmy desperately needs. If the mirror is smashed, the spirit of Jimmy's deceased girlfriend might be lost forever. The ghost flings the mirror and vanishes with an evil laugh. Jimmy races to catch the prized possession. The Storyteller calls for a Dexterity + Athletics draw. Jimmy's Dexterity is 3 and his Athletics is 3. He has no special tools or benefits to apply to the effort. Meanwhile, there's a whole room full of furniture for Jimmy to navigate to get to the mirror in time (the Storyteller imposes a –3 penalty). The result is a test pool of four (6 + 1 – 3). The draw turns up a 6, for a total of 10 – just enough to meet the standard difficulty of 10. One success. Jimmy dives and just barely makes it, catching the mirror a split second before it hits the ground. Elsewhere in the house, a disembodied wail of frustration echoes as the malevolent spirit sees its plan thwarted.*

EXTENDED ACTIONS

Some actions demand time and effort to be performed. They can't be completed on the fly or in the moment as instant actions are. Activities such as conducting research into a politician with a shady past, or canvassing a neighborhood for strange sightings are extended actions. Rather than require one draw, they demand several draws before overall success can be determined. Successes earned per draw are accumulated. The period that passes between draws varies depending on the activity performed.

Each draw is a step toward achieving the end goal, such as hacking a computer or hot-wiring a car. A failure on any single draw means you accumulate no successes at that stage and your character's time in that period is wasted. The project continues, though.

It's also possible that penalties could be imposed on your test pool at any stage, reducing you to a chance draw. Say a research effort is made ever more challenging because important documents are lost in a fire. (The Storyteller imposes a high penalty to subsequent draws made.) A failure on such a draw cancels all accumulated successes. This may also mean that your character must start the extended action from scratch, and has to make some change in his approach. Maybe he has to find a new source of information, get new tools, read the automobile repair manual or find new parts.

The Storyteller determines how many total successes are required to complete an extended action; players may also set their own totals for certain tasks without direct Storyteller guidance, if the Storyteller allows them to do so and they do not abuse this privilege. He also decides what period of time passes for each draw that you make, and translates what each stage means for your character. Chapter 3 indicates likely extended actions, the number of successes they require, and how much time passes with each draw. Relatively easy tasks such as stripping, cleaning and reassembling a gun may demand four successes, with each draw constituting 10 minutes of game time. Early stages involve pulling the pieces apart, intermediate stages involve ordering and cleaning them, and final stages indicate re-assembly of the weapon. A more demanding project such as building a computer can demand 15 successes. Each draw can represent minutes or hours. Early stages indicate acquisition of parts. Middle draws represent assembling the machine. Final draws indicate that last touches are applied and software is installed.

Unless a particular task or draw is described as an extended action, consider it to be instant.

Example: Marcus barricades himself inside a machine shop while that thing stalks him outside. Marcus realizes that he needs a weapon, but there's nothing but engine parts and tools lying around. Then his eyes fall on the partially disassembled chainsaw on the worktable. He sets to work right away trying to make the saw run again. The Storyteller calls for an extended series of Wits + Crafts draws, since so much improvising of parts is involved. The Storyteller also decides that each draw signifies the passing of five minutes, and that a total of 10 successes is required. Secretly, the Storyteller knows that the creature outside will grow tired of waiting and smash the door down after 20 minutes (four draws) of toying with its prey.

Marcus' Wits + Crafts total is seven, and the Storyteller says his player gets a +3 bonus per draw thanks to the facilities available. In the first five minutes, the draw produces three successes. Two more are gained in the second draw. The third draw achieves no successes at all. It looks grim for Marcus. However, in the fourth draw, an amazing six successes are achieved – one more than the 10 required, and just in the nick of time. When the creature bursts through the door, Marcus whirls around with a functional weapon in hand.

Optional Rule: Increasing Successes

One of the joys of the Storytelling experience is making up events on the fly, in response to characters' actions or to entertain players. A great opportunity to do just that lies with the successes that players draw. In an instant action where one success completes a task, and five successes mark an outstanding result, the Storyteller can have fun with everything in between. Take a research effort, where one success means the basic information sought is found. Perhaps two successes also turn up a link to some affiliated people who don't seem completely on the up and up. Three successes definitely indicate that these folks have their fingers in illegal pies. Four successes show that their circle includes some real movers and shakers in town. Five successes — an incredible amount — could reveal that the mayor herself is involved!

The effects of such increasing results apply primarily to actions that are completed when only one success is needed. Tasks such as combat attacks and extended actions that are specifically measured in terms of successes drawn call for less innovation. The number of successes drawn automatically shows you how well a character does; adding more onto that is potentially unbalancing.

So, when a player needs one success but gets three, the Storyteller should feel free to elaborate on any extra accomplishments, beyond what a character absolutely needs. Players should remember such increasing benefits are a Storyteller option and should not *expect* them.

RULE OF THUMB: EXTENDED ACTIONS
Draw Limitations

Tasks described throughout **Mind's Eye Theatre** involve extended actions. Examples include rebuilding an engine or writing a computer program. By definition, an extended action calls for a total number of successes, which a character tries to meet. His successes from draw to draw are accumulated until they equal or exceed that number. At that point, the project is completed. The total time required is determined by the number of draws made. If each draw involves 10 minutes and six draws are made, an hour passes.

Yet, on its own this system implies that almost any project can be accomplished given enough time. A crook can work on a lock indefinitely until she breaks in. A writer can work for an extended period on a movie script until it's finished. In reality, people rarely have unlimited time in which to accomplish their goals. The crook hears a security guard approach and needs to pick the lock before she's spotted. The scriptwriter must beat a deadline. A Narrator can therefore impose a limit on the number of draws that are allowed in an extended action. He might say that the crook has time for three attempts to break in before the guard arrives in three minutes (each draw takes one minute). The writer's deadline is in five days, and one draw in the extended action encompasses one day. The author's required successes all need to be gathered in five draws. In these cases, time is the great equalizer.

Time isn't the only limit to an extended action. A character's inherent capabilities could be a limit, too. A Narrator can rule that the maximum number of draws possible in an extended action is equal to a character's pertinent Attribute + Skill. If he can't get the job done in that number of draws, the project simply confounds him. Take the would-be burglar above. Say she has 3 Dexterity and 2 Larceny. Assuming she has unlimited time in which to break in, the Storyteller can rule that if she doesn't get enough successes in five draws (Dexterity + Larceny), she simply can't do it. Maybe the lock is jammed, she gets frustrated, she can't think straight or her hands ache from an earlier accident. Whatever rationale the player and Narrator can apply that explains the turn of events.

Just because this attempt fails doesn't mean the effort eludes the character forever. Taking some time to cool off, clear the mind and prepare for another attempt may make it possible to try again. A Narrator decides how much time must pass before another attempt can be made. If the effort involves a short period of time, such as picking a lock, it might not be picked this scene but the character can try again in a subsequent scene. If a project involves considerable time, such as each draw occupying days or weeks, a new attempt at the project might not be possible for a month or more.

If the Storyteller does allow a subsequent effort at the project, he may impose a penalty on all of its draws. If this is the second attempt, all draws might suffer a –1 penalty. If this is a character's third attempt, the penalty might be –2. Such modifiers are akin to "Successive Attempts" (p. 176) and are the only case in which such penalties might apply to an extended action.

Example: *Pete attempts to reinforce the backroom of his bar as a hideout, complete with booby traps and secret compartments. The Storyteller rules that it's an extended effort, and since it's during downtime, he decides that each draw represents one day of work. Fifteen successes are required. Pete's Intelligence + Crafts is 7, and he has some high-quality tools that offer a +1 bonus.*

If time were of the essence, the Storyteller might decide that Pete needs all 15 successes in four days – in four draws. If he doesn't have them in time, the hideout is useless when that creature in his neighborhood comes looking for food.

Alternatively, if time is not an issue but Pete's own capabilities are, all 15 successes need to be accumulated in seven draws (the total of his Intelligence + Crafts). In seven draws, Pete has only 13 successes. He hasn't been able to overcome certain design snags and his backroom is cluttered with boards and gear. The Storyteller lets him try again in the future, though. It's decided that the process can begin again in a week. This time, however, all draws suffer a –1 penalty because this is a subsequent attempt.

To stave off frustration on this second attempt, Pete stacks the odds in his favor and gets some self-help books and even better tools. The bonuses gained from this new equipment help him get 15 successes in seven draws, despite the –1 penalty that each draw suffers. Had even this attempt failed, the Storyteller could have allowed a third series, but all draws in it would have incurred a –2 penalty.

It's also possible in some cases that a character really does have unlimited time to work. His Attribute and Skill dots are not necessarily a limit to how many draws can be made to finish a project. A character might rebuild a classic car, for example. The old hulk sits in his garage for months as he tinkers on it on weekends. There's no deadline or imminent threat, and the character does it for pleasure rather than out of fear or pressure. The Storyteller decides that each draw represents a week of work, and the character will eventually succeed given enough time and successes.

Here are some guidelines for the amount of time to assign per draw in an extended action. Note that the times are divided according to what is generally advisable during a chapter, and what is more realistic during downtime. Chapter times are short in order to keep play moving and to avoid players getting bored with being forced to perform a particular task for hours of game time.

6.2 – ACTIONS DURATIONS

Pace of Activity	Time per Draw (Chapter/Downtime)
Quick	1 turn (3 seconds)/1 minute
Short	5 minutes/10 minutes
Long	15 minutes/30 minutes
Lengthy	30 minutes/1 hour
Consuming	1 scene/1 day
Exhausting	1 chapter/1 week or month

Target Successes

The extended actions detailed throughout this book all call for a total number of successes required to finish a project. Whenever possible, totals are derived from the traits of the characters involved. A competition between characters might require a target number of successes equal to the opponents' Speed, Dexterity + Crafts or double Dexterity + Crafts, for example. The goal in choosing these traits and setting a target is twofold:

1) Using traits to set success targets keeps those targets relevant to the people involved or to the activity performed.

2) A target is sought that doesn't allow an extended action to be resolved too quickly, but the task shouldn't drag on and on, either. A target should reflect the overall difficulty of a task, but it should still involve some kind of prolonged challenge. Otherwise, it would be resolved as an instant action.

Ultimately, the Storyteller decides how long an extended action should last, and therefore how many successes it requires. If the prescribed target listed in this book will make for too quick an effort or competition in your game, feel free to increase the number of successes needed. A number normally based on Speed or double an Attribute + Skill can be turned into an artificial target of 15, 20 or 25, instead. Whether the number is based on participants' traits is ultimately unimportant. How it's resolved in-game is what really matters. An increased number could allow for a demanding effort or an intense creative process. It could also heighten the tension of a competition between characters (in an extended and contested task — see below).

Here are some guidelines for target numbers that you can assign to extended actions. These are based on the complexity or sheer scale of the job, or on the drama that you want to evoke.

6.3 – ACTION TARGET NUMBERS

Challenge	Target Number
Simple/Relaxed	5
Involved/Trying	10
Elaborate/Demanding	15
Ornate/Daunting	20
Intricate/Epic	25

CONTESTED ACTIONS

Some activities that your character performs are conducted in direct competition with someone else. It could be another player's character or one of the Storyteller's characters. A race is a good example. Trying to crack the hard-drive protections created by someone else is another. You pit your character's capabilities against someone else's directly.

Contested actions are easy to resolve. You simply determine your test pool, apply all modifiers and draw. The same is done for your character's opponent. Subtract the number of successes the defending party got from the number of successes the aggressor has, resulting in the final number of successes in that contested action. In case of a failure, the players involved or the Storyteller decides if an effort can be attempted over and over until one competitor wins. If both try to grab a fish that swims downstream, they both probably have only one chance before the fish is gone. If one tries to hack into another's computer, the effort might persist as long as the intruder likes or until the owner's fail-safes shut the intended intruder out. If the contested action was directed at another character and used social or mental traits, then it can't be attempted again for an hour.

In some cases, draws aren't made for opponents in the moment of the contest. Sometimes one participant sets up a defense or creates a situation that a challenger later tries to overcome. The draw for the defender is made when he creates the object or defense, and any successes achieved are recorded for future reference. Challengers' draws are made as they approach, and are compared to the defender's original score. So, if an IT manager creates a firewall for a server and gets four successes, a hacker who comes along a year later needs five or more successes to get in.

The Skill descriptions in Chapter 3 indicate when contested actions are appropriate for various tasks. Draws made are based on the activity performed, as always. Hacking a computer might involve Intelligence + Computer for both sides. Running a race may involve Dexterity + Athletics or Stamina + Athletics.

Note that in a contested action, the total successes drawn for each participant are compared and the attacker's successes minus the defender's successes represent the final number of successes. The difference between successes drawn is thus the "margin of success." So, if one participant gets two successes and the other gets five, the latter of the two wins with three successes, the difference between the two totals.

Contested feats can be based on instant actions or extended ones. Activities that take only a moment – a turn – to perform between competitors are considered instant actions and are resolved with one draw each. Wrestling over a fallen gun probably involves only one action's effort to decide who ends up with the weapon. If draws tie or neither results in successes, the struggle can continue into the next turn. It's still considered an instant action, though, because it can once again be resolved in the space of one turn.

Time-consuming or demanding activities that are performed in competition are considered extended actions. Use the rules detailed above. These feats are also contested, though. Draws are still made for each competitor in each stage. He who gets the most successes wins that stage. Successes achieved by each side are added to a running total. The winner is the first competitor who accumulates enough successes to complete the project. Examples of such competition are a long-distance race, a car chase, a debate or an effort to be the first to find a vaccine. Essentially, any effort that demands more than a single turn's effort to decide a winner involves an extended *and* contested action. If the progress made by the 'slower' party in such a contest doesn't impact the progress made by the 'faster' party, don't subtract the lesser number of successes from the greater successes every turn, merely continue adding them up for every contestant: it doesn't matter if Bob has chopped less wood for the last couple of minutes, his achievement still counts since he may yet catch up to George's lead.

Example: *At first, Leeds and the poacher quarreled over the dead deer. Now that a giant wolf has descended upon them, they both run for their lives. The two race, because the slower of the two will be the wolf's victim. The Storyteller decides that the race is an instant action – decided in the space of a turn. The wolf is satisfied with whoever is closest when it pounces. Dexterity + Athletics draws apply for both. Leeds' Running Speed trait is two higher than the would-be poacher's, so the Storyteller awards a +2 bonus to the draw made for Leeds. He's wearing a lot of hunting gear, though, which imposes a –1 penalty. Leeds' player draws, and the Storyteller draws for the poacher. Leeds' draw nets four successes while the poacher gets three. The wolf has its victim, the slower of the two hunters.*

Now, what if the wolf holds back and allows its victims to run, judging which is the weaker of the two? The Storyteller could decree that the race is a contested and extended effort. He decides that whoever gets six successes first is allowed to escape – the wolf ignores the victor and chooses the loser as its prey. One draw marks a turn's time and the loser is dinner. The Storyteller also decides that since this isn't a measure of pure reaction time, but of endurance, Stamina + Athletics is drawn. Leeds' Stamina is 4 and his Athletics is 2, for a total of 6. The same modifiers above still apply, so Leeds' test pool totals seven. The poacher's test pool total is five. In the first turn, Leeds gets one success to the poacher's three. The poacher has the lead. In turn two, Leeds gets three successes, while his opponent gets none. Leeds is a step ahead now, but neither party has gotten away. In turn three, Leeds gets a tragic zero successes while the poacher gets another three, for the required total of six. Abject panic gives him a burst of speed, leaving Leeds to fend off the beast that howls greedily and leaps in his direction.

If participants in an extended and contested action accumulate their required number of successes at the same time, no winner is determined. They could both finish their separate projects simultaneously with no clear leader. Both scientific teams present their successful findings at the same time, for example. Alternatively, the competition could continue until someone overcomes the other. Draws continue to be made, perhaps to improve upon efforts that have already been achieved. Say, debaters both make valid points, so they continue their discussion to see who can get the last word.

If an extended and contested action is a tie, the Storyteller could rule that ongoing competition is worthless. Perhaps time has run out or the goal that both sides pursue is no longer available. Debating teams could refuse to quit, but the panel of judges has already decided that neither has won. As a last resort, the Storyteller may also rule that the character with the higher natural test pool is the victor. If they remain tied under such circumstances, the character with the higher relevant Ability (or primary Attribute, in the case of Attribute tasks) is the winner. If a tie persists beyond even that point, the characters must either accept the uncertain outcome or a final victor is determined randomly.

REFLEXIVE ACTIONS

In addition to instant, extended and contested actions are reflexive ones. These actions differ from the others, because your character doesn't take time to perform them — or even think about them. They're performed automatically, almost like the autonomic functions of your body. Accounting for them in a turn would be like drawing for your character's heart to beat or lungs to take in air.

Reflexive actions are best considered defensive or reactionary activities that don't intrude upon other behavior. They include resisting poison, seeing through a deception, defying social pressure and spending Willpower points. These activities do not preclude your character from taking his normal action in a turn. They are performed *in addition* to that action. Resolve reflexive actions immediately after the instigating action (when the poison is injected, when the threat is pointed or when your character decides to go for broke).

Various actions discussed in Chapters 2, 3 and 7 are termed "reflexive."

Action	Example
Instant	Throwing a punch, controlling a vehicle
	A one-shot chance of success or failure; success is determined by a single draw.
Extended	Mountain climbing, tracking in woods
	Task stretches over a period of time and each stage renews the chance for failure or success. You make several draws with the goal of collecting a stated number of successes.
Contested	Pick-pocketing or sneaking by a guard
	An instant action that pits two characters against each other. The two compare successes. The highest total wins.
Extended and Contested	Chasing someone, a pie-eating contest
	Players draw repeatedly in order to accumulate successes. The first to reach the total set by the Storyteller wins.

DOWNTIME ACTIONS

The unique nature of actions taken inbetween game sessions deserves some discussion, especially in live-action, where the time between games can often be almost as important as the chapters themselves. Here, downtime play can often be as important as what happens during an chapter. Quite simply, downtime actions are efforts undertaken by a character in the time between game sessions. These activities are not normally portrayed through roleplaying (though they can be), but simply talked through with the Storytelling staff to determine their results.

What kind of actions can constitute downtime actions? Quite simply, everything a character can normally do in a session *except attack other characters directly.* Most players prefer to use their downtime actions for less than glamorous but still vital actions.

These could be research, building or repairing equipment, doing investigative legwork, arranging certain favors through Allies or other Merits, and similar deeds. Generally speaking, a downtime activity requires an action only if it has a substantial in-game effect, especially one that impacts another character. The Storyteller has the final say on which actions have enough in-game weight to justify costing a downtime action.

As a rule, each character gets one downtime action between game sessions. Storytellers may raise this number if the time between sessions is particularly long. Certain Merits such as Allies and Retainers may also increase this number, as might particular supernatural powers, according to their respective descriptions. Without specific supernatural augmentation, no character should ever be able to *personally* take more actions in a single period of downtime than she has Resolve dots. There is only so much a character can focus on getting done in one period of time. A character may have dots in a half-dozen different kinds of Allies, but it's unlikely that she alone will be able to call upon them all in single downtime period.

Characters' wealth and power are represented by influential Merits such as Allies and Retainers, and by "raw" assets like Resources. Such a support base allows these characters to make full use of the options at their disposal, accomplishing various downtime actions simultaneously (see "Handing off Downtime Actions" in Chapter 5). Of course, turning to others to get work done runs the risk of assistants being impeded, attacked, killed or perhaps being subverted to serve enemies.

Note that downtime actions are possible even if a player is unable to attend a particular game session. One who misses two games still gets his normal downtime actions between both of the games. This is so that players who cannot attend as often as they would like can still be involved in the game, at least to some degree. Downtime actions are still subject the usual Resolve maximum and cannot be "saved up" over the course of multiple chapters. If they are not used before the next session, they are lost.

Some downtime actions are usually assumed to be free. Training to acquire new traits or to raise existing ones is represented by spending experience points is usually considered a free downtime action. The main exception to this rule is if the time between sessions is severely limited, in which case the Storyteller may restrict the number of traits that you can improve at one time. A couple of months of downtime may give you all the time you need to improve your character. He could hit the dojo to improve his Brawl, hang out at the firing range to raise his Firearms, and lose himself at the library to increase his Intelligence and Occult ratings. Trying to do it all in, say, two weeks stretches the bounds of plausibility.

Likewise, in-character meetings with Narrator-controlled characters or other players' characters held during downtime are generally considered free actions. That is, unless the players involved intend to use them as a springboard for more than just a bit of roleplaying. In such cases, the usual costs and restrictions apply. So, if you meet with fellow neophyte witch-hunters to discuss the various threats facing town, that's fine. Attempting to do more active things through the meeting such as conduct research, create new weapons, or other actions with more tangible in-game results probably requires you to spend a downtime action.

Barring exceptional circumstances, routine maintenance of equipment and fetching supplies is considered a free downtime action. A character without a Resources Merit may have to spend a downtime action scrounging up or even stealing supplies to replace those he's lost. He doesn't have any standing assets to cover his costs, so has to spend time figuring out how to get what he needs without being arrested. That extra effort is reflected in the expenditure of a downtime action.

Optional Rule: A Matter of Resolve

A Storyteller may opt to raise the number of downtime actions available to each character from one to a number equal to her Resolve dots, in order to show how more focused and dedicated characters make the most of their time. That means each character has at least two downtime actions, some get four or five per interval, and since certain actions can be handed off for supporting characters to perform (represented by Merits), which means that characters with high Resolve and a support network of Allies and Retainers may have a truly impressive number of actions at their disposal. Needless to say, Storytellers should carefully before applying this optional rule in large games. It can quickly generate a flood of downtime actions that can bring the game to a grinding halt unless the Storytelling staff is prepared to handle them.

Downtime Kills

Inevitably, a situation will arise in which a player wants to take downtime actions that endanger, impair or outright destroy a Narrator-controlled antagonist, or even another player's character. Perhaps the attacker wants to use Status in local politics to arrange for a vampire's daytime resting place to be torn down, exposing the creature to a (hopefully) fatal dose of sunlight. Maybe he wants Allies on the police force to have another character arrested on trumped up charges, essentially removing that character from play indefinitely. Perhaps he simply uses his Contacts to locate a hitman and puts a contract out on a rival. The character could even use inside information on the subject to give the hitman a "foolproof" assassination plan. Faced with such cunning plots and the fact that they're backed by in-game traits that players have bought with experience points, what's a Storyteller to do?

As a rule, no player's character can *ever* be killed in a downtime action. If a plan involves the potential for a character to be killed, arrested or otherwise seriously harmed, the player of that character is entitled to resist the attempt. And yet, the Storyteller should remember that the character initiating the attack merely uses official traits and systems. Disallowing him to use his traits to his best advantage is unfair. Ideally, the Storyteller should strike a balance between the two positions. She should allow the target a chance of surviving, while allowing the attacker use of his capabilities.

The best way to handle such events as a side session: a small in-character gathering at which the target has a chance to escape, if not unharmed then at least alive. Narrators or trusted players can assume support roles while the two opponents hash it out. Note that the Storyteller is under no obligation to forewarn the subject about the nature of the session. The point is probably that the victim is blindsided. However, once the scene starts, the subject should have some chance of surviving, no matter how supposedly "foolproof" the attacker's plans might be. After all, if you've already decided the target can't escape, why bother with the side session?

Sometimes a player or the Storytelling staff can't find time to hold a side session before the next game. Such episodes may also become so common that they drain the troupe during downtime (a particular problem with large games). The Storyteller may therefore make a ruling that any characters targeted for death by downtime actions automatically survive. They may be injured, possibly even seriously. They might also lose some other significant asset that is targeted in the downtime action, perhaps explaining survival by this loss (a Retainer takes a bullet meant for the character, for example.). The result could be actual loss of traits such as Resources or Allies, depending on the power and planning behind the attack.

If the Storyteller makes a decree that characters cannot be killed in downtime actions, some reward must remain for the attacker. Players whose characters lose valuables or traits should remember that the Storyteller is being kind. They might lose dots, but enemies aren't allowed to kill them with the figurative push of a button.

Imagine a character who uses connections to target a prominent vampire antagonist. The victim's haven is demolished by a wrecking crew, threatening to expose the Storyteller character to the sun. That night, the target emerges from the ruins, battered yet extant. It has lost its hiding place and anything the building might have contained. These are some pretty serious drawbacks for the antagonist to suffer in return for its ongoing existence.

Or imagine a character targeted by a crooked police raid. He's tipped off to the danger and slips out minutes before the invasion. The good news is that he's not in jail. The bad news is that he loses whatever was in his apartment, he can't go back any time soon, and chances are there's a warrant out for his arrest. He might be able to straighten the situation out with some downtime actions of his own. He could call a lawyer or pull some strings on the force. Thanks to the Storyteller's decree, he's alive. He has simply suffered considerable setbacks.

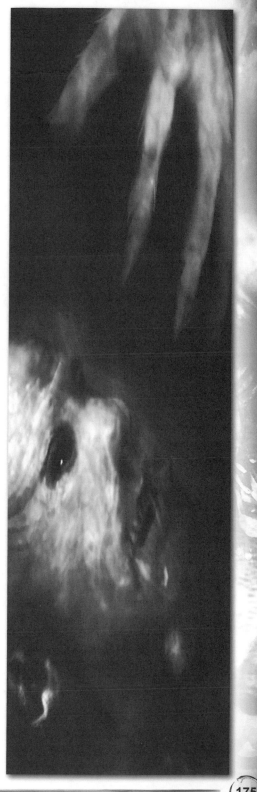

Sample Downtime Actions

Each of the following activities is considered to cost one downtime action to perform. This list is by no means exhaustive, and the Storyteller should feel free to add, alter or subtract from it as she sees fit. Consider the following as a rule of thumb for determining if an action has a downtime cost.

• An action that serves to influence a plot or build up a character in a mechanical way should have a cost. If it's simply done for a player's entertainment without immediate relevance to the story, it's much less likely to have a cost, though don't let players abuse this privilege.

• Training to learn a new trait or to improve an existing one. (The first trait trained per downtime interval is free and does not cost an action. At the Storyteller's discretion, each additional trait trained in a single interval may cost an action. This requirement reflects how demanding it is to train so many traits at one time.)

• Researching an important piece of information

• Maintaining a semblance of normality at a regular job/school after a brief time of extreme stress. (Failure to do so may result in being fired/expelled, followed by loss of Merits such as Resources.)

• Creating a work of art — music, prose, sculpture

• Conducting serious business/professional negotiations or demands

• Performing investigative legwork such as a background check or minor surveillance

• Taking a trip to a relatively distant location with significance to the plot

• Building or repairing an important piece of equipment. This does not include routine maintenance work, which is considered a free action.

• Running laboratory tests on materials with story significance

• Getting in touch with a Contact for information relevant to a current plotline

• Scavenging for the bare necessities if a character has no ready income or other means of basic support. (Characters who have to plot and fight for every meal and place to stay have much less time to devote to other activities.) Note that this does not necessarily apply to a character with no Resources Merit, as even without that trait characters are normally assumed to have a job that covers their necessary expenses. Rather, only characters who are explictly designed as homeless or reduced to a similar existence below this minimum level need to worry about this sort of action.

SUCCESSIVE ATTEMPTS

If your character fails an action in a turn, he can try again in the next turn if time and circumstances permit. He can throw darts for fun over and over again until he hits a bull's eye. Other situations don't allow for repeated efforts. Your character might have a limited opportunity to break down a door to get out of an inferno before he's burned alive. When time is a complete luxury and your character is under absolutely no pressure, the Storyteller may allow you to make successive attempts with a full test pool. No penalties are imposed.

If, however, time is short and/or the circumstances are tense, a repeated effort can be attempted in each subsequent turn, and the Storyteller can choose to levy penalties on successive attempts. Generally, a –1 penalty accumulates with each attempt after the first: –1 for the second try, –2 for the third, and so on. The Storyteller is free to make the penalty more severe if the stress is particularly high. The Storyteller allows successive attempts to break down the door, for example, but each draw after the first might be at a cumulative –2 penalty.

The nature of the action determines whether second chances are possible. They might be if your character attempts to pick a lock, parallel park or wriggle free from ropes that bind her. It does not apply if your character fails an attempt to shoot someone, detect an ambush, catch a baseball or to do anything else at which she has only one chance to succeed.

Note that Mental and Social-based traits have their own limits when it comes to attempting them multiple times against a target in a particular scene. See the rule on failed Social and Mental tests under the Failure heading, p. 162. If a character performs an action and succeeds with a low number of successes, for instance to activate a supernatural power, he should not normally be allowed to retry that self-same action to get more successes.

Example: Nick struggles to remember the punch-code to the laboratory door as the security guard's footsteps grow closer. The Intelligence + Composure draw made for him comes up with no successes. Nick's player asks the Storyteller if he can try again. The Storyteller allows one more attempt before the security guard appears, but at a –1 penalty because it's a successive attempt. Nick's Intelligence + Composure test pool is normally five, which is reduced to four due to the –1 penalty.

Note that successive attempts cannot usually be made in the stages of an extended action. If one draw in an extended action nets no successes, you can't re-draw it in a successive attempt. No progress is made at that stage of the project, the time is wasted, and the next normal draw in the effort is made. If, however, a *whole* extended action fails (the total successes required are not met), the Storyteller may allow another attempt to be made at it. All the draws in the new attempt may be subject to a penalty. See "Rule of Thumb: Extended Actions," above, for more information.

HEROIC EFFORT

Sometimes just trying to accomplish a feat isn't enough for your character. It's do or die. He has to make a leap or catch a falling child or a last desperate attempt to avoid the grasp of a devious predator . That's when he puts his all into it. You can have your character make this extraordinary effort by announcing that he "goes for broke" before the activity is performed. You then spend a Willpower point in a reflexive action to gain a +3 bonus on your test pool. That bonus can't be used for combat attacks or any other type of aggressive maneuver or power: it is assumed that you're already trying as hard as you can to strike someone in a fight, or to incapacitate them using a supernatural power. It can, however, be used for defensive purposes – a desperate scramble to get out of the way of a devastating blow or a last-ditch attempt to steel your mind against supernatural manipulation.

Willpower should be spent and three added to your test pool before all penalties for your draw are applied. So, form your pool, add all bonuses — including your three from Willpower — and then subtract all penalties. Yes, that means if penalties are sufficiently extreme, you could be reduced to a chance draw even if you have spent Willpower. Circumstances are stacked so heavily against your character that not even sheer determination can improve his odds of success.

Example: Your character tries to bandage a wound, but he has no first aid kit, and he's literally in the dark. His Intelligence + Medicine total is 3. A spent Willpower point adds three more, for a subtotal of six. The Storyteller decides that darkness imposes a –3 penalty, for a final test pool of three.

Now, if your character had no Medicine dots at all and he still tried to bandage the wound, your draw would be based on Intelligence alone and would suffer a –3 penalty since Medicine is a Mental Skill (see. p. 57). You therefore decide to spend a Willpower point. If your character has

2 Intelligence, your test pool starts out at five (2 + 3 for Willpower), but the –3 untrained penalty and –3 darkness penalty reduce your pool to zero. You must make a chance draw for your character to succeed, even though you spent Willpower on the task.

If you spend Willpower for a +3 bonus and your pool is still reduced to zero by penalties, the Storyteller may allow you to reclaim the Willpower point. After all, without that bonus you were still going to be reduced to a chance draw. Before making the attempt, your character realizes that the effort is nigh impossible, with or without all his determination. Alternatively, the Storyteller may insist that your Willpower is spent, even though its benefits are lost due to penalties. He may say that your character must go through with his focused effort once the point has been spent.

It's the Storyteller's prerogative to rule either way. Generally, this decision is best made before the game and announced to players to avoid hard feelings down the line. If the Storyteller intends to judge this rule on a case-by-case basis, that's fine. Players should still be made aware of the situation to avoid accusations of favoritism, and rulings should be consistent under similar circumstances. If one player can withdraw a Willpower point before making a hopeless shot, another player calling for a similar shot should be able to reclaim any point spent before a draw is made.

It's too late to spend Willpower if you've already drawn for an action. That is, if you compose your pool, remove points for penalties, draw and get no successes, you can't announce that you spend a Willpower point to add three more to your total. It's too late.

Only one Willpower point can be spent per turn no matter how it's used.

Willpower can be spent on only one draw at a time in an extended action. If your character goes for broke at each stage (for each draw), you have to spend a Willpower point at each stage.

If for some reason your character's Resolve and/or Composure temporarily increase during play, perhaps as a result of a mystical spell, he gains one Willpower point per dot increase. Essentially, he has access to one or more free Willpower points for the duration of the effect. When his Attribute returns to normal dots, your character loses any extra Willpower points. If they were never spent, he no longer has access to them.

RESISTANCE

Willpower can also be used to reflect your character's efforts to resist influences and dangers imposed upon him. Your character might be determined to resist a poison that depletes his Strength, or to avoid harm through sheer force of determination.

In these cases, you can spend a point of Willpower in a reflexive action to gain a bonus to Resistance efforts. In combat, a point of Willpower spent adds two to your character's Defense to resist harm against a single attack. You simply announce that you're spending Willpower to resist when the attack is staged. (Your character could even dodge in a turn — see p. 216 — and you could spend a Willpower point to gain a further two points of protection against a *single attack*.) Remember that Defense (and therefore Willpower) does not usually apply against attacks from firearms or bows.

Otherwise, Willpower can be spent to bolster one your character's "Resistance" Attributes — Composure, Resolve or Stamina — against a single draw when he is threatened.

Say your character is exposed to a supernatural power that diminishes his cognitive capacity. The power steals one Intelligence point per success achieved, and your character's Resolve is subtracted from the attacker's test pool. Spending a point of Willpower increases your character's Resolve by two to resist the power. That is, your character's Resolve +2 is subtracted from the test pool of the opponent.

Example: A monster's thrall tries to hit Stein, who hopes to get by to save a child. Stein stops at nothing to get to the kid, so her player spends a Willpower point to better resist the effects of the thrall's attack. Stein's Defense increases from 2 to 4 for the attack, diminishing the minion's test pool.

In another turn, Stein negotiates for the release of the child from the terrifying being. The creature seeks to cripple Stein with a magical power that saps life force, and Stein's Resolve is subtracted from the test pool formed for the creature. She fights back with all her might, and her player spends a point of Willpower to resist the power. Stein's Resolve is normally 3 but it increases to 5 in this instance. That number is subtracted from the test pool for the creature's trick.

Remember that only one Willpower point can be spent per turn, total, no matter how it's used. You cannot, for example, spend one point to gain a +3 bonus on a draw and another point to increase your character's Resolve in the same turn. Those points must be spent in separate turns.

Wound penalties (see p.235) do not apply to your character's Defense or other Resistance traits when those traits are subtracted from opponents' test pools.

Storytellers are encouraged to read "Rule of Thumb: Resistance," p. 179, to better understand when Resistance traits such as Stamina, Resolve, Composure and Defense are subtracted from attackers' test pools in play.

Rule of Thumb: Resistance

As you read this book and play a few games, you probably recognize that there are two basic ways in which characters can resist efforts applied against them. That is, two systems are used to allow characters to fight back when pressures and attacks are directed against them. It's important for you to see how these systems are used throughout this book so you can apply the same rules on the fly in your games.

The first type of resistance involves a contested draw. Say a creature intends to ply its will over a character, and a contested draw is made for both target and aggressor. The target's draw is probably based on a Resistance trait such Stamina, Resolve, Composure or a combination of two of them, such as Resolve + Composure. In these cases, the target's contested draw is typically reflexive. The effort to resist is automatic and doesn't interfere with the character's own action in a turn (unless he loses the contested action, which might have its own consequences).

In general, "contested" resistance is called for when the effect being used takes full effect if as little as one success is drawn for the aggressor. A monster's attempt to use mind control over a character is a good example. A contested draw is called for because it gives the target a reasonable fighting chance. Successes drawn for him are compared to those drawn for the monster. If the attacker has any successes left after subtracting the defender's successes from his own, he wins. If no successes remain, the action fails. So as a rule of thumb in your game, if a supernatural power or other phenomenon can have a sweeping effect on a character if even one success is achieved, allow the target a contested (and reflexive) resistance draw.

The second type of resistance is more "automated." A target's Resistance trait is subtracted from an aggressor's test pool before the draw is made.

The best example is in close combat. When an attacker tries to strike an opponent, the target's Defense is subtracted from the attacker's test pool before a draw is made.

In general, "automated" resistance is called for when the effectiveness of the effort is measured in successes drawn. Under these circumstances, one success doesn't invoke a sweeping result. Rather, successes drawn are added to determine the final result. Again, the best example is combat. Successes achieved in an attack draw each inflict a wound on the target. The overall degree of effectiveness achieved is therefore incremental based on successes gathered, rather than being "all or nothing." Automated resistance is applied against these kinds of effects, because it puts aggressor and target on relatively equal footing game-systems wise.

So, as a rule of thumb in your game, if a supernatural power or other phenomenon has incremental effect on a character based on each success achieved, allow the target automated resistance. One of his Resistance traits is subtracted from the test pool of the aggressor before a draw is made.

A character's wound penalties are not applied to his Defense or Resistance traits when those traits are subtracted from opponents' test pools.

For more information, see "Resistance."

TEAMWORK

Characters can aid one another to achieve the same goal. They might work together to assemble an engine, break down a door or break a crook's will. Choose which character is the primary actor. A normal test pool is assembled for him based on the action. Say, Dexterity + Medicine to administer first aid. The same draw is made for each secondary actor. Any successes collected from assistants are added to the primary actor's test pool as bonuses. *So, contributors' draws are made before that of the primary actor.*

A failure on a secondary actor's chance draw levies a –4 penalty to the primary actor's test pool — it hinders rather than helps his chances. The primary cannot decide to abandon his action if a contributor's draw contributes few successes or a penalty. He must proceed.

The Storyteller decides how many secondary actors can participate in teamwork, and can limit the actors however he desires. Three people might find space around a patient in order to provide first aid, for example, while five people might be able to work together to build a house. Teamwork rules don't normally apply to combat in any way.

Example: Corey is performing first aid on an injured friend, with the help of Rebecca. It's basic treatment rather than a diagnostic situation, so the Storyteller decides that Dexterity + Medicine is called for. Corey has 3 Dexterity and 4 Medicine, while Rebecca has 2 Dexterity and 3 Medicine. Corey is the primary practitioner at work. The Narrator running the scene decides that since the pair has only a simple first-aid kit at its disposal, no bonus is gained. In fact, a –5 penalty is imposed because it's late at night (-3 for darkness), the patient is struggling slightly (-1), and there's only one flashlight for them to use while they're working (-1).

Rebecca's test pool starts at 5 but is reduced to a chance draw by those modifiers. An Ace is drawn – a failure. The Narrator announces that Rebecca drops the flashlight and it breaks. Since Rebecca was helping Corey, that means his effort suffers an additional –4 penalty, the standard penalty for an assisting character suffering a chance draw failure. Corey starts with a test pool of 7, loses five from

the existing factors, and loses four more from Rebecca's failure on chance draw. He's also reduced to a chance draw. His draw produces a 6 – a failure. . The Narrator rules that without the flashlight, the two cannot properly dress the wound and have to wait until they have more light to try again.

If Rebecca's draw produced, say, two successes, a +2 bonus would have been added to Corey's pool for his own draw. His final pool would have been six (7 + 2 – 3).

SYSTEMS PERMUTATIONS

Mind's Eye Theatre involves composing a test pool based on your character's capabilities (Attribute + Skill). Modifiers are then added to or subtracted from this pool based on the tools used and the circumstances of the action performed. Typically, one success drawn indicates an overall productive effort, while multiple successes can indicate an increasingly rewarding result.

This approach to activities — from driving a car to swinging a sword to smooth-talking a receptionist — can resolve many of the events that might happen in your game. At times, however, you may want to throw a curve or create a unique situation that bends or breaks the traditional rules. Maybe the weapon your character wields can be used in unique ways, or a supernatural power invoked by an inhuman monster warps reality. In these cases, you can introduce system variations to spice up your game.

The following are optional rules and possible adaptations that your Storyteller can apply when she pleases. Perhaps your character's weapon receives these benefits, and the Storyteller puts the rules in your hands during play. Or she decides that an antagonist's spell has certain advantages outside the normal rules. If you think your character should have access to any of these special systems, petition your Storyteller. She has final say on whether (or when) they can be used.

Unless a Narrator says otherwise or it is specifically stated in a trait description, always assume that none of these optional permutations apply.

• **9 Again:** You can re-draw 9's as well as 10's. The result is effectively a "9 again and 10 again" rule. This rule might be applied to a power that brings luck or to a particularly useful tool.

• **8 Again:** You can re-draw 8's, 9's and 10's. Essentially, you have a "8 again, 9 again and 10 again" rule. *Extremely* powerful — allow with caution.

• **Ace Again:** Sometimes what starts as a simple failure has the potential to start spiraling out of control. Rather than counting the draw of an ace as an automatic failure, count it as −1 to the test pool and draw again. Subtract the value of the second card from the test pool as well. So, if you have a test pool of 9 and draw the ace, and then draw a 6, your final total is 2 (9 − 1 − 6 = 2). If the ace is drawn a second time, it counts as a −2 and a third card is drawn and subtracted. If the ace is drawn a third time, it counts as −3 and a fourth card is drawn, etc. According this rule, then, the worst result you can have is −12 to the test pool, which results from drawing two aces in a row.

• **Advanced Actions:** Your character has amazing quickness at his disposal such that others seem to move in slow motion. He exists outside the normal flow of time and can perform feats while others are essentially "frozen." Or maybe he has the luxury of trying an action over without repercussions for failed results. Whatever the case, you get to make two draws for an effect, and choose the most beneficial one. The same mechanic is used for the Gunslinger Merit.

• **Double Trouble:** Drawing an ace or 2 imposes an automatic failure. This rule might be applied to truly dangerous situations in which there's a very thin margin of error between success and utter disaster.

• **Extra Talent:** Your character can bring extra faculties to bear in an effort. An additional Attribute or other trait is added to your character's test pool for an action. Perhaps a supernatural power allows his Intelligence to be added to his Strength + Skill draw. The force of his mind literally bolsters his muscles. Maybe a blessed weapon has its own preternatural speed that's added to your character's own martial prowess. The weapon has a Dexterity rating that's added to your Strength + Weaponry pool.

This permutation should be used carefully in **Mind's Eye Theatre**. It can quickly make many actions extremely easy. It is even more impacting if a defender cannot call upon a similarly high rated trait in their defense.

A recommended means of balancing an extra talent without negating its benefit is to count the extra talent solely for the purposes of offsetting negative modifiers, without actually adding it to the test pool. This approach makes it far less likely for the character to fail, so the extra talent has a definite benefit. At the same time it does not make automatic success a certainty. Extra talent does not therefore allow one character to run roughshod over another.

Example: Jim has a Strength of 4 and a Weaponry of 3. He wields a magic sword that channels his inner determination, allowing him to add his Resolve of 4 to attacks. If the Storyteller feels this bonus is too powerful, she can rule that Jim's Resolve dots count only for offsetting negative modifiers, and are not added directly to attack pools. So, if Jim is penalized −1 for fighting in tight quarters and another −2 for low light, his Resolve of 4 cancels out these penalties (4 − 2 − 1 = 1). His player would not, however, add the remaining point to his test pool of Strength + Weaponry. The extra talent counts only for canceling penalties, not increasing test pools. Jim can fight under some amazing circumstances without hardship, but isn't automatically guaranteed to hit.

• **Lower Interval:** Normally, every interval of five starting at 10 indicates a success. This permutation reduces that interval to three. So, a draw total of 10 to 12 equals one success, 13 to 15 equals two successes, 16 to 18 equals three successes, and so on. This rule makes for a large number of successes on average, while still retaining the basic notion of difficulty. It is useful for actions that are challenging to carry out but bound to be potent if they succeed.

- **Limited Modifiers:** Storytellers who don't want to deal with a lot of modifiers may declare that the maximum total bonus or penalty any character can face at one time is +/-5. Any modifiers in excess of those values are simply discounted. For example, if a character has a weapon that provides a +4 bonus, and a magic charm that provides a +4 bonus, he gets no more than +5, total.

What if penalties also apply? Remember, add all bonuses first, making sure that they do not exceed +5. Then, add all penalties, making sure they do not exceed –5. Let's expand on the above example. Normally, bad weather (–2) and a voodoo curse (–4) would be subtracted from the total bonus (+8). This would result in a total modifier of +2 (8 – 6). However, with limited modifiers, the bonus and penalty are each capped at five. They therefore cancel each other out for no overall modifier.

The Storyteller may declare that certain bonuses or penalties exist outside of this structure. Wound penalties, for example, should not be subject to a cap. A character who's penalties are –3 for weather, –3 for darkness and –2 for injuries therefore suffers a total penalty of –7 (–6 is capped at –5 and –2 is applied after the cap). Such exceptional modifiers should be few; they can empower or cripple characters quickly.

- **Modifies Resistance:** This permutation offers an advantage over opponents not because it overpowers them, but because it undermines them. Targets of the effect lose a certain number of points in any Resistance trait that they might pose (Stamina, Resolve, Composure or Defense). A power to control a victim's mind might also reduce his Resolve, for example. The target's diminished Resolve is subtracted from the attacker's test pool. A victim's Defense may be diminished in combat by an entangling weapon such as a lasso or rope (see "Defense," p. 215 in Chapter 7).

Alternatively, the effect bolsters the user's own Resistance, giving him bonuses to traits such as Resolve, Composure, Stamina or Defense for countering harm or influence over him. Protective devices might work this way, without encumbering the wearer with actual armor. Or a spell might erect walls in your character's mind to help him resist outside control.

- **Rote Actions:** Sometimes the steps or work involved in a feat has been laid out by those who preceded your character. He follows in their footsteps or follows instructions to achieve a result. The plans make success easier than if your character tried the effort under his own power or inspiration. Treat this permutation as teamwork (see p. 180), except your character essentially assists himself. First you make one test to see how well your character understands the plans. This is generally simulated by making a test with Intelligence + a relevant Skill. Then, make the actual test draw itself, adding the successes achieved on the first test as a bonus to your pool for the second draw.

Say your character wants to build a robot and downloads intricate, authentic plans from the Internet. The Storyteller decides that it's a rote action. Make an initial Intelligence + Crafts draw to see how well he understands the plans and prepares to work (with modifiers imposed by the plans, and other factors). Plans of average helpfulness and complexity might offer no particular bonus or penalty, while exceptionally clear and well-written ones could grant a small benefit to the character's test pool, while poorly written, incomplete or plans with clear pictures but which have instructions in a foreign language might penalize the character's draw. Each success on this draw is a bonus to the actual Attribute + Skill draw required to perform the feat.

You may be reduced to a chance draw on the first step of a rote action. For example, suppose that your character is in a hurry and the plans themselves are in a foreign language (but have recognizable pictures). If so, a failure indicates that something has gone horribly wrong from the outset. You get nothing helpful out of the plans or make a crucial early mistake, and may in fact have a penalty due to the confusion suffered. If nothing else, you must make the Attribute + Skill draw unaided.

The Player's 10 Commandments

• **It's Only a Game:** Never forget that it's all a game. Other players and Storytellers can't be held responsible for their characters' in-game actions. If you froth at the mouth over a rules dispute or get so heated that you have trouble separating your feelings from your character's, take a time-out until you can continue with a clear head.

• **Don't be a Jerk:** If you're tempted to do something because the rules technically permit it, but you know it isn't what they really intend, don't do it. If you feel like upsetting another player and then hiding behind your character to justify those actions, don't do it. If you feel the urge to initiate a mass combat just because you can, don't do it. If you feel the need to steal the spotlight and leave everyone else in the dark, don't do it. The game will be better for your restraint.

• **Trust Your Storyteller:** It's the nature of a grim place like the World of Darkness for bad things to happen to your character, sometimes even things that may seem inexplicable or outright unfair at first. Remember that the Storyteller is not "out to get you," but trying to craft a tale that frightens, excites, intrigues and surprises you. That means you must sometimes take it on faith that the he has good reasons for what happens, even if all you can see are the repercussions for your character.

• **Be Honest:** A significant amount of live-action activity occurs outside of the immediate supervision of the Storytelling staff. That means an honor system is in place to keep the game running smoothly. If you feel compelled to cheat in a fictional world being created for *your* amusement, why play at all?

• **Stay In-Character in a Game Session:** You're at work or school all week and you have long periods of downtime between sessions. Why bring reality into the limited time of the chapter? Try to use every possible moment of a game session to remain in character. It's entertaining for you and it motivates other players to do the same.

• **Take an Active Role:** Don't wait for the Storyteller to lead you into a new plotline. Each character has her own ways to get into the action. Don't hesitate to track down leads, dig up dirt, shake down informants, conduct research, crash parties, tail suspects, grease palms, pick locks, play politics, hack mainframes, jump fences, analyze evidence, seduce strangers, translate texts, take chances, play hunches and otherwise have your character do whatever it is she does best to get involved. You won't regret it.

• **Avoid "Perfect" Characters:** You wouldn't want to watch a movie or read a book about a character who never failed, had everything she ever wanted and wasn't afraid of anything. So why try to create that character for yourself? "Perfect" characters are really rather boring. They lack for nothing, and so lack motivation to do much. Instead, invest your character with shortcoming and needs, and set goals in each session to resolve or overcome those challenges. Doing so not only ensures you never lack for something to do, but provides the Storyteller with story hooks involving your character.

- **Embrace the Mystery:** The World of Darkness doesn't play by the same rules as the real world. There are mysterious forces at work that ordinary people — and supernatural beings — simply cannot comprehend. Don't quibble over "right" and "wrong," but enjoy the chance to learn about this shadowy reality through a completely new pair of eyes. It's hard to top the drama and tension of having your character perform actions that you wouldn't, or that you know to be patently dangerous.

- **Come Prepared:** Make sure you have your costume, character sheet, cards, Health counters/tokens, rulebooks and any relevant props or makeup that you need for a session.

- **Make the Game Fun for Everyone:** Remember the "Only Rules That Matter," on p. 18, and portray your character in a way that not only entertains you, but other players as well. If other players love your character even as he screws theirs over, he and you are a hit. Play to build the overall story, not just your own personal glory.

ADDITIONAL SKILL SYSTEM: TASK CARDS

One way for Storytellers to help immerse players into the environment and to diminish need for Storytelling staff to always be on-hand is to use props called task cards. At the most basic level, a task card is simply an index card or small piece of paper with the following information marked on it:

- What the task is and any necessary description to set the scene
- The test pool required to perform it
- Any inherent modifiers that apply to the task
- The in-game time the task takes to perform. Players should spend this time roleplaying the action appropriately, when possible.
- Descriptions for the possible results

Some task cards may include a "cool-down period," which is a length of in-game time that must pass before another attempt may be made to complete the task, though these should be relatively uncommon. Thus, players who come across a task card during a session can perform the required test and adjudicate any results without necessarily needing to involve the Storytelling staff, free those folks to be active elsewhere in the game.

Example: Lee and Retta's characters investigate a haunted house, and come across a task card on a library shelf. If they wish to inspect the shelves for particularly interesting books, it directs them to make a Wits + Investigation draw, with a −2 modifier due to the haphazard organization and faded contents of the library. Furthermore, each time they attempt this action, they must spend five minutes roleplaying their search of the library. Lee draws a failure, while Retta draws a success, so they both flip over the card and read the section that details the result they got. For Lee, it's nothing special (he doesn't find anything). For Retta, the text for "success" directs her to pull down a particular book on a high shelf and flip through it until she finds the loose papers hidden inside. In effect, Lee and Retta run their own interesting and plot-significant scene entirely by the rules, without a Narrator in sight.

Nothing says task cards must always be mental tasks. Physical task cards are certainly possible as well. For example, a Storyteller could place a task card on a staircase, describing how it has rotted through in-game, and how those that wish to climb safely must make a Strength + Athletics draw to traverse the rotted section without falling through. Every time a player wishes to climb a draw must be made, but there's no need to post a Narrator there to handle the danger. The task card conveys everything players need.

Even social task cards are possible, though generally used with minor characters in out-of-the-way places where other players' characters do not witness the imaginary conversation. For example, the Storyteller could post a task card on the back porch describing how a few minor servants of the manor take cigarette breaks and gossip. A Manipulation + Socialize draw allows players to learn a few choice bits of information. Or in the case of failure on chance draw, servants alert their employer to the nosy character. Beyond such exclusive and remote circumstances, social interaction is best handled between players and Storytellers.

TASK CARD CONDITIONS

When task cards are present, it's naturally assumed that players are prohibited from performing the task through means other than those presented. The very presence of the task card means there's only one way the Storyteller wants the action to be resolved. (Players who believe they have truly compelling alternate means of resolving a situation can certainly present them to the Storyteller, but that's a whole new set of circumstances.) For example, if Lee's character fails the library search, Lee himself is prohibited from physically searching the library books, and must ignore any discoveries even if he comes across them by accident. Even if the shelves hold only a half-dozen books out-of-character, a failure means Lee's character doesn't locate the right one in the "full" library. It's cheating for Lee to go through the props until he finds the correct volume.

Task cards may remain indefinitely, representing challenges that do not go away (such as the rotted staircase). Or they may address areas where certain information can always be obtained (such as an Intelligence + Academics draw at the door of a manor to recall details about its history). It's also possible that task cards may have a limited number of uses. They disappear when acted upon the requisite number of times . For example, after searching the library successfully, Retta may be directed to take down the entire task card or just remove the part detailing a "success" result and give it to the next Narrator she finds. The task has essentially been completed and there's no point to other characters attempting it. Likewise, the servants might disappear after one interaction to "return to the kitchen," requiring the player who found them and attempted the task to give the card to the Storyteller no matter what the result. Not only does a use limit prevent players from attempting tasks that shouldn't net results, it alerts Storytellers that a given task has been performed, which may set other events in motion.

Task cards should be as visible as the task is obvious or necessary. The task card for the broken staircase should be large and hard to miss; no character should be able to pass in-game without being subject to the stairs. Meanwhile, the card for searching the library can be a bit less obvious if the Storyteller wants the library's contents to be less conspicuous to the casual observer. Just remember that if task cards are too difficult to find, players may miss them or even achieve the same results without performing the required actions. Avoid being too sneaky for your own good! For example, if the library-search card is too well-hidden, players looking for the book may actually inspect the shelves in good faith and find the hidden papers before they discover the card (if they find it at all). That could cause problems, because they shouldn't have found the papers without performing the test. So now what happens?

Simplified Task Cards

A simple variation names the task that can be performed, such as "Search the library shelves" or "Try to sense signs of anything unusual," and possibly the required test pool, so players can judge whether their characters would be interested in or even capable of performing the action. On the reverse side of the card is a direction to seek out a particular member of the Storytelling staff, who runs the test and gives any associated descriptions for the scene. This approach allows Storytellers complete control over the tests involved, but permits them to roam freely through the game until a player actually finds out about the action and needs to resolve it.

Storytellers should feel free to make task cards as simple or as intricate as they desire, especially when it comes to the descriptive portions. They may even attach particular behavior or announced descriptions to different results. A failure on crossing the decomposing staircase might not only inflict a few points of damage, but might require an unfortunate player to loudly announce, "You hear a loud crash from the stairs and the sound of rotting wood crumbling." Other players can therefore have their characters respond accordingly. Or a successful result on a task to re-start an old boiler might require a similar out-of-character announcement along the lines of, "You hear a deep rumbling sound from the basement, and then hot air flows from the nearby vents." In some cases, the Storyteller may not even consider a task successfully completed until they hear such announcements, or a player delivers a completed card to him, or both.

TROUBLESHOOTING TASK CARDS

Task cards assume that players can be trusted to obey them, to abstain from re-doing failed tests, or to avoid reading the descriptions for results that they do not achieve. Basically, players shouldn't consider these cards as an opportunity to cheat. (Since at least one other person is generally required to be there to perform the draw process itself, even if out-of-character, cheating shouldn't be common.) Storytellers should feel free to discipline players who abuse the task card system. If even one person does it, the viability of the entire concept is threatened.

Objects

It's inevitable that people in traumatic, tense situations turn their attention to objects. They wield weapons, grab tools or they need items such as cars to make getaways. Objects are often the tools with which we get things done, and characters in your game use tools to fulfill their goals. It's therefore important to know how difficult it is to break loose a chair leg, shatter a lock or forcibly bring another car to a stop.

If your character ever seeks to do damage to an object by striking it unarmed (he smashes his shoulder into a door, punches through a wall or kicks a steel gate), he suffers a bashing wound in the attack. This injury can be negated with appropriate armor worn (see p. 178).

Inanimate objects have three traits: Durability, Size and Structure. These qualities typically encompass whole objects, such as statues, couches or cars.

Durability: A factor of the object's material hardness. Successes achieved in an attack draw against an object must exceed the item's Durability before any damage is actually inflicted. Thus, if a door has 1 Durability, any successes achieved in excess of one are counted as damage to the target.

The Durability rating of supernaturally enhanced items can reduce any aggravated damage done to them (see Chapter 7: Combat). If an object is mundane or ordinary, its Durability is considered zero against attacks that inflict aggravated damage. This excludes objects that are specifically made to withstand such assaults: vault doors do not have a Durability of zero against cigarette lighters and swords don't automatically shatter if touched by vampiric claws.

Durability Rating	Material
1	Wood, hard plastic, thick glass
2	Stone, aluminum
3	Steel, iron
+1	per reinforced layer

Size: Objects smaller than Size 1 can fit entirely in one's palm; they have negligible Size.

Size	Object
1	Pistol
2	Sword
4	Spear
5	Door
10	2-seat sports car
15	SUV
20	Dump truck

Structure: An object's Structure is the equivalent of its Health and equals its Durability + Size. An object suffers "wounds" due to damage. Once its Durability is exceeded in total Structure damage suffered, it malfunctions and incurs a –1 penalty when it operates or is used by a wielder. Therefore, if a chainsaw has 2 Durability and 3 Size, it has 5 Structure. If the item suffers one or two Structure damage, it's still functional. When it suffers three or four Structure damage — anything in excess of its Durability — using it imposes a –1 penalty on a wielder. At five damage it cannot function at all.

When all of an object's Structure is lost to damage the item is destroyed. Bashing and lethal damage are considered the same for objects. It doesn't matter what kind of wound is inflicted. If Structure drops to zero, the object is destroyed. The exception applies to a more severe kind of harm called aggravated damage that inhuman entities can inflict. The Durability of mundane objects is reduced to zero against aggravated attacks, as discussed above. In addition, while ordinary damage inflicted on an object can be repaired by conventional means, harm done through aggravated damage cannot be repaired without some sort of supernatural agency unless the mundane object is trivial to repair: although a sorcerer's fireball may have burned a hole in a wall, mundane means will be sufficient to repair it.

An object's lost Structure points cannot be healed; they must be repaired. Doing so usually requires the Crafts Skill. The Attribute combined with the Skill depends on the task performed. Dexterity applies for delicate clockwork. Intelligence is applicable for innovation or design changes. Bonus points may be gained depending on the quality of any tools or the workshop used for the project. Repair is usually an extended action. Each success gained on a draw repairs one Structure point. Once sufficient Structure points are repaired, the object is back in working condition. The Storyteller declares the amount of time that passes per draw, based on the complexity of the task. Fixing a gun might involve draws made every half-hour, while repairing an engine could call for draws made every hour or even day. At the Storyteller's discretion, some broken objects may be declared irreparable.

Sample Objects

Baseball Bat: Durability 1 (reinforced to 2), Size 2, Structure 4, Damage 2

Board, 2"x4": Durability 1, Size 3, Structure 4, Damage 1

Cabinet, Wooden: Durability 1, Size 4, Structure 5, Damage 1

Chair, Wooden: Durability 1, Size 4, Structure 5, Damage 1

Coffin: Durability 1, Size 6, Structure 7, Damage 1

Crate, Wooden: Durability 1, Size 4, Structure 5, Damage 1

Door, Bank Vault: Durability 3 (reinforced to 10), Size 8, Structure 18, Damage 8

Door, Wooden (Exterior): Durability 2, Size 5, Structure 7, Damage 2

Door, Wooden (Interior): Durability 1, Size 5, Structure 6, Damage 1

Door, Metal (Security): Durability 3, Size 5, Structure 8, Damage 3

Fence, Chain-link: Durability 2, Size 4, Structure 6, Damage 2

Fence, Steel: Durability 3, Size 6, Structure 9, Damage 3

Lamppost, Steel: Durability 3, Size 8, Structure 11, Damage 3

Manhole Cover: Durability 3, Size 3, Structure 6, Damage 3

Steel Bars: Durability 3, Size 2, Structure 5, Damage 2

Tempered Steel: Durability 3, Size 2 (variable), Structure 5, Damage 2

Window: Durability 1, Size 3 (on average), Structure 4, Damage 1

Damage: Indicates how dangerous the item is when used as a weapon or to do harm. Damage is the lower of the item's Durability or Size. This rating is added to attack draws as a bonus to inflict harm. If the weapon is improvised, it suffers a −1 penalty. So, a manhole cover used as a weapon has a Damage of 3, but since it's an improvised weapon (it's not designed or weighted to be used in melee), it suffers a −1 penalty, for a total Damage of 2. Although some items may have Damage ratings listed, those don't apply to being wielded by characters – they denote the harm someone would take if a car were to knock down a lamppost, hitting a character, or if a vault door were to be blasted outward, knocking you down. As a rule of thumb, items with a Size of 5 or more can't be used as weapons.

BREAKING OBJECTS

It's easier to destroy than to create, and your character will probably want to destroy things relatively often if he ever gets into scrapes, or if he confronts things that humanity was never meant to face. The following are some examples of breaking items.

If an attack is staged on an object, successes achieved on the attack draw must exceed the Durability rating of the item to cause any Structure damage. So, if a wall has 1 Durability, any successes achieved in excess of one remove Structure points from the target.

Note that damaging and destroying an object isn't necessarily an all-or-nothing endeavor. Attacks on an item aren't always a matter of instant actions alone. Damage can be inflicted to a target over time through an extended action, if one can scratch the surface at all. Doing so assumes the attacker has the time to beat, batter or abuse the object. Points of Structure damage inflicted are accumulated until the item buckles and then breaks completely. If the attacker inflicts harm through unarmed attacks, remember that he incurs a single bashing wound per attack made on the target. Explosives and demolition gear are an excellent means to damaging and destroying objects instantaneously, if they're available.

Breaking down a door: Draw using a Strength + Stamina test pool. Each success gained in excess of the door's Durability is a point of Structure damage inflicted. Overcoming all of the door's Structure breaks it down completely. Exceeding Durability in damage done breaks the lock; the door remains on its hinges, but can be opened.

Holding back a door: Your character seeks to hold a door closed against others who want it open. Draw using a Strength + Stamina test pool. Successes earned are added to the door's Durability rating (which also increases its Structure). A holding character suffers half of any damage that exceeds the door's total Durability rating (that from the door itself and from the reinforcing character; fractions are rounded down). So, if your character holds a door with 1 Durability and two successes are achieved on your Strength + Stamina draw, the door's total Durability is 3. If an attack staged on the door nets five successes, the door suffers two damage and your character suffers one Health. These rules can also be applied to breaking and holding windows, cabinets and coffins. No more than two people can work together to break down or reinforce a normal-sized door.

If damage done to the door ever exceeds its total Durability (its own rating, plus points added by characters holding it), the door is forced open. If damage done ever exceeds the door's total Structure, the door is destroyed altogether.

Blowing up an object: Explosives must be acquired before they can go boom. Getting them is not an easy process, not even for characters with connections, and using high explosives in any serious volume is bound to attract persistent federal attention. Draw Intelligence + Science to configure explosives correctly, or Dexterity + Athletics to throw them where intended. Explosives have an inherent Damage rating that is inflicted automatically, and may also invoke a draw to do additional harm. See "He's Got C-4!", p. 244 in Chapter 7. That damage must exceed the target's Durability for the object to be harmed in the explosion.

Smashing one object into another: Your character rams one object into another with the intent to break the target. It's possible that either object could break, however. If the effort is made under stressful circumstances or the target resists, the Storyteller calls for a Strength + Weaponry draw as per normal combat (see Chapter 7), with any situational penalties applying to the attack. If there's no stress involved, the attack may be drawn without situational penalties. Add the Damage rating of the item wielded to your attack pool (-1 if the weapon is improvised — see above). Any successes achieved in excess of the target's Durability are suffered as damage and are subtracted from the target's Structure.

If insufficient successes are achieved in an attack draw to do a target harm (successes drawn are less than the target's Durability rating), the object used to make the attack may be broken, instead. Compare the successes drawn to the attacking item's Durability score. Any successes in excess of the item's Durability are incurred as damage by your character's tool.

Example: Pete's character Jimmy swings a baseball bat to break down an industrial-strength door. The door has 3 Durability. The bat has 2 Durability. Jimmy's attack draw nets three successes — not enough to do any appreciable harm to the door. The bat is damaged, though. The three successes drawn exceed the bat's Durability by one, so the bat loses one Structure point. It normally has 4 Structure and is now reduced to 3, but the bat can still be used normally. So, Pete's character keeps swinging. In a subsequent attack, Structure damage done to the bat rises to 3, which exceeds its Durability rating. The bat cracks and imposes a -1 penalty on Stack's remaining test pools. If four Structure points are ever incurred, the bat breaks altogether.

Were Pete to get one or two successes to damage the door, the door would be unaffected (it's Durability is 3). And yet, the bat would also go undamaged. One or two successes do not exceed the bat's 2 Durability.

Targeting items: Sometimes combatants use items such as swords in combat to defray attacks. Such weapons are used to deflect and redirect blows, rather than be the specific targets of them (see the "Weaponry Dodge" Merit, p. 138). That is, an attacker doesn't usually aim at an opponent's sword when trying to hurt that opponent. Thus, parrying weapons generally stand up to the abuse inflicted on them in combat. It's when they're the specific targets of attacks that they may be broken. In this case, an attacker specifically focuses on the item carried by his opponent. That might be a sword, but it could also be something carried in hand such as a videocassette. A normal attack test pool is formed, but the Storyteller imposes a penalty based on the size of the target (see "Specified Targets," p. 226). Any successes drawn are compared to the Durability of the item, with excess successes removed from the target's Structure. The target item might be damaged or destroyed as a result. Remember, if a tool or weapon is used to make the attack, and successes achieved do not exceed the target item's Durability, the attacking weapon may be the one to be damaged or broken (see above.)

Kicking out a grille: Draw Strength + Stamina. Successes gained must exceed the grille's Durability score to do it harm. Overcoming all of the grille's Structure points knocks it out completely. Exceeding Durability rating in total damage done bends the grille. In order for someone to crawl through a bent grille, Structure damage done to the target in excess of its Durability must also exceed the person's Size. Say a grille has 3 Durability and 10 Structure. Seven damage has been inflicted to the grille, which exceeds its Durability by four. Anyone who is Size 3 or lower may crawl through.

Falling objects: If one object falls into another, determine the damage done in the fall to both objects equally (see "Falling," p. 245). Add the Damage score of the opposing item to the falling damage suffered by each. Any total damage suffered in excess of an item's Durability is subtracted from the object's Structure. Thus, if a chair with Damage 1 falls on a statue with Damage 2, both take the same damage from the fall, but the chair suffers an additional two and the statue suffers an additional one. These totals are compared to the objects' respective Durability scores to see if they lose any Structure points.

When an object falls and lands on a person, treat the lowest of the person's Size or Armor rating (if any protective gear is worn) as his "Damage" score. That number is added to the abuse incurred by the falling item. So, if the aforementioned chair falls on a person (5 Size, 0 Armor), each party suffers the same falling damage (say, three points for a fall of nine yards). However, the person incurs an additional one damage from the chair's Damage rating, while the person adds no extra points to the chair's total. The person therefore suffers four damage and the chair suffers three.

Piercing Durability

No matter how many layers of protection are built into an item — say a tank or vault door — some invention can overcome them. It might be an armor-piercing bullet or a diamond-bit drill. Tools created to bypass Durability demand their own special rules. They ignore points of Durability equal to their rating, but do no extra damage. Thus, a diamond-bit drill rated 3 eliminates three Durability points in a vault door. Successes drawn to overcome the door are therefore compared to a diminished Durability score. In combat, the rating of an armor-piercing bullet diminishes the rating of any armor worn by a target.

Neither of these tools increases the damage done to the target, however. Their ratings are not added to dice pools for attack draws. They simply make the effort easier to accomplish.

Example: A vault door with a 10 Durability (reinforced steel) is the focus of intruders wielding a diamond-bit drill rated 3. The door's Durability is automatically reduced to 7. Successes achieved on a Dexterity + Larceny or Intelligence + Science draw must now exceed seven to do any damage to the door. At no point, however, is the drill's 3 rating added as bonus dice to a test pool.

In combat, an armor-piercing bullet rated 2 automatically reduces a target's armor by two for the purpose of making an attack draw. Two bonus points are not added to your attack pool. If a target wears no armor, your character's shot gains no special effects or bonuses from the ammunition used (the gun itself still applies a point bonus, though). See "Armor Piercing," p. 229 in Chapter 7 for more information.

In general, objects and vehicles are considered to have Durability ratings (which must be exceeded to cause damage to them). People and sentient targets who wear protective gear have armor ratings that are subtracted from attackers' test pools (see "Armor," p. 227). A person wearing a flak jacket is not considered to have a Durability rating, for example. The rating of his armor imposes a penalty to an attacker's test pool (see Chapter 7: Combat).

If you want to determine if someone beyond a barrier or inside an armored vehicle can be hurt, see "Cover," p. 223.

Equipment

The following items are indicative of just some of the gear that your character may acquire or use when dealing with the mysteries of the unseen world. The creatures that haunt the shadows may have miraculous capabilities, but modern technology can be used to even the odds somewhat. Sometimes beings in touch with humanity turn to these items to ply them against rivals, and some shepherd the way to new innovations that are *eventually* shared with the masses.

Unless otherwise noted, all relevant equipment must have an item card attached to it to show that it exists in-game. If a player does not possess an object or it's something that's not normally permitted to be carried in-game (such as a weapon), the item card serves as a prop for the object. Minor personal effects such as watches, wallets or jewelry do not normally require item cards. As a rule, any items that confer a game benefit (or penalty), allow the use of any special mehanics or that otherwise have a system effect should always require item cards. This can also apply to a number of commonly carried items that can have a strong impact on the progress of a story. Cell phones, laptops, cameras, PDAs and the like should require item cards or they are not considered to exist in-game even if the player has one one hand.

POOL BONUSES

Using equipment and tools to accomplish feats generally improves your character's chances of success. Gear is typically rated 1 to 5 in terms of quality, and that number of points is added to your test pool when pertinent actions are performed. For example, an attempt to break into a car involves Dexterity + Larceny. Your character can try it without any tools or devices, but the effort is difficult and probably crude (he busts out a window to get in). If your character uses a crowbar to help the effort, however, the Storyteller might grant a +1 bonus. You add one point to your test pool. If your character has a high-quality, precise set of tools designed specifically for breaking and entering, the Storyteller might grant you as much as a +3 or higher bonus. The better tools brought to bear are simply more effective than a crowbar.

Most conventional equipment offers +1 to +3 bonus points. These items are commercially available and not necessarily unusual. Note that using a tool does *not* automatically give you a benefit as opposed to working without one — the most basic, rudimentary or improvised of tools may add nothing to your character's efforts. A bent coat hanger isn't really so useful in giving your character a bonus at breaking into a car, for example, nor does a box of small bandages really help treat a serious gunshot wound.

Indeed, some activities require tools or devices to be attempted at all. In these cases, bonuses are gained only for using particularly good-quality equipment. You can't play in an orchestra without a violin, for example. Possessing any old violin doesn't grant your character an automatic bonus to Expression draws. When tools are required to perform a task, the instrument needs to be special to confer bonuses. A finely crafted antique piece might be +2, while a Stradivarius is +4 or +5. Likewise, you can't drive without a vehicle. A beat-up old sedan may offer no bonuses to Drive draws, while a new sports car can offer four.

Generally speaking, useful but simple items and tools offer a +1 bonus. Most specially made gear that's designed and fabricated for a particular purpose is rated +2. Say, a slimjim for auto theft. Tools at +3 are reliable and precise. Tools rated +4 and +5 are top-of-the-line, craftsman-made and probably expensive devices. Add one dot to the listed costs for items rated +4, and two for items rated +5. Thus, if your character has a set of lock picks (which normally have a cost of 3) with a bonus rating of +4, his tools have a cost of 4.

Equipment created or altered by supernatural or advanced means can be rated +4 or +5 (or higher!), but is probably always assigned an equal cost — if available for purchase at all. An inventor who works beyond the realm of ordinary human technology might design a universal lock set, for example. One tool can open doors of any kind. It confers a +5 bonus to B&E efforts, and costs five dots to be acquired. Of course, cost has little bearing if someone can steal or barter for an item rather than buy it.

The relative costs of items are listed in dots. Compare these to the dots in your character's Resources Merit (if any) to see if he can afford them with disposable cash. See "Resources," p. 144, for more information.

The items listed here tend to be somewhat unconventional — things you might not see everyday, but that your character might intentionally seek out. It's assumed that you can assess the utility (and bonuses) of ordinary items such as computers, household tools and handy items such as Swiss Army knives.

Pool bonuses can apply to instant actions — feats performed in the space of one turn. They can also apply to draws made in extended actions. A project occurs over a period of time, with draws made at intervals to gauge progress. Having tools (getting pool bonuses) definitely improves your character's chances of success at an extended action, and may help him accomplish it more quickly than without the gear.

When a failure on a chance draw occurs, something may have gone horribly wrong with the tools used. The Storyteller decides just what has happened. One of your character's picks could be broken, lost, hopelessly jammed in a door, or simply dropped making enough noise to draw attention. In the case of damaged or broken tools, consider their bonus ratings to diminish by one thereafter, along with their cost dots if they're sold.

Cost dots for equipment are ultimately relative assignments. In the free world where commerce is largely open, costs are as listed. In a politically or religiously oppressed locale, forbidden items are rare and more expensive. Illegal items in any region are certainly expensive and must be acquired through underground channels. Consider any illegal or black-market purchase to be at *least* one dot more expensive than indicated in these rules, if not higher. After all, it's a seller's market. There could also be a cost to life, limb and liberty for dealing with shady merchants, but that's for your Storyteller to decide.

NORMALIZING EQUIPMENT

Sooner or later, a player tries to procure exotic arms or equipment. Maybe he claims that his character has phosphorus rounds that burn a target, or something out of a science-fiction movie. He could claim that such exotic items do exist and can be ordered from a catalog, pieced together from plans available online, or cobbled together from existing items. Yet you don't want the game to become an arms race, and you want to keep all the characters on roughly the same level equipment-wise. So what's a Storyteller to do?

Ideas for handling such situations are listed below. Each has its own advantages and potential drawbacks. The default "tech level" of **Mind's Eye Theatre** is intended to be low, to help emphasize the horror and desperation inherent in the setting. That is, everyday, mundane items are probably available, while bizarre or unusual items probably are not. Characters — even supernatural ones — possessing all manner of exotic weapons and gizmos seriously detracts from the drama and turns a game into an arms race.

If nothing else, remember that just because an item has stats in a book or exists in reality does *not* mean a player is automatically entitled to have it for his character. All weapons, armor and equipment in a chronicle must be approved by the Storyteller. If she does not permit an item, it is not allowed. Period.

Default: Normal Equipment Only

This is no cop-out. The World of Darkness is designed to portray personal horror, not ultra-realistic modern espionage and warfare. This can sometimes limit player creativity when it comes to equipment, but it also levels the playing field because the players do not have to worry about one person gaining a big in-game advantage because he reads exotic scientific trade journals or *Soldier of Fortune*. By default, **Mind's Eye Theatre** characters are limited to "normal" items — mundane weapons and ammunition, not too much in the way of armor, what surveillance equipment and survival gear is commonly available, etc. It's not that more advanced technology doesn't exist, it just doesn't come into play, with the possible exception of rare storylines. As a rule of thumb, if the Storyteller hesitates even slightly before approving it, an item probably doesn't qualify.

Option 1: Advanced Equipment

This option pushes the envelope a bit to include some more high-tech gear, such as armor piercing ammunition, night vision goggles and other sophisticated gear, but stops well short of high explosives, most toxins, exotic ammunition (like phosphorus rounds), heavy weaponry (like machine guns), etc. Think of the upper limits of this kind of chronicle as being high-level police equipment, or mid-level military and espionage technology. It's not quite at the outright fantastic/devastating level of laser wristwatches or depleted uranium ammunition, but at the same time it's more sophisticated gear than the average person can typically acquire. This technology level is most likely to be found in games featuring characters with deep connections to the police, military, the espionage community or perhaps a very well-funded witch-hunting organization.

Option 2: Exotic Equipment

With this option, the players are pretty much free to bring any weaponry or equipment into game that they desire, provided their characters have the appropriate traits, Resources or other connections necessary to do so. This is the also the equipment level normally required to regularly bring uncommon poisons or high explosives into the game. This technology level is discouraged for World of Darkness games, as it tends to quickly replace the horror and mystery of the setting with a brutal arms race to acquire the most useful gear and the most powerful weaponry. However, troupes that wish to handle such unlimited access to technology are welcome to do so if that is their desire. Note that even at this level, it is *highly* recommended that truly powerful or outrageous items like nuclear/biological/chemical warheads or EMP generators be forbidden. Even in extremely liberal Mind's Eye Theatre games, some things are just too much.

Automotive Tools

Durability 2–3, Size 1–5, Structure variable, Cost • to • • • •

Function: Tools useful for working on vehicles and engines can range from handheld wrenches and pliers that can be used to perform minor jobs such as changing oil, to hydraulic lifts, diagnostic computers and complete garages. The Storyteller may rule that no tool that offers a bonus of +2 or less is any help on a significant repair job such as rebuilding an engine. A fully stocked machine shop is required for that (rated 3, 4 or 5). Otherwise, efforts to repair busted hoses or punctured radiators might be made with lesser tools. Bonus points are added to Dexterity or Intelligence + Crafts draws.

Climbing Gear

Durability 2, Size 2, Structure 4, Cost • •

Function: Ropes, bungees, pitons, hammers and clamps — the tools helpful in climbing a sheer surface, whether it's a mountainside or building. Bonus points are added to Strength + Athletics draws.

First-Aid Kit

Durability 1, Size 2, Structure 3, Cost • or • •

Function: Anything from your standard bandages-and-alcohol kit to an advanced set owned or carried by people such as EMT's who work in the medical profession or who anticipate serious work-related injuries. The kit's rating in bonus points is added to Dexterity + Medicine.

Flashlight

Durability 1, Size 1, Structure 2, Cost n/a

Function: Unlike most tools, flashlights don't offer bonus points. They simply diminish the effects of darkness, reducing the penalties of "Fighting Blind" (p. 227). Using a flashlight while performing actions makes the feats possible, but still challenging. Rather than be reduced to a Storyteller-controlled chance draw, you are still able to make your own draws, only at a penalty of –3 or –4 depending on the degree of darkness. So, if your character tries to shoot a target by flashlight, and he has 2 Dexterity, 3 Firearms and a gun rated 3, your test pool might add up to four points (2 + 3 + 3 - 4).

Alternatively, the Storyteller might decree that performing a task in the dark imposes a standard penalty of –3 and having a flashlight diminishes that penalty to –2.

No Resource dots are required to be able to afford a flashlight.

GASMASK

Durability 1, Size 2, Structure 3, Cost • •

Function: A device worn over the face and/or head that filters air, hopefully saving the wearer from airborne poisons or toxins. Bonus points (as many as four or five) can be added to Stamina-based draws to resist such threats.

GUNSMITHING KIT

Durability 2, Size 2, Structure 4, Cost • •

Function: The tools helpful in cleaning, maintaining and repairing firearms, from pistols to machineguns. Bonus points are added to Dexterity + Crafts draws.

LOCK PICKS

Durability 2, Size 1, Structure 3, Cost • • •

Function: A set of tools used to trip locks and open doors and windows. One kind could be intended for vehicles and another for buildings. The tools typically add points to Dexterity + Larceny draws.

MACE OR PEPPER SPRAY

Durability 1, Size 0, Structure 1, Cost n/a

Function: Contained in spray bottles that fit in the palm of the hand, these devices debilitate targets who are sprayed in the face. A Dexterity + Athletics draw is made at a –1 penalty to hit a target. Range is one pace maximum, and the target's Defense applies. If it is successful, all of the target's actions suffer a –5 penalty for the remainder of the scene as his senses are overwhelmed and breathing is made extremely difficult. A chance draw is not made to use a spray on a target over one pace away; the effort fails automatically. Beings that are no longer alive but that walk and talk are not affected by such devices, while other creatures with rapid recuperative abilities may still suffer the normal effects, but shake them off much more quickly than a human would. A single spray canister can be used three times before it's empty.

No Resource dots are required to be able to afford a spray.

NIGHTVISION GOGGLES

Durability 1, Size 1, Structure 2, Cost • •

Function: This headgear allows a wearer to see in darkness, eliminating penalties for operating blind. See "Fighting Blind," p. 227. Exposure to any bright light source while wearing the goggles actually causes blindness, imposing the Fighting Blind rules.

SILENCER

Durability 3, Size 1, Structure 4, Cost • • •

Function: Killers who try to work discretely can add silencers to their guns. These devices muffle (but do not eliminate) the noise made. Bystanders might still hear a shot fired with a successful Wits + Composure draw, with a penalty equal to the rating of the silencer. Some weapons such as revolvers and shotguns can't be fitted with silencers. Note that silencer ratings are not added to Dexterity + Firearms draws.

SURVEILLANCE EQUIPMENT

Durability 1, Size 3, Structure 4, Cost • • •

Function: Wiretaps, long-range cameras, listening devices — the things your character needs to spy on someone without being noticed. Small sets offer small bonuses, while large ones (that fill vans) have higher scores. Points can be added to Stealth-based draws to trail someone.

SURVIVAL GEAR

Durability 1–3, Size 1–4, Structure variable, Cost • to • • •

Function: Your character can be trapped or lost in the wilderness with a handful of tools such as a canteen and a sleeping bag (+1 bonus). Or he can bear an array of cutting-edge survival gear from a GPS receiver to a four-season tent to freeze-dried meals (+3 or more). Bonuses can be applied directly to Survival-based draws. Such equipment also forestalls penalties or damage normally inflicted upon your character by exposure (see "Temperature Extremes") for an additional hour per point of the equipment's rating. Thus, gear rated 2 spares your character action penalties for two hours before the effects of the environment kick in. Gear rating is also added to your character's Stamina + Resolve to determine how long he can go before suffering harm from exposure. Indeed, the Storyteller might decree that survival equipment rated 3 or higher might preserve your character from harm completely for days on end, assuming conditions aren't too severe. Gear rated 3 can keep a person active and alive for a few days under freezing conditions, for example. In general, assume that the rating of survival gear equals the number of days of food and water that the kit provides. After that period, your character must forage for food and water or go without (see "Deprivation," p. 241).

Chapter 7: Combat

From Hell's heart
I stab at thee;
for hate's sake
I spit my last breath
at thee.

— Herman Melville,
Moby Dick

What would a Storytelling game be without conflict? Storytelling is founded on dramatic and entertaining events. The essence of drama is conflict, whether it's a struggle with one's own flaws or competition between characters. The most extreme form of conflict is combat. Two or more characters fight, seeking to hurt or kill each other. In the World of Darkness, a bleak place where the wellbeing of others is taken for granted or utterly dismissed, violence is pervasive. All too often, problems are solved with violence. It might be a random mugging, an argument gone out of control, the result of road rage, or the frustration of an unfulfilling life vented on whoever gets in the way. Add to that reality the existence of strange and hidden beings that prey upon humanity, and violence is a fundamental part of life.

This chapter is dedicated to rules for combat. It covers everything from throwing punches to drawing a knife to opening up with a shotgun. While people certainly struggle with each other in the World of Darkness, some fight back against the things that stalk them. In turn, those creatures almost certainly wage secret wars among themselves.

Readers familiar with the **World of Darkness** Storytelling System rulebook will quickly notice some differences in this chapter. It is organized and presented a bit differently than its tabletop-roleplaying counterpart. This is no accident. **Mind's Eye Theatre** is an entirely different environment than tabletop play. The standard combat system has been streamlined to better suit this format. It's designed for quick if somewhat simplistic resolution of any fights that occur in a live-action roleplaying game.

Many factors addressed in the **World of Darkness Rulebook** are made optional rules here. This allows a Storyteller to use or ignore them at her discretion. That helps keep modifiers unobtrusive and maybe even eliminates need to consult the rulebook during play.

Don't despair if you're a Storyteller who likes combat to pack a bit more punch, however. There are optional rules here in abundance. They provide that extra detail on everything from automatic-weapon fire to grappling moves to range measurements. Such extra factors make for more rules to memorize, numbers to keep track of and time spent totaling modifiers; but some players don't mind the trade for more realistic combat. The default **Mind's Eye Theatre** combat system is simply intended to be as simple and quick as possible. Players should assume that no optional rules are in effect unless told otherwise by a Storyteller.

DESCRIBING THE ACTION

One of the main responsibilities of players involved in a combat scene is to make sure that everyone has an accurate mental picture of what's happening. Initiating combat carries responsibilities beyond bringing a katana and enough silver bullets to do the job. Environmental or circumstantial factors surrounding characters need to be described. Some may already be obvious through props, costumes and special effects. Players need to know the dangers their characters perceive. They need to know what's going on around them so that they can respond.

At the end of each combat turn, a Narrator or the characters involved should offer a *brief* descriptive re-cap of what has happened (or at least what other characters would know has happened). Such description should eliminate any confusion about what a particular character does. That way, players aren't confused about where others are and what they're doing. Whether a Narrator provides such description for everyone or players do it for themselves, these accounts should be as detailed and creative as possible. This is a chance to show off descriptive talents. It also keeps combat exciting, and perhaps most importantly turns a series of draws into a dramatic, and entertaining scene.

MEDIATION

Mind's Eye Theatre is a social game. Characters interact personally as players do. It therefore enjoys a unique way to resolve combat and other challenging situations. Mediation keeps play flowing smoothly and keeps long periods of test resolution from interrupting events. Before cards come out and battle ensues, all players involved in a scene are *highly* encouraged to discuss what's happening. That gives them the chance to resolve the conflict without resorting to cards. Doing so allows for the most dramatic and exciting combat possible, without worrying about bad draws or lucky breaks. Although such "social resolution" may seem like an unlikely step in combat, most of the time it is not nearly as unthinkable as it may appear. It simply requires that all players be both reasonable and creative about the situation.

Successful combat mediation involves balancing two factors: what players want for their characters and what their characters are capable of doing. It may seem that characters involved in a combat scene have motives that are downright incompatible. Two characters apparently bent on killing each other may not seem to have much room for mediation, after all. However, this is often not as true as it first seems. About the only outcome that players are unlikely to settle on is the death of a character. Yet this extreme result is less common then you might expect. Quite often, a player that initially intends to kill an enemy realizes that she is best served by her enemy's survival. Perhaps she can cow him into joining her cause instead, or she can force another character to get an entire group to back down or face dire consequences in the future.

Take a situation in which one player's character wants to kill another player's character. The target just wants to escape. A fair negotiation might result in the attacker roughing the victim up, but the target ultimately gets away. The intended victim's player might point out that the consequences of murder just aren't worth it. Possible legal problems or potential retribution by the victim's allies make it unrewarding. The victim's player could offer to spread word not to challenge the aggressor. By this negotiation, the attacker gets to display his prowess and send his enemy packing, while the subject lives to see another day. Furthermore, neither side has to deal with consequences like police action or the creation of a new character. Everyone benefits.

Negotiation as an alternative to combat can be as simple or involved as players' desire. Remember that while this is a resolution mechanic out-of-character, nothing says it can't be handled as in-game conversation as much as possible. Indeed, experienced players can often work negotiation into a scene rather seamlessly, its presence only apparent if they have to refer to traits and numbers as part of the process. If players wish to keep the negotiation process as in-character as possible, it is recommended that one party announce "Negotiation" at the beginning of the exchange to make sure the other players involved are also aware that this is system is being used, so no one mistakes the conversation for purely in-character banter. See the example below for an idea of how this discussion might go between two players.

Note that some players may still not want to reveal their characters' motives, but have trouble figuring out how to conduct the negotiation process without doing so. That's fine. Simply talk in terms of the results your character hopes for rather than revealing the reasons and intentions behind them.

SAMPLE MEDIATION DIALOGUE

In this example, Player 1's character springs a surprise attack on Player 2 as his character enters a secluded area away from the rest of the group. Before they pull out cards, they try mediation, demonstrating the essence of the negotiation system. Two characters with different motivations can reach a satisfactory result for both of them by spending a minute or two discussing the matter.

Player 1: "I'm going to kill you!"

Player 2: "Whoa! Negotiation?"

Player 1: "Sure."

Player 2: "Wh-Why do you want to kill me?"

Player 1: "I want you dead for making fun of me in front of the rest of the group. That's going to be your last mistake, you coward."

Player 2: "I understand — but honestly, killing me really won't help you. The rest of the group will find out, and then you'll be in jail or stuck on your own with all the monsters out there. So what do you say we just call it even with an apology from me and a nice scary warning from you? I guarantee I've gotten the message!"

Player 1: "Nice try, but that won't quite cut it. I think it's time someone taught you a lesson that you'll remember for a long time. I've been training pretty hard lately, so this is going to hurt. A lot."

Player 2: "Ouch. Guess I should've taken those self-defense classes after all. I guess I don't have much chance of a chance, so go ahead, get it over with. Break my arm or something — just not the face, OK?"

Player 1: "Sounds good to me. We'll call that two levels of lethal damage, plus you can't use that arm and have a -2 penalty on all actions that normally take two hands until the next chapter?"

Player 2: "Rough, but considering you've got me pretty thoroughly outmuscled, I'll say that's fair."

Player 1: "Cool. Ready to take some pain?"

Player 2: "OK. Let's do some extra staging, real quick. Stand behind me, and I'll put my arm behind my back like this to simulate an arm hold. So when you want your character to break my character's arm, I give you permission to tap my palm as the signal. Until then, we'll keep playing this scene out. Sound good?"

Player 1: "Fine with me. Now about those jokes you were telling..."

Adjudicating Negotiation

Characters' traits can impact the negotiation process, as seen in the preceding example. Dots are not nearly as important as character motivations, though. A successful, motive-based mediation can easily result in an outcome that satisfies everyone involved. If the terms contradict characters' raw traits, so be it. A mediation that reflects the traits represented but that leaves players involved unhappy is a failure. As with motivations, if players want to keep their actual trait dots secret, they may do so. Simply refer to characters' traits in descriptive terms. For example, "I'm a skilled marksman" or "I'm really not that tough."

Regardless of whether traits are revealed or not, a character who is outmatched by his opponent should accept that fact. A player must consider how likely it is that his opponent can, say, land a blow. If the defender has Defense 2, no combat Skills and no powers to protect himself, he should realize that it's not really fair or reasonable for him to demand to just walk away untouched when confronted by a capable attacker. For her part, the character with the upper hand should not always be compelled to insist on outcomes based on the fullest extent of her potential. Just because her character with Strength 5 and Brawl 4 *can* kill her opponent doesn't mean she *must*.

Mediation can also take place in conflicts involving Storyteller characters, assuming all parties are willing. Indeed, it's recommended that characters work with a Narrator to mediate battles against nameless thugs and other lesser threats. The Narrator acts on behalf of the thugs, making determinations based on their general strengths and weaknesses as opposed to more in-depth consideration of traits and the like. It's acceptable to have players' characters get past fairly large crowds of extras in this fashion — doing so saves time and builds a dramatic atmosphere. Characters can show off some of their prowess dispatching lesser enemies. That saves the excitement and uncertain outcome of the drawing process for confrontations with the real villains.

Note that this system does not mean to replace purely roleplayed outcomes. Characters can always attempt to a mediate a conflict in-game before it erupts into violence. Indeed, if the players can stay entirely in character and beg, threaten, or persuade their opponent not to harm them without invoking negotiation, that's not only the default assumption, but a wonderful outcome besides. In-character mediation does not use the rules and guidelines presented in this section.mediation takes place entirely out-of-character. This exchange is between the players involved in the scene as opposed to their characters.

Mediation Results

At the conclusion of mediation, players have agreed on the actions taken and their results, such as damage. They then go back and roleplay the events agreed upon. Needless to say, agreements made are good-faith arrangements. An agreement is reached to increase the drama and speed the flow of the game. Mediation is *not* a tool for crafty players to confound others in legalese. The spirit, not the letter of an agreement is always most important if a dispute arises. Do not "rules lawyer" another player by using the literal terms of an agreement.

Since mediation is an entirely voluntary system, players are naturally expected to abide by any agreements they make. Those attempting to take different actions should be disciplined. There can be extenuating circumstances, however. If a combat changes in a drastic, unforeseen way, the negotiated outcome may need to change accordingly. It's one thing if you improvise a little, alter what you agreed to do but still get the same message across, or to act slightly different but still achieve the final result. It's something else entirely to try to kill a character you agreed to let escape, or to shout a warning when you agreed to stay silent. The former possibilities are simply the spontaneous nature of live-action roleplaying. The latter are cheating and agreement breaking.

Obviously, mediated agreements apply to only to a specific conflict. *Game system* consequences such as damage do not fade until they are fixed within the system. *Roleplaying* consequences depend entirely on the characters involved. Using the two characters from the interaction, above, Player 2's character would be free to make fun of Player 1's character again later if he desired. That would be the *character* going back on his word in-game. Player 2 still upheld the out-of-game agreement for that conflict. If Player 2 decided his character would fight back after agreeing not to, the player would be breaking the mediation agreement. This is an excellent reason to be clear about the difference between in-character agreements and player agreements, to make sure everyone knows what's expected.

TROUBLESHOOTING MEDIATION

Remember, players cannot have their characters use any knowledge gained during such conversations in play. That is, unless the result of the negotiation reveals that information. Say a negotiation displays the full extent of the fighting prowess of a character with Weaponry 4, as she performs an impressive weapon flourish to intimidate an opponent. It's not a stretch for other characters involved to talk about how skilled that character is with a knife after such a display. Now, let's say the mediation resulted in the character with Weaponry 4 never even threatening to pull her blades. It would be cheating for another player to have his character suddenly know that his opponent is skilled at wielding melee weapons.

Since it is an out-of-character negotiation, players are also expected to be honest during the mediation process. A player may not exaggerate her character's capabilities as part of the process. However, she *is* allowed to undersell her character's talents if she likes, and pretend that she is weaker than she actually is. She might wish to keep her character's true strength or skill hidden until a later time, for example. (Of course, underselling herself too much might convince an opponent to go to cards and take a shot after all, so this can be a risky tactic at times.) She cannot, however, attempt to bluff the negotiation by claiming her character has higher traits than she actually possesses. Doing so is cheating, and wrong.

Mediation assumes that two or more characters are in conflict with each other, whether a physical fight, a social showdown or even a contest of supernatural powers. Therefore, it cannot be used for static actions such as breaking down a locked door, nor can it be used between two characters who work together to get around the need for ordinary draws. Say that Player A has access to a magic ritual that benefits Player B, but it's very risky, can be attempted only once per night, and it has a high chance of failure. The two of them cannot use mediation to ditch the game mechanics and circumvent the risk. They are not in conflict and therefore mediation does not apply. If, however, Players A and B are fighting a common enemy, they may use negotiation because the other players involved have to agree to the results.

Mediation is an optional part of combat. No player can be forced to mediate a conflict. A player or Narrator can also opt to end negotiation and go to regular systems at any time. Some players enjoy the rush and unpredictability of relying on traits and systems to determine the results of actions. Others might feel that a circumstance offers no room for negotiation. Even well-intentioned players might find that they can't reach a solution. They can then fall back to standard game rules to resolve the situation.

Lastly, remember that while the word "happy" has been used resolutions made, it's a relative term when it comes to mediation. If every character came out smiling without a scratch, there wouldn't be any conflict. Nobody *likes* his character being hurt or suffering some setback. As mature individuals, players are expected to recognize that the World of Darkness is a dangerous place. Sometimes their characters are going to suffer losses or get hurt in one sense or another. With the negotiation process, they at least have a chance to actively decide what happens to them. They can also make it dramatic and interesting to roleplay. So "happy" means *players* involved are satisfied with the result of the mediation, even if their *characters* are not.

Combat Time

As soon as one player initiates a combat test, it's generally best to make a general announcement of "Combat!" Doing so lets players in the immediate area know what's going on. At that point, play is considered frozen in order to determine who's involved in the fight. This is the time to call for Initiative draws. Once Initiative has been established, combat time usually proceeds in turns unless otherwise noted. Anyone whose character is not engaged in combat should be polite and not distract players in combat. This helps achieve the fastest resolution possible. Bystanders should also pay attention so they're aware of what's happening. They may wish to get involved later in the fight. If a Narrator declares a few moments of "Real time," players may roleplay and interact before combat time resumes. Once a fight ends, someone should announce, "Combat time off!" Regular, real-time roleplaying then resumes.

Combat Turns

Combat scenes can sometimes be extremely confusing. So much can go on at one time that keeping all actions and results straight is a challenge. Combat usually progresses through a series of three-second turns. The system for handling combat turns is further divided into two basic stages: initiative and attack. (For the other measurements of time that can be used in your game, see "Time" on p. 152.)

INITIATIVE

Initiative is used to determine who acts when in combat. At the beginning of a fight, draw a card for your character and add his Dexterity and Composure dots to the result. The total is his standing in the Initiative for the entire combat.

The Storyteller draws and records Initiative for any characters she controls. All players' totals make up the Initiative roster, in order from highest to lowest. He with highest has the best command of what's going on. He acts quickly or doesn't lose his cool. She with the lowest Initiative cannot keep up with events or has trouble making a decision.

If there's a tie between players, compare their Initiative scores (including any Merits or supernatural bonuses). The highest total breaks the tie. If there's still a tie, a card is drawn for each rival with the highest draw winning. If even card draws result in a tie, continue drawing until an order is established.

Example: *Joshua Musgrove has Dexterity 3 and Composure 2. He draws a 6 for Initiative, for a total of 11. One of the Storyteller's thugs also gets an Initiative total of 11. Their respective Dexterity and Composure totals are both 5. A card is drawn for each. Both get a 3. Another card is drawn for each, this time with a 4 for Joshua and an 8 for the Storyteller. The thug acts before Joshua throughout the fight.*

DELAYING ACTIONS

Your character does not have to act in the order of his Initiative standing. He could refrain from acting until something happens. Maybe he waits until an opponent shows his face, or he wants to sprint across the street during a lull in the shooting. In this case, your character delays his position in the Initiative roster, activating it when you choose. His Initiative rank for the turn changes to that at which he acts. This doesn't mean that you can pre-empt another character's action to prevent that action from taking place unless you go on an Initiative rank higher than that character and state that you wish to do so before that player declares his action.

Example: *Chris' character has an Initiative rank of 10, but he holds his action in a turn. If Lucci's character has an Initiative rank of 6 and Chris acts immediately after him, the Storyteller slots Chris in at 5.*

If Chris had prepared an action and said, "My character hits Lucci's if he attacks," then Chris' character goes on 7, right before Lucci's character.

If two or more characters delay their actions until the same moment in a turn, resolve their order as if their Initiative totals had tied.

A delayed action *can* be held over into the next turn for a temporary benefit. The delaying character sacrifices his action in the first turn (he can do nothing except move up to his Acting Speed) in order to act *any* time he chooses in the next turn. The player still has to declare what he wants his character to react to before the action takes place, otherwise he's slotted in after the action in question, as above.

Example: *Savastano and Marcus are in a fight. Savastano has an Initiative of 12 and Marcus has an Initiative of 8. From turn to turn, Savastano always act before Marcus. If he wants to, however, Marcus can forfeit his action in turn one. He can do nothing but move up to his Acting Speed. In the next turn, he can act at any point in the Initiative roster that he likes. He acts on Initiative 13 to precede Savastano. In turn three, Marcus' Initiative ranking returns to 8. If he wants to "get the jump" on Savastano again, he has to forfeit an action again.*

A character might delay an action from one turn to the next in order to attack a specific opponent. A gunman might wait for a target to cross a street, for example.

SURPRISE

A fight doesn't always start with two or more would-be combatants standing face to face, knowing what's about to happen. Sure, that occurs when tensions rise through dialogue. A stand-up fight is the very foundation of a duel, showdown or an invitation to step outside. All participants realize that a physical struggle is about to commence, and all can react.

Other times, a fight gets started with at least one party caught by surprise. Someone arranges an ambush for a victim or enemies encounter one another by accident. Under those circumstances, only the quick and the alert react in time to act or defend themselves. Any time an ambushing party feels that it meets this condition, it may declare "Surprise" and then Initiative is determined. A Narrator or other parties involved need to agree that surprise is possible. Any characters potentially being surprised must check to see if they can respond. Wits + Composure is drawn for characters who are ambushed. Any

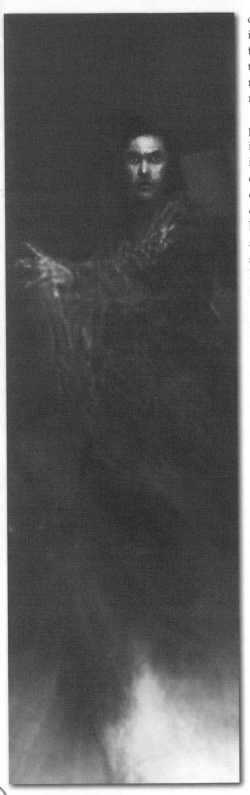

character for whom no successes are drawn is taken unawares and cannot act in the first turn of combat. Initiative is drawn for them normally in the next turn. One or more successes allow a character to behave normally and respond to the encounter.

A Narrator may very impose penalties on a surprise test if the attack is particularly well planned. For example, if assailants are thoroughly hidden or disguised, or target players react with obvious shock to the announcement of an attack. Someone attacking from behind and from invisibility would almost certainly have the element of surprise, requiring a test, unless the target had a very good reason to believe that an invisible assailant might lurk nearby.

A character taken by surprise has no Defense in the first turn of combat. His Defense trait is not subtracted from attackers' test pools. His armor (if any) still is, though.

Targets already involved in combat cannot normally be ambushed. It doesn't matter where an attack originates. Furthermore, a certain amount of dramatic license must be considered when declaring surprise. Players should remember that in live-action, characters might generally hide much better than players can, especially since playing areas tend to be rather small and relatively well lit for safety reasons.

If a character suspects an ambush, the surprise draw made for him may get a bonus. It is generally best to inform a Narrator or an impartial third party of any suspicions before entering the scene in question. The result is a record that the character knew what he was walking into. A Narrator may also give subjects a bonus to react if an ambush is ill prepared or poorly executed, typically between +1 to +3 depending on just how inept the attack really is.

In order to count as prepared for an ambush, players must demonstrate reasonably *specific* knowledge of the impending danger. Simply saying vague and general things like, "I have a bad feeling about this," or "I think we're going to get jumped along the way," isn't enough. If such open-ended predictions were considered prepared, the paranoid would never suffer from surprise attack.

FAIR ESCAPE

Sometimes all a character wants to do is get out of a dangerous situation. Perhaps she has a supernatural power that grants superior speed or she can teleport out of harm's way. Maybe she's just willing to put on a burst of speed and hope for the best. Regardless of how she intends to make an exit, fair escape determines if a character can avoid dangerous in-game situations. It allows her to get out of the way without being hurt. Sometimes, the "fishbowl" phenomenon of a small play areas can be a hindrance. Fair escape attempts to balance out this drawback, by allowing a character to evade someone without a player needing to run amok to do so.

Anytime you see a character approach and with whom you do not wish to interact, you may declare "Fair escape" to leave the area without being pursued. This assumes that your opponent is not already within conversational distance. Use common sense in nightclubs and other very loud places. If he is within that range, he may counter your attempt to flee. To do this, he initiates a regular combat action. You must take your chances using the Foot Chase rules in the Skills Chapter.

For example, suppose your character is attending a posh society party, when all of a sudden he spots a hated rival approaching him from across the room. Now, in-game the place is supposed to be a grand ballroom packed with a couple hundred members of the city's upper crust, but out-of-game it is a small student center activity room and there's only the thirty other players in there. To simulate that your character would be able to get away in the crowd well before your rival arrives, you may call a "fair escape" to slip away without being challenged. It also avoids the need to actually run through the play area in an unsafe fashion just to avoid your enemy.

There are other circumstances that can affect the ability to declare a fair escape, as listed below. The Narrator ultimately has final say on when fair escape applies. The maneuver cannot be declared once a character has been targeted with a combat challenge in a turn. Nor can a character usually fair escape from the middle of a melee. She must work to the edge of the fight and have some way to leave the area before she may attempt a complete departure.

• Situations like ambushes, where all exits are blocked, can negate use of fair escape. Use common sense.

• If an opponent has supernatural powers that increase his Running Speed, he may activate them to negate fair escape. If both characters have supernatural Speed, whoever has the highest relevant trait wins.

• Characters who possess supernatural powers of invisibility may attempt to use them to achieve fair escape. They must do so before a combat turn begins. If a pursuing character who has the ability to see through this invisibility succeeds in breaking it, the fair escape is negated.

• Certain other supernatural powers such as teleportation, stepping into parallel realms of existence and the like may allow the user to achieve fair escape.

• Ranged weapons are not normally sufficient to cancel fair escape. Otherwise, the rule would be useless against anyone with a gun. The Storyteller may still rule that certain powerful attacks or types of terrain such as flat, featureless land may allow attacking characters to use ranged attacks to cancel fair escape.

The fair-escape rule is intended to avoid accidents with players running around in a small play area, and to help the story move quickly and smoothly. If it takes several minutes to explain why a fair escape is justified, it probably isn't justified. Also, note that fair escape normally functions despite any differences in the Running Speeds of parties involved. That is, unless the Storyteller wishes to use the optional foot pursuit rules. In which case, the attacker may declare his Running Speed against the target's and attempt to initiate a foot pursuit to counter a fair escape.

Example: *Orlando and Bradley are in a fight. Orlando has a supernatural power enhancing his speed rated at • • • and Bradley has the exact same power. If Orlando is in front of Bradley and can conceivably take a straight route to an exit without having to move past Bradley, he will be able to declare fair escape since Bradley doesn't have the ability to catch up with him. If Bradley had a supernatural speed rated at • • • •, Orlando wouldn't be able to declare fair escape.*

ATTACK

An attack draw determines if your character manages to strike and harm his intended target. The type of attack he launches determines the test pool that you draw, as follows.

• **Close Combat:** Up close and personal, this includes unarmed combat (Strength + Brawl) and melee (Strength + Weaponry). Unarmed combat includes something as raucous as a barroom fight or something as organized as a boxing match. Opposing characters use their bodies to fight and must be within reach of each other. During melee, opponents use hand-held weapons. These may include knives, broken bottles, tire irons, swords or hastily snatched chairs. Maximum melee distance ranges from one to two steps.

Note that the Fighting Finesse Merit (see p. 133) may allow an attacker to use Dexterity instead of Strength with Weaponry. Your character uses precision rather than brute force to strike home and supernatural means of strength enhancement can't be used in conjunction with that Merit. The intent is still to inflict harm, though.

• **Ranged Combat:** This type of armed combat involves projectile weapons (Dexterity + Firearms) such as guns, crossbows or spear guns. Or it involves thrown objects (Dexterity + Athletics). Range for firearms varies based on the weapon. Range for thrown weapons depends on the attacker's capabilities. (See "Throwing," p. 74.) In either case, the target must be in sight.

ATTACK TEST POOLS

All combat actions require a successful draw to hit and do harm. As with any other draw, your character's Attribute and Skill dots are combined as the basis for your test pool. For example, Strength of 3 and Brawl of 2 adds to five points. This test pool represents your character's raw combat potential.

Other factors apply, however, such as any weapons he wields or special effects that he might use. That is, a number of bonus points are added to your pool equal to the rating of the tool or effect used. So, a sword rated 3 adds three bonus points to your pool. A mysterious supernatural trick that benefits your character's attack may add four. These modifiers increase the total number in your pool, making it more likely that your character succeeds.

Meanwhile, your character's target probably tries to avoid being harmed, and may wear protective gear of some kind. In close combat, the target's Defense trait and the rating of any applicable armor worn is subtracted from your attack test pool. If penalties imposed on your character's attack exceed your character's Attribute + Skill + any bonuses involved, the action is exceptionally challenging. The only way to accomplish it at this point is to make a successful chance draw (see p. 164).

Example: *The aforementioned character brings a sword into close combat. His 3 Strength and 2 Weaponry give him a starting pool of five. His sword, rated 3, adds three more. His opponent has a Defense of 4 and wears armor rated 1. That means five points are removed from the attacker's pool. The attacker is left with a base of three two which a draw is added.*

In ranged combat, you calculate test pools in much the same way. The attacker's Dexterity and Firearms (or Athletics for a thrown weapon) are combined. The rating of the gun or weapon used is then added to that pool.

Example: *If your character has Dexterity 2 and Firearms 1, you have three in your pool. If she fires a gun rated 4, four more are added for a total of seven.*

Firearms and Close Combat: a target's Defense does not usually apply. It's not subtracted from the attacker's pool. People don't try to avoid arrows or bullets like they do punches or sword swings. They run and look for protection, instead (see "Avoiding Getting Shot," p. 222). The exception is if Firearms-based attacks are staged within close-combat range (within a step or two).

A target's armor does apply against ranged attacks.

Example: *Continuing from above, the Defense score of the target is not subtracted from the test pool of your character's Firearms-based ranged attack. His one point of armor is, however. Assuming the target stands stock still, without diving for cover, your test pool loses only one point. You're left with six in your pool.*

A target's Defense does apply against thrown attacks made by drawing Dexterity + Athletics, such as with a rock or spear.

Optional Rule: Circumstance Factors

Beyond a target's Defense and/or armor rating, other conditions can affect your character's efforts in combat. Extreme weather might make it difficult to stand or draw a bead on an enemy. Darkness could obscure vision. The Storyteller or Narrator decides what "ratings" these environmental conditions have, which are subtracted from attack draws. This chapter, Chapter 3 and Chapter 6 all discuss a variety of circumstances that might diminish attack test pools. It's possible for some conditions or events to be extremely debilitating, inhibiting your character's ability to function. The effects of wounds, poisons, drugs, diseases and vicious supernatural powers may apply.

It's also possible for circumstantial conditions to improve your character's chances of making a successful attack. You already gain bonus points for your character's use of a weapon or special effect. In addition, the Storyteller can announce extra benefits. Maybe your character's hand is guided by a supernatural spell or he has a scope on his rifle. These conditions grant you bonuses, the number usually being stated in these rules or decided by a Narrator or Storyteller.

If no Narrator or Storyteller is present to manage a combat, assume that no circumstance modifiers apply. Only count those modifiers defined as the results of capabilities or powers, or which are concretely covered in regular systems, such as wound penalties, cover or blindness modifiers. If a given modifier relies mostly or entirely on Storyteller judgment, such as weather conditions, and its value has not been defined beforehand, players should either reach a common agreement or ignore it completely.

The Rule of Five

As stated in Chapter 6, each tool, weapon or circumstance does not normally add or subtract more than five from any pool. Such ratings range from one to five. Only truly impressive phenomena or devious supernatural tricks may increase or decrease modifiers to more than five, and the Storyteller usually dictates when that happens.

DAMAGE

The number of successes that you get on your attack draw determines the amount of damage that your character does. Each success inflicts one Health point of damage.

Example: *You have a pool of six for your character to stab an opponent and you draw a 9, for a total of 15. You get two successes. Your character's opponent therefore loses two Health points.*

The nature of the attack or the weapon doing the damage determines what type of damage is dealt (see "Damage Types").

If you get no successes on your attack draw, your character does no harm to his target. The attack misses altogether or is ineffectual.

After you determine the damage that your character inflicts upon her target, either you or a Narrator describes the damage to those present. Be creative! Rather than simply say, "Okay, I hit you and you lose three Health," make events more interesting. Instead say, "I plunge the knife into your dead flesh and pull upward, wrenching until the blade hits bone." By being evocative, you help create atmosphere. This entertains everyone on the scene and lends a sense of narrative continuity to what would otherwise be a series of draws.

Just remember that your descriptions cannot introduce or enforce any in-game effects that you didn't earn with your attack. For instance, you cannot say "I knock you off your feet" as part of your description if your character didn't actually use a knockdown attack (see p. 230), because that particular result has its own specific set of rules and consequences that must be accomplished through special maneuvers.

DAMAGE FOR FLAVOR

If your opponent specifically agrees to it, you can achieve the results of combat actions without performing "official" maneuvers, all in the name of "flavor" for the scene. While such effects occur in-game, your opponent doesn't suffer the usual results. You essentially expand the possibilities of events to make the game more vivid and exciting. Maybe your opponent thinks it would be cool if her character is knocked off her feet with a supernaturally powerful punch. She might allow you to achieve that effect, even if your character doesn't use a power that inflicts a knockdown effect. If so, she should be allowed to get back on her feet without losing her action for the turn.

The result can be some highly cinematic and impressive fights without the normal systems and modifiers. This approach keeps combat mechanics simple, and combat itself exciting, allowing players to use their creative potential without worrying about rules.

Naturally, not all forms of damage or other combat repercussions can be achieved using such cinematic storytelling. If it's too difficult to explain how a type of damage can be inflicted in this fashion, consider it impossible under those circumstances. For example, it's hard to justify how slicing off an arm or permanently blinding an opponent can really be "just for show."

DAMAGE LIMITS

While draw successes normally suffice to determine the amount of damage delivered in an attack, there is an upper limit to how much harm that can be inflicted to avoid "one-shot kills" and other fluke results. Use the highest trait available out of the relevant base Attribute or Skill applied, or based on the weapon's damage rating (if any) to determine the damage limit for the attack. So, if a character with Dexterity 2 and Firearms 1 uses a gun with damage rating of 4, he can inflict a maximum of four points of damage per attack (the highest value of the set). After all, even an average marksman can still put large holes in people with a powerful gun.

Or a wizened old sensei with Strength 2 and Brawl 5 has a damage limit of five, because his exceptional training allows him to make more devastating strikes than his humble physical stature might suggest.

And character with Dexterity 5 or Firearms 5 who uses a gun with a damage rating of 4 still has a damage limit of five, because his natural accuracy or lethal aim makes that weapon ever more deadly.

Note that supernatural means of enhancing an Attribute, Skill or weapon don't increase the base statistic used for establishing damage limits unless a power specifically states otherwise. The sole exception is the supernatural shifting ability of werewolves – the additional Strength granted to them by their alternate shapes does increase the limits for inflicting physical damage from melee weapons, brawling attacks or thrown objects. If this rule inspires players to boost their raw Physical Attributes for the sole reason of always inflicting a great deal of damage in combat, Storytellers may choose to determine damage limits on Skills and damage ratings alone. For supernatural attacks, the same limitation applies. If a voodoo practitioner uses his voodoo doll to shoot a lance of stabbing agony through a victim's head, the amount of damage he can inflict with a single ritual or a single supernatural attack is limited by the highest of his applicable Attribute, Skill or relevant sorcery rating.

Players should remember that damage limits exist because **Mind's Eye Theatre** is intended mainly as a social game. Roleplaying comes before action.

Combat Summary

Stage Zero: Mediation

If players involved in combat can come to mutual agreement about the outcome of the conflict, they may apply those results. Then, describe and roleplay the combat within the bounds of **Mind's Eye Theatre** safety and decorum. If a Narrator or the players decide that regular combat is required, combat proceeds to the next stage.

Stage One: Initiative

• Initiative draw: The result of a card draw + Dexterity + Composure. The character with the highest Initiative performs her action first. In any given turn, you may yield your character's action until later in the Initiative roster or into the next turn.

Stage Two: Attack

• Unarmed close combat: Strength + Brawl, minus target's Defense and armor

• Armed close combat: Strength + Weaponry, minus target's Defense and armor

• Ranged combat (guns and bows): Dexterity + Firearms, minus target's armor

• Ranged combat (thrown weapons): Dexterity + Athletics, minus target's Defense and armor

Add bonuses based on weapon used or effect performed, and then subtract penalties for circumstance conditions. Draw a card and add it to your remaining test pool against standard difficulty of 10. Normal intervals of success apply.

Attackers reduced to a zero pool make a chance draw.

Stage Three: Resolution

Each success on the attack draw equates to a Health point of damage inflicted to a limit based on the attacker's traits. Type of damage inflicted is determined by the nature of the attack.

The aggressor or Narrator describes the attack and wound in narrative terms, subject to the limitations of the attack itself.

DAMAGE TYPES

Each success gained on your attack draw inflicts one Health point of damage to a victim. Based on the nature of the attack, one of three different types of injury results.

• **Bashing:** Your character punches, hits with a blunt instrument or otherwise pummels her victim. This type of damage probably doesn't kill the target instantly, though repeated application could. Bashing damage heals fairly quickly (see p. 240 for more details).

• **Lethal:** Gunshots, blades and even crushing damage may prove fatal. Lethal injuries take quite a while to heal for ordinary people.

Note that firearm attacks that normally deliver lethal damage do only bashing damage to vampires. The creatures are undead; their organs are inert, their blood is congealed. Their bodies simply don't suffer harm like those of the living. Other supernatural creatures may likewise convert certain forms of lethal damage to bashing. Such alterations will be described as part of the creature's physiology.

• **Aggravated:** Different beings are vulnerable to different forms of attack, such as vampires to fire or werewolves to silver. Such assaults inflict aggravated damage, which those beings heal very slowly. Humans are not especially vulnerable to certain kinds of attacks. Fire or a silver dagger does lethal damage to them, for example. Some supernatural effects can inflict aggravated harm on ordinary folks, however. Wizards' spells or vampires' blood-based powers can cause injuries to normal people that take extensive time to heal. Any person or being who is so badly injured that she is comatose, bleeding to death or fading altogether also incurs aggravated wounds. Therefore, all denizens of the World of Darkness are subject to aggravated damage under one circumstance or another.

ZERO TEST POOL TO ATTACK

If a target's Defense, armor or other factors reduce your attack test pool to zero, you still get to make a chance draw to pull off a long-shot attack. Any successes gained inflict

Health points of damage on the target, as usual. See "The Chance Draw" in Chapter 6 for complete details.

MASS COMBAT

Sooner or later, a large group of characters will decide to mix it up. Given the number of players that attend many live-action games, the thought of running such huge fight scenes can cause Storytellers no small amount of anxiety. And yet, players and Storytelling staff who cooperate and avoid needless rules disputes can get through even the largest combat scene quickly and easily.

Both players and Narrators have a responsibility to help move these scenes along. Players should remain as quiet and attentive as possible so they know what's going on and can act quickly and react to attacks and Initiative changes. It helps even more to prepare your character's actions ahead of time.

Narrators can speed the process along by anticipating points at which large fights might take place. They can therefore have the materials needed on hand. That includes pens and paper to draw up an Initiative roster, combat cards with lists of common modifiers, and item cards for weapons. In addition, Narrators should do their best to keep the action moving, with a minimum of rules debate. (Players with concerns may take them up after combat unless a situation is truly dire.) Narrators need to do all this while still doing their best to describe what goes on. Players need to feel as though events involve more than just a series of card draws and rules calls.

The following steps help everyone resolve mass combats quickly, with a balance of action and description.

Step Zero: Upkeep (Optional)

This step occurs as soon as a new turn is declared but before any actions are performed. Make sure any supernatural powers that have ongoing costs and/or durations are addressed. See that continuous damage and similar effects are adjudicated. Acknowledge any characters approaching the narrative perimeter (see below). Announce characters who join the fight. Note any characters struggling to stay conscious. Perform any bookkeeping required by the capabilities or powers used in the scene.

You may also initiate mediation (see p. 200) at this stage, if parties involved are willing as an alternative to conventional combat.

Step One: Determine Targets

Before learning the order in which characters act, it's best to find out who they act against. The simplest way to do this is to count to three, at which everyone points at the person he or she acts against. If a character targets multiple opponents, the player may point with both hands or declare her intentions to a Narrator. The players of characters who target no one, such as those who dodge, should point at themselves.

As a general rule, no more than five people should be allowed to attack a single target at one time. Possible exceptions can be made for targets who are particularly large or otherwise vulnerable.

At a Narrator's discretion, anyone who is not targeted by another character may declare a fair escape, provided he is near the edge of the battle and has the means to flee the area.

Step Two: Initiative Roster

Have players draw Initiative (see p. 100).

It helps to keep track of Initiative on a sheet of paper. Narrators can use this paper to note who does what. Such notes help keep track of complications such as held actions (p. 205).

Remember that some actions such as dodging or going prone may take place outside the normal Initiative order. Also, if you use the optional ongoing Initiative rule, you must make a new Initiative draw each turn.

Step Three: Actions

Once the Initiative roster is complete, do a countdown. Begin with a high number such as 15, 20 or the higyhest Initiative total of the group and proceed down from there. On a player's turn to act, he may take one action and move up to his character's Acting Speed in steps. Resolve any actions accordingly. A Narrator can describe the results of the action then, or save it for the final step.

Remember that some actions require a player to waive Defense for the turn. If Defense has already been used in the turn, the character cannot take such an action and he must do something else.

A player may use an action to move up to his Running Speed. He can do nothing else that turn, not even declare a Dodge or go prone, though his Defense and armor still apply.

Step Four: Descriptive Results

After every character has acted, a Narrator should *briefly* recap what happened in the turn. This ensures that everyone involved knows exactly what's going on (or at least as much as their characters know). If players were not explicit about how their characters actions unfolded earlier, a Narrator may invite them to be more descriptive now.

Doing such a narrative recap enhances the drama and roleplaying intensity of the scene. It also helps avoid arguments later on about who did what, where they went or what happened to them.

If the optional on-clock, off-clock rule is in use (see below), the Narrator may call for a clock break.

Mass Combat Summary

Step Zero: Upkeep (Optional): Handle the costs/effects of any ongoing powers and conditions. Acknowledge new participants in the combat and perform any required bookkeeping.

Step One: Determine Targets: On the count of three, everyone points at the character or characters targeted. If you don't target anyone, point at yourself.

Step Two: Initiative Roster: Each player draws one card and adds it to his Initiative trait. Highest Initiative totals go first. In the event of a tie, the highest Dexterity + Composure. If players are still tied, draw another card each; high draw acts first.

Step Three: Actions: Count down Initiative from highest to lowest. When a players place in the roster comes up, she perform any necessary draws. Determine the outcome of each action and apply results.

Step Four: Descriptive Results: After everyone has acted for the turn, the Narrator takes a moment to describe the results in narrative terms so players understand what's happened before the next turn begins.

Basic Combat Modifiers and Complications

- Dodge: Double target's Defense, takes full action that turn
- Drawing a Weapon: Requires one action (one turn) without a Merit
- Offhand Attack: −2 penalty
- Prone Target: −2 penalty to hit in ranged combat; +2 bonus to hit when attacker is within close-combat distance
- Rising from Prone: Requires one action (one turn) without a Merit
- Surprised or Immobilized Target: Defense doesn't apply
- Specified Target: Leg or arm −2, hand −3, head −4, eye −5
- Touching a Target: Dexterity + Brawl or Dexterity + Weaponry. Armor may or may not apply; Defense does apply.
- Willpower: Add +2 to a Resistance trait (Stamina, Resolve, Composure or Defense) in one draw or instance

Close Combat Factors

The basic combat system is easy, with the simple stages discussed previously. Any complication comes from determining the factors that increase or decrease your test pool. That might mean the weapon wielded, the type of armor worn or the likelihood of hitting a target underwater. What follows are issues that can arise in close combat. Some of these circumstances are also addressed as Fighting Style Merits (see pp. 134-135). Ranged and General Combat factors are discussed on p. 221 and 229.

DEFENSE

Only someone caught completely by surprise, a fool, a masochist or a martyr stands still and takes whatever an enemy has to dish out. Most combatants seek to avoid being hit and hurt.

A target is automatically allowed a degree of evasion when an opponent uses a Brawl, Weaponry or thrown weapon attack against him. Such a response is a reflexive action and applies even if your character is attacked before his place in the Initiative roster. This reaction is called your character's Defense, a trait equal to the lowest of his Dexterity or Wits. Your character's Defense is subtracted from an attacker's test pool. In essence, your character bobs and weaves to avoid the blow.

This automatic Defense does not normally apply against Firearms attacks. (See p. 222 for how they may be avoided.) The only time that Defense does apply against Firearms-based attacks is when the attacker shoots within close-combat range, within a step or two of the target. (See "Firearms and Close Combat," p. 209, for more details on guns used in close-combat range.) Defense applies normally against thrown weapons, such as rocks, knives and spears.

A target who is tied up, unconscious or simply unmoving does not receive Defense as protection. Nor does one who's taken by surprise. That is, the attacker's test pool is not modified by the target's Defense trait.

A completely dormant target — a person who is completely tied up or who is unconscious — is a sitting duck for a killing blow (see p. 230). The attacker need not make a draw; he delivers damage equal to his test pool. If the target wears armor, its rating is automatically subtracted from the damage inflicted.

You may also spend a Willpower point to increase your character's Defense by two against a single attack. If his Defense is normally 2, it increases to 4 for the incoming attack. Basically, your character puts special effort into avoiding a particular assault. See "Resistance," p. 179 for more information.

At the start of each new turn, your character's full, normal Defense trait is restored unless he is still somehow unconscious or unmoving (see above) .

Your character's automatic Defense does not interfere with any actions that he performs in the turn.

Defense is *not* reduced by your character's wound penalties (see p. 235).

Combat Cards

Even in its streamlined form, **Mind's Eye Theatre** combat can still involve more numbers and factors than some players want to manage, especially if a number of optional rules are in play. Storytellers who want to avoid combat delays or the need to carry rulebooks can create and distribute index cards displaying a brief list of the standard combat modifiers that are have approved for the game. That way, players can simply check these "cheat sheets" to verify what bonuses apply when. This technique is much quicker than stopping play to consult a rulebook or to argue about the total modifier granted in a particular situation. Such combat cards are relatively easy to make and duplicate, and also easy to change during play if rules are new added or removed. They can save a great deal of hassle and confusion in the long term, especially for new players.

DODGE

Sometimes your character knows he's in over his head. Too many opponents are arrayed for him to hope to defeat them all. Maybe he's been hurt badly and needs to avoid any further injury. In such cases, he can dedicate himself to avoiding harm by declaring a dodge. Your character's action for a turn is spent anticipating attacks and moving out of harm's way. Double his Defense trait. Thus, if the lowest of your character's Dexterity or Wits is 2, his Dodge trait for the turn is 4. That number is subtracted from incoming close-combat and thrown attacks.

Dodge operates somewhat outside the normal Initiative order of the turn. You can declare a dodge for your character at any time in the turn, even before his place in the roster, assuming he hasn't acted yet. Your character's action for the turn is dedicated to dodging for the whole turn. Say you get an 8 Initiative and your character's opponent gets a 10. He attacks your character. You can declare a dodge at "10" in the turn, even though it precedes your "8," and your character is assumed to spend the whole turn evading.

Assuming your character hasn't acted yet in a turn, you can still declare a dodge for him late in the turn. Maybe your Initiative is 6, but you know that a dangerous foe has an even lower standing. Other characters have already acted in the turn, but your character has done nothing thus far. Your dodge applies to incoming attacks for the remainder of the turn.

Your character can do nothing else in a turn in which he dodges except move up to his Acting Speed. He can make no attacks. Dodging does not apply against incoming Firearms attacks (unless they are staged within close-combat range; one or two steps — see p. 209).

As with Defense, you can spend a Willpower point to add two to your character's Dodge against a single attack. So, if your character's Defense is 3 and his Dodge is 6, his Dodge increases to 8 against that single attack when a Willpower point is spent.

Your character may also possess one or both of the Brawling Dodge (p. 133) and the Weaponry Dodge (p. 138) Merits. These traits elaborate on the possibilities of dodging. They cannot both be used in the same turn, however.

OTHER COMPLICATIONS

• **Drawing a Weapon:** Pulling, sheathing or otherwise preparing a weapon takes one action. Thus, if your character draws a knife in a fight, he spends an action doing so. He retains his Defense for that turn. Having a weapon in hand before a fight breaks out allows your character to start swinging without delay. Walking around with a brandished weapon could have social and possibly legal implications. If a weapon is hidden on your character's person (under a coat or in a purse), an action is spent drawing it *and* your character loses her Defense for the turn. The Quick Draw Merit (see p. 137) allows your character to draw and attack in the same turn.

• **Offhand Attacks:** If your character makes attacks with his offhand (say, he's right handed but is forced to use his left), they suffer a -2 penalty. The Ambidextrous Merit (p. 133) negates this penalty.

• **Touching an Opponent:** An option of close combat is *intentionally* touching a target without doing harm. This could be by hand or with a hand-held item. A character might do this to plant a bug on someone, to count coup, to deliver the effect of an occult incantation or to knowingly spread an infection. It's assumed that a target doesn't want to be touched. If there's no resistance involved, the Storyteller can decree that a touch is performed automatically. Otherwise, Dexterity + Brawl or Dexterity + Weaponry is drawn to perform a touch. No damage is delivered through an intentional touch, even if multiple successes are drawn.

If actually making contact with the target's skin is not an issue — any part of him or his person can be contacted to achieve an effect — armor does not apply to efforts to touch. Armor rating (see p. 227) is not subtracted from test pools to make a touch. If making contact with skin is necessary, a target's armor applies normally.

A resisting target's Defense always applies against a touch, subtracting from your Dexterity + Brawl or Dexterity + Weaponry pool.

No successes drawn in an effort to touch a target means your character misses altogether.

UNARMED COMBAT

Not all fights involve knives and clubs. In fact, bringing a weapon to a fight implicitly states that the struggle is serious. Someone will not only be hurt, but possibly killed. The alternative is to go into a fight unarmed, using only one's body as a weapon. Unarmed combat applies the Brawl Skill and usually inflicts bashing damage. Going unarmed into battle doesn't have to put one at a disadvantage over opponents. Training in this style of combat can make your character fully capable of disabling others.

There is a variety of options possible in Brawl combat. The fundamentals available to anyone include punches, kicks and grapples. More versatile and even exotic maneuvers, such as throws and nerve pinches, are learned by studying the martial arts. See the Boxing and Kung Fu Fighting Style Merits (pp. 134 and 135) for examples of such training. The average guy on the street with no martial training can perform any of the following basics.

Strike: The basic unarmed attack — a blow with a fist, knee, head, foot or elbow. Draw Strength + Brawl without any bonuses. Unless a Narrator declares otherwise, a regular strike *cannot* be used to disarm an opponent or knock her down. Characters without combat Merits that allow them to perform such maneuvers must use a grapple to achieve those kinds of results (see below).

Bite: Your character's teeth, whether human-sized or gigantic fangs, clamp down on a target. Draw Strength + Brawl, with a bonus based on the size of attacker's jaws and teeth. An ordinary human's offer no bonus. A large dog's teeth offer +1. A wolf's confer a +2 bonus. A great white shark gets a +4 bonus. Generally, a bite from a person inflicts bashing damage, while that from an animal or supernatural creature inflicts lethal harm. The Narrator may decree that a human combatant can bite an opponent only after successfully grappling (see below). Note that a vampire cannot normally feed from a bite attack. The undead must grapple or otherwise subdue a target in order to feed. The bite can still inflict lethal damage normally.

Grapple: Your character gets a hold of or tackles a target and may apply a clinch with various effects, from immobilizing the victim to crushing him. Draw Strength + Brawl to achieve a hold. The target's Defense is subtracted from your test pool, as normal. If you get at least one success, your character has a hold of the target.

If the victim has yet to act in the turn, he may try and break loose at his stage of Initiative. Alternatively, the target may try to turn the tables on his attacker and perform an overpowering grappling maneuver of his own. In either case, draw Strength + Brawl, but the attacker's Strength is subtracted from the test pool. Even one success breaks the hold or allows a maneuver to be performed, as explained below. If the attacker's hold is broken, the grapple is over (although the attacker can attempt to grapple again). If the victim's test fails, he does not free himself or does not accomplish a maneuver. The attacker still has a grip on him. The victim of a grapple can try to free himself or perform a maneuver in subsequent turns, unless he is immobilized (see below).

If in the next turn the attacker still has a hold, he can try to overpower his opponent. A Strength + Brawl draw is made. The target's Strength rather than Defense is subtracted from the attacker's test pool. If no successes are gained, the attacker still has a hold, but accomplishes nothing more in the turn (he does not overpower his victim). If even one success is gained, one of the following overpowering maneuvers can be accomplished in the turn.

• Render opponent prone — Both combatants fall to the ground. Either party must relinquish or break the hold in order to stand again in a subsequent turn. Rising is considered an action in a turn. (See "Going Prone," on p. 225.) If one combatant manages to rise, close-combat attack draws to hit the prone opponent gain a +2 bonus.

• Damage opponent — Successes achieved on this turn's Strength + Brawl draw are applied as points of bashing damage inflicted on your character's opponent. Your character crushes, squeezes, bends or bites his victim.

• Immobilize opponent — Your character seeks to interfere with his victim's actions. Even one success renders the target immobile. The victim's physical actions are restricted to breaking free (he cannot attempt any overpowering maneuvers of his own), although he could bring mental or some supernatural capabilities to bear (Storyteller's discretion). Furthermore, the victim's Defense does not apply against attacks from opponents outside the grapple. So, if your character immobilizes a victim, attacks on him from your character's allies are not penalized by the victim's Defense.

Once an opponent is immobilized, he remains so from turn to turn until he breaks the hold. You do not need to make further overpower draws from turn to turn to keep the victim immobilized. He is automatically considered immobile thereafter. Your character can do nothing except maintain the hold, however. If he dedicates an action to any other effort, the target is no longer immobile. Your character still has a grip, but a successful overpower effort is required in a subsequent turn to immobilize the opponent all over again.

Trying to break free from immobilization is handled like a contested action between grapplers. A Strength + Brawl draw is made for the victim, and it's penalized by the holder's Strength. Successes achieved are compared to those that were gained by the holder when he applied the immobilization maneuver. If more are gained, the hold is broken and the victim is free again. Say that Greer manages to immobilize Sloan and gets three successes in the effort. To break free in subsequent turns, draws made for Sloan (Strength + Brawl - Greer's Strength) must achieve four or more successes.

• Draw weapon — With one or more successes, your character reaches a weapon on his person, on his opponent or nearby. Drawing or acquiring the weapon is an entire turn's action. The weapon has to be small, such as a knife or small gun (a pistol), in order to be brought to bear in grappling combat.

• Attack with drawn weapon — An attack is made with a drawn weapon. Each success achieved on your Strength + Brawl draw inflicts a point of damage. The kind of damage is appropriate to the weapon used — bashing for brass knuckles or lethal for a knife or pistol. A Weaponry or Firearms draw is not made under these circumstances, because it's your character's ability to overpower his opponent in grappling combat that dictates how well the weapon is used. The advantage of bringing a weapon to bear manifests in a bonus to your Strength + Brawl draw for the attack, and in the severity of damage that might be done (say, lethal for a knife).

• Turn a drawn weapon — If your character's opponent has a weapon drawn in a grapple, your character may seek to turn the weapon on her enemy. Her action is dedicated to gaining control of the weapon and turning it, even while it's still in her opponent's hand. Your character's action in a subsequent turn must be a successful attack in order to turn the weapon completely. If your character's opponent manages to regain control of the weapon in his action, before your character's attack is completed, no attack can be made in a subsequent turn. Thus, control of a weapon can be wrestled over from turn to turn in a grapple, with each combatant seeking to gain control and then make an attack.

• Disarm opponent — If you get one or more successes, your character manages to pry an object from his opponent's hand. Taking possession of the item thereafter (in another turn) is the equivalent of drawing a weapon (see above). No damage is inflicted.

If multiple people seek to grapple a single target, and they get a hold, the target can try to break free of all holds simultaneously. Draw Strength + Brawl and subtract the highest Strength among the grapplers, with an additional penalty for each grappler after the first. So, if Anton tries to break out of a hold imposed by three opponents, and the highest Strength among them is 4, Anton's breakout draw suffers a –6 penalty.

Grappling with an opponent has its drawbacks. Grapplers lose the capacity to dodge (see "Dodge," p. 216) and can perform only close-combat attacks. Ranged attacks are not allowed. (Wrestling over and using a small gun in a grapple is not considered a ranged attack for our purposes here

Example: *Drew seeks to grapple with Anderson. Drew first needs to get a grip on Anderson in his part of Initiative. Doing so requires an action and a successful Strength + Brawl draw, penalized by Anderson's Defense. If Anderson's order in Initiative comes later in the turn, he can try to break out with a successful Strength + Brawl draw, in this case penalized by Drew's Strength. Or Anderson can immediately try to perform a maneuver on Drew since the two are already locked. The same draw (Strength + Brawl – Drew's Strength) is applied and any successes achieved allow Anderson to perform a task, from doing damage to prying an object from Drew's free hand.*

If in the next turn Drew still has a hold on Anderson, a Strength + Brawl draw, penalized by Anderson's Strength, is made to see if Drew can perform any maneuvers on Anderson.

Anderson can keep trying to break free each turn, or he can attempt maneuvers on Drew each turn. Until Anderson breaks free, the grapple continues and Drew may continue to inflict his own maneuvers.

Grappling Summary

• Draw Strength + Brawl – opponent's Defense for attacker to get a grip on target.

• Target's next action can be dedicated to breaking free. Draw Strength + Brawl – attacker's Strength. Any successes indicate breaking free.

Or, the target can attempt to apply an overpowering maneuver to the attacker, participating in the grapple rather than trying to break free. Draw Strength + Brawl – attacker's Strength. Any successes allow for a maneuver (see below).

• If the attacker's grip on the target persists, and he is free to do so, the attacker can try to apply an overpowering maneuver to the victim. Draw the attacker's Strength + Brawl – opponent's Strength. Any successes allow a maneuver (see below).

• Possible maneuvers. Choose one:

    Render opponent prone

    Damage opponent

    Immobilize opponent

    Draw weapon

    Attack with drawn weapon

    Turn a drawn weapon

    Disarm opponent

    Use opponent as protection from ranged attacks

Attempting to break free is always an option instead of performing an overpowering maneuver.

Ranged Combat Factors

Ranged combat factors apply specifically to thrown weapons and firearms, the latter of which being the most common.

People in tense, potentially violent situations often resort to guns to defend themselves or to kill enemies. Depending on the country concerned, guns can be bought at the corner pawnshop or through dealers, with the formality of some paperwork and a waiting period. Personal arms such as pistols are acquired this way. Rifles, shotguns and bows can be acquired at sporting-goods stores. In other countries, gun possession is unheard of outside of the authorities. In some nations, going unarmed is more dangerous than going armed, be it with a pistol, rifle or automatic weapon. Finally, no matter what part of the world you look at, guns are always available illegally. They're quicker to get than through conventional channels, but definitely more expensive. Acquiring pistols and street guns through the black market can demand Resources dots of anywhere from 3 to 5, depending on what your character wants.

People with the Firearms Skill have spent time learning to use and understand guns — anything from pistols to machineguns to maybe even bows or other archaic weapons. Owning a gun and knowing how to use it are two different things. Homeowners can possess but may have never fired a weapon. These people could be as much a threat to themselves as to intruders. Attacks with guns are made by drawing Dexterity + Firearms. If the Skill is not possessed, Dexterity alone can still be drawn with a –1 penalty (the standard for untrained Physical Skills). A failure on a chance draw indicates anything as minor as a jam to something as severe as shooting one's self in the foot or shooting an innocent bystander, at the Storyteller's discretion.

RANGE

Normally, **Mind's Eye Theatre** combat does not need to consider range modifiers. Most games take place in relatively small areas that make range determinations unnecessary. For the purposes of clarity, however, some basic range categories are provided. These can be used if questions of effective range arise in combat. Some examples of what normally qualifies as the distance in question are included, though these should by no means be considered utterly binding nor completely exhaustive.

Short range: In the same immediate area. Within the same room, the next room over or at the end of a hallway in a typical house; across a hotel lobby; across a small forest clearing or average backyard. No penalty to attack draws.

Medium range: At the far end of conversational distance. Across a very large (ballroom-sized) room; across a medium-sized forest clearing; one or two houses away on a typical suburban street; at the far end of a long hotel hallway. Attacks at this range suffer a –2 penalty to the draw.

Long range: Any distance beyond those listed for the other categories, but still within line of sight, subject to the Narrator's discretion on whether a target is so far away that extreme range applies instead. Across a huge room such as a convention floor; up to the far end of a suburban block; across a truly large open clearing or field. Attacks at this range suffer a –4 penalty to the draw.

Extreme range: Targets that are still visible but at the absolute upper limit of what can realistically be attempted are considered to be at extreme range, at the Narrator's discretion. No modifiers are used; instead, the attack is reduced to a chance draw. The only exception to this for firearms purposes is the sniper rifle.

By default, thrown weapons can be used at only short or medium range. They normally cannot be used at long range in **Mind's Eye Theatre** unless they are aerodynamic (such as a football or a spear), the throwing character has superhuman Strength, or other mystical powers are used to enhance the throw. Any targets at long range are considered at extreme range when it comes to thrown weapons, unless as noted the attacker possesses superhuman strength or the object is particularly aerodynamic.

Call and Answer

Players and Narrators looking for a quick and dirty way to determine range can use the following. If players involved in a attack can speak normally to each other without raising their voices, it's short range. If they have to speak loudly or frequently repeat themselves to be made clear, it's medium range. If they have to shout or gesture to communicate with each other, it's long range or possibly extreme range, at the Narrator's discretion. Needless to say, this scale may require adjustment in a very loud area such as a nightclub or a particularly quiet location like a library. If the players have to shout to be heard over the music of the club, conversational distance must be approximated differently.

CONCEALMENT

The old adage "You can't hit what you can't see" is true. Visibility and an opponent's efforts to hide make it difficult to target someone with a ranged attack. Anything that makes a target difficult to see in ranged combat — fog, mist, darkness, obstructions — offers concealment. There are four degrees of concealment to consider, and the penalties associated with each may be applied to ranged attack draws. Concealment does not apply when opponents are engaged in Brawl or Weaponry combat. They're too close to hide from one another.

Barely concealed: –1 (Example: crouching behind an office chair)

Partially concealed: –2 (hiding behind the hood of a car, but with upper body exposed, using a resisting human shield)

Substantially concealed: –3 (crouching fully behind a car, using an unresisting human shield, or poking up out of a foxhole)

Completely covered: Completely protected by an intervening barrier (all shots hit the cover automatically; see "Cover," below)

As a rule of thumb, consider the concealment penalty equal to the quarter of the target's body that is concealed. So one-quarter concealment imposes a –1 penalty, half cover a –2 penalty, and three-quarter concealment a –3 penalty. Obviously, total concealment is a bit different.

Avoiding Getting Shot

Since your character doesn't normally apply his Defense against Firearms attacks, his best method to avoid being shot is to seek protection and go prone. These actions levy penalties against the attacker.

Example: *Tony is about to fire a shotgun at a demonic cultist. The cultist acts first in Initiative. He decides to run for the concealment of a nearby car. It's within his Running Speed in steps, so he can make it there in one action by running. When Tony's action comes, he suffers a −3 on his attack draw (−3 for the car's substantial concealment). In the next turn, the cultist goes prone, hoping that the arrival of more followers will chase Tony off. Tony's penalty becomes −5 (−2 for the cultist being prone and −3 for the car's concealment). Tony needs to close the distance or flush his target out if he wants to get rid of those penalties.*

See "Going Prone."

COVER

Cover provides protection for targets hiding behind it. Cover doesn't usually apply to close combat; opponents are within a step or so of each other. In a ranged attack against a completely covered target (someone behind a closed door or inside a closed car), the cover is hit automatically (the bullets rip into the door or car).

A powerful gun or other ranged attack might penetrate cover to hit a protected opponent. Follow these steps to find out if an attack passes through. Note: These rules don't apply to hitting barely, partially or substantially concealed opponents (see above). Penalties (−1, −2 and −3) already apply to hitting them. These rules apply to targets that are fully protected by a barrier between them and the shooter.

• Deal damage to the full cover. (See Chapter 6 for objects' traits.)

• If the successes on the ranged attack exceed the cover's Durability, the attack passes through the cover. The attack then hits the first target behind it. Note that he damage is still dealt to the cover. If multiple targets are in roughly the same proximity, determine who is hit randomly. Damage that exceeds the cover's Durability is then drawn as a new test pool against the target, but any armor worn by the target is subtracted from the pool. It is possible that the new damage pool might thus be reduced to a chance draw. Once cover's Structure has been exhausted, the object provides no more protection.

Example: *A lurking creature hides completely behind a wooden door. Rae can still shoot at the door in hopes of hitting the thing beyond. The door's Durability is 1. Rae's attack draw nets five successes. The shot passes through the door, with an excess of four. Those four points form a test pool that is re-drawn as a direct attack against the monster, which wears armor rated 2. That reduces Rae's test pool to two for the purposes of doing harm directly to the creature.*

Since Rae got four successes in excess of the door's Durability, and the door has a Structure of 6, two more points of damage done to the door will destroy it and make it useless as cover thereafter.

Someone in a closed car or room who can be seen through a window is still considered to be under full cover from ranged attacks. Shots fired must pass through the window before the target can be hurt. All the rules discussed here for being behind full cover apply. A typical window has Durability 1, Size 3 or 4 and Structure 4 or 5, and an attack to hit a window specifically suffers a –1 penalty. Any successes drawn in excess of the window's 1 Durability are then drawn as a new test pool to hit the hiding target.

FIRING FROM CONCEALMENT

Being concealed helps protect your character. It also makes it difficult to shoot back. Your character must pop up, fire, and then duck down again. If he fires back from shelter, the penalty to your draw is one less than the concealment rating of your character's protection. Thus, if he's substantially concealed (–3 to be hit) and fires back while maintaining that protection, your attack draw suffers a –2 penalty.

If both combatants are concealed, modifiers are cumulative. If your character is substantially concealed (–3) and his target is partially concealed (–2), your attack draw suffers a –4 penalty (–2 for firing at a partially concealed target, and –2 for his own protection). The opponent also suffers a –4 penalty (–3 for firing at a substantially concealed target, and –1 for firing from her own protection).

A character who is completely covered (under full cover) cannot stage ranged attacks at opponents. Doing so compromises his cover and reduces him to substantially concealed, instead. Attacks made against him suffer a –3 penalty.

OTHER COMPLICATIONS

• **Drawing:** Drawing or otherwise preparing a gun takes one action. Thus, if your character draws his gun in a fight, he spends an action doing so (unless he has the Quick Draw Merit — see p. 137). Having a gun in hand before a fight breaks out allows your character to start firing without delay. It carries the possible social or legal implications of openly brandishing a firearm, however. If a weapon is hidden on your character's person (under a coat or in a purse), an action is spent drawing it *and* your character loses her Defense for the turn.

• **Offhand Attacks:** If your character makes attacks with his offhand (say, he's right handed but is forced to shoot with his left), they suffer a –2 penalty. The Ambidextrous Merit (p. 133) eliminates this penalty.

• **Reloading:** Your character must spend one or several turns to reload an empty gun. Since you are paying attention to the bullets, shells or magazine, your Defense does not apply during those turns.

General Combat Factors

Some battle conditions apply to both close and ranged combat, or to circumstances of each.

MOVEMENT

Your character's Acting Speed of 5 indicates how many steps he can travel in a single turn by walking or jogging. He can travel that many steps and still perform an action, all in the same turn. He can move and perform an action, or perform an action and then move. He cannot, however, move, perform an action and then move again all in the same turn.

If he wants to move more quickly, he can travel his Running Speed (Strength + Dexterity +5) in a turn. Doing so is considered a full action. No other feats can usually be performed while running, including a Dodge. A special Merit or supernatural power is required to accomplish such combined tasks. The only exception is Charging (see below).

CHARGING

Your character can charge an opponent in close combat with a Brawl or Weaponry attack. Essentially, he runs up to a target and attacks. Your character can move his Running Speed and stage an attack at the end of his movement, all in the same turn.

Your character's Defense score is not subtracted from any attacks made against him in the turn. He makes a relatively easy target of himself by making a beeline to a specific opponent.

Your character cannot charge and perform any special attack that requires him to give up his Defense as a drawback to the maneuver. He can perform one maneuver or the other.

If your character's Defense is applied against any incoming attacks in a turn, he cannot perform a charge in the same turn. If he is attacked before his Initiative, he cannot use his Defense without losing the ability to charge in the same turn.

GOING PRONE

Sometimes there's no cover to be found when your character comes under fire, and he dives to the ground as a last resort. Maybe your character has been crawling to avoid being spotted, or he simply just lies on the ground. Regardless of the reason, it all boils down to going prone.

Ranged attacks suffer a –2 penalty when the target is prone.

A standing attacker gets a +2 bonus to hit a prone target in close combat. This bonus is also applied to a ranged attack if the attacker is within a step of the target. The ranged attack performed nearby is also subject to the target's Defense, even if it's a Firearms attack. See "Firearms and Close Combat," p. 209, for more details.

Your character can willingly drop to prone as a reaction to ranged attacks or other events in his surroundings. Doing so constitutes his action for the turn. He may even go prone before his rotation in Initiative, if he has not yet acted in the turn. Thus, if an opponent starts firing on Initiative 12, your character with Initiative 8 can go prone when the shots are fired (on 12). Your character loses all other actions for the turn, however. If he goes prone before his normal stage of Initiative, your character cannot move up to his Acting Speed. He must "hit the dirt" where he stands. If he goes prone at his normal Initiative, he may move up to his Acting Speed and go prone in the same turn.

If your character has already acted in a turn, he cannot go prone thereafter. Say he acts on Initiative 11. On Initiative 7 in the same turn, someone starts shooting. Your character cannot go prone, because he has already acted in the turn.

Rising from prone is an action and must be performed in its own turn. Your character could therefore rise from prone and remain stationary or rise from prone and move up to his Acting Speed in the same turn, but he could not perform any other action without the aid of Merits or special powers.

Flank and Rear Attacks

If your character attacks from the side or rear of an unsuspecting target, a reflexive Wits + Composure draw is allowed for the target to recognize the imminent attack (see "Surprise," p. 48). If the draw fails, the victim doesn't respond and his Defense is not applied to the attack. If your character intends to use a ranged attack against at the target, the reflexive Wits + Composure draw is still allowed at the Storyteller's discretion. Perhaps the target could see the sniper out of the corner of his eye or in a reflection. If the intended target's Wits + Composure draw succeeds, Initiative is drawn between combatants and Defense applies against close-combat attacks.

If your character attacks from the side or rear of an opponent in an established fight (Initiative has been determined all around), the attacker's angle or vantage point offers no bonus. The combatants are aware of each other and/or on their guard from all angles.

Specified Targets

Sometimes your character wants to direct an attack at a particular part of an opponent. You might need to target an object carried by an opponent to achieve a specific effect. Your character might want to shoot a gun-wielding robber in the hand, for example, or swing a tire iron to hit an opponent in the head. The Storyteller imposes penalties to your attack draw based on the size of the intended target. A torso region might be at -1, a leg or arm -2, a head -3, a hand -4 and an eye (or the "off" button of a machine) -5. If no successes are gained, the attack misses altogether.

A Narrator determines the secondary results of a successful attack, beyond simple damage inflicted. A successful Strength + Athletics draw might be required for a victim to hold onto a held object, with a penalty to the effort equal to the damage from the attack. A successful attack on a body part might ignore armor (see p. 227), because none is worn there. A blow to the head with a blunt object that normally inflicts bashing damage might inflict lethal damage, or stun the victim (see p. 230). A shot to an eye might impair ranged attacks due to loss of depth perception. Crippling both eyes causes an opponent to fight blind. As an example of how specified targets work, consider the classic stake through the heart:

Stake through the Heart: Ordinary people can rarely identify the supernatural creatures they encounter, let alone know their weaknesses. And yet, there are the classic Hollywood solutions to monsters: fire, garlic, religious symbols — and a stake through the heart. Whether the last actually works is unknown without extensive research or occult knowledge. After all, wouldn't a stake through the heart kill just about anything?

To stake an opponent, an attacker must target the heart. Wielded in hand, a stake calls for a Strength + Weaponry draw. Fired from some kind of projection device or thrown, a stake demands a Dexterity + Firearms or Athletics draw. The damage that your character inflicts is lethal and must also be sufficiently high to pierce muscle, bone and organ. All totaled, efforts to stake a resisting target are at -3 and a minimum of three points of damage must be inflicted in a single attack. If less than three points of damage are done, the stake sinks in but doesn't reach the heart. Damage is done, but not enough to have any special effect on a monstrous target. If any type of supernatural strength is used in such a failed staking attack, the stake splinters, breaks off and becomes useless for any successive attacks.

A stake must be hefty. A mere pencil, wooden hair needle or flimsy stick does not suffice, not even if shot from some sort of firearm. An arrow or crossbow bolt suffices, as does a sharpened chair leg, a broken pool cue and a pointed fence post. If in doubt, consult a Narrator on whether a particular object qualifies as a stake.

ARMOR

Your character's primary protection in combat is armor. Any form of protective clothing can classify as armor, from heavy work gear to a knight's outfit. In the modern World of Darkness, armor is functional. Anything that's worn for an extended period, such as reinforced clothing, is designed to be light and sturdy. Soldiers, police and anyone else who can get their hands on bulletproof vests wear them. Those who want to resort to metal plates can do so, but the bulk can hinder movement.

The armor rating is subtracted from the test pool of an incoming attack. If your character wears armor rated 3, an attacker's test pool suffers a –3 penalty. Armor is rated in terms of the kinds of attacks against which it protects: ballistic and all other kinds. Thus, protective gear has two ratings separated by a slash on the Armor Chart (p. 234): general/ballistic. The first applies to most attack types. The second applies to those made with attacks from firearms. So, a flak jacket rated 2/3 imposes a –2 penalty on, say, punch and sword attacks, and a –3 penalty on gun and bow attacks.

Types of armor designed to be "bulletproof" on the Armor Chart (a Kevlar vest, flak jacket and full riot gear) downgrade lethal damage from firearms to bashing. So, if a target wears a Kevlar vest and a shot is fired at him, the attack draw suffers a –2 penalty for the armor. Any successes drawn in the attack do damage, but it's bashing instead of lethal.

Attacks of a magical nature that inflict aggravated damage might not be hindered by armor; it depends on the type of attack. A sorcerous bolt of energy might pass right through armor. Mundane objects are simply not designed to withstand pure mystical assault. A silver letter opener stabbed at a werewolf, however, must still overcome armor to harm the creature (assuming it wears any armor). The werewolf's legendary Achilles' heel against silver doesn't give a letter opener a supernatural ability to ignore armor. The Storyteller decides if an attack that inflicts aggravated damage also ignores armor. More generally, characters shouldn't casually carry around silver weaponry since the softness of the metal makes it thoroughly unsuitable for almost any type of weapon.

If the specified-target optional rule is in effect (see below), draws may be made for attackers to hit unprotected portions of a defender and thus ignore armor. The Storyteller assigns the attack's penalty, depending on the size of body part targeted. In the case of bulletproof armor, an attack to an unprotected body part not only ignores the target's armor rating, but damage is not downgraded to bashing.

Ordinary people must wear armor to gain protection. Some supernatural creatures are naturally armored by virtue of tough hides, or they have magic enchantments that help protect them like armor.

Cumbersome gear imposes Initiative penalties. Some armor penalizes Running Speed and even efforts involving Strength. The Armor Chart (p. 234) provides stats for various forms of gear.

FIGHTING BLIND

Sometimes circumstances arise when your character cannot see, but he still needs to defend himself or seek out a threatening opponent. Maybe he's in pitch darkness, dense smoke fills the area or he's suffered vision damage. Such situations make your character easy prey for the things of the world that stalk him. All the more reason for him to try to fight back, even blind.

Characters who cannot see at all must attack enemies almost as if those opponents are fully concealed. They cannot be targeted at all; shots are taken in the dark, literally. This penalty reflects the fact that your character chooses a direction in which he stages

his attack — whether close or ranged combat — and guesses where his intended target might be. A chance draw is made by the blind character; success means he hits normally, while failure means his attack is sent in the wrong direction perhaps going tragically wrong: hitting a friend or bystander, damaging an important item, etc.

Remember that safety is paramount. Sighted players whose characters are blind must not actually close their eyes and stumble around. The affliction is roleplayed to the best of one's ability while keeping his eyes at least partially open. Play areas should never be so dark as to be a hazard. Areas of in-game low light or utter darkness should be marked with appropriate signs around the perimeter, so that players can roleplay conditions accordingly.

There are, however, ways to try to sense where a target is rather than stage attacks aimlessly. Ordinary people have some chance of bringing their other senses to bear. Supernatural creatures with inhuman capabilities may have stronger senses, may be able to function unimpaired without vision, or might be able to see in the dark.

LISTENING

Your character can attempt to listen for a target. The subject must be making noise, no matter how slight, to be heard (walking, fighting or breathing heavily makes *some* noise). Your character must spend an action listening and the Narrator or an impartial player makes a Wits + Composure draw. Survival may be substituted for Composure if the situation applies. Modifiers are based on how noisy the target is (+3 if he walks on dry twigs, +1 if he walks on a leaves, -5 if he stands perfectly still and only breathes lightly), and on how noisy the environment is (no modifier if the area is eerily quiet, -3 if heavy traffic passes by).

Failure: Your character cannot locate the target but can attack blindly where he believes her to be. The Storyteller may make a secret chance draw, as per the rules above, assuming your character attacks in the right direction at all.

Success: Your character can attack the target as if she is substantially concealed (-3 penalty).

Once your character has succeeded on an attack, a draw must be made for him each turn to keep an *ear* on the target. This is a reflexive Wits + Composure draw (although Survival might substitute for Composure). A Narrator decides if the same listening modifiers apply from turn to turn.

SMELLING

Characters with a heightened olfactory sense (or more likely bestial creatures) can try to sniff a target out by taking an action to smell. The Narrator or an impartial player then makes a Wits + Composure draw for the smelling character. Again, Survival may be substituted for Composure if the situation applies. A Narrator may apply factors based on the strength of the target's odor (+3 if the subject has gone unwashed for days, +1 if she wears strong perfume, –3 if she has showered recently and put on clean clothes), or based on surrounding odors (–1 at a gym, –3 near a paper mill).

Failure: Your character cannot locate the target but can attack blindly at where he believes she is. A chance draw may be made for the attack, as detailed under the rules for fighting blind.

Success: Your character can attack the target as if she is substantially concealed (–3 penalty).

Once your character has succeeded in an attack, a draw must be made each turn to keep a *nose* on the target. This is a reflexive Wits + Composure (or Survival) draw. A Narrator can decide whether the same smelling modifiers apply from turn to turn.

OTHER COMPLICATIONS

Combat can be complicated by numerous possibilities, some of which are addressed below. These are often special features of weapons or attack types that confer unique bonuses or rules variants. Your Storyteller should feel free to come up with others as situations warrant.

• **Armor Piercing:** A weapon or ammunition type that is capable of overcoming targets' armor or protective layers. The item is typically rated 1 to 3 and that many points of armor are ignored in an attack. Armor piercing rating is not added to attack pools as a bonus. It simply diminishes the number subtracted from an attack pool due to a target's armor. (See "Piercing Durability," p. 191, for more information.) The Damage rating of a gun from which an armor-piercing bullet is fired is still added to a Firearms draw as a bonus.

If armor-piercing ammunition is fired at a target wearing "bulletproof" armor (a Kevlar vest, flak jacket or full riot gear), the bullet might penetrate that armor. If the rating of the ammunition (1 to 3) exceeds the armor's rating against Firearms attacks, the armor is ignored altogether in the attack. No points are lost due to armor in the attack draw, and damage inflicted is not downgraded from lethal to bashing (see "Armor," p. 227).

If a target wears no armor, your character's shot gains no special effects or bonuses from the ammunition used (the gun itself still applies an equipment bonus, though). Armor piercing ammunition should be rare and many places outlaw it entirely.

• **Attribute Damage:** A poison, drug or supernatural power that doesn't cause Health points of damage, but reduces a victim's Attribute dots. The kind of Attribute is probably specific, such as Physical or even Strength. Attributes may be recovered as if they were Health points lost to bashing damage (see "Healing," p. 240). So, one is regained every 15 minutes. More harmful Attribute loss would be recovered as if it were lethal damage (one point every two days). Crippling Attribute loss would be recovered as if it were aggravated damage (one point a week). See the "Attribute Dots" sidebar on p. 44 for the effects of an Attribute that falls to zero dots.

• **Continuous Damage:** A mystical power or cruel weapon continues to deliver damage over successive turns, like a continually burning flame. It might be a fixed number, such as three. So, an attack draw is made normally with successes determining damage inflicted, but every turn thereafter an additional three damage is inflicted automatically, ignoring the victim's Defense and armor. Damage is ongoing until a time limit such as two turns is passed, or until some recovery action such as cleaning the wound is performed.

• **Immobilization:** When your character attacks someone involved in a grapple (see p. 220), the target's Defense applies against the attack. For example, your character approaches two people who are grappling. If he makes a close-combat attack on one of them, the target's Defense penalizes his attack.

If, however, the target is immobilized in the grapple (see p. 220), the target's Defense is lost against outside attacks. So, if your character's intended target has been immobilized in the grapple, your attacks on him do not suffer a Defense penalty.

Killing Blow: A target who is tied up, unconscious or paralyzed not only gets no Defense, but he can be felled by a single blow. A draw need not be made for an attacker; the damage points he inflicts equal his test pool, modified by any armor worn by the target. Damage done is automatic, as is the armor's protection. No attack draw is required.

• **Knockout:** A single blow delivered to the head (–3 penalty to hit if the specified targets optional rules is used) that equals or exceeds the target's Size in damage might knock him unconscious. A Stamina draw is made for the victim. If it succeeds, he behaves normally. If it fails, he is unconscious for a number of turns equal to the damage done. Supernaturals that aren't easily knocked out, such as vampires and werewolves, are immune to this effect.

• **Knockdown:** A power, weapon or effect forces a target off his feet. A successful Dexterity + Athletics draw allows him to maintain his footing as a reflexive action. If the draw succeeds, the character behaves normally. If the draw fails, the character is forced to go prone (see "Going Prone," p. 225). If he has not performed an action in the turn, he loses his action that turn. He cannot perform any tasks and cannot travel that turn. He just hits the ground. He can rise again as an action in a subsequent turn. Or once he lands, he always has the option of remaining prone.

In case of a failure on a Dexterity + Athletics chance draw, a character falls hard or at an odd angle and suffers one Health point of bashing damage (which may be absorbed if armor is worn).

• **Stun:** Some weapons pack such a wallop that if damage successes inflicted in a single attack equal or exceed the target's Size, he loses his next action. Supernaturals that aren't easily stunned, such as vampires and werewolves, are immune to this effect.

• **Wound Type:** The power or weapon delivers a different type of damage than normal: bashing, lethal or aggravated. A sword with a silver blade does lethal damage against an ordinary person, but does aggravated harm against a werewolf, for example.

NARRATIVE PERIMETER

In context, combat is supposed to occur in the blink of an eye. At the actual game, it can take several minutes to resolve a fight, particularly if multiple characters are involved. You may also find that combat undergoes a "popcorn ball" effect. Players in nearby rooms hear what's going on and come to investigate or even join the fray. A minor scuffle could therefore bloom into a full-on brawl of 30 characters or more, especially of in-setting tensions run high among characters. The trick is determining when (or if) latecomers can join a fight. Do you allow them to jump in at the next available turn, even if their characters came from far away in-game? Or do you make them wait before they can take part?

One way to solve this problem is to establish a "narrative perimeter" at the beginning of any fight that you anticipate might require stringent oversight. This is a quick and easy way to determine how long it takes newcomers to join the fray. Post Narrators and/or experienced players that aren't involved in the combat at any entrances. If the room has too many access points to cover, simply tell any arriving players to report to a single Narrator in charge of the perimeter. For every room a player must pass through to get to the fight, *including the room in which a player originated*, she must wait one turn before her character can enter combat, starting with the next turn to begin after her arrival.

Other factors may apply as well, at a Narrator's discretion. Changing elevation, such as climbing a staircase or ladder adds at least one turn per floor. Traveling down a short hallway such as one in an average house is worth a single turn. Medium-length hallways, like one in a hotel, add two turns. Long hallways such as those in a convention center add at least three turns. Each closed *and* locked door along the way adds an additional turn, and assumes a character can get through quickly with keys or by smashing through (Narrator's discretion). Outdoors or in truly large indoor spaces, each range increment above short (see p. 221) adds one turn. Characters at short range can join the fight immediately. Characters at medium range arrive one turn later and those at long range arrive two turns later.

So, a character who hears that a fight has broken out in the study attached to the master bedroom at the end of a short hallway could head there immediately out-of-character. His character, however, has to wait three turns before joining the fight. One turn for the room in which he starts, one turn for the short hallway, and one turn for the bedroom he has to cross through to get to the study. The player is expected to wait quietly at the narrative perimeter and not distract those involved in combat. He can take note of only those descriptive effects his character would notice along the way, like flashes of light or gunshots. A Narrator on the perimeter is normally responsible for keeping players informed.

Characters with supernatural speed may use it to arrive quickly. The power or trait's dots are subtracted from the number of turns that must be waited before entering combat, to a minimum of one turn. No matter how fast a character might be, there is always some delay when traveling to the scene of a fight. The same goes for characters who can of teleport or have other means of near-instantaneous travel.

Storytellers should never reverse turns just because a player arrives late without a very good reason, regardless of what powers his character might be. This is not done to be unfair to that player, but simply because turning back the clock frustrates players already involved in the scene. Basically, always move forward, never back.

Weapons

Firearms and melee weapons in live action role-playing are both a boon and a curse. They can sometimes provide an exciting element of game-play, a cinematic type of action that is otherwise difficult to replicate. Unfortunately weapons are also sometimes a short-cut away from roleplaying and towards violence-intensive play that disrupts the flow of the game and alienates those players who stand by, unable to interact with a scene that degenerates into a hail of bullets and never-ending explosions. A more abstract ideal of weapon types is provided here that standardizes a few general kinds of firearms and melee weapons and leaves the customization up to the imagination of players and Storytellers alike.

Anyone who enters a violent confrontation is quick to resort to weapons. One's own body can be used as a weapon, but often far more effective are tools such as bats, bottles, knives, swords, axes and guns. When dealing with mysterious creatures, sometimes wielding weapons is essential to survival — or completely useless. Weapons are generally classed as melee and ranged.

7.1 – MELEE WEAPONS CHART

Type	Damage	Size	Cost	Special
Stiletto	0 (L)	1	•	*
Dagger	1 (L)	1	•	
Short sword	2 (L)	2	••	
Small Axe	2 (L)	2	••	
Sword	3 (L)	3	•••	
Large Axe	3 (L)	3	•••	
Greatsword	4 (L)	4	••••	**
Great Axe	4 (L)	4	••••	**
Wooden Club	2 (B)	2	n/a	
Mace (metal)	3 (B)	3	•	
Rapier	2 (L)	2	••	***
Stake	1 (L)	1	n/a	

Type: Your character may use many other types of weapons (meat cleavers, halberds, hammers). Use the traits from the above lists that best approximate those weapons. See p. 189 for determining the traits of improvised weapons. Note that improvised weapons automatically suffer a −1 penalty.

Damage: The number of bonus points added to test pools when using the weapon. The type of damage inflicted is also indicated: aggravated (A), lethal (L) or bashing (B). A damage of 0 indicates that the weapon itself doesn't add any bonus traits.

Size: 1 = Can be hidden in hand or any clothing, 2 = Can be hidden in bulky clothing, 3 = Cannot be hidden in clothing, but carried in a large bag, 4 = Can't be concealed. Size is also used to indicate the minimum Strength needed to use a weapon effectively. A wielder with a lower Strength suffers a −1 penalty on attack draws.

Cost: The minimum dots in the Resources Merit usually required for purchasing the weapon. The "n/a" entry indicates that the item can be created rather than purchased.

*The stiletto's small size makes it trivial to conceal almost anywhere: a character can wield the stiletto by sliding it out of her sleeve and attack in the same turn without requiring the Quick Draw Merit.

** If a character attacking with such a huge weapon draws an Ace on her Weaponry test to strike, she will be off-balance and unable to attack using a weapon or her bare hands for the next full turn as she steadies herself, regaining her footing. She may defend and move as normal, however.

*** The rapier-wielder gains a +2 Defense bonus when fighting enemies who are using melee weapons themselves due to the foil's suitability to that style of combat. If the character wielding the rapier draws an Ace while attacking an opponent using a melee weapon with a Size of 3 or higher, the rapier breaks.

Type	Damage	Ammo	Strength	Size	Cost
Derringer[1]	0	2	1	1	•
Semi-Auto Pistol[2]†	1	12	2	2	••
Heavy Revolver[3]†	2	6	2	2	••
Breech Shotgun[4]	4	2	3	3	•••
Shotgun[5]	4	6	3	3	•••
SMG[6]	3	10 bursts	3	2	•••
Assault Rifle[7]	4	10 bursts	4	4	•••••
Sniper Rifle†[8]	4	1	2	4	••••
Crossbow[9]	3	1	2	3	••

Damage: Indicates the bonus added to your test pool for using the weapon. Firearms deliver lethal damage against ordinary people. The type of damage may vary against supernatural enemies such as vampires, which suffer only bashing damage from conventional firearms. Ammunition that inflicts aggravated damage on supernaturals is not normally easy to come by.

Ammo: The number of consecutive shots (1 per action) that can be fired before the weapon needs to be reloaded.

Strength: The minimum Strength needed to use a weapon effectively. A wielder with a lower Strength suffers a −1 penalty on attack draws.

Size: 1 = Can be hidden in hand or any clothing, 2 = Can be hidden in bulky clothing, 3 = Cannot be hidden in clothing, but carried in a large bag, 4 = Can't be concealed.

Cost: The minimum dots in the Resources Merit usually required to purchase the weapon.

† This weapon can be silenced with a (usually illegal) silencer that halves the effective range of the sniper rifle.

[1] Because of the size of the derringer, it's very easy to hide and reveal: you can quickly slide it out of your pocket and attack in the same turn without requiring the Quick Draw Merit. The derringer can be reloaded in one full turn.

[2] The semi-automatic pistol has a range of up to 50 yards/150 feet. It takes a full turn to release an empty magazine and slide in a new one.

[3] A large-caliber chambered revolver has an effective range of 30 yards or 90 feet and can be reloaded in two full turns.

[4] The breech-loading shotgun has a range of 10 yards or 30 feet and fires one shell per shot. It takes three full turns to break open the shotgun, eject the empty shells, reload and re-acquire aim.

[5] The effective range of the shotgun is 10 yards or 30 feet. Due its recoil, it can only be fired once every two turns. The intervening turn has to be spent reacquiring aim. It takes five full turns to reload the entire magazine, or one turn to reload only one shell.

[6] Sub-machine guns are illegal to own and operate in many countries or regions. The SMG fires a short burst every turn with a range of 25 yards or 75 feet, requiring two full turns to reload the magazine. Up to two SMGs can usually be carried on a character at any given time, with a maximum of six additional magazines.

[7] Civilian ownership and use of assault rifles is illegal almost anywhere, especially outside of strictly controlled shooting ranges. The range of an assault rifle is 75 yards or 220 feet. Because of the bulk of the rifle and its magazines, only one can weapon can usually be carried, with a maximum of four additional magazines.

[8] The hunting rifle or sniper rifle has an effective range of almost one kilometer, a thousand yards or three thousand feet. The rifle is very difficult to conceal although it can be taken apart and stored in a bag in about thirty full turns, the same time it takes to re-assemble. It's impossible to carry more than one sniper rifle on you at any one time because of its size and shape.

[9] Crossbows require three turns to reload. A character may use a crossbow to attempt to stake a vampire with a targeted shot (−3 penalty and a minimum of three points of damage must be inflicted in a single attack).

Class	Rating	Str.	Ini.	Speed	Cost
Modern					
Reinforced/ thick clothing	1/0	1	0	0	n/a
Kevlar vest* (thin)	1/2	1	0	0	•
Flak jacket*	2/3	1	−1	0	••
Full riot gear*	3/4	2	−2	−1	•••
Archaic					
Leather (hard)	1/0	2	−1	0	•
Chainmail	2/1	3	−2	−2	••
Plate	3/2	4	−3	−3	••••

Rating: Armor provides two kinds of protection: against general attacks and against Firearms attacks. The number before the slash is armor rating for most kinds of attacks (for close combat and thrown ranged attacks, whether bashing, lethal or perhaps aggravated). The second number is for Firearms attacks — guns and bows. Bulletproof armor (Kevlar vest, flak jacket and full riot gear) also downgrades damage done in Firearms attacks from lethal to bashing.
Strength: Armor is often heavy and cumbersome. If your character does not have sufficient Strength to wear it, she cannot perform at peak efficiency. If your character's Strength is lower than that required for armor worn, her Brawl and Weaponry attacks suffer a −1 penalty.
Initiative: The penalty imposed on your character's Iniative trait for the armor worn, reflecting limited mobility.
Speed: The penalty imposed on your character's Running Speed for the armor worn.
Cost: The minimum dots in the Resources Merit usually required to purchase the armor.
*This type of armor is bulletproof.

Each weapon has a Strength requirement to be used effectively. A sword or shotgun might be too powerful for a weak or frail person to use properly. For melee weapons, compare a wielder's Strength to the item's Size. For ranged weapons, a Strength requirement is stipulated on the Ranged Weapons Chart. If your character's Strength is lower than that required for a weapon, attacks suffer a −1 penalty.

No weapon with a Damage rating of 3 or higher can be used with any type of Fighting Style or Merit that allows for dual-wielding, such as Two-Weapon Fighting or Gunslinger. Holding two melee weapons or firearms only provides special benefits or bonuses from one of the weapons, even if the character has the Ambidextrous Merit or any applicable Fighting Style.

States of Being

Combat is about hurting and killing opponents. You therefore need a means of gauging your character's physical condition during and after a fight. You need to keep track of whether he's bruised and battered, crippled or dead. And there are other states of being (and forms of injury) beyond those resulting from combat. The World of Darkness is a dangerous place. All forms of harm may befall your character, from fire to disease to electrocution. Yet, when he's faced with the horrors that lurk in the night, and supernatural creatures threaten his very existence, he may dismiss the pain as best he can to forge ahead against the unknown.

HEALTH

Chapter 4 quickly captures your character's vigor with the Health trait, which is determined by adding Stamina and Size. Typically, the bigger and more resilient your character, the more punishment he can endure before he goes down for the count. The average person is 5 Size and has 2 Stamina, for a total of 7 Health.

Your character sheet offers a chart for keeping record of your character's changing state of being. The dots are filled in from left to right, one for each Health that your character has. The squares shown are used to gauge his current condition: his Health *points*. If he has no injuries at all — no squares are checked off— your character is in perfect condition. Each time he suffers damage, mark a square from left to right across the row. Multiple points on a damage inflict extensive harm. For example, if your character's opponent achieves one success on an attack draw and your character is currently unharmed, that damage is marked in the leftmost box on your sheet. If in a subsequent turn he suffers two more damage, you mark off the second and third boxes.

The more injuries your character suffers, the more impaired his actions are. Penalties are imposed on your draws thereafter. The more damage your character takes, the more difficult it is for him to act at full capacity, as follows. Remember that wounds are marked off from left to right on your character's Health chart. The wounds on the right indicate whether he suffers any penalties from injuries.

Health Box Marked	Penalty
Third-to-last	–1
Second-to-last	–2
Last	–3

Subtract the penalty listed for your character's current Health from your test pools for every action he performs (including Initiative draws, but excluding Stamina draws to remain conscious — see "Incapacitation," below) until the wounds heal.

So, if your character starts with 7 Health and suffers five points of damage (there's a wound mark in his third-to-last box), his actions suffer a –1 penalty. This continues until that fifth Health point is recovered.

Should your character take more damage, he suffers a –2 and then a –3 penalty as the second-to-last and the last of his boxes are checked off.

Wound penalties also affect movement, reducing your character's Running Speed and Acting Speed alike. Wound penalties do not apply to your character's Defense or other Resistance traits — Stamina, Resolve or Composure — when those traits are subtracted as penalties from opponents' test pools.

Tracking Health

The injuries that your character suffers are recorded on your character sheet by filling in the squares of his Health chart. Bashing wounds are marked with a "/," lethal wounds are marked with an "X," and aggravated wounds are marked with an "*." As injuries of different severity are suffered, lesser wounds shift right. You don't have to erase and re-draw every wound on your Health chart, though. You can transform a bashing mark into a lethal one by drawing a crisscrossing line to create an "X." You can turn a lethal wound into an asterisk by drawing a horizontal and vertical line through the center of the "X." Just be careful not to "lose" any wounds in the translation.

To avoid carrying around pencils to keep track of health, some troupes may wish to experiment with different ways to keep track of Health points. For example, players could carry a number equal to their Health points of small tokens such as glass beads or signed slips of colored paper, and hand them over to a Narrator or other impartial observer as they get injured. When they run out of beads or slips, they've run out of Health. Provided it doesn't present more problems than it solves, they might even carry three different colors or types of tokens, one for bashing, one for lethal and one for aggravated.

When your character heals and recovers from wounds, you need to erase those marks, recover the tokens from a Narrator, etc.

APPLYING DAMAGE

Three different types of damage can be inflicted: bashing, lethal and aggravated. Bashing damage includes any wounds inflicted by blunt instruments, punches, kicks or other similar trauma. Lethal damage comes from knives, bullets or any type of attack that actually pierces or cuts flesh. Aggravated damage is usually reserved for supernatural sources. These forms of harm exceed the mundane or even reality as people know it. Anyone can incur aggravated harm, however, when bashing and lethal injuries turn so grievous that a victim falls into a coma and/or bleeds to death.

All types of injuries are cumulative and the resulting total determines your character's current Health points. Specifics on each type of damage are provided below.

When marking your character's damage in the Health chart on your character sheet, record a "/" for bashing, an "X" for lethal and an asterisk ("*") for aggravated damage. The last is best described as drawing a cross ("+") on top of an "X," for an eight-pointed star. These marks go in the boxes of your character's Health chart.

When it comes to your character's long-term survival, lethal damage is crippling and aggravated damage is ultimately fatal. If your mortal character's Health chart is filled with X's, he's on death's door. He's horribly beaten and in a coma, barely holding onto this mortal coil. Any subsequent injuries upgrade boxes with X's in them to asterisks. Once all boxes are filled with asterisks, your character is dead and gone.

When your character acquires a mixture of bashing, lethal and/or aggravated damage, mark the most severe damage at the left in his Health chart; it pushes any lesser damage right. For example, if you mark that your character has taken a point of bashing damage in the leftmost box, and she then takes a point of lethal damage, mark the leftmost box with an "X" for the lethal damage and move the bashing damage right one square by putting a "/" in that box. Any further bashing damage goes in the third box and keeps going right. Any further lethal damage pushes the entire thing right again until all the boxes are marked with either an "X" or "/."

Aggravated damage works the same way. Say your character has already suffered a point of lethal damage (first box) and a point of bashing damage (second box). He then suffers a point of aggravated damage. As the most severe injury that he's incurred, the aggravated goes in the leftmost box, the lethal moves right to the second box and the bashing moves to the third. Any more aggravated points suffered continue to push those lethal and bashing injuries right.

That's the first rule of tracking your character's Health: A more severe wound always "pushes" a less severe wound to the right. Wounds that are "pushed off" the right edge of the Health chart as a result are ignored.

Tracking your character's Health may seem complex at first, but it's easy to learn once you try it out. The system also makes recovery from injuries easy to record. While wounds are taken from left to right, they're healed from right to left. That way, your character's least severe, fastest-healing wounds are always healed (erased off your character sheet) first. The system also makes supernatural effects that temporarily grant extra Health easy to record (see the "Temporary Health Dots" sidebar).

Say your character with 7 Health is in bad shape with a chart that looks like this:

He takes another lethal wound. The new injury pushes his bashing wounds to the right. Since your character's seven Health boxes are all full of injuries, one of his bashing wounds is essentially pushed off the right edge of the chart and is ignored. Your character's Health chart becomes:

Or, if your character's Health chart looks like this:

and he suffers another point of aggravated damage (*), his Health chart changes to this:

His less severe lethal and bashing wounds are pushed to the right by the newest aggravated one, and one bashing wound is pushed off the chart and ignored.

Once all the boxes on your character's Health chart are filled and there are no less severe wounds to push right, *any* new injury upgrades the least severe wound that he already has. These upgrades occur from left to right. That's the second rule of tracking your character's Health.

So, say your character's Health chart looks like this:

He then takes a point of bashing damage. There are no empty wound boxes left to fill, and there are no less severe wounds to push to the right (your character's least severe wound is bashing and the new one he incurs is bashing). The new point of bashing damage therefore "upgrades" his leftmost, least severe injury by one kind. In this case, it means the bashing wound in his fifth Health box is upgraded to a lethal wound and his Health chart looks like this:

If your character then suffers three more points of bashing damage, the first two of those points upgrade his two existing bashing wounds like this:

The third point upgrades the leftmost, least severe wound that he has remaining. In this case, the lethal injury in his third Health box is increased to an aggravated wound, like so:

●●●●●●●○○○○○
⊠ ⊠ ⊠ ⊠ ⊠ ⊠ ⊠ □ □ □ □ □

If your character continues to take more bashing or lethal damage, another lethal wound is upgraded to aggravated for each new point of damage. If he incurs any more aggravated injuries, they push his lethal wounds right, as stated by the first rule of tracking Health.

With bashing and lethal injuries being upgraded as more harm is suffered, it's possible to be beaten to death. This might happen even if the damage is only bashing. Say all boxes of your Health chart are filled with slashes. When they're full, you go back and upgrade each to an "X" from left to right as your character continues to suffer more bashing injuries. Once all the boxes are full of X's, he's utterly overcome, comatose and dying. Suffering even more harm upgrades each lethal wound to an aggravated one. X's change into asterisks.

Remember that before any wounds are "upgraded" in severity, all of your character's Health boxes must be filled. There can be no less severe injuries to push to the right.

TEMPORARY HEALTH DOTS

It's possible that your character might acquire extra Health dots that make him more robust for a temporary period of time. A spell or supernatural effect might increase his Stamina, Size or even his Health trait directly. These bonus Health dots are added to the right side of your character's Health chart, and each also has a corresponding box where any wounds are recorded.

The question arises, though, if he incurs wounds in such extra Health and then the spell wears off, what happens? While his extra Health dots are lost, any wounds in them are not. Your character returns to his normal Health dots. Any wounds that were assigned to his bonus points now upgrade the least severe wounds that he already has, from left to right on his Health chart.

Imagine that your character gets two extra Health dots from a supernatural effect applied to him. His normal Health of 8 increases to 10. He now has 10 Health dots and boxes in his chart. He's been beaten up pretty badly, and has wounds in nine of his 10 boxes, as follows:

When the spell wears off, he loses his right two bonus Health. That means all of his normal Health boxes have injuries attributed to them. Since a bashing wound was assigned to one of his bonus Health, it upgrades the least severe wound that he has remaining among his normal Health boxes. In this case, that would be the bashing wound in his seventh box, which becomes a lethal wound. His Health chart then looks like this:

If he had suffered a bashing wound in both of his two bonus Health, his chart would have been filled with aggravated and lethal wounds when the two extra dots were lost, as follows:

● ● ● ● ● ● ● ● ○ ○ ○ ○
⊠ ⊠ ⊠ ⊠ ⊠ ⊠ ⊠ ⊠ □ □ □ □

In the first case, your character could fall unconscious (see "Incapacitation"). In the second case, he would be dying.

INCAPACITATION

Anytime all of your character's Health boxes are marked, regardless of damage suffered, and he has a bashing slash remaining in his rightmost box, a reflexive Stamina draw is made each turn for him to remain conscious. This draw does not suffer your character's –3 wound penalty. It's made at the beginning of your character's action each turn. So, if your character's last Health box is filled with a slash, you must make a Stamina draw when he acts next, whether in this turn or the next, and in each turn thereafter.

A failure means he falls unconscious. A success means your character is conscious and can continue to act in that turn. The standard –3 wound penalty *does* apply to any action he performs.

These Stamina draws continue from turn to turn until your character passes out completely or is healed and his rightmost Health box is emptied. Of course, if that last box is marked with lethal or aggravated damage, your character is on death's door or leaves this mortal coil.

A character who falls unconscious from a failed Stamina draw remains incapacitated until he regains at least one Health (his rightmost box is emptied again — see "Healing," below).

Of course, the danger of putting one's self in harm's way is getting hurt or killed. A mortal being who has lethal marks in all of his Health boxes is utterly overwhelmed and dying. Maybe he's bleeding internally, his lungs are punctured and he can't breathe, or he has suffered burns over most of his body. Each *minute* thereafter in which your character receives no medical attention — mundane or supernatural — he suffers one more injury. One Health box currently marked with an X is upgraded to an asterisk for aggravated damage, from left to right on your character's Health chart. Once all boxes are filled with asterisks, he's dead.

If a dying character receives successful medical attention before he fades completely, he can survive. (See "Healing Wounds" in Chapter 3, p. 67.) He's still a wreck, though. He requires ongoing medical or supernatural attention for the time it takes him to heal his rightmost wound. He's surely in a coma or is bedridden throughout the period. After at least one Health point has been healed completely, he can safely leave intensive care and recover on his own. See "Healing," below.

BASHING DAMAGE

Any kind of damage that does not pierce the body but that batters against it is considered bashing damage. This includes most harm from brawling combat, punches, kicks, beatings with a blunt instrument, and even falling or being thrown into a brick wall. Certain targeted bashing attacks may cause lethal damage, at the Storyteller's discretion and if that optional rules is used (see "Specified Targets," p. 226). Use a "/" when marking bashing damage on your character sheet.

Once all your character's Health boxes are full and the rightmost is occupied with a slash, begin making Stamina draws to see if he remains conscious. (Remember that your character's –3 wound penalty does not apply to these draws.) If he suffers any more harm, mark any further damage over your character's existing injuries (using X's or asterisks this time), from left to right. Once your character loses all Health from lethal damage, he's comatose. Once all is lost to aggravated damage, he's dead.

LETHAL DAMAGE

Attacks made with piercing or cutting weapons — knives, guns, crossbows or swords — deliver lethal damage. Fire also causes lethal damage to ordinary people. Mark lethal damage on your character sheet with an "X." Lethal damage is "upgraded" to aggravated once a mortal being's rightmost Health box is occupied by an X.

AGGRAVATED DAMAGE

The creatures that lurk in the world's shadows work in ways that most people cannot comprehend. They have their own mysterious agendas and miraculous capabilities. Among the latter is the capacity to inflict crippling harm on other beings and mortals. These otherworldly attacks sometimes prey upon enemies' inherent weaknesses, such as silver for a werewolf. If they involve dark magic and unfathomable might, they may inflict horrifying injuries.

A character's Health points lost to aggravated damage are marked with an asterisk. As the most severe harm a being can suffer, they always appear in the leftmost squares on your character's Health chart. If some boxes are already marked with asterisks from previous injuries, you continue filling the remainder in, from left to right. All lesser injuries — lethal or bashing — are pushed right as more and more aggravated damage is taken. This continues until your character's Health chart is full of aggravated marks.

Once the rightmost Health box on your mortal character's chart is filled with lethal damage, all subsequent injuries are upgraded to aggravated, from left to right. He also bleeds to death or simply fades from life at this point. One box, from left to right, is upgraded to aggravated damage per minute that passes without medical attention. Once your character's Health chart is full of asterisks, he's dead.

HEALING

Characters who face danger and who live to tell the tale still need time to recover physically. They need to heal their injuries. Short of being fatally injured or falling unconscious (see "Incapacitation," above), your character can continue to act while any of his Health boxes remain empty. If any of his last three Health boxes show injuries, he is debilitated with penalties to his test pools, but he can still be up and around.

Wounds recover at the following rates.

Bashing: One point is regained in 15 minutes.

Lethal: One point is regained in two days.

Aggravated: One point is regained in a week.

Note that some supernatural beings can recover from injuries at abnormally fast rates, even regenerating them automatically or healing them at will. Humans, of course, do not have that luxury.

Your character doesn't have to rest or receive special attention to clear Health squares. They are cleared automatically as the prescribed amount of time passes. The exception is if he is ever reduced in Health such that he is dying (see above); this requires intensive medical care.

Lost Health is recovered on your character sheet from right to left – in the reverse direction in which wounds are recorded on your sheet. Your character's least severe injury (that in the rightmost box) is recovered first. The damage marked in each box is erased as your character becomes progressively healthier, until his last (leftmost) box is empty and he is fully healthy again.

Example: *Your character's Health chart looks like this:*

His rightmost wound is healed first. It's from bashing damage, so is recovered in 15 minutes. (If your character had been unconscious from this wound, he regains consciousness upon healing it.) His next three lethal injuries each heal over two days. One is erased from right to left as each two-day period passes. All lethal wounds are gone after six days. Finally, each of your character's three aggravated wounds is healed after one week. It takes three weeks for them all to heal, each asterisk being erased from right to left.

Of course, receiving medical attention increases your character's recovery time. See "Medicine" (p. 66) in Chapter 3 for the Skill's effects on wounds. Supernatural treatments such as spells, powers or ointments might restore lost Health more efficiently (at the Storyteller's discretion).

DEPRIVATION

People go hungry and without proper drinking water everyday in the World of Darkness. They might eke out a meager existence in poor or war-torn countries, or could struggle to survive in inner cities where brown water drips from corroded pipes. A person might fall ill, be unconscious, or be imprisoned and starved for days on end. He could even send his spirit on an incorporeal journey during which his body languishes. Regardless of the circumstances, denied proper food and water for an extended period, a mortal being suffers.

Your character can go a number of days equal to his Stamina before being inhibited by lack of water. Once that threshold is exceeded, he suffers one point of bashing damage for each day that passes. He can go without food for a number of days equal to his Stamina + Resolve. After that point, he suffers another point of bashing damage a day. Denied both food and water, he suffers two bashing wounds a day.

Without food and/or water over an extended period, your character becomes susceptible to disease. Any draws made to resist disease suffer normal wound penalties when your character's Health falls to 3 or lower. The Storyteller might also call for draws to fight off disease where he would not have done so when your character was healthy and immune.

The Survival Skill (p. 81) may allow your character to forage for sustenance for himself and any companions. The Iron Stomach Merit (p. 137) may also help him to persevere by drinking and eating substances that do not normally have any nutritional value.

Health points lost due to deprivation cannot be healed until your character gains access to a sustained supply of food and/or water. If he has gone without both and comes upon a water supply alone, the Health he has lost to thirst heals normally. Still denied food, however, he continues to lose Health to starvation and cannot heal damage lost to it until he gets a steady food supply, too.

Using the Survival Skill to find food and water for one day — or even a few consecutive days — doesn't constitute a "steady supply." It only suspends the loss of Health for those days, after which points are lost again.

DISEASE

Diseases ravage the World of Darkness. Sadly, normal people are their primary victims. Beyond the threats that nature poses, such as Ebola, cancer and even the common cold, a creature that feeds on people might transmit ailments. Other beings might even control the spread of disease to keep humanity cowed and afraid.

The Storyteller can use the threat of infection as a plot device to increase tension and introduce socially relevant topics to a story. She could introduce biological warfare or serial killers using disease as a weapon to take danger to new heights. Moral issues could arise as characters face unwitting disease carriers, or they deal with the infection of a friend, family member or ally.

Characters with appropriate training can research antidotes and cures for diseases. Perhaps the "disease" that drives people to drink blood or that keeps their bodies alive after natural death can be undone. Although finding a cure for HIV should not occur within your game, an Intelligence + Medicine draw can detect the presence of HIV, hepatitis or other diseases. This, of course, requires access to the appropriate equipment and a sample of a subject's blood. Developing a cure can take hours, days or years. Developing an antidote is an extended action (Intelligence + Medicine), with a goal of 20 or more successes depending on the elusiveness of the ailment.

If your character suffers from a disease, she may take damage over time based on her rate of decline, on her Attributes or on the nature of the illness. The Storyteller determines how often your character must face damage from the disease — every hour, day or week. Each period typically imposes a number of Health points of damage that are suffered automatically. Stamina + Resolve (see "Resisting Poison or Disease," p. 53) might be drawn to resist harm from illness. This draw is modified by the severity of the disease in question.

Damage from illness can be treated as bashing or lethal (or aggravated if the ailment is supernatural in origin). The effects of the ailment might also pose penalties to Stamina + Resolve draws — say from -1 for a cold to -3 for tuberculosis. These penalties might apply to all other test pools as well. The Storyteller could decide that symptoms can be ignored until damage suffered from illness begins to impose wound penalties. It might also be impossible to heal damage from illness until the disease itself is overcome.

Beating an illness can involve extended Stamina + Resolve draws. A common cold might call for a total of three to five successes, with one draw made per day. Fighting cancer might demand 30 or more successes, with one draw made per month. Bonuses gained might reflect medications taken (+1) or extensive medical treatments (+1 to +3).

DRUGS

People take drugs all the time to escape the hardships of their lives. In the World of Darkness, humanity has a subconscious, ingrained awareness that it is prey for monstrous predators. Drugs are a frequent means of short-term happiness and oblivion.

It's impossible to discuss every drug that your character might take or be exposed to, but the list below offers directions on how to handle various kinds. The intent here is to address the effects of recreational and habitual drugs taken in tolerable doses. An overdose, whether self-induced or inflicted upon a victim, is covered under "Poisons and Toxins" (p. 247). The former use simply alters a character's perceptions and ability to function normally. The latter leaps straight to threatening to kill the character.

A tolerable dose of a drug alters a character's awareness and capacity to function. Your character might take the drug willingly or it might be slipped to him, but the application is not immediately life threatening. It could be possible to fight the effects of a drug by making Stamina + Resolve draws. See "Resisting Poison or Disease" (p. 53) for details. The potency or dosage of drug taken can influence such draws. A potent drug imposes a –2 to –3 penalty. A mild drug or small dose can impose a –1 penalty to ignore the effects.

The Storyteller might rule that a drug's effects are a genuine challenge to overcome; extended draws are required to do so. Draws might be made every hour, and penalized by the potency of the drug. The total number of successes required to overcome once and for all is dependent on the strength of the drug, perhaps from five to 12. Drugs never provide any benefits to test pools for supernatural powers or in combat, although a few of them may indeed weaken you in some respects.

• **Alcohol:** Subtract one point from any Dexterity-, Intelligence- and Wits-based test pools for every drink your character consumes in excess of his Stamina in an hour. Defense is also reduced accordingly. Meanwhile, Social draws can gain a +1 bonus per drink (maximum +3). If your character is a mean drunk, turn this modifier into a Social penalty. These effects fade at the rate of one per hour until all the alcohol is purged from your character's system.

• **Marijuana:** Lose one point from any Dexterity-, Intelligence-, Resolve- and Wits-based test pools for every hit your character takes from a joint or bong within an hour. Defense is also reduced accordingly. This effect fades completely an hour after the last toke, unless your character continues to "medicate" himself.

• **Hallucinogens:** All test pools lose one to three and traits such as Defense lose one to three depending on the strength of the hallucinogen. Your character may experience confusing, frightening or enraging hallucinations, although he may manage to realize that they exist only in his drugged mind. (Draw Intelligence + Streetwise or Empathy, with the –1 to –3 penalty in place, to gain any such "clarity," after which Stamina + Resolve draws can be made to resist the effects.) Composure is likely to be affected by a "trip," with a bonus or penalty depending on whether your character hallucinates when he sees anything, or he assumes that anything he sees is a hallucination. He might see an ordinary person and interpret her as a monster, or see a monster and interpret her as an ordinary person. The effects of hallucinogens persist for (8 minus Stamina) hours.

• **Cocaine/crack/speed:** Your character may gain a bonus point in Strength- or Stamina-based draws, although he may also become edgy and paranoid (–1 to Social draws). The Storyteller bases the effects of the drug on the volume that your character takes, on how pure it is and on your character's state of mind.

• **Heroin/morphine/barbiturates:** Pain subsides (wound penalties are ignored), but your character enters a dreamy state for (8 minus Stamina) hours. All test pools and Resistance traits such as Defense are reduced by two during that time.

For most players this goes without saying, but **Mind's Eye Theatre** *is a Storytelling game of make-believe. Elements such as violence and drug use are included purely for their dramatic roles in stories. Actual consumption of illicit substances not only breaks the fundamental rules of the game, it breaks the law.*

ELECTROCUTION

Lightning strikes, a live wire hits your character or he touches a conducting item. Some supernatural beings even possess mastery over electricity and can direct it at your character. Electrocution automatically causes bashing damage per turn of exposure. No attack draw is made.

If harm from electricity is more than just instantaneous — there's a constant flow such as through power cables — a victim may not be able to escape. His muscles contract, which can prevent him from pulling away. Draw Strength as a reflexive action in each turn of contact. Failure means your character is still connected to the source and suffers its damage each turn until a successful draw is made.

Source	Damage
Minor; wall socket	4 (B)
Major; protective fence	6 (B)
Severe; junction box	8 (B)
Fatal; main line feed/subway rail	10 (B)

Worn armor provides no protection against electrocution. Magical protection conjured up by supernatural beings might, at the Storyteller's discretion.

"He's Got C–4!"

The best way to do a lot of damage in a short amount of time is with an explosive. They're often used commercially to clear rock, to demolish buildings, or by the military to take out structures or vehicles. The Storyteller must remember that these devices aren't widely available. Many of them are strictly illegal to sell or possess, let alone use. Truly *massive* police manhunts result if a character uses serious explosives, especially in public places. The officers are going well armed, well trained and as persistent as they are humorless. In game terms, the Status Merit (p. 146) is required to have personal access to explosives. The Resources, Allies or Streetwise traits might also be applied to acquire these weapons. Of course, characters can always steal what they need, but remember that missing explosives attract a *lot* of attention.

No other hard-and-fast statistics for explosives are included in this book. Bombs and **Mind's Eye Theatre** characters just don't mix. Narrator-controlled characters are a slightly different story, because the Storytelling staff has total control over them and what they do with such devices. It is a conceit of live-action that most if not all action takes place in a confined environment. All players' characters would therefore be wiped out with a single, well-placed charge. No matter how "realistic" that might seem, it's hardly fair and never entertaining for one player's character to devastate the rest. Likewise, if characters bring hand grenades or sticks of dynamite to a fight, something has gone terribly wrong somewhere along the line. Maintaining an immersive setting is difficult under normal game circumstances. It's downright impossible when large chunks of setting are blasted apart.

Storytellers are encouraged to view explosives solely as plot devices. An explosive either destroys its target or it doesn't, depending solely on the needs of the story. If characters have dynamite to blow a safe and they're skilled enough to know how much they need to do the job, don't worry about math. It works unless something about the situation changes unexpectedly. If a Narrator playing a madman has the players' characters trapped in a building wired to explode, does it really matter how much damage the explosives do? The characters will either die if they don't get out in time, or live if they do.

Never be afraid to tell a player "no" when he asks to use explosives against another player's character. Urge him to find a different, more cunning, less direct means of attack.

FALLING

Your character tries to jump between buildings, but doesn't make it. He tries to scale a ladder but someone above pushes it away from the wall. Your character is thrown from a height by a powerful opponent. Regardless of the reason, your character plummets and may be hurt on impact. Falling damage is bashing, unless your character lands on a fence spike or broken glass, or hits the ground at terminal velocity. A person suffers one bashing wound for every three yards fallen. Terminal velocity is achieved in a fall of 30 yards or more; damage is lethal at that point. So, if your character falls 30 yards, he loses 10 Health points to lethal damage.

Once your character reaches terminal velocity, the damage he suffers remains 10 Health no matter how far he actually falls. Thus, falls from 30 yards and 100 yards both inflict 10 lethal damage.

The Storyteller may allow armor to be subtracted automatically from damage taken, assuming it can absorb the kind of damage incurred, and if it makes sense. Generally speaking, no protective clothing helps once someone reaches terminal velocity.

The Storyteller may allow your character to try to break his fall by some means, perhaps by grabbing for awnings or twisting to strike soil rather than concrete. A single Dexterity + Athletics draw may be called for, with each success gained diminishing damage taken. There may be a limit to how much damage can be shaved, though — say, three. There's only so much that desperate flailing and grabbing can do when someone falls from a significant height. Efforts to slow one's fall are usually useless at terminal velocity.

Falling into deep water, snow or a pile of pillows might diminish damage taken automatically, if the Storyteller allows it. No such "soft" landing is possible once terminal velocity is achieved. At that speed, hitting water is like hitting concrete.

FATIGUE

Sometimes the demands of dealing with the world and the threats it poses do not allow for such luxuries as sleep. Your character may need to remain vigilant or on guard over a person or item. He may need to get across country as soon as possible, but an airplane ticket is out of the question. So, just how long can he remain awake, and to what effect?

Your character can push himself beyond normal limits, but exhaustion soon impairs his abilities. Almost anyone can go without rest for 24 hours, but to continue is challenging. For every six-hour period that your character persists beyond 24 hours, make a Stamina + Resolve draw. If it fails, he falls asleep. If the draw succeeds, your character remains alert and active. Spending one Willpower on a draw adds three to your test pool. No more than one Willpower point can be dedicated to a single draw to remain awake.

Burning the candle at both ends impairs your character's performance. For each six-hour period in excess of 24 hours in which he foregoes sleep, his test pools suffer a cumulative –1 penalty. He has trouble focusing and might suffer mild hallucinations. This penalty also applies to successive Stamina + Resolve draws to remain awake.

If your character performs physically demanding activities such as running, fighting or performing a magical ritual, the Storyteller can impose an additional –1 to –3 penalty on your draws to remain awake.

The longest a person can go without sleep is a number of days equal to the lowest of his Stamina or Resolve, at which point he passes out.

Once your character does sleep, it's for eight hours, plus one hour for each six-hour period (in excess of 24 hours) that he remained active.

FIRE

Your character is exposed to a candle or an inferno. Either way, he gets burned. Fire automatically inflicts lethal damage per turn of exposure (no attack draw is required). The larger and hotter the flame, the more it hurts.

Size of Fire	Damage
Torch	1
Bonfire	2
Inferno	3

Heat of Fire	Damage Modifier
Candle (first-degree burns)	—
Torch (second-degree burns)	+1
Bunsen burner (third-degree burns)	+2
Chemical fire/molten metal	+3

So, a fire the size of a bonfire (2) and with the intensity of a torch (+1) inflicts three damage per turn of contact.

In general, if exposure to fire persists for more than a turn, it catches anything combustible. Your character continues to take full damage, even if he escapes the original source of the flame.

Depending on the accelerant involved, the size of a fire can be reduced by one point per turn. Your character might stop, drop and roll or be targeted with a hose or fire extinguisher. The Storyteller might rule that a fire goes out immediately under some circumstances, like diving under water. Or a fire could continue to burn despite efforts to put it out, such as with a grease fire when water is poured on it.

Most armor can block its rating in fire damage automatically for a number of turns equal to the gear's rating. Damage that exceeds armor rating in that period is transferred directly to your character. Once exposure exceeds armor's rating in turns, all fire damage is inflicted directly to your character.

So, armor rated 2 against most harm eliminates two points of damage in the first two turns that your character is on fire. As of turn three, your character gets no protection from his armor.

Characters who are reduced to zero Health by fire but who still manage to survive might suffer more permanent effects. They could develop a permanent impairment (reduced Physical Attribute), nerve damage (reduced Mental Attribute) or severe and disfiguring scars (reduced Presence), at the Storyteller's discretion. Such impairment can be defined as a Flaw (see p. 311) gained during play.

POISONS AND TOXINS

While some poisons or toxins might affect behavior and awareness as drugs do, most simply inflict lethal damage. These substances threaten a character's very existence. Indeed, drugs can do so too when overdosed. Poisons, toxins and drug overdoses must be delivered to a victim by a required means: injection, ingestion, inhalation or touch.

Injection: The substance is introduced directly into the bloodstream by a needle or through injury such as by a sword coated with venom. At least one success is required on an attack draw to deliver the injection on a resisting target. Unless the poison is designed to damage or destroy the blood itself, vampires are probably immune to these toxins.

Ingestion: The poison is administered in food or drink. These substances usually take longer to activate than others (say, an hour as opposed to immediate effects). Vampires are immune to most ingested poisons.

Inhalation: The poison is breathed in as a gas. Vampires are immune to most inhaled poisons.

Touch: Mere skin contact is all that's required to activate the poison. A touch is often sufficient to deliver the toxin (see p. 217), and a target's armor may apply as a penalty to the draw.

Once delivered, the poison automatically deals damage (usually lethal, but a knockout gas could cause bashing) equal to its toxicity level. Some substances inflict damage only once. Others might inflict it for a number of turns or once per hour until purged or until the effect runs its course. It could be possible to resist the effects of such substances by drawing Stamina + Resolve in a reflexive action with a penalty equal to the toxicity of the poison in question. Storytellers may call for extended rolls to overcome long-term exposure.

Poison/Toxin	Toxicity
Ammonia (inhalation)	3
Bleach (ingestion)	4
Cyanide (ingestion or inhalation)	7
Drug/Alcohol Abuse (ingestion, inhalation, injection)	3 to 7
Salmonella (ingestion)	2
Venom (injection or ingestion)	3 to 8

As with explosives, Storytellers should beware players who want to poison other characters by doctoring food or drink available in-game. At some venues, food might be considered entirely out-of-game and not a valid means to dose a target with a poison in-game. Even if food is considered in-game, allowing players to use it as a means of attacking each other eventually makes everyone paranoid about touching the food at all. It's recommended that Storytellers forbid in-game tampering with food provided for a session. They can, however, allow characters to do the doctoring away from the food table. Your character can't spike the whole punch bowl, but in rules terms she could spike a glass of punch that another character left unattended. If poison becomes a pain to track or causes more harm than good to the story, don't hesitate to rule that poisoning can be performed only through a Narrator.

TEMPERATURE EXTREMES

Extreme heat or cold has an adverse effect on your character. It may impose penalties on Dexterity- and/or Strength-based draws. It may even affect his mental acuity by penalizing draws involving Wits. (Defense might be reduced, too.) Penalties could be a cumulative –1 per hour of exposure. If test pools are reduced to zero as a result of exposure, your character is physically exhausted and immobilized, or delusional. An Attribute dot could even be lost permanently for prolonged exposure. Frostbite, hypothermia and heat exhaustion have dire consequences.

The Storyteller can also represent extreme weather conditions through the accumulation of damage. Such damage may be resisted for a number of hours equal to your character's Stamina + Resolve. Every hour after that inflicts a point of bashing damage that can't be healed until your character is no longer exposed to the extreme condition.

Chapter 8: Storytelling

What Is Storytelling?

Many roleplaying games are more concerned with rules and statistics than the drama created within the game. **Mind's Eye Theatre** certainly provides for a simple and consistent set of rules, but it seeks more than just card draws and character sheets. Storytelling is about drama, the wonder of a make-believe tale told by players. Good Storytelling is always surprising, taking unexpected twists and turns, and players often find their characters speaking and acting in ways that are strange and novel, taking on a life of their own.

Unlike child's play or corporate roleplaying, Storytelling can strive to be an art form. This might sound pretentious, but anybody who's played roleplaying games long enough has experienced more than one epiphany, a moment when the game seems to become a living entity, a Muse dictating strange and wonderful things to the players. These moments are worth striving for.

Throughout this chapter are tips and hints that will hopefully lead to these epiphanies. But it's not a recipe that, if followed exactly, will always produce the same result. It's the collected wisdom of a number of people who have spent many years enjoying live-action roleplaying. This chapter is designed to spark ideas for your own games, to offer tips on how to make it come to life, and to offer advice on how to avoid some common problems. Remember that a successful chronicle takes active work on everyone's part, and a desire to achieve more than the mundane.

Just don't get lost in the Ivory Tower. Don't deride those who see gaming as a fun hobby (which it is), or whose roleplaying stories don't aim higher than just getting together and having a good time. Instead, *encourage* and *persuade* players to stretch their boundaries. Storytelling is about achieving something great through an interactive tale, but not at the expense of fun.

Telling Tales

In **Mind's Eye Theatre**, what we call Storytelling isn't about standing before an audience and reciting

> The whole neighborhood abounds with local tales, haunted spots, and twilight superstitions; stars shoot and meteors glare oftener across the valley than in any other part of the country, and the nightmare, with her whole ninefold, seems to make it the favorite scene of her gambols.
>
> – Washington Irving,
> *The Legend of Sleepy Hollow*

memorized lines. It's a shared experience in which every player is involved in creating the story as it unfolds. Unlike interactive computer games, there is no set script. Players don't just stumble along triggering occasional video playbacks. They *create* events as they go, in competitive cooperation with the Storyteller. The only limit is your imagination. This has been said many times before about many different media, but roleplaying is the truest example of it. Since Storytelling takes place in a collaborative imagined space, uninhibited by the limits of screen pixel count or broadband connection speed, anything can happen as long as it's agreed upon by the players and Storyteller. There are certainly some rules, but they're intended to aid consistency and believability. They can always be thrown out if the Storyteller thinks they impede the actual story.

The majority of this book presents information for both players and Storytellers. With the exception of sections on costuming, props and setting materials, this chapter is aimed at the Storyteller alone, the single player most responsible for forming the shape and scope of the story. Players fill in valuable details, and can take the game in interesting directions, but the Storyteller, like a film director, ultimately decides what parts of the collaborative script are made a part of the story. He does so not in the editing room, but on the fly as the game is played.

There are a number of tools and structures that writers traditionally use to create stories, novels, plays and films. Some of them can be quite handy for organizing the Storytelling experience, to keep a session from becoming a random series of encounters. The most useful of these are presented below. Storytellers are encouraged to experiment with their own techniques and crafts.

THE PARTS OF A STORY

Most long-form stories are divided into segments of one sort or another, to allow actors and the audience a breather between major plot points. Storytelling games are no different.

The different units of time within a story — a turn, a scene — are covered in the Dramatic Systems chapter (see p. 152). Below we introduce the concepts by which we enhance the sense of connection between game sessions. With the real-world pressures like school, jobs and family, you might be able to get your friends together only once a week or even once a month, making it easy to lose the big picture of your tale. By dividing your games into chapters, stories and chronicles, you can better maintain a sense of cohesion and purpose over time.

CHAPTERS

A chapter is the shortest part of a story, and most stories are made up of many chapters. A single chapter typically represents one game session or night of play. Like a chapter in a novel or an episode in a matinee serial, a chapter is long enough to establish one or more key events in the story. The players' characters discover that their rival is smuggling black-market goods through a warehouse by the river, and go to investigate. If exploring that discovery takes too long to resolve (perhaps the players spend a lot of time preparing for their outing), the chapter might end on a cliffhanger, leaving the characters' situation unresolved at a point of danger or uncertainty.

A chapter comprises whatever events can take place within the span of a single game session. This can be handled rather loosely and chaotically, or the Storyteller can attempt to weave the disparate threads of player activity into what appears, by the end of the night, to have been a tightly plotted tale. Doing so requires guiding the players as they go, keeping them from veering in directions incidental to the plot. Tips on doing so are given below, in the section "How to Tell Stories" (see p. 267).

Side Sessions

Sometimes you might have a scene that involves only a few characters from the troupe, or maybe you want to give a new player a chance to try the game in a scaled-down setting before introducing her to the rush and confusion of the average group session. Perhaps a player has missed a few games and wants to have his character do some in-game catching up before the next chapter. Or you might want to run a special type of session such as a prelude or dream sequence that doesn't necessarily require all players to attend. On these occasions, you may wish to schedule what's known a side session.

Quite simply, side sessions are miniature chapters, typically used to further a particular plot line in greater detail than would be possible with a large group of players. Anything that can happen during a regular chapter can happen during a side session, though it should be noted that side sessions do not normally count as full chapters unless they are the only sessions a player can attend. Thus, side sessions do not re-set factors such as downtime actions per month. Nor can they allow a player to exceed a monthly/session-based experience limit if one is in place (see the "Experience" later in this chapter). Aside from those concerns, there is potentially no limit to the number of side sessions possible in your chronicle.

Scene Days

One variation on the side session that can greatly reduce the complexity of handling subplots, downtime actions and other small but vital aspects of the chronicle is to hold a "scene day." Players arrive and sign up to run short scenes for their characters, generally on a first-come, first-served basis. (Scenes that are required to move along the chronicle as a whole may be bumped to the head of the line, if necessary.) Other players waiting for their own scenes or just there to help out assist the process by assuming Narrator characters or other necessary roles, switching places to play their own characters when the time comes to run their own parts. It might even be possible to have several small scenes running at the same time, if the location is large enough and there are enough players and Storytelling staff members on hand. Players should remember that while scene days are great fun and offer a number of opportunities, they must be considerate of fellow troupe members and not take up too much time.

A scene day thus allows players a chance to flesh out their characters , running vital scenes for personal story lines and allowing the Storyteller to give players individual attention and to get a lot of chronicle business out of the way.

STORIES

A complete story introduces and resolves a single plot (see p. 256). A simple plot might unfold in a single game session, or 10 sessions might be required for a grand, epic plot. There can be many subplots within a story, but overall a story has a single, major focus, such as a mystery to uncover or a death to avenge.

To continue with the example of the rival's warehouse, perhaps the story is about discovering and shutting down the business. The first chapter is spent seeding clues for the players' characters to uncover. The second chapter involves their discovery of the warehouse and its location. The third and final chapter sees them shut it down — or fail to do so.

CHRONICLES

A chronicle is a series of stories, most often interrelated or that build toward a grand plot. A chronicle can also be identified by its cast of recurring characters. It's like a television series made up of individual stories (episodes) all about a group of characters or their mission. Some series strive for complicated plots spread out over a season of episodes (such as *The Shield*), while others prefer self-contained episodes whose plots have little effect on successive episodes (such as *The Simpsons*).

Perhaps your chronicle is about toppling the warehouse owner's crime empire. Discovering and shutting down the warehouse is only one stage of that quest. There are many more cesspools of crime to expose before the boss can be hauled off to jail.

THE MEANING OF A STORY

The *parts* of a story help to organize the roleplaying experience and give it cohesion over a series of game sessions. The *meaning* of a story reveals what the story is about — not what happens in it (that's the plot, described below), but how events matter.

THEME

Stories and chronicles have themes (sometimes chapters can also have themes). A theme sums up what a story is about, the so-called moral or lesson it tells. It might be "Crime never pays," "Violence begets violence," or "A hero shall rise." Theme is useful in reminding the Storyteller where he stands as events unfold. The wild give and take of ideas and events in a game can often be overwhelming, and the Storyteller might find that his story takes a direction he didn't anticipate or doesn't even understand. The best way to get back on solid ground is to remember the theme and steer events back to it. It doesn't matter what happens, as long as events illustrate the theme.

For example, in our crime-fighting chronicle, the theme might be "Crime corrupts even the just." In other words, it's about the characters' struggle to remain moral when confronting corruption. They'll be tempted to resort to all sorts of expedient but unjust (even sadistic) methods of overcoming their enemies. The bottom line is they must follow the law lest they risk becoming as bad as their rivals. If they destroy the criminal empire but tarnish their own reputations and souls through violence, lying and theft, do they really win?

This theme gives the Storyteller a tool by which to focus any scene on the overriding purpose or vision of his story. Perhaps he expects the players' characters to be tempted to mete out their own style of justice, but to ultimately take the thugs they capture to jail. Instead, the characters succumb to temptation and take the thugs out to the desert and bury them up to their necks in sand, leaving them to bake, ripening for a confession. The Storyteller didn't expect this, but, remembering his theme, he knows just how to run with it. When the players return, they find one thug dead of exposure, another half-dead from scorpion poison, and the third delirious and raving out of his mind. The characters' own actions have led them into the trap of being corrupted by their own crime-fighting zeal.

MOOD

Just as important as theme for organizing a story is mood, or atmosphere. Keeping a story cohesive over the course of many different sessions is made easier if a consistent mood is evoked. Each scene, chapter, story and chronicle can have its own mood. Mood isn't the atmosphere of the actual gaming environment (that's covered below under

"How to Tell Stories"). It's the key images, symbols and even tension that the Storyteller consistently invokes to set the stage for the story. Mood reinforces theme.

Our crime-fighting chronicle might have a mood characterized as "dark and gritty" or "film noir." Things are described in blurred contrasts, in grays rather than in black and white. For example, the night is often fog-bound and full of shadows rather than clear. This mood implies that answers never come easily and that choices are never simply right or wrong. Or the Storyteller might go for something more subtle, such as "ominous significance," wherein everything hints at a darker meaning beneath the surface, much like the mood evoked in the *Twin Peaks* television series. Threats lurk everywhere. Nothing and no one can be trusted. Even the swish of pine trees in the wind seems to forebode a sinister revelation.

Mood isn't as easy to orchestrate as theme. It's more ephemeral and requires some off-the-cuff creativity to implement, especially when players surprise you by taking their characters to places you weren't ready to introduce. But don't sweat it. Consistent mood is just a tool, not a requirement. It's there to help you focus on the theme through imagery and other sensory data — sounds (moaning wind, piercing screams), tactile sensations (greasy, sharp) and even smell (peppermint, rotten eggs). If your mood is "film noir," you might avoid describing smells or tactile sensations and concentrate solely on sight and sound, to reinforce the stark nature of the story, devoid of any real human touch.

Ultimately, mood makes it seem like your story's theme pervades every part of the world. Not even the night sky, wind or the shadows appear to escape the significance of the story's events or meaning.

The Importance of Atmosphere

Think about the scariest movie you know, and how you would react to watching it all alone on a dark night, or perhaps with one or two equally scared friends. Then try to imagine how scary it would be if you watched it on a sunny afternoon while hanging out with friends and cracking jokes about it at every turn. The difference that you have just observed is one of atmosphere, and in a live-action game atmosphere is primarily composed of two elements: theme and mood. Without these ephemeral yet vital components, **Mind's Eye Theatre** can quickly become little more than a wisecracking splatter fest rather than an engaging personal exploration of fear, mystery and supernatural horror.

It's human nature for someone to crack jokes when he's scared — it's one way to avoid acknowledging how frightened or disturbed he really is. If such humor is in-character, that might just mean a player is roleplaying. It might also mean that he's not really in character and is disturbing the experience of you and other players. Talk to him about it. A player who thinks of a joke or witty remark can always save it for the end of the session.

Despite your best efforts, the game's atmosphere will be broken from time to time. You or another member of the Storytelling staff may be the one responsible. Don't let it become a habit, though, or something of inestimable value to your game may be lost.

WHAT HAPPENS IN A STORY?

Apart from the meaning you impart in a story, you must consider what happens in a story. Everything is tied together; meaning and the events that evoke it. Considering the events of your story as separate units is a useful means of getting a handle on them. In the end, they form an unbroken continuum.

PLOT

Plot is what the characters *do*. They act out a series of events that, considered as a whole, tells a story from beginning to middle to end. No Storyteller is completely in charge of his plot; the players provide many twists. However, a basic plot is helpful when presenting a story, even if it's doomed to be derailed, hijacked or shanghaied into new lands of development.

In **Mind's Eye Theatre**, several major plot lines are run simultaneously in a game session, each divided into separate acts. Some plots are open to everyone or naturally involve all the players in the troupe, while others might be followed by only a small group.

Regardless of how many plots you have running at any given time, it's wise to sketch each of them out so you have an idea of what can happen as the story proceeds. Players have a knack for doing things you don't expect, so be prepared to shift the story around if necessary. Indeed, that's why a general outline is sometimes better than a specific one. The simple plot of a crime-fighting chronicle might be broken down like so:

• First Act (Beginning): The characters are made aware of the problem: the city's crime boss.

• Second Act (Middle): The characters work to overthrow the boss.

• Final Act (Conclusion): The characters win (but at what cost?), or the crime boss wins.

Plots don't have to be confined to three acts; they can have many. But three is a nice, easy way to keep to a thread simple without confining events that inevitably veer in new directions during play. The above plot could be complicated as follows.

• First Act: The characters are attacked by thugs.

- Second Act: The characters investigate who the thugs are and why they attacked. The characters find out about the crime boss.
- Third Act: The characters work to overthrow the boss' empire.
- Fourth Act: The crime boss threatens a character's loved one, and cruelly kills her even if the character capitulates to his demands.
- Fifth Act: The characters win, or the crime boss kills them or sends them packing to a new city.

The fourth act is a bit tricky (the characters might rescue the loved one and send her far from harm), so it might be amended: "If thwarted, the boss takes out his ire on an innocent and makes sure the characters know they're to blame." Otherwise, none of these acts is too hard to achieve, even if the players have different ideas about what to do. For example, even if the players' characters refuse to investigate the thugs who attacked them, they can still be drawn into the crime war in other ways, willingly or not.

Another complication might be that the crime boss is really a supernatural being who wields sorcery to maintain his empire. This secret could be discovered in any of the acts, depending on character ingenuity. Or the characters could win without ever really knowing what they're up against. Or maybe by destroying the boss, the characters unwittingly release a ghost whose restless soul was appeased by the boss' sacrifices. Now it wants revenge against those who thwarted its servant.

The bottom line is that plot is merely an outline of what the Storyteller wants to have happen, a series of events that helps to illustrate the theme.

SAMPLE PLOTS

The following section contains some sample ideas suitable for both main plots to sustain a story or perhaps even a full chronicle, as well as subplots to give individual characters more depth. Storytellers should feel free to alter, adapt and otherwise tinker with these ideas to make them suit their chonicle; even if the Storyteller does not wish to use any of these ideas, they can still serve as examples of the kind of conflicts that drive different levels of the chronicle.

Main Plots
- Individuals all over town are starting to experience bizarre periods of "missing time," including the characters. They keep winding up in increasingly bizarre situations, and it's getting worse. Who's causing this, and what do they hope to accomplish by it? Can it be stopped?
- A sinister creature has managed to insinuate itself into the city's political structure. The characters must remove this high-profile menace before it does serious harm to the community. But how do they take down a public figure without winding up in jail or worse?
- Strange lights have started appearing over a local forest or body of water around midnight each night, and the people who live in the vicinity are acting oddly, sleeping during the day and watching the lights all night. What does it mean? And what can be done about it?
- A series of murders has begun in the area, each one involving strange occult designs traced around the body. Each death is more savage than the last, as though the killer is getting bolder — or *stronger*. The death toll will continue to climb until the killer is caught... but is it even human? And if it's not, what can they do?
- A strange new drug is working its way into the local club scene, one which supposedly gives users "mystic insight." It's obviously a scam... until a friend tries it and makes some uncanny predictions. Now the question is: Where does it come from? And what else does it do?

• Sensitive characters or similarly gifted allies start noticing a large number of ghosts in the area, and they seem to be drawn to a particular house in a nice part of town. Can the characters figure out what's going on before the town is flooded with spirits (or worse)?

• A famous television "psychic" comes to town and promptly begins visiting all manner of local supernatural hot spots, riling the anger of the unseen forces with his shameless grandstanding. Can the characters find a way to drive off this publicity-seeking fraud before someone actually gets hurt, and without getting their faces on the national news in the process?

• A traveling museum exhibit comes to town, containing a number of supposedly "cursed" relics. When one of the items is stolen, the town is plagued by a rising number of strange "disasters." It's apparently critical the item be returned to its resting place — but who has it?

• A non-lethal but rather debilitating illness is sweeping the area, and rumors are starting to fly about its source, each more fevered and illogical than the last. Can the characters avoid getting sick, tend bedridden loved ones and still figure out some sort of solution to the problem before the town explodes in a full-blown panic?

• Every year some local teenagers go out to a secluded spot at the edge of town and hold a wild party to celebrate of the school year. The problem is, this year the site is right in the middle of the territory of a group of savage creatures the characters have seen roaming the area. Can they fight or drive off the beasts in time to keep the kids safe?

Subplots

• A close friend or family member becomes romantically involved with a mysterious stranger almost overnight. The loved one is absolutely smitten, and refuses to hear anything to the contrary. Is it really love at first sight, or does this suitor have a sinister agenda?

• A character begins having disturbing dreams in which seemingly random events occur, only to see them played out during her waking hours. This is merely curious, until the character has a dream of some terrible event: a friend dies, the town suffers some disaster, etc. Is it just a string of coincidences, or is this a chance to change the future?

• A character who recently committed some criminal or otherwise suspicious activity and got away with it receives an anonymous package in the mail. It contains evidence of her guilt, along with a demand for money — blackmail! Does she pay and hope they go away? Try to turn the tables? Or take the heat and turn herself in?

• A character has managed to luck out and find someone who's totally perfect for him. The interest is definitely mutual; the only problem is the time his involvement in the main storyline requires is threatening what is otherwise a perfect relationship. Something has to change. Does he try to strike a better balance, turn his back on the love of his life or tell the other characters to get lost to be with his beloved?

• Concerned by the odd habits the character has developed, his family members fear he is an alcoholic or drug addict, and stage an intervention. Now that they're watching him closely, can he keep up his new activities without them finding out (or dragging them in too)?

• Chronicle events are taking their toll on a character's productivity, and she gets called in by the boss and warned that any more missed shifts or shoddy work will mean the end of her employment. This is especially powerful if the character needs the job to support a family or outfit a team of her fellow characters. When it comes down to it, will she choose to lose the job to do what she feels is right?

- Just before or after witnessing supernatural or otherwise inexplicable events, a character keeps bumping into a particular person, apparently by accident. There doesn't seem to be anything notable about this person otherwise, but over time these meetings are really starting to add up. Is this person as normal as they seem to be? Or is their presence around these events anything but accidental?

- A trusted and important figure in the character's life — lover, Mentor, best friend — comes begging for aid, calling in old favors to get help with an urgent personal matter. While the matter is indeed quite important, what they're ask the character to do for them involves some extremely shady if not outright illegal actions, and carries some real risks as well. However, refusal will mean breaking ties with this person, possibly forever. What does the character do?

- Someone is leaving roses and little personal notes on the character's doorstep at all hours of the day and night, but none of the neighbors ever seem to see anyone around, and casual efforts to try to catch the culprit likewise turn up empty-handed. Is this just a sneaky would-be paramour, or is there something more supernatural going on here?

- A character finds an immensely valuable object in the course of another storyline. Does she tell anyone about it? Selling it could solve a lot of her financial problems, but what if it's stolen? Or famous?

GETTING THE PLOT OUT

When organizing a live-action game, remember that it doesn't function like a conventional roleplaying game. Simply throwing a plot in front of a large group of players is likely to leave many of them with nothing to do. It's like feeding fish. Sprinkling a little food on the top just means the big, aggressive fish eat while small or timid ones wait for whatever's left. In a live-action game, active or aggressive players take control of the plot. This leaves your reactive or laid-back players in the cold. It's therefore best to consider multiple approaches to get the plot out to all players.

Repeat Yourself

You'd be surprised how often players don't get involved in a story, not because they're disinterested or their characters aren't capable, but because they don't know what's going on. With all that happens at the average game session, it's really easy for players to miss an important announcement, be absent for the arrival of a vital Narrator character, or to otherwise find themselves out of the loop. Part of getting a plot out to the troupe often involves repeating it several times in several different ways and in several different places. Perhaps the group first hears about a development through a mentor or trusted ally, then later on as a shadow of it works its way onto the local news, and perhaps yet again as several of the characters' friends and relatives witness related phenomena. This ensures that all the characters are exposed to the plot several different times, without hitting them over the head with it either.

A good rule of thumb is to somehow prominently announce a major plot development at least three different times. That generally ensures that everyone hears it directly or players recognize how important it is and spread the word. If this approach seems heavy handed in the shadowy World of Darkness, remember that even the best story line is no good if none of the players knows it's there.

And yet, use common sense. Not all story lines and plot twists need to be shouted from the rooftops. In fact, doing so may ruin any surprise or secrecy surrounding them. Use your imagination and think of more subtle ways to disseminate your more secretive plotlines.

Multiple Offerings

Perhaps the simplest way to hook all players is to give them frequent opportunities to get immersed in events in different ways. After all, different characters have different motives. Perhaps the majority of the troupe run off after the police when word of a missing girl is spread. Meanwhile, a more contemplative group hangs back to see what happens next. While the first group is out and about, a mysterious stranger arrives and offers more reluctant characters a hefty reward for their aid in finding the child. Finally, the grieving parents arrive on the scene and beg for help from emotionally sensitive characters. Here we have three different approaches to getting players involved in the same problem, each likely to trigger the desired response from a general character type (proactive or helpful adventurer, mercenary and sympathetic).

As mundane as it sounds, sometimes getting all players involved in a plot really is just a matter of making another story hook available an hour or two after the initial one, when the more aggressive players have had time to run off and prepare their responses. Sometimes it just takes other players that long to weigh their characters' options and decide whether they want to get involved.

Group Targeting

Sometimes characters gather in formal or informal groups, whether out of friendship, happenstance, political convenience or even just personal safety. Tailoring a plot hook for each of these groups (and perhaps another general hook for all "unattached" characters as a whole) can work wonders in getting everyone involved. A group of college kids hears about a contest to bring back photos from a haunted house. A group of parapsychologists and investigators happens to pick the same night to do some research. Meanwhile, neither group suspects that some of the locals are out for a night of drinking in the nearby woods. Thus, three very different groups are drawn to the same location without the need to try to rope them all together with one clumsy plot hook.

Just be sure that you don't favor one group over the others. While not every group of characters will be on even footing every time, routinely giving one advantage makes other players feel secondary. Make sure each group gets a chance to shine. Maybe the college kids have contact with a sympathetic professor who can help shed some light on the mysterious happenings, while the parapsychologists bring much-needed investigatory equipment and even an air of "legitimacy" to the group that keeps them out of jail when they're caught exploring someplace they shouldn't be. Of course, for their part the locals know the area better than anyone else, and can help the group dig up area history or avoid getting lost in the woods, not to mention maybe find local townsfolk willing to unofficially support the group's activities.

Team Building

This approach to character involvement encourages experienced or aggressive characters to partner up or form groups with new or more reluctant characters as part of the plot. Perhaps elder characters are made responsible for overseeing the progress of rookies in the field, or maybe they're punished with a "babysitting" assignment. No matter what the in-game rationale, the result is mixed groups of active and reactive characters. This technique keeps an involved plot from falling into the hands of just a few highly active players.

Be careful not to use this tactic too often or too overtly, though. Players dislike few things more than being led around by the nose or being forced to do things that seem out of character. Use it sparingly, and make sure characters have convincing reason to organize in this fashion when it is used.

Guided Plot Lines

One approach to immersing characters in a story is having Narrator characters control access to all or at least important events, and confronting specific characters with these details. By stationing Narrators as "guards" over the story, you regulate who gets involved and can have Narrators approach players individually if they look lost or bored. At the same time, remember that Narrators serve the story. They're not obstacles intended to slow down active players. Narrators coax out some players with information to share, and can challenge other players with tests or dangers that keep all players active to a similar degree. A Narrator character portraying the local eccentric who knows all about the creepy house on the other side of town can approach some players that look lost and give them some information that helps them get back on track. Of course, that same Narrator character can also show up as an added distraction or challenge to players who might be threatening to leave the rest of the group in the dust, so that one group doesn't run through and solve all the mysteries themselves.

Multiple Plots

Rather than just offer one plot that can be engaged from different angles, offer up various story lines at the same time. While this is by far the most work of all the options, it ensures that no player can monopolize the action, and it gives all players something to do. Various plots may or may not be connected. Either way, characters will encounter one another in their various pursuits and may devise connections between plots whether they exist or not.

Just be aware that this tactic not only takes a lot of work in creating and keeping an eye on unfolding events, but if the plots are too disconnected, scheduling large games may become difficult. Characters are very likely run off in many different directions. Getting them under one roof, whether real or imagined for the purposes of events, may be quite a challenge.

Continuing with the previously mentioned examples, the college kids and the parapsychologists might both be handed plot threads related to uncovering the history of the haunted house, the kids for their contest, the researchers for their expedition. Chances are those groups won't have any trouble coming together. At the same time, the Storyteller can give a semi-related plot thread to another group of players portraying investigative journalists, who are shadowing one or both groups as part of an exposé for the local news. They're not interested in the haunted house itself, but their actions will still lead them to go along with much of what the two other groups are doing.

Lastly, the Storyteller can put the locals on an apparently unrelated plot dealing with strange people lurking in the woods near the house, prompting members of the community (namely the characters) to go out there and investigate. The haunted house isn't immediately relevant to them at all — they only care about running these shady types out of their woods. Of course, what they believe they're in for and what will actually happen are two very different things ...

Subplots

Subplots are nearly as important to the success of a live-action game as main plots. They're minor events or activities, triumphs or tragedies that help round out a character's existence. Note that the term "minor" is used only in reference to a troupe's overall story arc. To the characters involved in a subplot, there's nothing minor about it! For example, a character might be fired after a string of unexplained absences from work and be faced with losing her house and all she's worked for. Does she get another job and pray she can keep it, or ignore such mundane concerns in favor of continuing to stalk the *things* out there? This subplot doesn't effect any other characters directly, but it has a profound impact on the character in question, reinforcing the consequences of her behavior under the main story arc.

Conversely, some characters just aren't interested in the main plot at times. Their goals might be too far removed from the primary one, or their personal motivations might be more important to them than collective ones. This may seem like a problem, but it's actually an opportunity. Character goals and motives are the very essence of great subplots, and can lead eventually to broad, more encompassing stories. Just ask what that character's goals are and you can weave a subplot for them. If a character wants to start his own business, confront him with a chance to make a large financial gain, but that involves some shady activity, or even just requires that he do less supernatural investigation at a critical time.

You may discover that subplots are also an effective means of introducing a new character into an existing story. Just give the newcomer a connection with one or more existing characters and let the sparks fly. Having two characters be relatives is a classic standby, of course, but friends, service buddies and co-workers work well, You can even have them be former (or current) rivals, either personally or professionally, though it's generally best to give them some reason to work together now unless you want them to be at each other's throats directly. Remember: Conflict is your friend! It makes the best subplots and is relatively easy to establish.

When running long-term stories, be alert for subplots that take on a life of their own and threaten to become major plots, engulfing many characters and dominating entire game sessions. Maybe your small business entrepreneur unexpectedly drags the other players into his financial schemes, preventing them from taking part in the story you had planned. This development may not derail your own story. Again, look at it as an opportunity. You might even be grateful to your players for this type of enterprising behavior, because it relieves you of some of the burden of creating stories. Work with the players involved to make a personal story line a thrilling part of the main plot. Perhaps he discovers that his potential backers are actually connected to some sinister conspiracy, and were attempting to bribe him in order to stop his investigatory efforts — but now that he and the others know their true nature, these new enemies attempt to destroy their reputations and livelihoods. Even if you can't tie the new subplot back to your story arc, let the players run with it for a while. Your plot will still be there when the characters are ready for it.

CONFLICTS

It's been said before and it's worth repeating: Conflict is the essence of drama. Conflict does not have to be physical (although it quite often is in roleplaying games). It can be as simple as a character striving to discover the location of a store in downtown New York. The conflict is represented by the obstacles he encounters, even if they're merely other shoppers or the temptations of other, easier-to-find stores. This is perhaps the most boring example possible, but it shows that conflict is simply about setting an obstacle before the characters, giving them some challenge that bars their way to easy victory.

Live-action roleplaying differs from most other forms of gaming in that its prime source of conflict is derived from social interaction, as opposed to combat and other acts of physical prowess. Given that the average troupe has 20 or more players and most if not all of those characters has the drive and personal strength of a central character in a novel or film, all manner of social conflict comes quite naturally to most games, without much prompting from the Storyteller.

This is not to say that physical conflict can't be part of **Mind's Eye Theatre**. Indeed, it can be a very compelling and exciting element as the result of social interaction gone wrong or negotiations stalled out. But combat in a live-action game should generally be a last resort, much as it is in real life. Introducing it just to stir things up runs counter to the social emphasis of the game.

The best source of social conflict is between players' characters. Giving them multiple objectives at cross-purposes, a limited number of items or positions for which they compete, or even just stirring up the hornet's nest of envy and pride is often enough conflict to inspire an entire chapter, if not several. Think of D'artagnan's first meeting with the Three Musketeers. A series of misunderstandings results in a grand sword duel. But that encounter forges an alliance of heroes whose like has scarcely been seen since. While the fight is cool, the characters' social interaction and eventual cooperation is most important to the story. Of course, your players' characters might not wind up being nearly as friendly in the end, but that's the World of Darkness for you.

Narrator-controlled characters are also ultimate sources of conflict, because you can make them as nasty and complicated as you like. Players' characters can search for clues to find them, gather evidence of such nemeses' crimes, and unravel their defenses. What fun is it destroying a crime empire if you never get to take on the boss himself? Would we know the name of Elliot Ness without his rival Al Capone? Robin Hood without the Sheriff of Nottingham? Woodward and Bernstein without Nixon? Facing a hated Narrator-controlled rival should be one of the most memorable events in any story. Sure, he can be a strict bad guy, a pure foil to the players' characters, but he could also be more complicated than that. He could have his own quirks and complications, motivations and fears. Defeating an antagonist because he's the enemy is one kind of resolution, but facing him only to discover that he's also doting father or a loving patron of the arts makes for a much more interesting and believable opponent. Defeating the first is a pure victory because the antagonist is two-dimensional. Defeating the second involves moral grays and emotional nuances, because on some level players' characters can understand or even empathize with him.

No matter who an opponent is, however, conflict — overcoming obstacles, whether they are people, things or even one's own conscience (think of Hamlet) — creates drama.

INTERNAL VS. EXTERNAL CONFLICT

One special topic that Storytellers should think about when constructing conflicts for a chronicle is whether they want the players to be confronted by external threats, fight internally against each other (literally or figuratively), or some mixture of the two. Most traditional roleplaying games assume that the players are primarily faced with external threats — enemies strike, disasters loom and so on. And there's nothing necessarily wrong with keeping that focus in live-action play. Creating a persistent yet multifaceted enemy like a crime boss and his empire or a dark magician and her sinister cult following is good for this sort of conflict, as it allows for a variety of different storylines and challenges while still keeping the players focused on a single set of enemies. Indeed, focusing primarily on external conflicts is good for chronicles where you wish to stress group unity, or simply do not feel like handling a lot of squabbling between players' characters. Just make sure these threats aren't too simplistic, or the chronicle will start to feel more like a linear video game instead of an interactive live-action roleplaying experience.

At the same time, the large groups of players' characters that comprise a lot of live-action troupes offer the potential for a lot of conflict between characters, whether in the literal sense of physical struggle or perhaps more commonly in terms of social and political maneuvering. Given how driven many players' characters are, it's only a matter of time before some of them butt heads, and quite a few stories can be sustained just by putting prizes or obstacles among the players and watching them play off each other. Centering a chronicle around a political or social hierarchy is a good way to encourage this kind of play; just be careful to make sure that there's always enough rewards and story hooks to go around, as opposed to letting a few characters enjoy the spotlight. Players who feel like they've been forced out of the action and have no way to get back in seldom stay in a chronicle, after all. Also, make sure the players aren't taking in game squabbles personally — internal conflicts can be very intense.

Mixing internal and external conflicts is a good balance for live-action chronicles that don't want the characters to constantly be at each others' throats, but also don't want them to get too cozy either. This kind of chronicle can be created by having the characters faced with some serious external threats, but also making them part of an organization or hierarchy that offers some real benefits to those willing to fight their way through the ranks (or deny their enemies the same). That way you can ramp up the external threats when you feel the internal conflict is stagnating, or intensify the need to pay attention to internal tensions if external threats are growing tiresome.

Player Surveys

Running a large live-action game requires a deep level of dialogue and interaction between players and Storytellers. Everyone comes to the game with his own aspirations and desires, such as stories based on problem solving or immersion in what it means to be a hero or monster. You can learn everyone's likes and dislike before starting a chronicle by issuing a poll. The one proposed here lists five basic elements of a "typical" live-action chronicle and asks readers to rate them on a scale of 1 to 10 based on how much they would like to see them in the game. A rating of 1 indicates very little interest and 10 indicates exceptionally strong interest. So, if a player really enjoys mysteries, and social intrigue only slightly less, she might rate Mystery/Suspense 9 and Social/Political Intrigue 7. If she doesn't enjoy fighting that much, she might rate Action/Adventure 3. And she might give the other two categories a 5 each if she didn't have strong feelings about them one way or another.

Action/Adventure — Chases, escapes, infiltration missions, battles and besting physical obstacles of all sorts. Good for those who like the adrenaline rush and visceral high of performing amazing physical feats and defeating foes head-on.

Mystery/Suspense — Riddles, ciphers, enigmas, mysteries and investigations into the strange and unknown. Good for those who enjoy new discoveries, unraveling puzzles and the thrill of acquiring forgotten (or forbidden) knowledge.

Social/Political Intrigue — Gossip, rumors, reputation, power plays, intrigue, double-entendres, political games and backroom deals. Good for players who like plotting and scheming and deciphering others' motives.

Personal Subplots — Romance is its most obvious form, but players who stress this aspect of Storytelling are interested in seeing subplots and "small" stories involving characters' daily lives and personal relationships outside of the chronicle's main storylines. Good for players who like moral dilemmas, tough personal choices and the consequences a characters' actions have on her "old life."

Supernatural Elements — This aspect is actually expressed through the others during the game, but it is rated on its own simply because some players like to see the supernatural world come into play often or directly, while others prefer it to be in the background, manifesting subtly.

Once you have these numbers collected, you can sit down with your staff and use the polls to not only run totals to see what overall elements players hope for, but also to break players up into out-of-character groups based on their various interests. (That is, write down who's an action junkie, who's a mystery fan, and so on.) You may even hand out this poll several times over the course of a chronicle to make sure you have a finger on the pulse of the group's interests. This way, you can anticipate who's most likely to be interested in a new story line, or who can be approached with a particular subplot. The result is stories geared specifically to certain players.

If the group as a whole values mystery and social intrigue, but a few players are really into action, you can design a main plot focused on, say, digging into the election campaign of a mysterious candidate who might have supernatural masters. At the same time, you can introduce a subplot or side session geared toward action, perhaps that requires breaking into the candidate's mansion or confronting his sinister backers. If an individual player loses interest, look at his poll results and see if you can't hook him back in by appealing to his strong suit. Maybe he's the only one in the troupe who really likes a good mystery, and you haven't offered anything along those lines in a while. Send a subplot his way involving a tantalizing enigma that eventually leads to the main story and you'll have him back in no time.

The survey provided here is by no means exhaustive. At risk of giving some things away, for example, Storytellers who want be as precise as possible might list specific story lines in the poll as opposed to general elements, so that players rate options like, "Checking into the history of the strange house," "Learning the identity of the weird family across town" and "Hunting the wicked *thing* that lives in the woods."

SETTING

The setting of your story is as much a character as the fictitious individuals who populate it. Before choosing your setting, consider your theme and mood. Are there settings that will enhance or detract from them? It's difficult to convey a brooding or somber mood when your setting is a circus or a car wash, while the right portrayal of an abandoned cathedral can convey its own mood of sorrow and desolation.

Setting your story in familiar territory is a good option. It's fun to pretend that your hometown might hide some kind of supernatural presence behind the storefronts and houses that you already know. There are strange legends in real life that we've all heard, places around town that seem tailor-made for supernatural stories. You know that old barbershop supply store downtown with the creepy owner who doesn't like customers? Some say he sells black-magic supplies in the back — just ask him and he'll show you. This kid went back there once, but he won't talk about what he saw. What's really going on there?

Providing an interesting and believable setting relies on balancing the real and unreal. Good horror relies on a contrast with the ordinary to give it substance, otherwise even the most bizarre events seem ordinary before long. Pick up that copy of *Weird U.S.* and mix urban legends with real places. Actual houses you've walked past at dusk, the alley near your workplace that nobody wants to go down, the old flooded quarry in the woods where everyone's afraid to swim. In a sense, this is a re-enchantment of the world, although in the World of Darkness the effect is more often chilling and terrifying than awe-inspiring.

A good place to start building a setting is to obtain some accurate information about your city history, government and municipal services, and to view it through the dark and distorted lens of the World of Darkness. Then choose some physical locations in the area that you want to replicate in the game. The advantage to setting your story in your own backyard is that you have minimal creation to do. The disadvantage is that players might know the city as well or better than you do.

Also remember that your stories needn't be restricted to familiar stomping grounds. Even the best setting can get a little stale, in which case feel free to shake things up. Take the characters to another side of town, another city or even to a foreign country. Libraries, bookstores and online sources yield a wealth of information on nearly any municipality of any size, including population figures, government structures and maps. Just remember that you have to make players feel as though they've been transported to, say, an old hunting lodge in Germany, rather than simply presenting them the same old location and props and giving all your Narrator characters bad German accents. For details on creating a convincing setting, see "Stagecraft" later in this chapter.

Thinking Mythically

Storytelling games are about amazing things that happen to characters in interesting places, described with passion and intensity by players. The details of a particular villain or an ominous graveyard are vital to evoking a scene. But don't get too caught up in the literal. Events resonate on deeper levels, the levels of myth and poetry. In other words, events can be *metaphors* for powerful ideas.

Storytelling allows us to make the metaphorical literal, to take what would otherwise be fantastic or unreal and make it seem real within the context of the story. For example, spirits and ghosts are very real in the World of Darkness. In our world, however, they seem to exist only in the imagination, as metaphors or dreamlike images signifying truths we can't consciously grasp, but truths important to us nonetheless. The great advantage of a Storytelling game is that we can bring these metaphors to life, to confront them and interact with them in the guise of Storytelling characters. Moments of epiphany come when the Muse speaks through us — a spontaneous encounter with art. This is *myth*, metaphor come to life. The literal or imagistic means used to convey it are just props and stage decorations.

This doesn't mean you should artificially construct their stories and characters around cardboard archetypes and prefigured "hero quest" templates, following some formula set forth in a screenplay-writing book. It means you should be aware of the power of myth — living metaphor — to greatly enhance a story, to add depth through resonance with mythic themes. To this end, think mythically, not literally.

How to Tell Stories

Now that you know the basic elements that make up a story, you should know the best methods for telling one. Just as with any art or craft, Storytelling techniques are innumerable. Everyone has his own style or methods. Here are the few of the most basic and useful ones that you should be aware of.

INSPIRATION

Perhaps the most often-asked question of any writer is, "Where do you get your ideas?" Perhaps the best answer is that given by Neil Gaiman: "I make them up." But how exactly do you do that? Anyone has the creative power to make up stories, but the best stories have ideas or events that appeal to others, that communicate something the audience can grasp. There are various means of finding inspiration — the creative spark — for stories that can enchant others. Some good sources are:

• **Current events and history:** Read about what's going on in the world or what happened in the past (since we seem doomed to repeat history). Feel free to steal ideas directly from actual events. Television shows about lawyers do this all the time, with stories "ripped from today's headlines," focusing on the legal implications of various social conflicts. Even if your game is set in our times, historical events can provide inspiration for current ones. Could, say, the Salem witch persecutions happen today?

• **Literature and movies:** We're all inspired by other people's stories, whether in fiction or movies. We read *Dracula* and want to play a more modern version of that vampire lord's tale. We see *Princess Mononoke* and wonder what it would be like to witness nature spirits in our own neighborhoods. We read or watch *The Lord of the Rings* trilogy and want to play wizards. Stories feed on themselves, sparking new ideas in readers who tell their own stories, which in turn spark new ideas in a whole new generation of readers. The key here is to let these sources *inspire* you to come up with your own fresh ideas, not to rip them off in every detail.

• **Games:** Besides other roleplaying games, there are numerous PC, console and arcade games from which to gain inspiration. If you like running through a government laboratory while being stalked by extra-dimensional aliens, then you might want to do something similar with your friends in a Storytelling game, but this time in an environment all of your own creation.

Inspirational Materials

The following is a list of sources to which you might turn to get inspiration for your settings, games or chronicles. These works have been selected for their relevance to humans discovering the supernatural. Specific recommendations for chronicles about other creatures such as vampires, werewolves or mages can be found in their respective books: **The Requiem**, **The Forsaken** and **The Awakening**.

Literature: Anything by Poe or Lovecraft. *The Haunting*, by Shirley Jackson; *Ghost Story*, by Peter Straub; *House of Leaves*, by Mark Danielewski; *Sin City*, by Frank Miller; *The Club Dumas*, by Arturo Pérez-Reverte; *The Shining, IT, Bag of Bones*, by Stephen King; *Turn of the Screw*, by Henry James; the early Anita Blake novels, by Laurell K. Hamilton; *Spider*, by Patrick McGrath; *Criminal Macabre, Savage Membrane*, by Steve Niles; *Weird U.S.*, by Mark Moran and Mark Sceurman; *Puppetmasters* by Robert Heinlein; *The Ax*, by Donald Westlake; *Hostage to the Devil*, by Malachi Martin; *Twilight Eyes*, by Dean Koontz; *Something Wicked This Way Comes*, by Ray Bradbury; *The House Next Door*, by Anne Siddons; *Exquisite Corpse*, by Poppy Z. Brite

Film: *Devil's Backbone, The Crow, Stir of Echoes, The Exorcist, The Sixth Sense, Donnie Darko, Lost Highway, Mulholland Drive, The Ring, 28 Days Later, Frailty, The Blair Witch Project, In the Mouth of Madness, Poltergeist, The Thing* (remake), *Session 9, The Fog, The Ninth Gate, Assault on Precinct 13* (original), *The Usual Suspects, The Changeling, Fight Club, The Others, Bringing Out the Dead, Halloween, The Haunting* (original)

Television: *Twin Peaks, Twilight Zone, The X-Files, Alias, Millennium, The Dead Zone, American Gothic, The Outer Limits*. Also, programs such as *Unsolved Mysteries, Haunted History* and *Sightings* can be good sources for story ideas, at least once you get past their rather sensationalized delivery.

Online: Thousands of websites dedicated to all manner of supernatural topics from hauntings to demonic possession and beyond are no farther than a web search away. For a singularly unusual resource, try www.snopes.com. It's a vast collection of all kinds of well-researched urban legends.

SCALE

The scale of your story is its relative size, the number of players who want to participate. You can run stories for one player or more than a hundred, but stories for 20 to 30 are the most common. The scale of many stories is often predetermined by the number of players involved when you begin, but it can and will change. Players bring their friends, spouses and significant others in, and some players drop out for various reasons.

This doesn't mean that your story's scale is at the mercy of chance — you can influence it in either direction. Actively recruiting more players increases the scale, and getting rid of some players decreases it. Some Storytellers establish a player cap, which is the maximum number allowed to participate, or make their games invitation-only, carefully selecting the players they want for various reasons. Your primary scale considerations should be the number of players you can comfortably handle, and the planned duration of the chronicle.

Scale can get out of hand if you're the only Storyteller and the number of players grows too rapidly. When you see this happening, get some help. If you don't, your game and players suffer as you try to handle all the Storyteller responsibilities by yourself. Ask for volunteers among your players and make them Narrators (see below). A good rule of thumb is one Narrator for every 10 players, depending on your group dynamic. Some very large games even have several Storytellers, each in charge of a different aspect of the game (main plot, subplots, Merits, Status, antagonists). Remember that the larger your scale, the more broad and encompassing your plot should be in order to allow every player the potential to be involved.

Give some special thought to scale if you're running a plot that requires months of continuous play. Anticipate how scale changes will affect your long-range plots. Sudden or dramatic changes in scale can wreak havoc on ongoing stories, requiring you to do some fancy Storytelling footwork to repair the damage and keep everything on track. Stories for extended chronicles must be flexible in order to withstand the changes in scale that inevitably occur as some players drop out and others arrive.

Ask yourself the following questions toward managing the scale of your game:
• How will the story be affected by the sudden departure of several players midway through?
• Can the story cope if a particular in-game group undergoes unexpected growth, or if you gain players at a faster rate than anticipated?
• If the outcome of a major plot hinges on one or a few characters, what will you do if relevant players leave the game, or if a key character dies before the story's climax.

Planning a few "escape routes" for long-term plots helps you take scale changes in stride. Perhaps too many inquisitive mortals poking around will force the local supernatural creatures into hiding for a time, giving you a chance to have the characters meet each other, form friendships (or rivalries), and otherwise give the game time to adjust before bringing back the main antagonists for an even more suspenseful second round.

Starting Troupes and Attracting Players

While you may already have at least a small gaming group with which to form a **Mind's Eye Theatre** troupe, chances are you need more people to achieve the group you want. Or you may be starting from scratch. Have no fear. Finding players isn't as difficult or intimidating as it might seem. Here's a quick checklist of things you can do to recruit new blood.

The Camarilla: White Wolf's official fan club runs its own massive live-action chronicle that links hundreds of troupes around the world. It's entirely possible that there's already a group in your area. Even if there's no active group, it's relatively easy to gather people to start a new chapter (see the ideas below) that is part of the organization. If nothing else, you're bound to meet a number of fellow Camarilla members and live-action players from all around your region. For more details on joining the Camarilla organization, check out White Wolf's website.

Be Social: Visit local game stores. If none are within easy driving distance, try bookstores, comic shops or video-game stores or any other location that sells roleplaying books. Other good places to find potential players are college game societies, community drama groups, Renaissance faires, coffeehouses, historical re-creation societies and even nightclubs. It may take some time before you're familiar and comfortable enough to approach people in these settings, but you may make friends in the process.

Go Online: There's always the option of looking online. The strength of starting a search here is that it's usually pretty fast and relatively easy to perform. The downside is that you may not be able to find people in your area without a more concentrated, real-world effort. Launching a search engine with words and phrases such as "White Wolf," "live action" and the name of your community is a good start. Aside from the resources on White Wolf's website, try searching related game discussion groups and chat rooms, or posting announcements on forums and bulletin boards announcing who or what you're looking for. Then be patient. Results may not come overnight, but if you're persistent, they will come.

Advertising: If you don't mind the up-front expense or if you've struck out using the other methods, consider being a bit more aggressive. Print up some flyers with a description of the kind of game you're looking for and some (preferably fairly anonymous) contact information, and approach local store owners about posting these flyers. You can even approach civic officials about posting on community boards. Just make sure that you secure the consent of any relevant parties before proceeding.

SCOPE

Your story's scope encompasses the range of possibilities for character action and impact. Essentially, it's what's at stake in your game. Are you telling a low-key tale in which characters are concerned primarily about personal agendas and small-town events? Or do characters have the chance to save the entire city from some dire supernatural threat? (Or to sell it out to it?) Scale can modify your story's scope to a degree. It's easy to create the semblance of a city full of various frightened mortals and the supernatural creatures that prey upon them if you have enough players to represent everyone and everything. In the end, however, the stakes can be as big or as small as you want.

Short stories often work best with a narrow scope, while extended chronicles can handle wide variations. If your story is only going to last for three or four chapters, don't try to move between a small goal like helping an old eccentric locate a missing item and defusing a series of bombs that threaten to destroy the entire city. Both can make compelling stories, but it's hard to do them simultaneously in a short story. Pick one and focus on it — the story will be that much better for your increased attention, since the players can focus all of their roleplaying energies on becoming involved in that one story.

By contrast, the key for long-term chronicles is balance. Vary the scope of games from story to story to give your players variety and a sense that their characters exist in an active setting. Saving the world story after story grows tiresome, as does fighting continuously between different player groups over what they want or how they should act. Change the value of story consequences and rewards periodically to keep things from stagnating. One good way to do this is to have little events generate larger repercussions later on; perhaps the little girl the characters rescue from the attacking zombies turns out to be the daughter of an important local politician, whose gratitude helps save the characters when they're facing serious jail time in a later story. Plot twists like this helps keep players focused on the story and discourages them from glossing over minor details because "they're never that important."

Conversely, a large event can often quite naturally lead to characters focusing on a much smaller task for a while. For example, in the wake of bringing a brutal serial killer to justice, the characters might find themselves caught up in a story about helping the widow of one of his victims put her restless husband's soul to rest, or even just help her recover the pieces of her shattered life and go on living in a totally mundane way. This is especially fitting if the characters were friends with the victim or his family before the killings, or happened to become close to the widow during the course of the previous storyline. Not only does it give the characters a bit of a breather in terms of scope, but it also helps reinforce that the events of the story have consequences extending beyond what affects the characters directly. It is also good for allowing the characters a chance to have a lasting impact on the world beyond just "beating the bad guy."

Large or small, scope is ultimately about making players care about the outcome of the story. Only when they care about what they're doing will the players feel real tension when their characters are in danger, or for that matter enjoy a genuine feeling of accomplishment from succeeding in overcoming challenges. It doesn't matter how high the stakes, how terrible the consequences of failure or how big the potential prizes are supposed to be — if the players are not emotionally involved, the final outcome of the story will never really touch them. Success is met with a lukewarm cheer (or worse, a feeling of complacent expectation), and failure is shrugged off or even regarded as upsetting because the players feel as though they're being punished for something they didn't care about in the first place. None of these potential outcomes are ones you want for your chronicle.

So regardless of the scope you've chosen, do your best to make players care, but not by strong-arming them. Have them befriend a Narrator character well in advance of his eventual murder; doing so makes it seem less arbitrary, and gives the players time to grow attached. Invest characters with personality, quirks and connections to the players' characters, however strange or transient. Anonymous victims are seldom as compelling as ones the characters had some contact or empathy with. This goes for places and objects as well — if the first time they show up in your story is when they become endangered, the players will care about them a lot less than if they've become attached to them in earlier stories.

Pacing

The value of pacing is clear when you accept the Storyteller axiom that nothing goes exactly as planned. Characters sometimes miss vital clues for no apparent reason and then spend an evening scratching their heads as the session drags on. Or characters can cooperate in a frighteningly efficient manner, solving all the puzzles and conundrums that you thought would take them the entire night. Occasionally the players can even feel so overwhelmed by information or be so uncertain of what to do next that they fail to take an active role altogether.

You can mitigate if not avoid these eventualities by considering your story's pace. Decide the rate at which you'd like the story to progress before any session starts. Fast-paced games throw new situations at players throughout a session, forcing them to deal with each new challenge and leaving little time to assess the big picture. A man barging in with a gun and a hostage, yelling for his demands to be met within the hour, doesn't give players much time to do anything but react. Slow-paced games lend themselves to extended communications between characters, not to mention subtle intrigues and plots. A society party where the characters suspect supernatural creatures have hidden themselves may require several hours of discreet conversation and astute observation before they can uncover the hidden monsters. You may want to vary the tempo of a game, starting slow and getting faster, or vice versa. Having the hostage-taker be a crazed monster hunter who barges in near the end of the society party and threatens to kill his victim unless the "the real monsters show themselves" represents just such a switch. The characters have been working all night, but they might find their patient investigatory efforts (not to mention the life of the hostage) destroyed by the madman unless they act fast. You can also influence the pace of stories by learning to narrate spontaneously. That doesn't mean you shouldn't prepare for game sessions, but also be ready to provide plot information on the fly. Characters often ask questions for which you don't have prepared answers, but that deserve a response in order to keep the action flowing. Try to give answers that satisfy a player's need for information, but that also advance — or at least do not impede — your plot. Perhaps your paranormal investigators unexpectedly decide to research the cemetary on the other side of town for signs of ghostly activity; you hadn't planned for it, but it's certainly a valid inquiry. So after a few quick research tests, you tell them they find that all the members of the family that used to own the haunted house are buried across town, rather than at the cemetary adjacent to the house itself. Evidently they went to a lot of trouble to avoid being buried nearby, but why? This sort of quick thinking adds to the mystery surrounding your main plotline without putting off your players or leaving your story in a bad position. An unexpected lull in the game provides the perfect opportunity to introduce a new plot thread that you cleverly prepared for just such an occasion. Perhaps things are quiet during a usually contentious meeting time, but that's nothing a cryptic warning from an old enemy can't liven up. Or you can reintroduce a plot line that the characters thought resolved in order to keep the game going without a break in the action. A mundane criminal they helped bring to justice appears on the local news after a sudden court twist sets him free. What's more, he's shown on-camera, smiling and shaking hands with one of their other enemies, whom they believe to be one of the town's secret supernatural masters. The connection is obvious... isn't it?

Although off-the-cuff Storytelling is essential to any successful game, good pacing is roughly equal parts planning and improvisation. Start each night's game with at least a rough idea of the speed at which you want events to occur and where you think the story will go. If you want your story to start slowly and build to an action-packed finish, have early scenes designed around more thoughtful activities (like carefully exploring a haunted house room-by-room), then build up some speed with faster scenes (players hear voices urgently calling for help and must search to find the source), until finally the really fast action happens (a confrontation with an angry ghost).

Even if events don't get there because something unexpected happens, you're prepared to deal with it if you have ideas ready to speed events up or slow them down. Knowing the general direction in which the story is headed helps you recognize when the pace is too fast or slow, and gives you clues about how to adjust it in ways that best suit your players and plot. If the players are racing through searching the house, have some events encourage them to slow down a bit — one of them is nearly killed by a falling object knocked down with a careless search, it becomes evident they've missed an important clue, etc. If they don't seem motivated to move quickly when they hear the cries for help, have them become more personal, or appear to be coming from a loved one.

Be sensitive to the ebb and flow of the story, watching carefully for periods of too much inactivity or hopeless chaos. If players clearly enjoy a scene, don't interrupt it just to introduce something new for its own sake. Few things discourage roleplaying more than cutting it off when the players were really enjoying it, and that's the last message you want to send players in a live-action chronicle. And yet, don't let a scene drag on until it dies a painfully slow death with all the players staring at their shoes or making awkward conversation. Let players enjoy the moment and be prepared to move on when the moment is over.

If you're forced to choose between extremes — too fast or too slow — too fast is recommended. Slow-paced stories can bore players. Prepare a couple of plot threads or dangers in advance that you can introduce in case the story slows unexpectedly. These curve balls can be as simple as a character's spouse or child overhearing the details of a secret life, or as complex as the emergence of an enigmatic group that the characters have never met before.

If you're *really* in doubt about what to do to alter pacing, take a few trustworthy players aside and ask what the story needs, what their characters want to do next. After all, the story is about their characters.

NARRATORS

You as Storyteller can't be everywhere during a game session. Sooner or later something critical happens to the story and you're not there or you learn about it a week later! Nor can you do everything yourself, especially if your story's scale grows. Unless you have an exceptionally small group of players, you probably need some Narrators. A Narrators are people who volunteer to help run the chronicle, and they can be broken down into two groups:

• Full Narrators, those who can answer rules questions as well as give out plot information

• Limited Narrators, who can resolve mechanical disputes or who have other forms of specialized authority, such as resolving combat or handling experience point expenditures, but who do not have any special knowledge of the chronicle's story line.

One of the most valuable and essential Narrator tasks is adjudicating rules questions. Your assistants should be very familiar with all the game's rules. Only the truly trustworthy or likeminded should be allowed direct supervision over plot events. One advantage to Narrators who do not have plot access, however, is that they can usually play

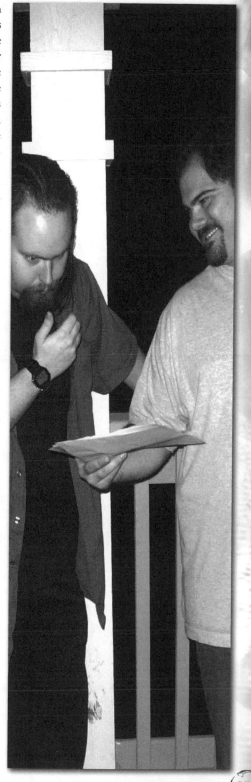

regular characters, as well. They have no inside information about the story that gives them an unfair advantage. Regardless of Narrators' specific roles, be sure to brief them thoroughly and establish the boundaries of what information they can impart and what should remain secret. Setting up a Narrator to be a colorful snitch is great, but if you forget to tell him that he's not supposed to pass along the name of the Mafia boss who's after the characters, he could accidentally do a lot of damage to the game. Give them clear expectations and good directions before each game starts, such as what actions you think the players are likely to take and how you want them to respond. If you set up a chapter designed around roleplaying and interaction, but feel some players might try to start a fight anyway, it's a good idea to tell the Narrators in advance and let them know how you want them to react. Don't be afraid to give them some coaching on the fly if you feel it's necessary. If you see a Narrator floundering in a part, or acting well but not getting the attention of the players, it's better for you to step in and offer some help than to try to fix the damage later.

Narrators don't have to be limited to rules questions and plot points. They can portray allies and enemies, help new players create characters, oversee experience-point expenditures and help keep track of the story's paperwork. Some particularly large games designate special Narrators to handle individual aspects of the story. One Narrator for all things relating to omens and portents, another for Influences, and still another to keep track of the various antagonists in the chronicle, for example. Each Narrator is responsible for managing that element of the story, and should do so with the goal of making less work for the Storyteller.

In the end, the more Narrators you have, the more work you can delegate, and the more you can concentrate on storytelling itself. Encourage players to approach Narrators with their questions first, especially on matters of rules adjudication. There's no reason why you must handle every draw resolution personally if your Narrators can do it. At the same time, make it clear that your Narrators should always ask for help if they ever feel they're in over their heads, and don't hesitate to step in if a situation appears to get out of hand. Just don't overrule a Narrator in public. Doing so undermines her authority and embarrasses her.

Limited Narrator Roles

What follows is a brief list of some limited Narrator roles that can be assigned, along with a common title for each position. Limited Narrator roles are useful, because they share the burden of running the game, without having to completely brief each Narrator about the entire plot. Limited Narrators need only worry about their own small jurisdictions. Outside of those, they're the same as any other player. Note that not every troupe needs to fill every one of these roles. It's fine to have general, all-purpose, full-time Narrators or even ones who "change hats" from time to time.

Judge — Rules, systems and other game mechanics, including combat situations. No ability to make decisions related to plots or story lines.

Mask — Portrays one or more supporting cast members, with Storyteller supervision. Less emphasis on rules than a typical Narrator position.

Muse — Plot determinations and rules adjudication, but only for a specific plot line or subplot. Outside of that particular story line, this Narrator has no authority.

Oracle — Recording prophecies, visions, omens, dreams and foreshadowing.

Reeve — Combat rulings *only*. Unlike a Judge, a Reeve has no authority to rule on any game mechanics outside of combat.

Rumor — Allies, Contacts, Retainers, Status, gossip, politics and intrigue.

Tutor — Experience points, character training and all other trait improvements.

Spirit Guide — Otherworldly beings and travel to other planes of existence.

Supernatural Keeper — Overseeing all things related to a particular type of supernatural creature. An eclectic game might have a Vampire Keeper and a Werewolf Keeper.

CHRONICLE FORMAT

Traditional live-action gaming puts all Storytellers, Narrators and players in one location, looses the characters on the plot (and each other), and allowed the chips to fall where they may. As live-action evolves, however, and different troupes seek different ways to run events, innovative approaches develop as discussed here.

Default Format: Ensemble Play

Also known as "group play," this basic chronicle structure focuses on large gatherings, usually held about once a month or every other month. While side sessions and smaller gatherings may be arranged from time to time, and downtime actions are vital, large gatherings are the key to distributing and advancing major plot developments. This is not to say that the in-game setting for gatherings must always be the same, or that the reason for gathering must remain constant. Both can change. What begins as ghost-hunter gatherings at a college library might turn into desperate meetings of paranoid survivors at hotels and safehouses.

Ensemble play is excellent for Storytellers of all experience levels because it ensures that everyone is present when you introduce new story twists and plot elements, and it allows you to take full advantage of group dynamics to foster drama, excitement and intrigue. Having a Narrator portraying a reclusive occult scholar arrive and announce the impending doom of the town is dramatic on its own, but when you add to it the fact that the different characters will have a wide variety of different reactions — shocked disbelief, angry warmongering, desperate curiosity, etc. — you have the seeds for a truly powerful chapter. It also reduces the number of logistical headaches associated with trying to schedule a large number of sessions for small groups, and allows you to get an immediate sense of the pulse of the troupe and its reaction to different story threads. Finally, if you see players being ignored or looking bored, you can try to introduce them to groups through plot hooks and story twists.

Perhaps the most serious challenge you face as Storyteller of an ensemble game is making sure characters always have interesting and compelling reasons to get together in large groups. If characters are all present in one location just because the players meet for the game, your atmosphere will seem forced and artificial. Ironically, you may find it difficult to justify gathering a large group of ordinary people who have learned about the supernatural — even more so than gathering creatures themselves. While beings such as vampires naturally meet to be with their own kind and to do business in their shadow societies, humans tend to be fearful as they learn about the hidden world. Provided you give rational reasons for paranoid characters to gather, such as safety in numbers or the need to exchange absolutely critical information or equipment, this shouldn't be a problem.

Another concern of ensemble play is "face in the crowd" syndrome. Players feel as though they're always left behind or overlooked by important events, or that their efforts go largely unnoticed. Don't worry if you can't spend time with everyone in a large game — you have a lot on your hands — but if you realize that you haven't noticed much activity from a player or group in a while, approach and ask how they're doing, whether they feel involved, and what plots they're interested in. Sometimes it's be a false alarm and characters have been busy behind the scenes or deliberately avoid the limelight. But if players do feeling left out, you can address their individual needs.

Option One: Crew Play

Crew play is a type of game in which players create several small groups of characters (known as "crews") and rotate responsibility for portraying supporting cast members and otherwise running games for each other. Say a troupe of 15 players decides to run a crew-style game. They break up into three crews A, B and C, with five people each. When crew A has a session, members of crews B and C act as Narrator-characters and work with the Storytelling staff to fill all needed roles — antagonists, allies and innocent victims. When crew B has a session, members of crews A and C help run the show. Sometimes crews may even rotate roles at the same session if the scenes that each group runs are short. All three might be work on the same plot from different angles or their stories might be completely independent.

Crew play's main advantage is that it allows you to customize plots and story elements to the strengths and interests of each group. Since you don't have to worry about alienating players, you're free to explore what they like as far as you want to. Having a potentially large Storytelling staff also allows you to create in-depth environments than might normally be possible. Narrators and extras from crews B and C might actually emulate a bar full of people for crew A's session, rather than just describing one.

Logistic concerns must be considered carefully before committing to this kind of game. Having a number of small groups means you have to juggle a number of different plots (or different aspects of the same plot), not to mention scheduling games for each crew and making sure they all get fair representation. Keeping a written record of the plotlines and where you intend to take them is not only useful but almost certainly required if you want to keep them straight, especially in a large crew play chronicle. Scheduling conflicts can be kept to a minimum by telling the crews the time frame they have to schedule a game, and then allowing the members of these crews to work out what dates are best for them. For example, you can schedule the game on a two month basis, and let all the crews know that they need to find a date that works for them within that time frame.

Option Two: Blended Play

There's always the possibility of compromising and doing a little of both crew-style and ensemble gaming. Break characters into several in-game groups and conduct sessions for each crew in one month, and then hold a large ensemble gathering of all characters the next month. Each crew gets individual attention, allowing you to write stories that allow it to show off members' talents and to satisfy their playing styles. You can even bring up incidents from past stories without fear of focusing on a few characters or alienating the rest of the group.

At the same time, large group gatherings are more important than ever. They allow characters to exchange stories and information and perhaps gain insights into a greater threats and problems. Last but not least, setting up an epic-level storyline is easy with this format, since it's simply a matter of tailoring each crew's goals individually instead of trying to steer the whole unruly mob of characters all at once every session. Just make sure not to neglect ensemble meetings in favor of small ones. The big get-together helps everyone maintain perspective on the overall troupe and any crossover story lines.

For all of its plot and character advantages, the main difficulty of blended play is logistic. You'll need several Narrators and perhaps fellow Storytellers. Getting in all the required crew sessions before the next ensemble session can be very demanding, for example, and requires an extensive Storytelling team. Also be wary of burnout when trying to handle so many different stories, one or several per crew. Fortunately, the nature of the crew sessions makes it likely that players give you a good deal of help since you can put so much emphasis on individual subplots with which players run, using character histories to spark ideas.

Format Twist: Incorporating Tabletop Play

Storytellers familiar with both conventional roleplaying and live-action gaming are aware that each has particular strengths. "Tabletop" play focuses on small groups, combat, physical obstacles and rapid transitions between locations, while live-action is ideal for large groups, intrigue, problem-solving and complex social environments. If the chance presents itself, why not switch between the two and take full advantage of both their strengths? Characters created under the Storytelling System can transition directly from tabletop gaming to live-action. The same character sheet is used in both venues! Furthermore, the only rules that are different between, say, the **World of Darkness Rulebook** and this one are those that need to account for characters *imagined* to be performing actions (tabletop), and actual players *performing or announcing* those actions (live-action). Some systems, such as those for explosives, just don't translate over well. Those exceptions are few, however, so your character in a monster-hunting roleplaying game is the same as your character in a live-action, monster-hunting game.

That consistency allows you to go back and forth to best portray the scenes you have in mind on a chapter-by-chapter basis. If you normally run an ensemble live-action game, but a small group of characters plans a daring raid on enemy territory, you might schedule a side session as a tabletop game. That medium allows you to employ tabletop's strengths in portraying combat and rapid location shifts. Then you can transition back to regular live-action play for the next group session.

COAXING PERFORMANCES

It's a simple fact that some players are more outgoing than others, or that some players tend to favor story and acting over rules and mechanics. Understanding how these different types of players approach the game, what kinds of situations they excel at, and what conflicts they avoid can help you to coax performances from your players.

Proactive: These players are both a blessing and a curse for the Storytelling staff. While they're quick to keep themselves entertained and to create new plots and story lines with their own explorations of the game environment, they tend to ignore prepared stories and go in directions you might not anticipate, sometimes even dragging the rest of the troupe with them. The key to channeling the energy these people is to understand what they looking for in a game and to offer plots along those lines or to steer their enthusiasm to propel the plot that you have already have underway. Offer them positions of in-game authority where they can move the plot along. Hint to them that some necessary clues are out there and need to be uncovered, but make sure you let them figure out how they want to carry out the search.

Reactive: This distinction is actually a bit of misnomer, in that it implies players never do anything until they are forced to react. Many "reactive" players are quite aggressive in resolving the conflicts in which their characters involved in. They may not be so progressive, however, to seek out or initiate new plots. They let the Storytelling staff and more active players forge ahead and create new stories, which they are more than happy to join. The advantage of these players is that they typically follow a plot hook sent their way. They're not likely to have personal agendas so strong that they conflict with supporting new threads. Just make sure you don't marginalize their efforts. Hand them important plot points that need to be handled in a particular way, and hint at what that way might be.

Roleplayers: Obviously, everyone involved in a live-action game is a roleplayer, but some go farther than others. They dedicate a great deal of time and attention to bringing their characters to life through complex histories, personality write-ups and stagecraft tools such as costumes, props and makeup. These players prefer to roleplay and mediate their way through conflicts rather than resort to rules and cards. Involving them heavily in the game's social and political plots puts their strengths to good use, and abstaining from too many mechanics in these realms allows these folks to explore the part of the game that they like best. Give them plenty of opportunities to use interaction and roleplaying to achieve results, or even where those are the only means a character can hope to succeed.

Rule-Players: These players enjoy the systems of the game, whether in the abstract sense to see how rules simulate reality or in a direct sense of using rules on a regular basis to achieve goals. Such interest doesn't necessarily mean these people are poor roleplayers. They just enjoy the clarity that rules bring to their characters' actions; an effort is completed or fails when a draw is successful or fails. If story conflicts call for traits and draws, these players thrive. Or if they can apply their knowledge and love of the rules for the good of the chronicle — say by acting as Narrators — they can be valuable assets to the game. Likewise, putting them in situations where their expert knowledge of the rules and how their various traits gives them an advantage is a good way to coax out the best performance from them.

ADVANCED TECHNIQUES — TIME

There are a number of special Storytelling tools available to you, often best used once you're comfortable with the dynamics of telling a collaborative story with a group of players. Some of the more interesting manipulate time. Storytellers have several options in scenes in which time is mutable: they can simply narrate them or write them out and hand them to the players; they can have Narrator representing the players act them out for the players; or they can have the players portray themselves, acting according to the script or directions you give them as they go along.

For example, say the Storyteller desires to do a foreshadowing scene where one of the characters is shot and killed. In order to accomplish it with maximum effect, the Storyteller writes up a brief script for a couple of her Narrators, detailing what she wants them to say and do in this brief vision of the future. The Narrators then learn the simple script and secure a few basic costume pieces to help represent the players' characters. When she decides to run it, the Storyteller has the players sit down and describes the setting of the scene in front of them, if it is not already created with stagecraft. Then the players watch as their characters (played by the Narrators) act out the script, ending with the stunning moment where one character falls, mortally wounded. Informing the players that what they've seen is still only a possible future that they have the potential to change, the Storyteller leaves them wondering what they must do to prevent this tragedy, not to mention speculating as to the killer's identity... and the dramatic tension of the game increases.

Flashbacks: Events that have already taken place can be played out to dramatic effect by using flashbacks. These are short scenes set in the past that inform players' understanding of present conditions. Flashbacks might involve players' characters before they became aware of the supernatural world, or they might even involve characters' ancestors! Players can temporarily observe or take the roles of other past characters, whether their own ancestors or some unfortunate people who "accidentally discovered the curse of the tomb." Flashbacks are like short scenes in a movie. Keep them short. If they're too long, they detract from the current story. As soon as a flashback offers some insight on a present predicament, end it and cut back to present time. Note that flashbacks don't actually involve tests or task resolution; everything has already happened and is scripted or narrated rather than played.

Cutaways: Events that take place at the same time but in different locations can create dramatic effect. The technique involves more than simply cutting back and forth between two groups of characters. It can be used to witness Narrator characters conniving against the players' characters, or striving to aid them. It's fun to let players assume the roles of "cutaway characters," whether it's a crime boss chortling with his captains about a death trap into which a character just fell, or disciples trying to understand a clue that will allow them to rescue players' characters. These cutaways serve to embolden the main characters. The protagonists hold the fort, waiting for reinforcements that players know will arrive. Tension is heightened as the players get a taste of just how dangerous their enemies really are. Or cutaways get characters to change tactics before they wind up dead. As with most other temporal tricks, events here are scripted; don't bother doing tests. Just impart the message or feeling that you want and end them before the players learn too much.

Foreshadowing: Events from a potential future can be foreshadowed by actually playing them out. The scene shifts to next week, where the characters attend the funeral of one of their own. This kind of scene really wakes players up! How did the character die? How do they stop it from coming to pass? Everything they do will be measured against the scant clues this glimpse into the future provides. It's best to make these visions and scenes short, cutting away before too many details are revealed. If you use players to portray their own characters, try to write up sheets in advance so the players know how they're supposed to act, but don't give away too much. It's sweet agony watching players try to avoid — or accomplish — the fate they witnessed. One important point: Visions must be of a *possible* future, not a preordained one. Character actions should be allowed to change (or fulfill) what players see.

BOTTOM LINE: HAVE FUN

There's no "right" way to play this game. You can tell whatever kinds of stories you like, by whatever systems you device, as long as everyone has fun. Indeed, it's every player's job to be lenient and patient with other players, Narrators and the Storyteller. If mistakes are made, point them out politely (if necessary) and move on. Don't belabor the point. It's impossible to avoid mistakes completely — you're all making this up as you go! Just don't mock someone mercilessly for an error. What goes around comes around. You'll make your own mistakes soon enough.

The point to remember is that you all create a spontaneous story experience. That's an amazing thing. Many professional actors, directors and writers would be scared to death to even contemplate the idea. As opposed the millions of dollars that can be lost by screwing up a film, there are no consequences to screwing up in Storytelling. It's a game, and in the end you produce a work of imagination that outshines any blemishes that go into its making.

THE 10 STORYTELLER COMMANDMENTS

• **Story First, Rules Second:** Rules are tools. Use them to help tell your story, but don't let them trap you. If a rule stands between you and a good story, there's nothing wrong with ignoring it. Making the odd rules change here or there to encourage the flow of the story is unlikely to upset players. Just make sure all rules changes are public knowledge, that players understand rules will never be changed just to screw them over, and that all changes are applied equally and consistently.

• **Involve Players Whenever Possible:** Incorporate players ideas and backgrounds into your setting and chronicle. Doing so interests players *immediately* and gives them a voice in your story. Players' characters should always be the most important — though not necessarily the most powerful — ones in your chronicle. It's well worth your time to work with players to develop their characters and their involvement in the story, even between game sessions.

• **Be Aware of Players' Expectations:** Giving players the general kinds of challenges that they enjoy is a good idea. Survey players before the chronicle starts and periodically thereafter to find out what they want in the game: horror, action, intrigue, romance, supernatural powers. But don't be predictable. Just because the players know you plan to feed their appetite for action doesn't mean they have to know exactly who or what characters will go up against — or why.

• **Work Things out in Advance:** Every erg of effort you spend preparing saves you 10 ergs of desperation during an actual game. Even if you like to improvise, know the basic outline of what you need to convey and try to think of potential ways in which players might react. If you know in advance what's in a locale or what motivates an important character, you pay more attention to portraying what you know instead of making things up on the fly.

• **Set the Stage:** Players truly bring a game to life and should be immersed in the environment from the moment they enter. Whether you use a full-on production with lighting, sound and ornate props, or simply item cards and a detailed description circulated before play, pull your players into the imaginary world as much as possible and maintain that illusion as best you can.

• **Avoid Stereotypes:** Perfect examples of type are rare. People who *try* to fit into a stereotype usually do so to cover up some secret insecurity, and may not be able to carry it off on close examination. People who naturally tend toward stereotypes often rebel against being just like everyone else, and may go to great lengths to show that they're unique. Even if you're pressed for time, try to give Narrator-characters quirks to set them apart from the ordinary.

• **Be Fair to Your Setting:** If players work hard and make smart decisions, characters' success should be in proportion to the challenges faced or players will feel cheated. Even if they don't always "win," they should feel as though something has definitely been accomplished. Conversely, don't reward characters if they don't earn it or the reward is hollow, and characters may become spoiled and complacent if they come to believe they can never fail.

- **Don't Tell Them Everything:** Much of the challenge of a game is in the mystery, the parts of the story that you hold back for the players and their characters to discover through effort. No matter how tempted you are to talk about how cool a future plot twist will be, keep your thoughts to yourself. Players will thank you for keeping it a surprise.
- **Don't Abuse Your Power:** Remember that your role as Narrator or Storyteller is to help entertainment the players. Respect your influence over their characters. You both initiate and arbitrate events. Use your power to move the story, not to force people to play out *your* vision of how their characters should behave. You're not trying to "defeat" the players, you're working with them to tell a good story. If you outsmart them or outmatch them, it should be to heighten the drama of the story, not to show off your fantastic Storytelling powers.
- **Don't Panic:** If the players pull the rug out from under you, don't be afraid to call a break and take some time to collect your thoughts. It may happen a lot at first, but after a while you'll be able to handle anything they throw at you, and players will appreciate having you take a moment to work out a good solution rather than hastily throwing something together.

Stagecraft

Now that you've learned how to create live-action stories and ways to bring **Mind's Eye Theatre** troupes together, it's time to learn about the more theatrical side of the game. That is, how take all the numbers on a character sheet and the plot elements scribbled in your notebook and make them into a living, breathing world for characters to explore. One of the most crucial aspects of hosting a live-action event is invoking a compelling mood using the play area and materials that you have available. That means focusing on the factors that make live-action different from any other type of game. Unlike tabletop games where your voice sets the stage, **Mind's Eye Theatre** sets the stage right before your eyes. What you do with the stage is at least as important as the story you tell on it.

As Storyteller, strive to bring to the surface all the somber, harsh qualities that define the World of Darkness. Immerse your players in the seedy nightclubs, mist-enshrouded graveyards and dangerous back alleys that epitomize the setting. Make it a total sensory experience that players will talk about for years. Let them explore the game area and use it as a tool to further their roleplaying. It takes a lot of work to achieve this lofty goal, but the results for both you and your players are richly rewarding.

This section covers a variety of topics to help bring your chronicle to life, from selecting a location and getting it ready for play, to handling sound and lighting, to costuming and prop use.

THE PLAY AREA

First, you need to find a place to hold your game. An ideal location has multiple small rooms or other areas where players and their characters can meet privately, as well as at least one central meeting area that's large enough to hold all the players at once. A room for costume changes and out-of-game materials is helpful, as is a kitchen for long games. The location needs to be relatively private and preferably somewhat soundproof, so that players don't disturb the neighbors or be disturbed in turn.

Provided the troupe is relatively small, it may be possible to use your own private residence or a player might volunteer her own. This is perhaps the best solution, as it allows you to control the setting as much as you desire and eliminates the worry of non-players intruding. Just make sure everyone leaves it in livable condition when the chapter is over, and that they don't do anything that causes neighbors to call the police or get the host kicked off condo association.

If a private residence isn't an option, there are still a number of options, although you might have to pass around a donation hat to cover the costs of securing some places. Examples of alternative locations are public parks, rented halls, dorm lounges, night clubs, convention centers, hotel conference rooms, apartment complex common areas, museums, student centers, restaurant meeting rooms, office board rooms and shopping malls. The more public the location, however, the more care you must take not to disturb or offend non-players with your choice of costumes, props, language and behavior. "Freaking the mundanes" may be fun for an immature few, but the potential consequences in terms of getting booted from the play area or having to deal with authority figures are never worth the payoff. Keep your presence as unobtrusive as possible, and tell players not to interact with non-players who approach them, but to come to you immediately and let you handle the matter.

In any event, always obtain explicit permission from the owner before utilizing any private property. If necessary, contact local civil or law enforcement authorities to reassure them ahead of time. Use common sense when dealing with any non-players who are curious about what's going on. Take the time to explain exactly what you're doing, but don't invite non-players to participate at that time. Consider printing up some inexpensive business cards to offer to curious passers-by, and encourage them to contact you later when you can speak at leisure.

Banishing the Familiar

Once you have your location, do your best to separate players from the ebb and flow of the mundane world. Constantly working to keep players focused and in character only interferes with managing the story that you want to tell. A huge part of maintaining mood and focus is removing any unnecessary distractions from the play area. No matter where you hold the game, a few things are going to draw players out of character. Unless you actually play in a haunted house or a seedy nightclub — possible, but you can't count on it — elements of the real world creep in.

As the saying goes, "out of sight, out of mind." Cover or remove any mundane objects or details that suggest your location's ordinary function. You can drape unwanted objects and furniture with dark, opaque sheets, take pictures off the walls and move unwanted pieces to areas where they won't do as much harm. Those leftover pizza boxes have to go, as do the stacks of rented videos or game books. Don't feel obligated to pack up everything and ship it off to some storage center, but the most obvious reminders of the real world should be addressed.

Anything that provides too much of a reminder to the real world that can be moved should be, and anything too big or otherwise too complicated to move should be obscured or covered up. If your play area is a regular out-of-game hangout, changing mundane features gives the location a subtly unfamiliar look that can help players to create and maintain the illusion of a new setting.

Use What You Have

A helpful tip on staging a live-action game is to use what you have to its best advantage. The old "What you see is what you get" rule is an excellent for immersing players into the world you fashion for them. For the most part, try to stick with what's actually present in the play area. That's not to say you can't stretch the imagination of your players — chairs arranged in a row could represent seats on a subway, for example

— but the more you use what you have to represent the reality of the setting, the more immersive and intense the game is.

For example, if you have access to a rough stone basement, don't try to play it off as the glitzy ballroom of the local luxury hotel. Use it for what suits it best. Perhaps it could be a moldering crypt that the characters suspect contains an unquiet spirit, or it could be a werewolf's cave dwelling out in the forest. If you have a nicely furnished living-room space, don't make it represent the back alley behind a strip club, use it for the sitting room of the mansion owned by that recluse on the far side of town. If your play area looks something like a dusty warehouse after you cover the furniture with sheets, why not write in a plot that involves that specific setting? Cut up long pieces of cardboard to "board up" the windows of the "abandoned factory" and watch players' imagination run rampant with the results.

This same principles work for the size of a room. Try to reserve small rooms for side rooms and secret meeting places where you anticipate only a few of players meeting. It's difficult enough for a player to be taken seriously as an obsessive scholar of the occult, but it's downright impossible if he's are squished up against the sink in a small bathroom that's supposed to represent the storm cellar of a haunted house. So, reserve large sections of your play area for what will be the most commonly used locales and gathering places. If you run short on rooms, certain large areas can be sectioned off using some clothesline and a couple of dark sheets. You can even create a small maze of rooms, allowing for any number of scenes and locations at your whim.

Basically, take a long look at what areas you're going to play in and come to a compromise with the space. It's a good idea to talk to players in advance to anticipate what locations will be needed for your story. There's no reason to designate a room the local library if there's not going to be any action there. Make every space that you have count for something important. If even the roof over your head can serve as a silent Narrator to your game, let it do so. Using and creating locations that suit the in-game environment you're intending to create can add a lot more to the chapter than you might suspect.

STATIC VERSUS DYNAMIC SETTINGS

One question you will need to address early on is whether you want your play area to represent a single static setting, or whether you want different rooms to represent other settings, possibly even ones distant enough to warrant in-game travel delays. Static settings such as a warehouse or haunted house keep the characters in one place the entire night, allowing you to prepare set dressing, lighting, sound and other effects to immerse the players in that single setting.

Dynamic settings assume that various rooms or designated areas represent different in-game locations that characters can visit. An upstairs room might have an out-of-game sign on the door that reads, "Blue Cat Nightclub, 10 minutes travel." Players who want their characters to visit that location must spend 10 minutes waiting out-of-game before they can enter, to represent the time it takes to make the trip. If they wish to return to the main play area, they must wait the same amount of time as their characters travel back.

Dynamic settings allow you to portray a wide variety of vital locations in relatively little real-world space. Care should be taken, however, to ensure there's good reason to visit each locale or players will be annoyed at spending travel time out-of-game for nothing. Also beware possible time discrepancies that arise when players try to carry out combat or otherwise interact between locations.

Deciding which setting format works best for your chronicle is generally learned by trial and error. In general, groups that focus on social interaction and creating an immersive environment prefer a static setting, while groups that enjoy action-adventure crave a flexible setting.

OUT-OF-GAME ROOMS

Don't forget to allocate a room that you and the rest of the Storytelling staff can use to take a break, store important props, talk over a sudden plot development or change costumes. Keep in mind when choosing your staff room that players are often just a room away. A closed-off location with a door and that's located away from the action works best, not only to keep your staff out of the way of the game, but to help keep your plans a mystery. Whether a mistake of innocence or design, nothing spoils a good surprise more than a player overhearing your carefully laid plans.

Players should have a similar space to get changed into costume, sneak a quick peek at the rulebook, eat a snack, store unnecessary out-of-game items and or to just plain take a breather from the actio. Designate such a room as the "reality room" and make sure all players are aware of its nature to prevent possible future arguments. At the same time, inform players that while you understand the need to catch one's breath from time to time, the reality room is for temporary breaks only. They shouldn't hide from in-game opponents there. (If a player genuinely has a hard time staying in character and uses the reality room as a recourse, give her some coaching on how to handle troublesome elements of the game.) Nor should players disrupt the game for others by holding loud out-of-game conversations in a reality room. Finally, such a space cannot be used to discuss in-game events that involve players still participating in the game.

If your play area represents multiple locations instead of just one, you may even wish to designate a reality room double as a "travel room" where characters moving between locations can sit and wait without disturbing play. The same is possible if you anticipate characters performing actions such as meditating, repairing complex equipment or performing lengthy arcane rites that require players to be out-of-game for extended periods. Such characters' preoccupation can be represented by players spending time outside of play.

A Hint of Rose

Although it may not always be an option when preparing your play area, consider burning incense or scented candles to help create atmosphere. Scent is a powerful stimulus and can encourage players to immerse themselves in their surrounding when they're literally reminded of them with each breath. An amazing variety of fragrances can be found in candle shops and herbal boutiques. Sniff around until you find ones that evoke the mood and location you want. Just remember the following guidelines. Learn if players have any allergies to smoke or specific odors. *Never* leave any burning materials unattended for any length of time. And remember that a little aroma goes a long way. Start small and gradually work your way up to get the intended effect.

LIGHTING

One of the quickest, easiest and most compelling ways to create the impression of a different setting is to change the light scheme. A room that's familiar and uninteresting to players is an entirely different place by candlelight. Clever use of different colored lights and light sources can suggest your story's mood and theme. Colored bulbs can be obtained at most novelty stores, while cheap lamps and fixtures are easy to find at bargain prices in secondhand shops. Some suggestions on uses of different colored lights are provided below.

Even if you don't have the budget or opportunity to create new lights, there are still a few basic tricks to creating a new game environment. Turn off overhead lights and use light sources closer to the floor. Doing so allows players to safely navigate the playing area, and provides illumination for them to read or examine clues, but keeps the room shadowy. Light sources close to the floor also means you can move them easily, allowing you to change the tone of the room quickly or to suggest new settings.

Avoid bright lights unless they would exist in a particular setting. You want players to be able to move around without groping for the walls (even if their characters are in the pitch-dark), but the mystery and uncertainty of the World of Darkness are portrayed by low lights. A Narrator portraying a hideous monster might very well look silly in bright light, where players can see the edges of the mask and the seams in the stitching, but the "monster" looks more intimidating lurching around in near dark.

By contrast, bright light reveals the corners of the room and the things that seek to hide, even in characters' souls. Bright light can therefore be appropriate in a laboratory or courtroom, but also when you want characters to feel exposed, insignificant or even violated.

LIGHTING PRIMER

White — For our purposes, "white" light is considered fluorescent lighting. Unless you're specifically trying to create a very drab and rather sterile environment such as an office building, laboratory or shopping mall, it's not your friend. It's not very flattering, it creates very little in the way of shadowy atmosphere, and fixtures have an audible hum.

Yellow — "Yellow" light is generated by most lamps and home light fixtures, and is an excellent all-purpose source. If it is diffused or muted it helps create a cozy, inviting atmosphere, reminiscent of old lamps or even firelight (especially with enough orange tint). If it's very bright, yellow makes an excellent substitute for sunlight. In general, think of this as "base" lighting.

Red — Red light creates a stark, dramatic atmosphere charged with raw passion, especially lust and anger. It can also be used to signal emergency lighting, such as a military-style "red alert," or a photographer's dark room. It does not interfere with night vision, either.

Blue — Blue light is an excellent substitute for starlight, especially if it's soft. On an emotional level, it tends to promote a subdued, mysterious atmosphere. It's excellent for evoking mystical, otherworldly locations.

Green — Green light tends to suggest visceral feelings of horror, sickness, contamination or corruption, making it ideal for rank sewers, toxic dumps or unquiet graveyards. Brightly glowing green lights are also associated with hazardous radiation.

Blacklight — Aside from being a natural choice for creating a rave environment, the contrast effect of blacklight is excellent for dream sequences, the appearance of monsters that seem to bend reality around them, trips to other planes of existence and other departures from mundane reality.

Strobe — Another natural choice for a rave or nightclub scene, strobe lights work very to play with perceptions of time and movement. Slow strobe lights make movements seem jerky, startling and abrupt, while fast strobe lights give the scene an edgy, not-quite-real feel. Just make sure that you don't have any epileptic players or others who are sensitive to such lights.

Firelight — Strong firelight creates a cozy atmosphere in the same manner as yellow light, while candles and lanterns create small islands of light that only serve to make the darkness around them all the more sinister. Fire is primal. It easily conjures up ingrained fears of the dark and what little that can be done to keep it at bay. Certain safety guidelines *must* be observed if any sort of fire is used in a game. Check to see if open flame is permitted in the play area. Clear any flammable objects from the area. Make sure the source is not anywhere where it can easily be bumped into or knocked over. Finally, make sure that even the smallest candle is never left unattended for any length of time.

Sound

Although human beings tend to focus on visual stimuli more than any other kind, never underestimate the impact that sound has on people, from music that fires players up to sound effects that create a much more visceral experience than simply announcing, "You hear gunshots." Creating an interesting and involving soundscape on top of the visual elements of your setting adds depth and realism to a scene.

Technology allows us to create our own custom music and sound-effect discs, arranged and mixed exactly as you want them for your games. You can even design discs for specific locations, characters or events, allowing you to switch between scenes or to suggest the presence of familiar characters with little more than the push of a button. Just be sure to add to your repertoire on a regular basis or the same old sounds and songs will become passe.

Music outside of your normal listening matter, as well as familiar favorites, creates a range from which to choose. Giving players something they've never heard before helps them get into character in its own way, because they have no prior associations with the music, so it belongs entirely to your new world.

Remember to make your sound system unobtrusive, especially if the music is an out-of-game element of a scene. A deserted haunted house loses a lot of its mystery if there's a shiny new CD player sitting in the corner.

Sound in **Mind's Eye Theatre** is broken down into two major categories: in-game and out-of-game.

In-Game Sound

As the name implies, this category covers music and sound effects that are considered audible in play, and which the characters can therefore react to upon hearing. If the session takes place at a jazz club, it's entirely appropriate for you to put on an album by a jazz trio and declare that it represents a live band. If the action takes place in a forest glen with a stream flowing by, a soundscape disc of forest noises or the sounds of a mountain stream adds realism to help players envision the location.

Even momentary sound effects can be used to heighten drama and tension, from gunshots and screeching tires to thunderclaps and wailing voices. Players aren't passively told what their characters hear, they actually experience it in real time! Engaging characters with sounds also motivates them to explore the in-game environment, as audible clues attract their attention without your direct prompting.

There are several considerations to take into account when selecting in-game music and sound effects. It should always accent the actions that characters take. It should never upstage them. Even if it's "realistic" for a nightclub setting, blaring music makes it hard for players to interact, for example. Prominent lyrics are also distracting; instrumental music is generally preferable, as it creates mood without being distracting.

Preview soundscape and sound-effects discs. A lot of "nature sounds" CDs actually feature instruments or even vocals that might be out of place in your game. And while many sound effects discs are fine, some are so cheesy that they will detract from the environment than add to it, so preview these discs carefully before using them.

Out-of-Game Sound

Quite simply, this category covers music and sound effects that enhance the mood of the session, whether it's an orchestra string section wailing ominously as characters enter a haunted mansion or a barrage of techno music to capture the intensity of a fight scene. This is essentially the "score" of a game. Characters can't hear it, but it builds atmosphere and provides players with audible cues about ongoing events.

Since out-of-game sound doesn't have to be justified by anything in the setting, it opens up a number of options. Film scores are a Storyteller's best friend here, since they are specifically designed to create mood with a minimum amount of lyrics or other distractions. You can often search for scores attached to a type of film your scene most resembles, such as a romance or murder mystery. Sacred and classical music are excellent sources of powerful atmosphere without intrusive lyrics. Many techno, ambient and industrial albums also create intense, frenetic mood without lyrics, and bring a very modern feel to your scene.

As with in-game sound, there are some things to be aware of when selecting cuts to play at your game. Once again, try to avoid music with prominent lyrics, and make sure you preview CDs to ensure they remain consistent in tone throughout. Nothing's worse than putting on some excellent mood music and having to run back to the CD player as it switches to something entirely inappropriate. If you can't make a custom disc, use the "repeat" and "program" play functions.

Finally, as cool as out-of-game sound can be, sometimes silence is the most eloquent soundscape of all, especially if you're playing a gritty, realistic game. While you might enjoy putting on "fight music" or spinning a few spooky tracks to try to get players in the mood, that approach isn't always appropriate, and can even detract from the atmosphere you want to create. After all, real life doesn't have a soundtrack. Sometimes a frightened hush is the most powerful sound of all.

Advanced Sound: LeitMotif

An erudite cousin of the "theme song," leitmotif is a musical term for a recurring melody used to represent particular characters, items, locations or even emotional states. Think of *Jaws*Just hearing the theme is enough to let you know the shark is back, and the fear builds as the audience dreads what happens next. By linking the presence of a particular supernatural creature or threat to a particular piece of music, you subconsciously train players to jump at the first few notes, even if the creature is nowhere in sight, just because they know it's around. This tool is even more devious if you can find multiple versions of the piece in different musical styles, allowing you to sneak it into many different situations without being very obvious about it. Just be careful not to overdo it. This sound technique spoils quickly if you use it too often. It dilutes the intended effect rather than enhancing it.

RECOMMENDED LISTENING

Classical: It can be hard to figure out where to begin with classical music. Troupes are encouraged to use these pieces as starting points: Berlioz's *Symphonie Fantastique*, Saint-Saëns' *Danse Macabre*, Orff's *Carmina Burana*, Bach's *Fugue in G Minor*, Barber's *Adagio* (choral), and the requiems of Mozart, Beethoven and Dvorak. Also, the album *Vision*, with the music of Hildegaard von Bingen. For more challenging classical fare matching the mood of the World of Darkness, try to find music by Georg Ligeti.

Soundtracks: Many of the films discussed earlier in this chapter have excellent scores and soundtracks that are worth looking into. *Twin Peaks* in particular has a still-available soundtrack that is perfectly suited to set the mood. For more ideas, try *One Hour Photo, Disturbing Behavior, Lost Highway, Truth and the Light, Fire Walk With Me, Black Aria, End of Days* and *Judgment Night*. The quasi-soundtrack albums of Cirque du Soleil and The Midnight Syndicate are also worth checking out.

Rock/Metal: David Bowie, Disturbed, Lennon, Black Sabbath, Tool, Linkin Park, Lacuna Coil, Metallica, Nirvana, Rammstein, Garbage, Static-X, Rob Zombie, CKY, Godsmack, Foo Fighters, Evanescence, Stabbing Westward, Mindless Self Indulgence

Rap/Hip-Hop: Eric B. & Rakim, N.W.A., Public Enemy, Beastie Boys, Wu-Tang Clan Busta Rhymes, N.E.R.D., Eminem, Ice-T & Body Count, Ice Cube, Ozomatli, Shootyz Groove

Punk/Hardcore: Black Flag, Bad Religion, Anti-Flag, Rancid, The Misfits, Murder By Death, Pennywise, downset, Strike Anywhere, The Damned, Rage Against the Machine, Ignite, Thursday, By the Grace of God, Hatebreed

Goth/Electronic: Sisters of Mercy, The Jesus and Mary Chain, KMFDM, Nine Inch Nails, The Cure, Crystal Method, Prodigy, Enigma, BT, Joy Division, Portishead, Bjork, Agent Provocateur, Poe, Aphex Twin, Propellerheads, Juno Reactor, Squarepusher, Lords of Acid

PROPS

Props are tools used to help tell a story, serving as little bits of reality with which players interact. There are two kinds of props in **Mind's Eye Theatre**: stage and character. As with creating a setting, the rule of thumb for props is to give the players as much they can work with as possible, provided you do so within the rules of safety.

If players can carry or wear items such as canes, headgear and, say, a golden chalice, super. They held create mood and ambiance. Weapons and items too large or unwieldy to be worn or carried should be represented through items cards or description tags carried by or pinned to players.

ITEM CARDS

To clarify, an item card is an ordinary index card or small piece of paper that's attached to a prop to signify that it exists in-game, and that the object can be interacted with in-setting. Item cards also serve as a replacement for items that characters carry, but which players do not actually hold. Minor objects such as glasses, watches or wallets do not usually require cards. Weapons always do. If in doubt, the Storyteller has final say on which items require cards.

A proper item card offers the following information: The type of item represented; any relevant in-game description of the item's appearance or function; all traits, powers or modifiers associated with its use, such as Durability, weapon damage or modifiers to draws made with specific Skills; the player carrying the card (if any in particular); the cost of the item in Resources dots (optional); and the initials of a Storyteller indicating that an item has been approved for use. Some troupes allow item cards to be used over multiple sessions, while others require players to receive new cards each game.

You may also use a color code for item cards to help players recognize and react to them quickly. As a default, you can use the following color scheme: white cards for ordinary items, blue cards for armor, yellow cards for weapons and purple cards for magical items or effects.

STAGE PROPS

Stage props don't belong to any particular character (or at least to any player's character). They're simply used to define the setting itself. Some examples include furniture, lamps, plastic plants, wooden chests, hanging vines, fake skulls, tombstones or other set pieces. Anything that helps set the mood of your game by forming the background environment before which characters' actions are carried out.

Begin by making a list of important items that you would like to see in your game, and hunt around for good physical representations of them. Get together with your staff and players to see what everyone can contribute toward the cause. You'd be surprised at the little interesting bits of property that a number of motivated people can donate.

Take time to haunt some local thrift stores, antique shops, church bazaars, yard sales or secondhand outlets. These places can provide a wealth of inexpensive objects that can be infused with purpose in your setting, with a little bit of patience and persistence. Afghans or throws can be used to cover chairs and couches. Inexpensive black cloth can be used to section off areas of play. Simple pieces of furniture can be transformed with a quick dash of paint or fabric. Cheap glassware might substitute for a millionaire's fine-wine glasses. A collection of economical but impressive-looking old books can be put on shelves to emulate the home of a mad scholar. With enough lead time, you'll find that you can come up with a reasonable substitute for almost anything you need in your game.

Once you've located appropriate props, don't hesitate to show them off! That wonderful antique music box you discovered at a garage sale doesn't make much impact if it sits in a corner. If you come across something really special or interesting, draw attention to it, perhaps even having it figure prominently in events. Whether it's a mystical relic, a key piece of evidence in a murder mystery, or just an item of great monetary value, a special prop can rally characters and players. Whole stories can be based on objects, whether their full significance is obvious or discovered only with time.

Also consider that you need to keep your newly acquired treasures somewhere between sessions. Sure, that old grandfather clock you got cheap makes a great cursed item for the characters to deal with, but if no one can store it outside the game, it becomes a burden. Small but important props such as jewels or rings that belong to players or the Storytelling staff should be kept by a reliable troupe member when not in use.

BUILDING YOUR WORLD

Of course, there are times when you just can't find the exact props you need. That's time to poll your staff and players to see what skills they can contribute. Some folks have amazing talent with paint, wood or metal and are willing to donate time to create special props. A portrait of a significant character or calligraphy on a parchment can be the centerpiece of a game session. If nothing else, craft and hobby stores carry inexpensive kits that can be adapted for use in making props. Anything that you can do to bring the game experience to life is worth exploring.

PERSONAL PROPS

Many of the same guidelines for stage props apply to personal ones. Haunting yard sales and secondhand stores in particular goes a long way toward achieving the look of a character. If troupe members are friends out of game, they can be an invaluable resource for each other when it comes to loaning or locating accoutrements. There are very few things that players and Storytelling staff can't find or at least approximate to portray characters.

There are some general rules of thumb to outfitting players with personal props. Remember that they should be used to *accent* a character, not *replace* one. If you have an amazing crystal wand you're just dying to bring to a game, feel free to work it into your character's background, but make sure there's more to your character than just showing off a neat tool and a few in-game Skills that accompany it. This seems self-evident, but sometimes players get so caught up in how cool a particular item or costume is that they forget it's supposed to belong to an interesting character! It's okay to have a "signature" prop like a diary in which your character always writes, or a necklace she always wears. Indeed other players (and characters) may recognize her by that prop. This technique is particularly useful for Narrator-controlled characters when Narrators have multiple characters to play in a single game. Just don't let personal props overshadow the characters who possess them.

Since you can carry only a few significant props with the average costume, choose your pieces carefully. Aside from necessary in-game gear, try to bring at least a few items that suggest your character's occupation or notable hobbies. A scientist can carry a clipboard and notepad with scribbled research observations on it. A college student could wear a beat-up backpack stuffed with textbooks purchased at the local used bookstore. Even if you don't have the budget to purchase all the accessories of, say, a wealthy businessman, bringing a cheap briefcase full of papers and a cellphone (working or not) can go a long way toward establishing an image in others' minds.

If your character doesn't have an occupation or any notable hobbies, or makes a point of disguising them, try implementing props that suggest his outlook or that play off his mannerisms. Perhaps he perpetually toys with a lighter while he waits for his turn to talk, or he checks his watch when he's nervous. A character who's fastidious might clean her glasses in view of others, while a character who lives on the streets might have chipped and dirty equipment.

Designating What's In-Game

One of the joys of live-action roleplaying is that it allows you to create a truly immersive environment. Players can almost become their characters when the stage you've set seems to transport them to another world. Sometimes, however, you run into a problem when players don't know what they're allowed to interact with in-game. For example, if you're running an investigation scene, you might not want players to rip apart your entire library trying to find a particular book, or to go into your closet looking for clues, or to search through all the drawers of your personal desk seeking evidence.

One way to handle this challenge is to place small, inexpensive colored stickers on all items, boxes, drawers and doors that the players may consider in-game. While they may still admire the books in your library, they know they're supposed to pull down and leaf through only those that have stickers on their spines. This technique allows players to know at a glance what's relevant.

Such labels can also be combined with task cards for maximum immersion value. Players might have to complete a successful test to be able to search a desk, and when they do they know to search only the marked drawers and to remove items with item cards or in-game stickers.

Proper Refreshments

One critical yet often-overlooked aspect of a live-action game is the kind of nutrition found in the refreshments that are served. It's very common for troupes to load up on snack foods like chips and candy as well as sodas and other sugary drinks. While such foods provide a brief rush of energy, they also go through the body relatively quickly and generate a lot of chemicals that can cause lethargy, headaches and irritability, especially if the players haven't had anything more substantial to eat all night.

To promote higher sustainable energy levels, then, try offering plain water and fruit drinks for beverages, as well as vegetables, whole grains and nuts along with the usual gaming menu. When planning longer chapters, remember that refreshments of some kind will be essential to keep everyone playing in top form as the night goes on. Ensure that snacks are available, and if necessary make plans for a full meal break either in or out of character at some point during the chapter. Just be mindful of any special dietary restrictions or allergies particular players might have, and prepare suitable refreshments accordingly.

Especially innovative Storytellers might even consider offering some foods designed to help evoke story elements found in the chapter, such as bagels and coffee to help suggest an all-night diner, or a selection of cheeses and finger foods to evoke a posh society reception. Likewise, if you're worried about breaking the atmosphere of the game, you should either restrict the food to an out-of-game room like the kitchen, or find a way to present it in a more in-game fashion. For example, if you're setting up a bar or nightclub scene, simply attach new labels to the bottles, so that root beer becomes "beer," water becomes "vodka," cola becomes a "rum and coke," and so on. That way players can walk up and order a drink while remaining entirely in-character, rather than being forced to step out-of-game for a moment.

COSTUMING

If a character sheet tells a player everything he needs to know about what his character can do, a player's costume is often a summation of everything others can expect from his character (or what he *wants* them to expect). With some basic awareness of different costume elements and how to put them together, a player can quickly create a very cool and distinctive look that says exactly what he wants about his character, without breaking the bank.

As with many stagecraft essentials, thrift shops and secondhand stores are your best friend when it comes to finding inexpensive costuming. Indeed the low cost allows you to radically alter pieces to suit your character's look, and they can get stained or damaged. The key to such stores is to allow yourself time to assemble pieces. Don't start your costume the day before a game and expect to find everything you need! You're limited to what a thrift has on hand, and there's seldom any way to tell what it'll get in the near future.

Players creating a rugged or adventurous look can try camping and army-navy stores. Those thinking along civilian lines can look into uniform shops, which make pieces like work shirts, coveralls, surgical scrubs and other working attire at reasonable prices. (You might even be able to have clothing made for you that bears the names and logos of in-game businesses, if you're willing to pay higher prices for custom work.) Arts and crafts stores also carry inexpensive if rather basic clothing, like T-shirts and sweatpants, which can be used as building blocks for more complicated outfits. If you have a seamstress in the group, it might even be possible to create all kinds of custom costume pieces to your exact specifications.

If all else fails, players without much in the way of costuming can dress the same way that most Narrators do when they play multiple roles over the course of a night. That means a base of dark clothing without prominent graphics or logos. Then you can add any accessories that identify who your character is. This trick allows you to feature what pieces you do have, while at the same time not calling too much attention to outfit alone.

PERSONAL COSTUMES

Fortunately the World of Darkness is very similar to our own in many ways, which means just about any modern fashions and many old ones apply. And yet, this is a game. Characters should stand out in some way, if not from mundane society then at least from how players normally dress. Too many players showing up in regular T-shirts and faded jeans undermine the game's atmosphere. Everyone looks alike, and unlike their characters, and it's hard to imagine them as explorers, scientists or creatures of the night.

A common trap is having only one or two costumes for a character. This isn't always a problem if a character naturally wears a uniform or games are held so far apart that it doesn't seem odd, but even the best costumes can become ordinary if games are held on a frequent basis. Players with elaborate or impressive costumes might try something different every once in a while, if only to avoid diminishing the impact of a favorite outfit. Below are some tips on building a distinctive costume.

Piece — A player may have such a fantastic costume piece that she insists on wearing it to every session. Perhaps it's a leather jacket painted with elaborate in-game symbols, or a stylish dress. Maybe it's not a specific costume, but one type of piece such as shawls or large black leather boots. Planning around a particular piece simply means accenting it as much as possible while still presenting enough diversity that the article doesn't grow tiresome. Experiment with different ways of wearing the piece, or with how other clothes or props call attention to or away from the piece. Have some outfits that really show it off, and others that conceal it to establish a theme yet to create diversity.

Style — It's possible you've always liked a certain fashion style and wanted to give it a try, or even a specific look from a movie or magazine. You can develop a coherent character image not by having a single costume, but by giving your character an overall style that's the basis for many different costumes. There are literally thousands of styles and looks — bohemian, tribal, grunge, hip-hop, yuppie, Goth, biker, Western, punk, raver. Choose looks that you know or to which you have access to various pieces. Once you have that basic look, you can accessorize as much as you like.

Another way to generate a definite yet changing look is to shop for all materials at the same store. Over time, your character projects a unity of style, not to mention making it a easier to search for new materials. Just be sure to select a store with enough variety to keep pace with the seasons or simply to keep things interesting.

Theme — Players who don't want to build around a specific piece or style can build a distinctive look based on theme. Common themes include colors, such as always wearing red, or a particular type of material such as always wearing a denim or animal hide. You might want to avoid black as your character's theme. Most everyone at your game will make that color a part of his costume.

GROUP COSTUMES

Giving all members of a group or character type a distinctive costume is an excellent way to save time for your Narrators and to indicate character affiliation. For example, a group of paranoid investigators might wear a particular type of clothing like a red cap as a subtle way of identifying each other. Gang members might wear distinctive bandannas

and tie them in a particular fashion. The result is recognizable roles or groups within the game, as we recognize in the real world.

Storytelling Shorthand

One excellent trick by which you can signify a great deal of information to players is to develop a system of makeup and costume shortcuts. For example, you can tell the players that any Narrator wearing a blue armband is a police officer in-game, or that one wearing a white bandanna is a local gang member. Or you might establish a troupe rule that Narrators with bright green paint on their faces are zombies, while Narrators with gray makeup on their faces are ghosts who should be ignored unless a character can somehow see them or they can make their presence known. Characters on other planes of existence might wear a distinctive black veil or a prominent gray armband.

Such shortcuts allow players to react immediately whenever they encounter suitably prepared Narrators, without having to stop play for descriptions or to ask out-of-game questions about Narrator identity. Meanwhile, Narrators are spared having to change into a complete police or gang costume with each new scene. Just make sure these shortcuts aren't something the players are likely to be wearing, and that they aren't so complicated they negate the point of a shortcut in the first place.

MAKEUP

One thing that's constant to your many costumes and characters is your face. If your face looks the same for every character you play, they blur into one. Even a little makeup can alter your appearance, and says a lot about a character's physical or emotional state. Some rather quick and dirty makeup tips on creating basic looks and effects are provided at the end of this section.

Even changes that don't strictly involve makeup can make a big difference when it comes to facial appearance. Men can experiment with going clean shaven or growing a facial hair. Members of both sexes can experiment with styling products to create different hairstyles or hair colors. Wigs or hair extensions change the color, look and length of hair.

As a rule of thumb, start with a little makeup and add more as you get comfortable using it. Slathering it on for your first game may backfire and create a horrifying circus clown instead of a suave vampiric predator, for example.

Seasoned or theatrical players might use makeup in combination with advanced tools such as liquid latex, spirit gum, bald caps, body paint, fake facial hair, blood capsules, pointed ears, specialty contact lenses and prosthetic pieces to craft divergent looks. While doing so is certainly encouraged, these pages focus on basic makeup tips using common components to help troupes get started.

MAKEUP PRIMER

A number of common conditions or looks can be simulated with makeup. The materials needed can be found in costume shops, beauty-supply outlets or drugstores.

Take pictures of elements such as scars, tattoos and other marks that you will need to create again and again so that they look the same each time. Having a intricate tribal tattoo is cool, but it's hard to explain why it changes from session to session.

Blackened Teeth: Costume shops sell makeup in a variety of colors that's designed to stain teeth in non-permanent ways: black for missing teeth; yellow or orangish-brown for a filthy or diseased look. Lipstick sticks to teeth, but it doesn't tend to last and isn't very palatable.

Blood: You can make respectable fake blood from a mixture of caro syrup, sugar, water and food dye, though it might take several mixes before you get the desired color and consistency. Unless an authoritative source says otherwise, *always assume fake blood is toxic, and never ingest it.* Also be careful of shocking bystanders, staining carpeting, damaging props or ruining costuming.

Bruises: Dark red, black or purple blush can create an excellent suggestion of a bruise. Eyeshadow in similar colors also works for this purpose. Using some other colors like green or yellow can suggest an even nastier mark.

Dirty/Haggard: Put black or gray eyeshadow under the eyes, perhaps mixed with a touch of light yellow, and darken until you reach the desired tone. Applying some burnt cork to the face and the backs of the hands creates a filthy, desperate appearance without actually going unwashed.

Dyed Hair: Dyes are available that can be rinsed out. If you don't want to actually dye your hair, use sprays. Note that spray colors tend to be faint unless very heavily applied, however.

Fake Fangs — Beware cheap plastic fang "retainers" from Halloween stores. They're as convincing as they are costly. Spend a few dollars more for fangs that fit over your teeth; some may not even require adhesive. Two fangs on top creates a vampiric look, while two on top and two on bottom suggest a more bestial character.

Feral Visage: Many stores sell cheap "animal face" makeup kits, which show how to create a bestial facial structure. Follow the instructions but use darker browns, blacks and other less cartoonish colors.

Ghost/Zombie: Put down a layer of vampiric pallor (see below), apply scars and cuts if desired (especially for zombies), and use black around the mouth, eyes and facial bones, especially on the cheeks. Outlining bones in slightly darker shades creates a sunken look.

Old Age: Use burnt cork or eyebrow pencils to darken natural furrows on the brow and to deepen lines at the corners of the eyes and mouth to suggest wrinkles. Coloring one's hair white or gray is another touch.

Scars/Cuts: Eyeliner pencils can be used to make patterns and they resist smudging. For particularly bright, dramatic scars, red or reddish-brown acrylic paint can be used. While waterproof, it can be rubbed off.

Sickly: Apply haggard makeup around the eyes and then apply faint blotches of yellow, green or other different (but still relatively natural) colors to the face.

Tattoos: For any area except the face, washable markers work well. For the face, don't take chances on designs that you'll have to explain at work or school, so use something impermanent such as eyeliner.

Vampiric Pallor: Use basic white grease paint. Alternately, a pale concealer works well, as does pale foundation if used to cover large areas of skin. They're all best if blended to create a natural pale, as opposed to a slathered, painted appearance.

CHARACTERIZATION

While costuming and props are a great start, there's more to crafting a truly memorable character than outward appearances. This section presents advanced tips for creating a unique persona, rather than just you with a slightly different wardrobe.

NAME

A character's name creates an immediate impression. A compelling name just feels right and helps reinforce an identity. Storytellers may be called on to create a number of names for supporting cast members, so it's worth coming up with of a few in advance so players' characters aren't always talking to Bob, Bob Jr. or Bob III. Players and Storytellers who want to nurture name selection can pick up baby name books or go online to learn the meanings of names in just about every culture around the world. Names have great symbolic meaning, which you can use to further individualize and distinguish your character.

A fairly common name like Jane or Larry tends to convey a more down to earth personality, while a less common name like Alexis or Stefan is often associated with an artier, trendier character. Don't hesitate to use unusual or obscure names, either. A name like Dorian, Wallace or Arturo calls attention to itself on its own, as well suggests multi-nationality of this world and the World of Darkness. Even the mere sound of a name can also conjure associations. A name with a lot of hard consonants tends to convey a very forceful personality, while a longer one with soft, sibilant sounds is often indicative of a more thoughtful or restrained character.

And yet, beware names that are so strange or unusual that they can't be understood, remembered or pronounced. "Favian" might mean "man of learning" in Latin, but if other players can't remember it, you don't make the cultured impression that you hope to. If you want to tell everyone that your bad-ass character answers only to "Juggernaut," be prepared for him to be mocked in and out of character, undermining your character's image. Finally, as cool as it might sound to you, insisting that your character's given name really is Nightravyn the Hellstalker just isn't very convincing.

VOCAL MANNERISMS

Your voice itself adds dimension to your character, whether you adopt an accent or simply use a different pattern of speech than your own. Even minor changes help you create the impression of a separate individual, and indicate when you're in-character. The key to all vocal work is to use it in moderation, unless you've really got it down pat. Too much of a trick is heavy handed. Ease into it and then increase your usage as you become more confident.

Accents are perhaps the most common voice characterization, but also the hardest to get right. Unless you were actually raised or trained in a particular accent, research how it sounds in daily use and remember the "less is more" approach to using it in-game. Rather than speak every word through the filter of that accent (and potentially coming off as a stereotype), pick a few relatively common words or phrases that you can do convincingly. This approach not only gives you an exotic sound, but it requires less concentration to maintain over the course of an evening than constantly maintaining an accent. Simply add more words and phrases as you improve.

Specialized vocabulary also helps create the impression of a character very quickly, especially if she belongs to a distinct subculture with its own slang. Trying to play a streetwise gang-banger is going to be a bit tougher if you sound like an ordinary suburbanite every time you open your mouth. Being able to talk the talk reinforces the image your costume and props present. Study books, films and music related to the group you want to emulate. Research can also identify "poser" lingo that's a mass-media distortion rather than genuine to your character's origins. As with accents, unless you're truly familiar with the source, it's best to use your vocabulary for spice, not stock. It's hard to come across as a gang member if you sound like a suburbanite, but it's also tough for others to take you seriously if you strain to make every sentence into an Ice Cube lyric. Balance your ordinary speech with your adopted lingo.

Common expressions or mannerisms are also good for defining a character, especially if they're not ones you normally use. If your character always replies to a request for help with a cheerful, "No worries!" or exclaims, "For the love of Mike!" when he's surprised, other characters will come to recognize it over time and recognize character. Just remember that we're talking about common expressions, not "catch phrases." You portray a character, a "real" person in a roleplaying game, not a two-dimensional mascot.

Finally, the cadence of your speech and the modulation of your voice creates character and reinforces mood. Speaking rapidly tends to indicate a passionate, energetic or high-strung character, while speaking slowly and precisely indicates a refined, deliberate or thoughtful mentality. Likewise, a high voice is equated with some measure of dignity and aloofness, while a low voice tends to make a character seem base or direct. These are not absolutes, but simply general concepts that you can manipulate to define your character. Just make sure you sustain or character's tone. A gravelly voice can be a wonderful twist, but if it causes you to lose your voice altogether it's really not worth the benefits.

BODY LANGUAGE

Only a small part communication is verbal. A great deal of it is conveyed by body language, and what a person does can often conflict with what he says. Players and Storytellers can use this truism to project character identity as soon as they walk into a room. Movement, posture and mannerisms can be used to portray a character's image throughout a session, even when a player says nothing.

Posture subtly suggests a character's very perspective and attitude. Drawing yourself up to your full height, raising your chin and setting your shoulders back slightly displays a strong, confident nature. By contrast, hunching your shoulders, ducking your head and keeping your movements small and close to your body suggests timid, nervous or shifty personality. Leaning forward slightly conveys a direct, forceful bearing, while drawing back suggests caution or aloofness. If you want to impart a feeling of power or control, always try rise above an audience. Actual height helps, of course, but if you stand while they sit, or you can find high ground from which to interact with others, you help convey a sense of command.

Gestures are another powerful tool, adding flourishes of mood to the emotional foundation of your posture. Wide, expressive gestures indicate a confident character or one in the grip of a powerful emotion, while small, subdued gestures convey a character who's less certain of his environment or that he can trust others. Animated hands implies an agitated state, while a raised chin indicates arrogance. Letting your eyelids droop conveys a languid or bored disposition. You can even create signature gestures for your character, such as a particular kind of heaving sigh when you come up against a particularly troublesome obstacle, which can eventually become one of her defining traits.

The key to remember is that unless you're using really obvious or over-the-top motions, other players may not even realize you're performing. So don't lose heart if no one approaches you with compliments about your convincing bearing or gestures.

They take time to establish as part of your character. Indeed, a sure sign of their success is achieving the results or influence you want without others even knowing how you accomplish them.

Business

Also known as the acting you do when you're not acting, business is the term for minor actions performed when you're not the center of attention, or little flourishes that make other actions more distinctive. For an idea of what this means, watch your favorite actors at work. Even when the action of the scene isn't directly focused on them, they maintain character with use of small gestures, quirks, body language and other fine touches. That's what business is all about. Staying in character and more importantly projecting that character to others even when you don't interact.

Devising a few bits of business to perform keeps you notably in character at all times. It could mean cleaning a pair of glasses with a handkerchief, nervously flicking a lighter, biting the tip of a pen or humming a tune. The personality qualities suggested could be ones that other players already recognize in your character, or they could be inner fears or desires that you have devised for your character but actually revealed to no one. A seemingly commanding character who bites pens could suggest a leader who's secretly afraid of failure or humiliation, for example.

Any time you find yourself in a bit of a lull in the action, without anyone to talk to or any actions to carry out, employ some business. Not only does it give you something to focus on to help you stay in character, but maintaining your character helps others do the same.

As with vocalizations, the key to business is to not overdo it. Roleplaying games last longer and are more continuous than most acting endeavors. Don't feel that you have to conduct some business at all times or it will become a hassle instead of a tool. Likewise, you're not launching an add campaign. Don't feel compelled to call attention to every bit of business that you perform and don't be discouraged if other players fail to notice it. As with other characterization tricks, it may take a while for other players to realize what you're doing, simply because it seems so natural! Rather, use business to entertain yourself by staying in character. You will contribute to the overall game without even trying.

An Evening's Events

Now that you've read all about how stories are created, settings are transformed into live-action environments, and what players and Narrators can do to get into character, here's a model for how a typical game session might go.

Before the Game

Forget trying to do anything but game preparation in the final hours before a session starts. You'll be too busy making final adjustments to plots and subplots, reviewing character sheets, preparing props and answering last-minute questions. Preparing for a game is little different than preparing for a lecture or work meeting. That also means meet with your Storytelling staff (co-workers) and making certain they know about any special characters, expectations or goals you have prepared (ensuring that they're up to date on your sale pitch). No matter how hectic things get, however, find a few moments to collect yourself before the main event. That way you can make sure that everything is in place and you capture the right mood instead if projecting your harried one.

Pre-Game Setup

Be one of the first people to arrive at the game site. Establish yourself in a convenient chair or corner and set a time when the game will get underway. Give players and yourself long enough to get ready, but not so much time that folks gets restless. Check out the game site. Is everything as it should be? Has everything been moved into place, the lights adjusted and the sound set up? Unpack and set up your props, enlisting aid from Narrators and players if necessary. Set aside some time to check in players; many of them will want to talk with you briefly to ask questions or to submit requests. Have your copies of character sheets handy, and be ready to write out item cards or sign off on character sheets as players obtain new gear or spend experience points. Check all props for safety.

"Game on!"

At game time, give players a minute or two to collect themselves and get into character. Advise them that they should remain in character thereafter unless an emergency arises or a pressing out-of-game question arises (and then players should to discreet about stepping out of character). If the play area permits, designate an area as the "reality room" where players can take breaks or can step out of character. Finally, announce how long you expect the session to last, dim the lights, cue the music and set events in motion.

Alternately, if space permits, have players exit the area (except those whose characters would already be on site) and re-enter in character. Moving off location and returning in character is a subtle, powerful means for establishing identity and setting.

During the Game

If you don't actively portray a support cast member or answer a player's question, you might wonder what to do with yourself while the game is on. The answer depends on your Storytelling style. You might hole up in a corner with a notebook and watch the action, jotting down notes on interesting events and watching for problems. You might remain at a check-in area so that players can find you easily. No matter where you are, be prepared to answer questions, adjudicate challenges and resolve plot complications at any moment.

After the Game

It's a good idea to get your players together before they leave the site for "decompression." Live-action roleplaying can be an energetic and intense experience. Give your players a little nudge back toward reality when the game is over. Encourage feedback. What were favorite and least favorite moments? Did everyone enjoy themselves? If not, why not? Did anyone feel lost or confused? Are there any questions about the night's events? Also, make any necessary announcements at this point, such as the date for the next game.

Police the site and clean up. If the location belongs to someone else, leave it in better condition than you found it. Pack up your props and make sure everyone does the same. Be one of the last people to leave, and give the place a final once-over to ensure that all is in order.

Many troupes enjoy going out for refreshments after a game session, which is a great way to relax and unwind. Don't feel obligated to continue Storytelling once the session concludes, though. A player might not be able to enjoy his food until you tell him how many experience points he earned, but it's important to encourage players to maintain perspective on the game.

Troubleshooting

No matter how expert a Storyteller you are or how friendly members of your troupe might be, problems or difficult situations will arise that require your attention. This section details some common complaints and tricky situations that occur in live-action play, and gives ideas on how they can be handled with minimal fuss.

PLAYER BOREDOM

You'll hear this refrain at some point, even if you've done all you can to see to their interests or needs. You simply can't anticipate every last hope that a player has of your game, so don't panic. The burden and responsibility of creating and maintaining interest in the story does not fall entirely on your shoulders. Players have responsibilities, too. When you hear such a complaint, try to help the player identify the source of the problem.

- Is she pursing her goals actively?
- Is she hoarding information that she should be sharing?
- Does she refuse to interact with other players during games?
- Did she miss one or more vital clues?
- Did she create an interesting character background?
- Is the pace of the game too slow for her?
- Is she achieving her character goals too easily?
- Is there something in particular that she dislikes or doesn't understand about the story?

Paradoxically, you might hear cries of boredom even when you go out of your way to provide allegedly bored players with a clear course of activity! In such cases the problem usually lies with players perceptions of the story rather than in any deficiencies in your Storytelling. Nonetheless, some players will claim to be bored and will have a legitimate complaint. Prepare plot threads for them that you can introduce into the story quickly, but that do not invalidate the plots and subplots already in progress.

The more players who participate in your story, the more likely it is that one or more will lose their way. A player may be bored because she's not pursuing her character's goals actively, or doesn't have any character goals. If you think this is the case, remind the player that the easiest way for her to exclude herself from the story is to remain inactive and silent. Characters who do not interact with other characters or who do not make an effort to participate in the action are quickly forgotten by their peers. While some players may be shy and prefer to participate passively, suggest that they locate at least one other character with whom to interact. Otherwise, they probably won't enjoy the game and there's probably little you can do to alleviate the situation.

Too Much Violence

Conflict is endemic to the shadow world in which the characters move. Sometimes conflict leads to outright violence. It's a part of the game, but it need not be the focus of every story. If you believe your story is plagued by unnecessary or ceaseless violence, talk with the players you believe are responsible. Do they truly believe they're roleplaying their characters' personalities, or are they simply using their character as an excuse to kick the snot out of everything that moves? If every session devolves into group combat or an extended series of tests, you probably have a problem.

Try moving the fictional location of the game to a place where characters must think twice about going berserk, such as an art gallery, museum, shopping mall or other public forum. If the extreme or unwarranted violence continues, players and their characters must pay the piper for their behavior. Perhaps a powerful supernatural creature seeks to punish them for drawing too much attention, or maybe a character faces justice from his peers for using his fists to solve every problem.

If the source of the bloodletting is a particular player who enjoys the game only if he's attacking or killing other characters, don't let this person ruin things for everyone else. Yes, the World of Darkness is a violent place and tragedies happen, but there are plenty of ways to play a vicious bastard without actually making the game a nightmare for others. Encourage the player to seek other means of contending with rival characters, such as threats, blackmail or attacks on loved ones. If the player persists in turning game sessions into draw tests and combat matches, ask him to leave the troupe.

Player Frustration

In the World of Darkness, there are bound to be times when characters feel as though they face impossible odds, or they don't know where to turn to get out of a jam. That's normal. In fact, it's often an integral part of the drama of a good conflict. If those same feelings of hopelessness carry over into out-of-game bitterness and frustration, you may have a problem on your hands. Frustration can grind players down and create a lot of bad feelings very quickly, so be sure to handle it as soon as possible to avoid it spreading.

Most of the time, these feelings arise for similar reasons as boredom, and can be countered with the same techniques. Players don't look in the right places for answers, aren't using solutions or evidence as intended, or do not see solutions that are right in front of them. Sometimes players get fixated on a dead end and pursue it despite your efforts to show they're barking up the wrong tree. The easiest way to handle all of these problems is to simply give them a slightly obvious nudge in the right direction.

It's easy to get annoyed with frustrated players, but remember that they don't see the big picture like you do. What looks like an obvious solution to you might be opaque to them, so be patient and do your best to put them on the right track without being patronizing.

NEW PLAYERS

If a newcomer has never roleplayed before, sending him into a game with only a five-minute rules discussion, a hand of cards and a character sheet is cruel. Sometimes these folks come in with friends, spouses or significant others, so they aren't completely unprepared, but the lone new person does occasionally emerge, trying something out for the first time. Consider giving him important plot points, letters of introduction to deliver to established characters, or even a veteran player or Narrator to act as a mentor. Basically, give the newcomer reason to interact with the rest of the troupe and help get him into the game. Some go-getters take that impetus and plunge right in, but the shy and inexperienced may need some extra motivation.

Sometimes new players forget what they should be doing, drop out of character at inappropriate times, or break a conduct rule. Your best option is to politely remind them to stay in character or to behave themselves, that either is a courtesy to others in the game. Point them to the reality room if they have questions or need a break.

A new player's first game can count as a "Mulligan." He can re-create his character completely for the next game. That way if he thought a particular Skill or Merit would be cool but found out it didn't work quite the way he hoped, he's not stuck with it for the rest of the chronicle. This also encourages him to experiment with traits and get involved in the story right away.

There's also a disturbing tendency among some longtime players to perceive new players as "fresh meat." There are few surer ways to drive off newcomers than by letting predators have their way. Keep an eye out for bullying or rules lawyering against new players. New players can be shy about approaching a Storyteller, fearing that their word won't be taken seriously because they're not part of the "in" crowd. If a new player does come to you with a complaint, listen to the grievance and investigate it seriously. Taking it lightly only reinforces the new player's perception that his voice is empty.

METAGAMING

If players seem confused about the difference between what occurs in-character and out-of-character, adopt a means of indicating when a conversation or action occurs outside the context of the setting, such as the "out-of-game" hand signal on p. 16. Or suggest that players remain in character at all times for the duration of a session, except when they enter a reality room. Essentially, if a player is on the game floor, he's assumed to be in character.

When it comes to players who have read other **Mind's Eye Theatre** games, talk to them before a session to remind them that their characters don't necessarily know what they as players know about the World of Darkness. It can be difficult to separate what a player knows from what a character knows, but it's a vital part of getting into character and being fair to uninformed players.

ARGUMENTATIVE PLAYERS

Don't allow the players to argue with you, particularly when doing so disrupts the flow of the game. Encourage players to take up problems or questions off to the side when the scene or session is over. That allows both sides to talk quietly and reasonably away from the heat of the moment. If it absolutely can't wait, listen to a player's grievance, make your ruling and stick to it. Once you make your decision it's final. If you respect the input of players who disagree in an appropriate manner, and then make a fair ruling, other players will approach you in the same manner.

Encourage players to respect the story. If the source of an argument is the death of a character, help the player deal with the situation maturely and rationally. Don't allow him to manipulate you through guilt or a tantrum. Humoring players in this fashion only reinforces their behavior and discourages other players who pursue grievances through appropriate channels. If a player simply can't cope with the reality that not all things go his way in the story, don't let him ruin the fun for everyone else. Politely but firmly ask him to leave so you can discuss the matter after the game.

Sometimes players argue amongst themselves about the game or their characters. You have the final authority to resolve such disputes. Don't let these situations grow into shouting matches or hysterics. Put a stop to them long before they reach that stage. If the arguing players can't resolve their disagreement, settle it for them as quickly and fairly as possible. If they don't accept your ruling, remove them from the game and try to help them work it out later. You have a story to run and those kinds of antics are unacceptable.

STORYTELLER BURNOUT

No game should not take precedence over your life. If you ever find running sessions a burden or chore, get some help or arrange to take a break from Storytelling until you feel like resuming the helm. Let someone else take over for a while, or try playing a new type of game to recharge your batteries. The game should be fun for you as well as for the players. Storytelling should never feel like a completely thankless task, a burden you grudgingly accept because no one else will. If you feel that way, it's vital to give yourself some well-deserved time off before taking up the mantle again.

ODD ONE OUT

Don't be afraid to say no to a character concept that just doesn't mesh with other characters or with the overall scheme of your chronicle. While it's always wise to think beyond common character stereotypes or to approve characters who will initiate conflict on one point or another, there are limits to the extremity of characters that you may want to approve for your game. That's part of your role as the Storyteller. The players look to you to make sure all characters are appropriate to the game. Doing so not only saves you the trouble of trying to adjust the events make the square peg fit, but also saves players the frustration of dealing with an odd man out. More than anything else, a character must be able to make a positive contribution to the game, or he just doesn't fit.

Watch out for players who are never happy unless they play an unusual character type, one that belongs to an obscure in-game group, or that has traits or powers that are rare or highly restricted. Such players typically create these characters to feel superior or to get attention. Don't let a player bully you just because he took the time to write down some traits. Just because a power is in a book doesn't mean it has to available in your game, especially if you feel it's being selected merely for one-upmanship or uniqueness.

Characters can be ordinary people or of common origins, and be made unique for their personalities. The best way to handle persistent problems of this nature is to take players aside and explain to them that are plenty of ways to make a unique and memorable character that have nothing to do with game traits or character types, and offer to help them tailor their concepts in other ways.

PLAYER CHEATING

It's an unpleasant reality that some players will cheat. A player might try to lie about Attributes, Skills or Merits that her character doesn't have, or might try to fudge the number of experience points she can spend. Take the alleged cheater aside and try to get to the bottom of the situation. Don't let accusations of cheating fester. They undermine players' confidence in you and their own enthusiasm for the game. Likewise, don't take accusations of cheating as the gospel truth. Investigate the matter yourself before leveling any blame. A player could have simply made a mistake. If you actually catch a player cheating, you have two options: Give him a warning and another chance, or remove him from the game.

Sometimes players "cheat" on a massive scale, "forgetting" to cross off Health points or to mark off Willpower points expended. You can combat these problems by having players carry cards or tokens for any trait that can be spent or lost, like Willpower, Health points or certain supernatural traits. When a character loses or expends such a trait, the player must turn over the appropriate token(s) to you or a Narrator. When a player runs out of tokens, she runs out of those traits. Tokens can thus be a physical reminder of how precious exhaustible traits are, and a physical reminder to cough "points" up.

LOOPHOLES

Though every attempt has been made to cross-check different traits in these rules to make sure that they don't combine in ways that unbalance the game, individual creativity can never be fully anticipated. Some players are bound to hit upon trait combinations and rules interpretations that nobody could have foreseen. This applies to other books in the **Mind's Eye Theatre** line as well. While they have been designed with each other in mind, some dangerous permutations are bound to arise. You may have to deal with a player who wants to exploit the letter of the rules for her own benefit.

Understand that there's a difference between a legitimate combination of traits and a loophole, however fuzzy the line between them might be. A loophole might feel wrong or unfair to everyone except the person who wants to use it, while a potent but permissible combination of traits doesn't inspire the same reflexive sense of unease. In the "legal" case, other players may be worried about crossing paths with a character with such a combination or power, but they don't feel the possessing character is outright unfair.

Other signs of a possible loopholes include: if a permutation requires references from multiple chapters or several different books to justify it; if it clearly contradicts the intent of some or all of the rules from which it springs (using healing powers to harm, for example); or if reaching the same conclusion about the loophole demands that you look at key rules passages "a certain way."

On an official level, the solution is to check for errata and other corrections from White Wolf directly to see if the problem hasn't already been addressed. If this doesn't solve the problem, remember that no matter what a book might say, if you determine that a loophole is destructive to the fabric of your game, feel free to forbid it. A rulebook should never have more authority over your game than you do, and players must understand that **Mind's Eye Theatre** is about group-based roleplaying, not finding a thirty-hit combo attack like in an arcade game.

FAILED STORIES

Keep an ear to the ground for murmurs of discontent about the direction of your story. Sure, some players always complain; you'll learn to screen unwarranted gripes. But don't dismiss all complaints as idle whining. Sometimes players have a genuine beef with the events you have laid out. Maybe the players aren't as interested in the main plot as you hoped they'd be. Maybe you miscalculated the characters' relative power and have confronted them with opponents who are too powerful. Encourage players to bring real problems to your attention, and be appreciative when they offer constructive criticism and suggestions to improve matters.

Don't let mishaps discourage you from telling future stories! On the contrary, it's important that you learn from these less-than-successful attempts and apply the knowledge gained to later endeavors. It's sometimes true that failure, as frustrating and disheartening as it may be, teaches us far more than success.

FIELD TRIPS

All veteran Storytellers have been there. You have the game area dressed, the players interact and the action is rolling, and then a group of characters tells you it's leaving to go to another in-game location. Normally that might not be a problem, but you have a major scene planned for later that night at the current location, not to mention several plot twists involving some of the departing characters. Yet there's no logical reason why they shouldn't be able to leave, and simply forbidding them from doing so robs them of their characters' free will. What's to be done to keep the game together?

The easiest way to prevent excursions is to give players compelling in-character reasons to stay. Too often the only reason characters have gathered is because players need to meet to play the game, so put some extra effort into it. Maybe now is the only time characters can gather and trade valuable information and equipment, or perhaps the leader of their particular faction demands attendance at these gatherings in order to handle the business of their shadow society (not to mention to keep tabs on everyone). Even something as innocuous as a plain old in-game party is still a better hook than an out-of-game "just because." Don't rely on harsh devices to keep the characters in one spot. Use the carrot, not the stick. Make it more valuable and appealing to them to remain where the action is for the duration of the chapter, and you'll find players are much less likely to go wandering in this fashion.

Though it's a bit direct, you can also appeal to players and let them know that you'd rather they left later in the session, or perhaps handled the task as a side session or downtime action. This approach works better than you might expect, if for no other reason than the players considered the trip because they didn't think much was happening at the current location. News that some exciting stuff in the wings is enough to keep them on site.

If the characters still insist on taking off for another location, let them know they're free to do so, but you wrote the plot for the evening around the main location, and you can't allow their unexpected trip to derail the entire chapter. Don't ignore them or belittle their action, but just let them know that your primary concern is the majority of characters still at the main setting.

FAVORITISM

The best antidote to accusations of favoritism is to not practice it. Explain your decision-making processes to players and share your criteria with them. Strive to make your decisions about the game as impartial and objective as possible without damaging the story. It's particularly important to adjudicate rules situations fairly and to not favor people or characters you like. If you place limitations on certain types of characters or powers in the game, rotate those limits so that all players are subject to them at some point. If only some characters have access to a specific trait, make sure that it either becomes more widely available later, or have another trait that those characters cannot have which the other characters have access to.

Unfortunately, no matter how careful you are to remain objective, accusations of favoritism may arise. Sometimes they're unjustified and mask other issues. A player's character died and he wants to blame someone for the loss. A player felt she was unfairly denied the opportunity to play a special role in the game. A player thinks your decisions are motivated by friendship rather than by the desire to tell a good story. Take the accuser aside and discuss why she feels like the victim of favoritism. Don't overlook the possibility that she might actually be right. Sometimes it's possible to practice favoritism unconsciously. If the problem is justified, apologize as necessary and amend your behavior accordingly.

POLICE ACTION

In a game universe where characters might find themselves forced to resort to breaking bones and kicking ass, it's important to address how and when the police come into play, especially when violence breaks out. As a general rule, the authorities should be a constant concern for characters acting outside the law or even the mundane. Police don't outright ignore gunfights, not even in the World of Darkness. And yet, they're sufficiently corrupt and apathetic to be slow to respond (unless they're being paid on the side or one of their own is in trouble).

Players can take some small comfort in the fact that generally speaking, like the protagonists in popular movies and novels, their characters should be able to avoid most trouble with the law. The police must remain at least a consideration for characters who break the law, however, or the characters' actions won't seem to have any consequences and the tone of the game will suffer. And if they are truly foolish, bloodthirsty, brazen or just downright unlucky, the characters *must* expect trouble from the police.

Instances that could inspire police response include:
• Committing a truly spectacular crime such as destroying a public landmark, stealing a national treasure or killing a police officer.
• Careless, habitual or flagrant violation of the law.
• Use of military-grade equipment and/or automatic weapons, shotguns, toxins or any kind of explosives.

Repeat offenders who ignore police threats might be dogged by the authorities and forced to scramble to stay out of jail. Even if you don't intend to actually have them get caught, players may not know that. Or police could decide to administer their own private justice on a criminal, never bringing him in for prosecution. Beatings, blackmail, extortion or attempted execution could result.

SUPERNATURAL OVERLOAD

If your game involves supernatural creatures, it's tempting to have magical powers and mystic treasures behind everything that happens. In fact, many players enjoy this kind of supernatural proliferation. There's nothing wrong with magical elements — they're part of the horror and mystery of the World of Darkness. Ideally, however, supernatural elements should *accent* good stories and strong characters, not *replace* them. Starting Storytellers may want to see what various powers are like in action, flooding their chronicles with supernatural effects. It's only too late when they discover they've lost control of their games, or that players have become bored with vast power because nothing challenges them.

If characters constantly have to resort to supernatural powers to create plot twists or to further the story, you might want to look for other ways for them to achieve the same goals. Characters using supernatural powers or devices too often robs them of their mystery and uniqueness. Whenever possible, try to save such phenomena for situations in which only they can achieve the result you desire.

If in doubt about how much is too much, keep the degree of supernatural powers and characters to a minimum, at least at first. Maybe all characters start out as mortals and become creatures as the story progresses. You can always add more inhuman beings as the troupe gets comfortable, but getting rid of existing creatures is far harder to accomplish.

MIXING SUPERNATURAL TYPES

At some point you or your players may want to run a chronicle in which players can portray several or even all of the supernatural denizens of the World of Darkness. While such games certainly have a great deal of dramatic potential (not to mention inherent conflict), consider a few essential points before getting started.

Supernatural creatures are defined not only by their individual powers and predilections, but also by their interaction (or denunciation thereof) with the shadow society they share with others of their kind. For example, a vampire with no connection to the Danse Macabre is only half-realized in many important ways. He lacks significant elements of his own culture to bring to interactions with other beings. By combining supernatural types, crossover games remove the unique cultural relationships and prejudices that comprise some of the most interesting facets of a character type's background. Without full grounding in their own shadow societies, it can be all too easy for different supernatural characters to develop a "Super Friends" mentality that allows them to ignore ancient feuds and reasonable suspicions in favor of titanic team-ups and bland unity.

Another important point to consider is that the different games are designed on different themes and moods. Mixing them without care can override many of the subtle elements that make each character type what it is. Removed from harsh lessons about the loss of identity to the Beast and immersed in the frenzied and bloody world of werewolves, for instance, vampire characters may soon slide down the Humanity scale and become unplayable, or may ignore a crucial mechanic that defines undead nature. Storytellers are thus encouraged to think of ways to keep each game's central themes active in a combined chronicle, so the identities of various character types are maintained. At the heart of the Storytelling system rests the question of humanity. Mortals protect their values (and sanity); vampires and werewolves try to hold onto what is left of their human nature; mages must avoid becoming so swelled with hubris they forget their innate humanity. Moral dilemmas and other such problems thus make excellent crossover plotlines.

Lastly, consider why a crossover needs to occur. If it's because a great story awaits with interesting characters that involves each supernatural faction in a compelling way, fantastic. If it's because the idea "seems cool," a few players aren't satisfied unless they play characters that are totally different from everyone else, or some motivation is at work that doesn't address the story, you're probably best off reconsidering a crossover. Just because various creatures *can* share the same stage doesn't mean they *have* to, or sometimes that they *should*.

CROSSOVER PROBLEMS

Each of the **Mind's Eye Theatre** games is designed to feature its characters as protagonists. Many of the powers in **Requiem** allow vampires to run roughshod over ordinary mortals, for example, because the **Requiem** is designed to showcase the undead and their terrifying superiority over humanity. While the various Storyteller games are designed to work together, you don't want any particular group running roughshod over other character types in your chronicle.

The easiest solution is to allow your game's composition to determine where the balance lies. If your game is about mortals hunting vampires, impose a cap in the number of players who can portray the undead, putting them at a disadvantage in numbers. Or consider powering down vampiric powers somewhat, and/or using optional rules such as resistance draws and other mechanics to give mortals a fighting chance. It doesn't matter what the **Requiem** book says, you get to keep your game balanced and fair. If, however, your game is composed mostly of vampire characters, let them rule their human herds with their powers as written, and warn anyone who wants to play a mortal of the risk faced.

If your game involves an even mix of character types — mortals, vampires, werewolves and mages — put everyone on a relatively level playing field, if not in terms of raw personal power then by making sure each faction has some sort of advantage. Mortals may not have the same individual power as vampires, but if you allow them to make good use of their ability to walk around during the day and to interact with other people without causing alarm, the game is balanced. Werewolves are fearsome combatants, but often have trouble navigating more delicate social and political situations, and thus can be outmaneuvered by clever mortals who keep their distance and work through intermediaries. Mages have fantastic powers to change the world, but often have equally persistent enemies after them for one reason or another, and mortals who develop their own Skills and Attributes are frequently much more of a match for mages than the wizards are willing to admit.

Problem Players

Don't be afraid to lay down the law with problem players. The integrity of your story is your responsibility, and everyone has equal opportunity to enjoy it. Most players usually present no problems, but someone occasionally crosses the boundary of acceptable behavior. The transgression could be accidental and requires only a reminder to keep players from getting out of hand. But you might encounter a player who actually enjoys going out of control and wrecking the game with constant disruptions. Maybe he likes the attention or the feeling of power. Whatever his motivation you must deal with him quickly, calmly and decisively. You're well within your rights to remove such offenders permanently.

This is especially true concerning players whose characters seem to confront every problem with lethal force. While this doesn't mean characters can't have decent fighting skills, bear in mind that constant violence as a means of solving problems doesn't mesh well with the **Mind's Eye Theatre** environment. This medium is designed to evoke Modern Gothic horror, not necessarily summer action movies. Simply put, real people do not solve all problems by firing guns and kicking heads in. Your players should be encouraged to explore other means of getting the results they want, too.

Experience Points

Characters grow and change over time, getting better at what they do. The more they undergo, the more they grow. This phenomenon is represented in the game by experience points, a measure of how quickly a character improves his traits or learns traits in which he didn't have competence before. Experience points are very important over the course of a chronicle. They allow characters to become more capable and trained at what they do, allowing the protagonists to take on greater and more difficult challenges.

Awarding Experience Points

The Storyteller is the sole decision-maker on how much experience to award each character at the end of a chapter or story. He judges awards based on a variety of factors, from how well a character performed to whether he truly learned anything from his encounters to how well the player roleplayed his character.

After a Chapter

At the end of each game session, the Storyteller awards between one and five experience points to each character. Every character who took part in the chapter gets one point just for being there, no matter how poorly he fared. Use the following guidelines when determining how many points to hand out to each character thereafter, adding one point for each category that applies. Some characters might be awarded more points than others. Extra points should be based on merit, not favoritism.

1 point — Automatic. Each player gets one point for participating in a chapter.

1 point — Learning Curve. Ask the player what his character learned during the chapter's events. If you agree with his response, award his character one point.

1 point — Roleplaying. The player did a good job of portraying his character, either entertainingly, appropriately, or both. If he veered too far from his character's concept, he might not deserve this reward, but don't be stingy here. Indeed, superlative roleplaying might be worth two points.

1 point — Heroism. Characters who rise to the occasion with truly heroic (or anti-heroic) actions or feats of survival or sheer persistence deserve a point. Do not reward characters who act in stupid, belligerent or suicidal ways just so they can gain the accolades of a hero.

After a Story

Once a story has concluded, its aftermath provides moments of reflection or self-awareness that might warrant extra experience points, beyond those awarded for the final chapter.

1 point — Success. The characters achieved all or part of their goals.

1 point — Danger. The characters survived against harsh odds and grave dangers.

1 point — Wisdom. The player, and thus his character, devised a brilliant plan or came up with a spontaneous solution that enabled the group to survive or succeed when it might have failed.

1 point — Group Play. (Optional) The player went beyond the norm during the course of the story, not only to help the game itself run smoothly but to encourage others to do the same. This point generally rewards out-of-character actions and can thus be awarded for any number of reasons, including but not limited to the following: leading other players to remain in-character despite outside distractions, assisting in calm arbitration of combat or rule disputes, helping new players and making them feel at home, and providing essential props or other materials for the game.

If you want characters to advance in talent more quickly, feel free to award extra points to get them to the desired level of competence.

Flat Rates

In large games, it may not be possible for you to pay attention to each player to fairly assign experience points as outlined above. Indeed, rewarding only those characters who catch your attention might send the wrong message to players, encouraging some styles of play over others and suggesting favoritism. When it's impossible to keep track of players well enough to assign points based on merit alone, give out a set amount of points for each session and waive the option of granting additional points based on subjective or attention-based factors such as roleplaying.

Of course, this doesn't mean you can't reward truly inspiring roleplaying that impresses everyone, or selfless efforts made for the group. Just save these rewards until the end of the story as opposed to the end of each chapter so that no one character can steal the limelight too often.

Experience Limits

It's recommended that especially large or long-running games institute limits or "caps" on how many experience points a character can earn each chapter and/or month. This limit prevents characters from becoming too powerful in a short period of time, and avoids the problem of newcomers facing a horde of veterans with maxed-out characters. There are still a number of advantages for longtime players in a game. They're aware of long-past and ongoing events, can probably act frequently per turn based on Blood Potency, and generally have an influential say in how any story unfolds. Putting a cap on experience earned per chapter simply means that the other characters do not fall hopelessly behind frequent participants.

The longer you expect the chronicle to run, the lower the experience cap should be. Start with a limit of six and subtract the number of years the chronicle is designed to run, to a minimum of two. So if you're planning to run a three year-long chronicle, by this reckoning the experience point limit per chapter is 3. If the chronicle has no definite end in sight — it runs until it ends — a cap of two experience points per session or calendar month is a good idea. The lowest cap recommended is two. One is generally discouraging for players.

A cap system can be adjusted a number of ways. The proposed model assumes an average of one full session per month. If your troupe plays more or less frequently, the cap should be raised for infrequent games and lowered for more frequent ones. Or you could institute limits on a sliding scale, allowing new players a higher cap and gradually lowering it over time (over a certain number of sessions, every six months or a every year). Such variable limits allow new or infrequent players to catch up or keep pace with longtime players, and encourage established players to manage their resources carefully as it becomes harder progress over time.

Players shouldn't look at experience limits as arbitrary restrictions on character development, but as a means to keep the chronicle from becoming unbalanced.

Spending Experience Points

The costs for increasing existing traits or gaining new ones are listed in the "Experience Point Costs" chart on p. 32.

Learning New Traits

It takes time and study to learn new things. If a character does not already possess some basic competence in a Skill, he must spend time training in it before any dots can be purchased. The Storyteller decides just what he needs to do to qualify. It might take days of study in a library, or enrolling in a semester-long night course at the local college. It could be a simple matter of days spent in the wilderness, or a week's worth of repetitive practice. Most Skills can be self-taught with time and effort, if a character is smart and diligent. Otherwise, a teacher might be required.

Learning a new Merit requires either training or time spent achieving whatever goal is most appropriate to that Merit. A Kung Fu Fighting Style requires training and a teacher, and time spent at a dojo with a *sensei* and other students. Political Contacts require time spent at City Hall or in whatever smoky backroom local conspiracies are hatched. In any event, the Storyteller judges new Merit acquisitions on a case-by-base basis.

Note that some Merits can be purchased all at once, while others must be purchased one dot at a time. Merits that increase incrementally and/or bestow different benefits at each dot, such as Fighting Styles, must be purchased dot by dot. Merits such as Inspiring that confer only one benefit are purchased all at once. For example, Peter's character has two dots in Fighting Style: Boxing and Peter wants to raise it to three dots. Later in the chronicle he wants his character to acquire the Inspiring Merit. Assuming he receives Storyteller permission and justifies the trait increases in-game, a third dot in the Fighting Style Merit costs six experience points (new dots x 2). By contrast, Inspiring's four dots are acquired all at once and cost eight experience points. Peter can't go from no dots in Fighting Style to three dots. He first needs to acquire one and then two dots on separate occasions.

Raising Attributes requires periods of self-training, or with the aid of a personal trainer. Strength might require regular visits to a gym, while Wits might need nothing more than a marathon week of playing video games to hone the ability to react to fast-acting stimuli. Again, the Storyteller can determine whether extra measures are required before a trait can be raised, but Attributes are less stringent than Skills in requiring specific conditions. As long as some activity can justify increased competence, spending experience points should be allowed.

Raising Morality through experience points is discussed under "Regaining Morality," p. 105.

OPTIONAL RULE: CHARACTER FLAWS

Flaws are considered an optional character-creation element. These traits are made available to codify the details of characters' possible weaknesses as well as strengths. Be aware, however, that Flaws can be very difficult for Storytellers to keep track of in large live-action games. Emphasis therefore lies on players to observe and portray their characters' faults realistically and honestly. In fact, Storytellers may refuse these traits because they believe players should portray flawed characters naturally. Players, ask your Storyteller is Flaws are a allowed during character creation.

Most people are flawed in one way or another, but some people have truly tragic weaknesses, hindrances that make it a challenge for them to achieve certain goals. A player can select one Flaw for his character during character creation from the list below. If that Flaw significantly hinders the character adversely during a game session, the Storyteller can choose to award the character one extra experience point for that chapter.

Note that a Flaw awards an experience point only if it adversely affects its bearer. If a character is crippled and requires a wheelchair to get around, but spends an entire game session hacking into a corporation's computer database, he does not gain an experience point for his affliction. It didn't affect his hacking in any way. Flaws reward a character for overcoming adversity. If there's no adversity to overcome, there's no special excuse for growth or improvement.

Flaws might be temporary or permanent, depending on the nature of the trait and your wishes. If the Storyteller deems that a Flaw has been sufficiently overcome, he can declare that a character no longer has it and no longer suffers from its effects (and thus no longer gains an extra experience point now and then). For example, a character who undergoes an experimental operation that heals his crippled legs no longer gets an experience bonus for being wheelchair-bound. Likewise, a character who suffers from Notoriety and who publicly clears his name in a dramatic manner (perhaps catching the one-armed man who was the real killer) no longer suffers social stigma, and no longer gains extra experience points.

Events in a game might also inflict a Flaw. A character who has been reduced to dying (losing one Health point per turn to aggravated harm) twice in one game session might develop a condition associated with his injuries, if the Storyteller thinks it's appropriate. Perhaps he is now Lame or has Poor Sight. If a fight is particularly traumatic, he might become a Coward or develop Amnesia. In all cases, only the Storyteller has the power the inflict Flaws (or to *not* inflict them), and he should do so only if a player agrees.

The ultimate key to Flaws, however, is roleplaying. A player must fully roleplay his character's Flaw. He can't pretend it's not there and demand an extra experience point. If his character is in a wheelchair, he needs to act like it, roleplaying all the frustration that entails. The Storyteller might tell the player that his character can't be in the same room with the rest of the characters right away, because he had to take the elevator to get there while the rest vaulted up the stairs. His character can arrive in the next turn. If the *player* whines about it, he's not in the spirit of his flawed character. If his *character* whines about it, grumbling about the horrible Muzak™ in the elevator when he arrives, then the player is doing his job.

For the most part, Flaws act as carrots rather than sticks, rewarding roleplaying rather than enforcing it. If a player doesn't incorporate a Flaw into his character's actions, he should not be made to do so. His only punishment is that he does not gain the extra experience point. If he ignores his Flaw too often, the Storyteller can declare him cured of it, and thereafter refuse to award extra experience points even if the player later attempts to play the Flaw and claim the points. Even a man with One Arm can be given an effective prosthesis.

The Storyteller is free to devise new Flaws not represented here, or to allow players to create their own provided the Storyteller gives final approval. In no instance should a Flaw ever grant more than one experience point when applicable, no matter how serious it is.

Mental Flaws

In addition to the mental conditions below that can be incurred by a character, he may have a derangement as a Flaw. Derangements are explored on p. 110 in Chapter 4. It's suggested that it be a mild case rather than a severe one. Unlike mental ailments developed through loss of Morality, derangements taken as Flaws cannot be eliminated by spending experience points. Indeed, the Storyteller may decide they cannot by cured at all (unless he concludes that such a Flaw is not being honored during play and he lifts it from your character).

Addiction: Your character is hooked on a certain substance or behavior. If he doesn't get it regularly, he gets anxious and goes out of his way to satisfy his need, even neglecting more important duties. If he goes three or more game sessions without indulging this addiction, he is assumed to have beaten it (your character loses the Flaw). The Storyteller is free to inflict harsh withdrawal symptoms, however. Note: Satisfying this particular addiction does not count as indulging a Vice such as Gluttony. No Willpower points are gained for doing so.

Amnesia: Your character cannot remember a certain significant period of her life. This might have been caused by physical or psychological trauma, and memories might come back at the most unexpected or inopportune moments. In addition, she might not remember allies or enemies from her past. This seeming disregard might insult others, make them abandon your character, or drive them to make her remember. For all she knows, there might be a warrant out for her arrest in a distant county or state.

Coward: Your character is afraid to confront unknown situations, and hesitates when he should act boldly. This Flaw is often as relevant to heated social situations as it is to actual physical combat. You get an experience point for this Flaw only when your cowardly behavior significantly harms your ability to achieve your goals, not just for running away from a conflict during a chapter.

Forgetful: Your character doesn't have amnesia (see above), but she does have trouble remembering particular details. *What was the name of that cursed book I was supposed to rescue from the library?* The player should avoid relying on her own memory or asking for memory draws for her character. The character doesn't forget *everything*, especially not truly important details like her identity or where she lives, but she should forget enough to make things frustrating for her companions on a regular basis.

PHYSICAL FLAWS

Crippled: Your character cannot walk. He has no natural Speed trait of either kind, and must rely on a wheelchair or vehicle to travel. A manual wheelchair's Acting Speed is equal to your character's Strength, but he must spend an action to move or suffers a -2 penalty to both Acting Speed and any other action performed (he uses one arm to spin a wheel). An electric wheelchair has an Acting Speed of 3 and allows for other actions in a turn without penalty (your characters' hands are largely free). A character in a wheelchair also has no Running Speed. Needless to say, this Flaw can be very difficult to simulate properly in live-action for players who do not normally require a wheelchair out-of-game, and the Storyteller should think carefully before allowing it.

Dwarf: Your character is much shorter than the average person. His adult Size is 4. This Flaw awards points only if the character's short size causes him physical or social problems (besides the obvious problem of having a low Health). This Flaw requires a suitable description tag if your actual stature does not already approximate this Flaw.

Hard of Hearing: Your character's hearing isn't so good. Subtract two points from any hearing-based perception draws, and roleplay asking others to repeat themselves or obliviousness to soft sounds, within the bounds of good taste. Even though your character suffers this penalty on all hearing draws, you get an experience point at the end of a session only if this Flaw causes him notable trouble.

Lame: Your character has a leg or foot condition that impedes his movement, slowing him down. He might require crutches or braces to walk, or even has only one (working) leg. His basic Acting Speed is 2 (instead of 5). Add two instead of five to his Strength + Dexterity to determine his Running Speed (see p. 108). You get an experience point at the end of a session only if this Flaw causes your character notable trouble.

Mute: Your character cannot speak and must communicate through hand signs, gestures or by writing. While this can be a very trying Flaw to roleplay in a live-action format, like other Flaws this drawback still only grants an experience point if it presents special problems beyond the norm during a particular session.

One Arm: Your character is missing an arm, which makes it hard to perform certain tasks. At the Storyteller's discretion, tasks that normally require two hands take twice as long to perform or are impossible. If your character attempts to perform a challenging task in the normal amount of time, he suffers a -3 penalty. You should simulate this Flaw as well as possible within the bounds of good taste.

One Eye: Your character is missing an eye. He has no real depth perception, so all penalties for ranged attacks are doubled. If he attempts to drive in heavy traffic, drawing an ace constitutes a dramatic failure regardless of the test pool, and you may not re-draw 10's. You may wear an eye patch, a special contact lense or otherwise obscure your affected eye, so long as it does not cause out-of-game safety problems.

Poor Sight: Your character's sight isn't so good. Subtract two from any sight-based perception draws. Even though she suffers this penalty on all visual perception draws, you get an experience point at the end of a session only if this Flaw causes your character notable trouble.

Social Flaws

Aloof: Your character is uncomfortable in social settings and avoids crowds and interaction as much as possible. She dislikes being the center of attention and recoils from center stage. Experience is gained when she avoids attention or social environments and misses out on potential rewards as a result. Maybe she doesn't get the job that she "deserves," because the boss is looking for a people-person rather than a hard worker.

Behavior Blind: Your character doesn't really understand human behavior and is blind to common social cues that communicate other people's basic feelings. Maybe he was raised by wolves or terrible parents, but he is socially maladapted. He can't tell when others use sarcasm or innuendo, or if he's boring them. An experience point is awarded only if this Flaw is directly related to a setback that delays or prevents your character from achieving his goals. Perhaps an important contact or ally refuses aid due to being insulted or disgusted by your character's behavior. Note: This Flaw does not preclude your character from having the Empathy Skill, but barring successful Skill draws, he cannot figure out other people's moods.

Deformity: Your character has a misshapen limb, a terrible visible scar or some other physical affliction that might cause revulsion in others. You must wear a prominent description tag alerting other players to your character's deformity, or better yet simulate it with appropriately hideous makeup and prosthetics. You suffer a –2 penalty on Social draws when your character makes new acquaintances.

Embarrassing Secret: Your character has a secret about her past that she must hide or else suffer shame and ostracism from her peers. An experience point is awarded only if your character harms her other causes by working to keep her secret. Perhaps she misses an important meeting with an ally so that she can distract a reporter from looking into her past. Extra experience can be awarded if the secret gets out, at which point this Flaw might be exchanged for Notoriety at the Storyteller's discretion.

Notoriety: Your character, like O.J. Simpson or Michael Jackson, is renowned for some heinous deed, regardless of whether he committed it or not. This Flaw could derive from his infamous family or from his association with a scandalous organization such as the Mob or a company known for environmental infractions. If recognized, he inspires a negative reaction in others. The Storyteller may ask you to wear a description tag noting your infamous nature, or she may simply inform other players of what they've heard about your character and let them take it from there. An experience point is awarded only if the negative reaction causes some harm to your character's goals.

Racist/Sexist: Your character has biased opinions of other races, genders, gender-preference groups or cultures. Unfortunately, he also has trouble keeping those opinions to himself, even in the presence of such people. Experience is gained when your character acts on his biases and is confronted, dismissed, ignored or even attacked for them.

Speech Impediment: Your character has significant trouble speaking properly. This might be due to a lisp, stutter, deep accent or wound. This Flaw should be roleplayed whenever your character speaks, within the bounds of good taste. If you consistently forget to do so, the Storyteller may warn you that your character's condition is improving and might soon be cured.

Running Convention Games

Although the majority of this chapter is designed for use with long-term chronicles run in rented public halls or private residences, one type of game deserves special attention, if only because it's how many people encounter the medium in the first place, not to mention how many long-running games attract fresh talent or revive fading interest. That is the convention game, or a live-action event that runs for several days during a roleplaying or sci-fi/fantasy convention. The unique circumstances of these games mean that many stories designed for regular live-action games will not work nearly as well for conventions, while other elements work better than usual, and Storytellers who desire to run one should take care to think about just how they can use the differences to craft a good game.

For the purposes of this section, a convention game is assumed to be taking place over the course of three nights — often Thursday, Friday and Saturday — during a large roleplaying convention. While some larger national conventions can begin play as early as Wednesday night and run as late as Sunday night, those are generally the exception rather than the rule, and in any event such games can still make use of the advice offered in this section with minimal alteration.

SETTING THE STAGE

One common mistake that many convention game organizers make is assuming that many of the same plotlines that work in long-running chronicles will work over the course of a single weekend. To combat this problem, focus on a few proven ways to craft a successful convention event, from writing stories that work to making sure your game is set up to run with minimal difficulty.

Have One Clear, Universal Conflict

Easily the single most helpful guideline for convention writing. Have your story based around one common conflict, which can be accurately summarized in a simple sentence: "Everyone wants to get the McGuffin," "If we don't reach a peace accord in two days, everyone will die," etc. It should also be something that can reasonably be expected to reach a conclusion in a matter of a few days. This is not to say that this basic conflict must be childishly simplistic, or folks will get bored with it; that all the characters must agree about what should be done about it, or there won't be much drama; and definitely that it shouldn't be easily resolved, or someone will do so the first night.

No, this just means that it's *extremely* helpful to have just one clear, universal conflict at the heart of your story. That way, even if all your secrets, subplots and other story flourishes fall through, you will still be able to build to a conclusion that doesn't leave anyone out. To that end, don't hesitate to script scheduled events to help move the story along — it can do wonders if the game is stuck or the players are confused — but at the same time don't be so enamored of these events you refuse to let the players interfere with them. Even if a group has a different goal than the resolution of the central conflict, they should still be aware of it and have some information or other important things to contribute to it, if only to bargain with others who do care to get what they want.

Have Subplots for Entertainment, Not Necessity

Be wary of having the success of one or more groups (or even the overall story itself) hinge on the completion of subplots and "side quests," especially those unique to one particular character or the acquisition of any item that is easily lost, stolen or destroyed in-game. It's a rule that important characters will die or vital items get destroyed in unexpected yet inescapable ways, so while subplots can do wonders to keep players entertained and help flesh out different aspects of the story, remember that you have only a couple of nights to see the story through to completion. Having too many subplots can distract from the main story and lead to a confusing resolution at best. Use them to give players something to do if they can't or don't want to work on the main storyline for a while, not in place of the main storyline.

Write Characters In Groups

Especially if you anticipate a large number of players attending, write out the characters for your story in groups, and task each group with at least one large goal that you foresee taking them most of the game to complete, as well as one or two minor goals that can be completed in the span of several hours each night. One excellent way to anchor such groups is to insert a Narrator character or two in each group as you go along — not only is this a great way to help guide players in the direction you desire and feed them information if they get stuck, but it also gives you an reliable ear in each group that can help keep you informed about what the players are thinking, any plot points they might be having trouble with or even if they're just bored and are looking for something to do.

Inserted Narrator characters need not always be present or have leadership roles in every group, but should be in roles where the players will have good reason to listen to them when they do appear. Think of this group system like a wheel, with the Narrator character as the hub and each player-controlled character as a spoke — the players are the ones that actually move around doing everything, but the Narrator is there to keep them centered and focused as necessary.

Every Character Is Interesting, But None Are Essential

Another common pitfall of neophyte convention Storytellers is writing every character so that they all have a unique and essential role in the game — while it arises from a noble motive, the main problem here is that if a player disappears on the second night or some roles go unfilled due to a lack of eligible players, the story immediately begins to suffer rather dramatically. This is another excellent reason to adopt the group-oriented character design structure, because it allows you to create a large number of characters who are all important and interested in the goals that further the story, but who are not individually essential to its success. It also allows you to write up extra characters quickly should you find yourself needing to do so, because you don't have to give them personalized goals or too much individual background to get started — you can simply "plug in" the new character to an existing group and let them help that group achieve its goals.

Beware of relying too much on your Narrator characters, either — while you can count on them to act as you desire, spread the information you need and otherwise help move the story along, their prominent status also makes them natural targets for aggressive players as the game goes on. If the players come up with a legitimate way to dispose of a Narrator character, don't fudge things so she survives, but accept it and move on. You can always introduce another character, after all, and cheating the players of a valid victory will cause them to believe you're never going to let them do anything that you don't like. On the other end, make sure your Narrators know their place is to entertain the players and help tell the story, not throw their weight around so they can show how cool they are or "win" the weekend.

The Big Five

Classic story models that just about every live-action veteran has seen at one convention or another, these five plots are used so often simply because they work so well in a convention format. Note that nothing says they cannot be altered, combined or otherwise changed to suit your needs — in fact, doing so is pretty much required if you want to keep them surprising and exciting — just that they form an excellent foundation for Storytellers to build a convention game on.

The Master — Events center around the presence of a powerful (supernatural) being, whether it is actively involved or simply looming in the background.

The McGuffin — Everyone is after an item of great power or significance.

The Meeting — Rival factions are gathered to negotiate a truce or agreement.

The Meltdown — Everyone must try to stay alive as a threat grows rapidly more serious, or prevent some event from occurring before the end of the game.

The Mystery — A serious crime has occurred, and the characters must solve it before the criminal either escapes, strikes again, or they get punished instead.

Running the Game

A lot of convention games doom themselves to headaches before the first players arrive by failing to take into account the basic parameters of the game they will be running, which in turns leads to organizational problems and possible plot complications down the line. Once you have the basics of story and perhaps a few important characters worked out, sit down and think about how you're going to deal with the following factors/complications.

Logistics

Make sure you have enough character sheets, makeup, item cards, costume pieces, description tags and other supplies to handle the size of the game. Always bring extras, because it's almost guaranteed that more people will show up than you expect. Encourage your Storytelling staff to bring a number of extra packs of playing cards for players to use. Learn the boundaries of your play area, and make sure the players know them as well so they don't accidentally wander off or interrupt another game. Check to make sure the location can hold the number of players you are anticipating, and if it can't, try to arrange for a larger space if possible or figure out some way to compensate.

Rearrange furniture, set up lighting and sound equipment if you have any and otherwise prepare the environment. If parts of the play area are going to represent different locations or be designated as out-of-game, make sure they are clearly marked so that players aren't confused about where they are in-game. If you provide refreshments, make sure they are set up in a convenient location, and don't feel shy about passing

around the hat to offset the expense — most players will gladly chip in a few bucks to have drinks and snacks on hand for the game.

Unless you are running a private game or one with a limited number of players, don't hesitate to advertise with flyers or other promotional materials, and be sure to tape up signs or have Narrators waiting to help make sure your players can find the game location. Conventions are notorious for misprinting information or changing game locations at the last minute, and quite a few games have a dull first night because the players can't find any sign of where the game was being held! It's also a good idea to have a volunteer from the Storytelling staff stationed at check-in throughout the night to handle any latecomers, answer questions from convention staff or non-players and keep an eye on all the materials at the logistics table.

Last but not least, in addition to any usual description tags, it's a good idea to have players wear stickers, ribbons, necklaces or other obvious props to signify who is playing your particular game, so that in the midst of a large convention or a hotel full of people the players can tell who they can approach and who to leave alone. You may even wish to hand out different colors or types of props based on what kind of character a player is portraying, though of course this is out-of-game information unless otherwise noted.

Telling the Story

Once play is underway, try to make sure you have Narrators attached to significant character groups or stationed at important in-game locations, and attempt to communicate with them at least every couple of hours to make sure that things are moving smoothly, players are entertained and that you can deal with if any problems that might be developing as soon as possible. While you must not allow yourself to micro-manage the events to the point that you interfere with player freewill to an intolerable degree, don't hesitate to take a slightly more active role than you might in a normal live-action game. After all, chances are most of the players do not know each other, have no familiarity with your Storytelling staff or your personal style, and might not even know that much about the setting or the rules either. Given those factors, it's only natural that you might have to do a bit more to stir up the story than you would in a regular game.

A good rule of thumb is to write so that each night builds to a mini-climax of sorts, which in turn build to a big finish on the final night. This allows you to keep things exciting and gives the players a strong finish each night to bring them back for more, while still giving them time to work on goals that take longer than one night to finish. Pay special attention to what the players enjoy and try to use it to move the story along; if a scripted scene just isn't working, don't drag it out, but instead cut it short and simply find a different way to bring across its important points to the players later. Likewise, make sure your Narrator characters aren't beating down the players or stealing their limelight, but keeping players involved and guiding them to the resolution you have in mind.

When it comes to the finale, try to prepare a suitably impressive scene – remember, this may be the only time you get to tell a story with these players, and that means it's your best chance to really show off your group's talents. (This is especially true if you want to hold more games at other conventions and wish to build a cast of regulars.) Try to come up with scenes that are difficult to prevent completely, just so that the wrenches the players inevitably come up with to throw in the works won't render your preparations useless. And when the time comes, remember that the *players* are the true stars of the show; too many convention games wind up ending with a scripted show where the players watch Narrator characters talking to each other and doing everything of consequence. Don't make the players feel as though they have simply been dancing on the end of your strings, but that they have really done something significant. Even if the characters fail, don't leave the players with a bitter taste in their mouths – try to give them some sign that they didn't spend money and hours of their time on nothing more than your personal amusement.

When it's over, try to make time for the players to hang around for a wrap-up after the last session. Have some refreshments ready, then tell them all the plot secrets they might have missed, reveal the hidden motivations of the Narrator characters, and then let them stand up and tell some good stories of their own. ("Remember that police raid that ruined your chance of getting the Scepter of Glory? All me, baby!") Take lots of pictures and hand out award certificates or other door prizes, from serious ones like Most Valuable Player and Best Sport to more humorous ones like Most Villainous and Best Cowardly Exit. Try to hand out as many as you can, and make sure you don't put anyone down more than you build them up. A good wrap-up time cements the players' sense of a positive gaming experience, not to mention helps build some great memories and makes it far more likely they'll be back for your next venture!

Convention Troubleshooting

Inevitably, problems will arise, and while the previous troubleshooting section covers a good range of possible complications, there are some that are unique to live-action play by their nature or how they should be handled.

Disappearing Players

Remember, your game is taking place at a convention full of other events that your players might be involved with, any of which might cause them to come late or even miss one or more nights of your game. Few things throw a game's plot off as fast as setting one player up as an indispensable Chosen One or Authority Figure on the first night of the game, only to find out they can't make it to the second night (or even being stuck waiting for them to appear for a few hours before assuming the worst). Don't take it personally — after all, it is just one weekend, and most people pack it as full of gaming-related fun as possible — but be ready for it in any event. The easiest way to do this is to heed the advice offered previously and make sure that while all characters have something to contribute to the game, no one outside of your Narrators and possibly a few trusted returning players are given characters utterly vital to the progression of the game.

Disruptive Players

Sadly, there are some folks who go to convention games purely because they enjoy their transient nature, and play them like they would an arcade game —they drop their money in, get a character and promptly go around the game fighting other characters and committing all manner of destructive acts, no matter how illogical it would be for their characters to do so. As pathetic as it is, some of these players even join just to see how much carnage they can get away with before the staff kicks them out of the game. And sometimes otherwise excellent roleplayers can wind up resorting to violence and other extreme actions more often than they otherwise would, because the short-term nature of the game sometimes makes a brief burst of violence seem more efficient than the less-certain route of trying to roleplay through a situation to achieve their goals.

The easiest way to deal with this is to announce your game's code of conduct at the beginning of each night and warn players that they can be removed for violations; if some players still insist on causing problems, politely inform them that they're not welcome and ask them to leave, and enlist convention or hotel security to remove them if they don't take a hint. When they're gone, fix the damage as best you can — don't hesitate to turn back time to "undo" their most recent damage or even bring other characters back to life if they were unfairly shafted by the problem players. Normally retroactively declaring that certain things didn't happen or happened differently isn't a great idea, but since convention games are so short, this generally doesn't cause too many problems.

By showing a willingness to stand up to jerks and problem players, as well as do whatever it takes to fix the damage they caused, you let all the rule-abiding players in your game know how far you will go to protect their fun and give them the most entertaining experience you can. This is bound to generate far more good word of mouth than the volume of gripes from any departing players.

Trespassing Non-Players

Many convention games take place in hotels or convention centers, which means there is a fairly good chance that either other convention attendees or ordinary people will wander by at some point, possibly even interact with your players or try to enter the in-game area. A two-fold strategy generally works best for keeping problems from such encounters to a minimum. First, tell your players to stay in the in-game area, and more importantly *never* to interact in-character with anyone who is not playing in your particular game; it is bound to be distracting to your players at best, and possibly downright offensive or disturbing to non-players at worst. No one wants to be bounced from the hotel because an overzealous player flashed his fangs at housekeeping or creeped out the vacationing family of four sitting next to him in the hotel lobby by discussing gory werewolf murders in grisly detail.

Second, if non-players approach your group or enter the game area, make sure your players know to get a member of the Storytelling staff to speak to them. Tell these outsiders what you are doing as politely and succinctly as possible, but also inform them that it is a private event and so if they don't want to sign up and play, they will have to move along. Even if the game is being held in a common area of the convention, you still have a right to keep out people who are deliberately interfering with your game. Persistent types may require you to summon convention or hotel security to escort them out, but generally most folks will either agree to stay and observe in a capacity you permit or move along when they're not welcome.

Appendix: Antagonists

This chapter offers profiles for a number of sample human and inhuman Storyteller characters. You can use these as quick references when narrating your stories, or as ideas for your own supporting cast members. The amount of detail provided in each profile depends on the section. Animals are listed with only a basic description of their pertinent capabilities (plus relevant test pools). Non-combatant characters are individuals who fill minor or "walk-on" roles in your game. They answer questions, sell equipment or become victims. These individuals have basic descriptions, Storytelling hints to help you portray them as distinct people, a quick costume that's easy to put together to represent them, and brief descriptions of their pertinent abilities.

Combatant characters are individuals who, as the name implies, could pose a threat to the main characters of your story. They can be cops, gangbangers, Mafia thugs or militia types. In addition to basic descriptions and roleplaying hints, they offer detailed profiles of relevant abilities. The final section presents supernatural antagonists in the form of restless and angry ghosts.

ANIMALS

The following specimens are animals commonly found in urban or rural environments. Note: Unlike humans, Defense traits for animals are determined by whichever dots are *higher* between Dexterity and Wits.

Skill Specialties are listed in parentheses following their associated Skills. Add one to a pool whenever a Skill Specialty comes into play. Each animal's attack is listed with a total test pool (including natural weapon modifiers) for your convenience.

BAT

Description: Bats are small, generally nocturnal animals that hunt for food using a sophisticated means of echolocation. Though unintelligent, they are swift, agile fliers. While most bats feed on insects or fruit, a few species in Latin America are known to feed on the blood of animals.

Attributes: Intelligence 0, Wits 1, Resolve 0, Strength 1, Dexterity 4, Stamina 1, Presence 1, Manipulation 0, Composure 1

Skills: Athletics (Flight) 4, Brawl 1, Survival 3
Willpower: 1
Initiative: 5
Defense: 4
Running Speed: 15 (flight only; species factor 10)
Size: 1
Weapons/Attacks:

Type	Damage	Test pool
Bite	1 (L)	3

Health: 2

CAT

Description: Cats are feline carnivores that stalk and pounce upon prey, killing it by snapping its neck with their jaws. Cats are intelligent animals and clever hunters, but difficult to train. They have exceptionally sharp hearing and keen night vision, plus well-developed senses of taste and smell.

The following traits are typical for a medium to large cat (9 to 12 pounds).

Attributes: Intelligence 1, Wits 4, Resolve 3, Strength 1, Dexterity 5, Stamina 3, Presence 3, Manipulation 1, Composure 3
Skills: Athletics 4, Brawl 2, Stealth 3
Willpower: 6
Initiative: 8
Defense: 5
Running Speed: 13 (Acting Speed 7)
Size: 2
Weapons/Attacks:

Type	Damage	Test pool
Bite	0 (L)*	3
Claw	0 (L)*	3

Health: 5

* A cat's attacks receive no damage bonus, but still inflict lethal damage.

DOG

Description: Dogs are pack-oriented carnivores that are capable of hunting and killing prey many times their size through teamwork and persistence. Dogs come in a variety of shapes, sizes and intellect, and are generally loyal and can be taught many different tasks. Dogs have highly acute senses of smell and taste, powerful jaws, and are tireless runners.

The traits listed below are representative of a large guard dog (80 to 100 pounds).

Attributes: Intelligence 1, Wits 4, Resolve 3, Strength 4, Dexterity 3, Stamina 3, Presence 4, Manipulation 1, Composure 3
Skills: Athletics (Running) 4, Brawl 3, Intimidation 3, Stealth 1, Survival (Tracking) 3
Willpower: 6
Initiative: 6
Defense: 4
Running Speed: 14 (Acting Speed 7)
Size: 4
Weapons/Attacks:

Type	Damage	Test pool
Bite	2 (L)	9

Health: 7

HORSE

Description: Horses are large herbivores with a long history of domestication by humans, serving as draft animals, farm workers and fighting mounts for thousands of years. Horses vary considerably in size, weight and temperament, but are generally intelligent and easy to train.

The traits listed below represent a medium-sized riding horse (725 to 1000 pounds).

Attributes: Intelligence 1, Wits 3, Resolve 3, Strength 4, Dexterity 3, Stamina 5, Presence 3, Manipulation 1, Composure 2
Skills: Athletics 4, Brawl 1, Survival 2
Willpower: 5
Initiative: 5
Defense: 3
Running Speed: 19 (Acting Speed 12)
Size: 7
Weapons/Attacks:

Type	Damage	Test pool
Bite	1 (L)	6
Hoof	3 (B)*	8

* Special: Knockdown (see p. 230)
Health: 12

RAVEN

Description: Ravens are large, omnivorous birds related to crows, and are common in rural areas (particularly farmlands). They are very intelligent, inquisitive animals that possess a penchant for stealing small, brightly colored objects such as earrings or other pieces of jewelry. Hand-raised ravens can be domesticated and trained, and are capable of mimicking human speech.

Attributes: Intelligence 1, Wits 3, Resolve 3, Strength 1, Dexterity 3, Stamina 2, Presence 3, Manipulation 1, Composure 3
Skills: Athletics 3, Brawl 1, Intimidation 2, Survival 3
Willpower: 6
Initiative: 6
Defense: 3
Running Speed: 14 (flight only; species factor 10)
Size: 2
Weapons/Attacks:

Type	Damage	Test pool
Beak	1 (L)	3

Health: 4

NON-COMBATANTS

The following are examples of non-combatant characters commonly encountered over the course of a typical story.

CLUB-GOER

Quote: "C'mon man, let me in! The manager's a friend of mine! Seriously!"

Background: Club-goers haunt the streets and alleys downtown, cruising the hip locales or hitting their usual hangouts and looking to get lost in a haze of music, smoke and booze.

Description: These characters fit a wide range of descriptions depending on the local culture and the kind of club in question. They can range in age and appearance from teenage poseurs to middle-aged iconoclasts, from ostentatious Goth attire to flannel shirts and jeans.

Quick Costume: Shirt of (currently) hip club or band, stylish pants.

Storytelling Hints: Club-goers are people out looking for a good time, or at least a distraction from their troubles. They aren't generally interested in long, deep conversations or answering detailed questions about the local nightlife. They're often good sources of local gossip relating to the club scene, and can provide useful information on local personalities, but quickly excuse themselves after more than a couple of questions.

Abilities:

Carousing (test pool 5) — Club-goers know how to party, and most are well-versed in the art of drinking the night away. These characters are adept at dragging others along on their club-hopping escapades, often to the detriment of their hangers-on. (See "Carousing," p. 95.)

HOMELESS GUY

Quote: "Man, you wouldn't believe some of the shit I've seen out here at night. Let me have one of those smokes and I'll tell you about it."

Background: The homeless can be found in almost every large city or town around the world, wandering the streets and back alleys in search of a meal, a fix or a warm place to sleep. Many times their disheveled appearance hides a sharp mind and the capabilities of a practiced confidence man or thief, or a proud, good-hearted individual who's simply fallen on hard times.

Description: Dirty, tangled hair, cracked lips, raw complexion. Most homeless people are thin and in poor health, and wear layers of dirty and ragged clothing. They often carry their possessions in a trash bag or threadbare duffel bag.

Quick Costume: Dirty brown pants, smudged/ripped shirt, ragged overcoat.

Storytelling Hints: Homeless people are often beggars, looking for some money to feed their addictions or just their bellies. These individuals can be eager to perform a simple job in return for a handout, like posing as a lookout or sharing information about the local area. In some cases, however, these people are experienced con artists who try to swindle as much as they can out of the gullible or overly compassionate.

Abilities:

Awareness (test pool 4) — Many homeless people have learned to be acutely aware of their environment and are quick to take advantage of whatever opportunities fate tosses their way.

Streetwise (test pool 5) — Homeless people develop an intimate knowledge of who and what goes on in their territory, mostly as a matter of survival. With the right incentive, they can be persuaded to share what they've observed with others.

SALES CLERK

Quote: "Let's see... four stakes, a mallet and a mirror. Wasn't Halloween like, last month?"

Background: They are the faceless masses that man every counter at every store and institution across the world. Most are young men and women earning minimum wage and working long hours while going to school, or trying to make ends meet with a second job. Frequently sullen and sarcastic, these characters have seen all manner of strangeness while working the graveyard shift at the local Mini-Mart.

Description: Sales clerks come in a variety of shapes and sizes, largely depending on the kind of store or institution at which they work. Late-night convenience store clerks are usually young men or women with pasty skin and red-rimmed eyes. A car salesman might be artificially tanned, with bleached-white teeth and an off-the-rack business suit.

Quick Costume: Brightly colored shirt with prominent corporate logo, slacks.

Storytelling Hints: Sales clerks can be sullen and sarcastic, distant and withdrawn, or outgoing chatterboxes eager to share the latest bizarre episode of their workaday lives. Longtime clerks are often keen observers, able to tell a lot about the people who come into their stores just by watching. Clerks can be a useful source of information with the right kind of motivation.

Abilities:

Awareness (test pool 4) — Sales clerks spend a lot of time watching people and gauging their moods. They can often discern a great deal about a person's intentions by observing what she wears and how she acts.

Empathy (test pool 5) — Successful clerks are adept at reading a customer's mood and manipulating it to make a sale.

SECURITY GUARD

Quote: "Who's there? Come on out where I can see you!"

Background: Often derided as "Barney Fifes" or "rent-a-cops," security guards are a ubiquitous presence at most medium or large institutions, from schools to warehouses to hospitals. Most times they're poorly trained and paid only minimum wage to walk a long, boring beat or to sit at a desk and stare at cameras all night long.

Description: Often middle-aged and overweight (many security guards are retired cops), with a sharply pressed uniform. Security guards carry a large flashlight, a set of keys, and sometimes wear a radio. They are frequently unarmed, though some carry non-lethal weapons such as pepper spray or a collapsible baton.

Quick Costume: White, button-down shirt; dark slacks; flashlight.

Storytelling Hints: Most security guards are tired, grumpy and bored out of their minds. When confronted with signs of trouble they typically have one of two reactions: try to pawn off the problem on someone else (calling the cops or hunkering down in their golf cart and calling for backup), or charging headlong into the situation, eager for some action.

Abilities:

Awareness (test pool 6) — Security guards are paid to pay attention to their surroundings and be alert for trouble.

Brawl (test pool 5) — The most action that many security guards ever see is manhandling the occasional drunk or shoplifter, and some are experienced in dealing with fistfights.

Intimidation (test pool 3) — In many situations, security guards are used to present an intimidating presence to deter troublemakers. Sometimes guards like to throw their weight around and abuse their authority out of boredom or frustration.

STUDENT

Quote: "I can't believe I let you talk me into this. I've got an exam tomorrow!"

Background: When they aren't going to class or sleeping in their dorm rooms, students can be found wandering campus grounds or haunting the bars, clubs or café's around town. Usually young and often night owls, students tend to look for out-of-the-way places to study — or to avoid studying altogether.

Description: Students are generally in their mid- to late teens, and typically wear whatever clothes they happen to find on the floor each morning. Nearly all carry bags overflowing with papers, books and snacks.

Quick Costume: Shirt with university logo, jeans, books, backpack.

Storytelling Hints: Students are often bored with college life and look for ways to blow off steam, usually by partying or hitting the local clubs, or hanging out with friends and watching movies. Full of new-found freedom after a lifetime under their parents' control, some students get involved in hare-brained stunts that no sane adult would ever consider, just because it sounds like a good idea.

Abilities:

Academics (test pool 4) — If a student can't recall something he's learned in class, he has ample facilities with which to go look it up.

Carousing (test pool 3) — When not studying or going to class, most students spend their nights hitting the bars.

Science (test pool 4) — Some students (like Engineering or Biology majors) possess this ability instead of Academics. Occasionally, some students possess both.

COMBATANTS

The following are examples of combatants whom your principal characters may encounter one time or another during a story. These people are arranged in an increasing order of competence, skill and rarity.

GANGBANGER

Quote: "Step off, bitch!"

Background: The most common member of any gang, this person is the enforcer and "soldier" who fights and dies in turf wars and drive-bys. Most gangbangers are teens or young men or women who have learned that violence is the only path to respect and power on the street. What they lack in finesse they make up for in ignorance and bravado.

Description: Gangbangers wear the "colors" of their gangs — sometimes a literal hue, sometimes a particular article of clothing or tattoo. Most bear scars from numerous fights, and sport ostentatious rings or other types of jewelry.

Quick Costume: White tank top, gold necklace, large jeans, bandanna.

Storytelling Hints: Gangbangers are thugs. Their standing in the gang is determined by how tough they act and how vicious they can be when provoked. Most fight at the slightest provocation. The others go and get 10 of their friends and *then* look for the guy who pissed them off. Most times, they prefer to ambush their opponents with a flurry of (mostly inaccurate) gunfire and then escape to safety. When faced with well-armed or capable opponents, they run and look for opportunities to even the score when their enemy least expects it.

Attributes: Intelligence 2, Wits 2, Resolve 2, Strength 3, Dexterity 3, Stamina 2, Presence 2, Manipulation 3, Composure 2

Skills: Athletics 2, Brawl 2, Drive 1, Firearms 1, Larceny 2, Stealth 1, Streetwise 2, Weaponry 2

Merits: Allies 2, Fleet of Foot 2, Status 1

Willpower: 4

Morality: 6

Virtue: Fortitude

Vice: Wrath

Initiative: 5

Defense: 2

Acting Speed: 5

Running Speed: 11 (13 with Fleet of Foot)

Weapons/Attacks:

Type	Damage	Range	Shots	Test pool
Glock 17 (light pistol)	2 (L)	20/40/80	17+1	6

Armor: None

Health: 7

POLICE OFFICER

Quote: "Please step out of the car, sir."

Background: Many people become police officers out of a desire to protect others. Some, often former soldiers, join the force looking for a chance to use their capabilities against live opponents. Police officers are generally well trained in criminology, investigative procedures, armed and unarmed combat, and basic lifesaving techniques.

Description: Most police officers are tall and broad-shouldered, with close-cropped hair (many have military-style haircuts) and muscular physiques. They actively cultivate an intimidating persona, an attitude they have a hard time letting go of when not in uniform.

Quick Costume: Navy blue shirt, dark slacks, flashlight, plastic police badge.

Storytelling Hints: Police officers are trained to be polite but detached when dealing with civilians. They can't afford to make friends or appear to favor one person at the expense of another. They tend to assume people are guilty until proven otherwise, and cops with many years' experience can be sarcastic and cynical when dealing with the public.

Attributes: Intelligence 3, Wits 3, Resolve 3, Strength 3, Dexterity 3, Stamina 3, Presence 2, Manipulation 2, Composure 4

Skills: Academics (Criminology) 3, Athletics 2, Brawl 2, Computer 1, Drive 3, Empathy 2, Firearms 3, Intimidation 2, Investigation (Crime Scenes) 3, Larceny 2, Medicine 1, Stealth 1, Streetwise 3, Subterfuge 2, Weaponry 2

Merits: Allies 2, Fast Reflexes 2, Status 2, Stunt Driver

Willpower: 7

Morality: 7

Virtue: Justice

Vice: Wrath

Initiative: 7 (9 with Fast Reflexes)

Defense: 3

Acting Speed: 5

Running Speed: 11

Weapons: Semi-Automatic Pistol, Shotgun

Armor:

Type	Rating	Initiative Penalty
Kevlar vest (thin)	1/2	0

Health: 8

SWAT OFFICER

Quote: "Get down on the ground and put your hands behind your head! Do it now!"

Background: SWAT (Special Weapons and Tactics) officers are police who receive special training in commando-style assaults when faced with hostage situations or when dealing with heavily armed suspects such as terrorists or militia members. These officers are generally more fit than their peers and receive extra training in guns and combat tactics. They are not typically activated except in extreme situations, and operate more like soldiers than police. When confronted with an armed individual they are likely to shoot to kill.

Description: SWAT officers wear specialized uniforms, usually black, with heavy ballistic armor and a web harness to carry equipment. Their faces are typically hidden behind shields or balaclavas.

Quick Costume: Black shirt, slacks and vest; dark face mask (not in public!).

Storytelling Hints: SWAT officers are much more gung-ho than their peers on the force. They often consider themselves an elite squad, and behave that way to civilians and fellow officers. When in action they perform like soldiers or commandos, operating with flawless teamwork and precise shooting.

Attributes: Intelligence 3, Wits 4, Resolve 3, Strength 3, Dexterity 4, Stamina 3, Presence 2, Manipulation 2, Composure 4

Skills: Academics (Criminology) 3, Athletics 3, Brawl 2, Computer 1, Drive 3, Empathy 2, Firearms (Submachine Guns) 4, Intimidation 3, Investigation (Crime Scenes) 2, Larceny 2, Medicine 1, Stealth 3, Streetwise 3, Subterfuge 2, Weaponry 2

Merits: Allies 3, Fast Reflexes 2, Quick Draw (Firearms), Status 3

Willpower: 7

Morality: 7

Virtue: Justice

Vice: Pride

Initiative: 8 (10 with Fast Reflexes)

Defense: 4 (3 with flak jacket)

Acting Speed: 5
Running Speed: 12
Weapons/Attacks: Semi-Automatic Pistol, Sniper Rifle, Shotgun
Armor:

Type	Rating	Initiative Penalty
Flak jacket	2/3	–1

Health: 8

MONSTER HUNTER

Quote: "They're out there, hiding among us, preying on the innocent and defenseless. I'm going to make them pay for what they've done."

Background: A "monster hunter" is a man or woman who has witnessed firsthand the terrors that plague the modern world, be they ghosts, vampires or werewolves. Some hunters have lost loved ones to these creatures. Others may be victims themselves who survived only by luck or the cruelty of their tormentors. Rather than shrink from the horror of what they've experienced, these individuals devote themselves to finding and destroying creatures. Monster hunters generally operate alone. Many don't want to put people at risk, while others are too consumed with paranoia to trust anyone. They often lead secret lives, working by day and stalking the streets by night.

Description: Monster hunters come in all shapes and sizes. Some, unhinged by their experiences, are dirty and disheveled. Others appear perfectly respectable until they pull a stake and a mallet from a briefcase. Like the creatures they hunt, these people work hard to blend in with the crowd.

Quick Costume: Normal (worn) clothing, prominent holy object, wooden stake.

Storytelling Hints: Most monster hunters are mentally disturbed to one extent or another by what they've experienced. They are frequently paranoid and suspicious of even close friends, whom they constantly fear might become "one of *them*." Some take to their mission with a sense of holy zeal, likening themselves to modern-day crusaders, while others consider monsters with the same dispassionate regard that a big-game hunter brings to his prey .

Attributes: Intelligence 2, Wits 4, Resolve 5, Strength 3, Dexterity 4, Stamina 3, Presence 2, Manipulation 3, Composure 4

Skills: Academics 2, Athletics 2, Brawl 3, Computer 1, Drive 1, Firearms 3, Intimidation 2, Investigation 2, Medicine 2, Occult (choose a specific monster) 4, Science 1, Stealth 3, Streetwise 2, Subterfuge 2, Survival 2, Weaponry 4

Merits: Danger Sense, Fast Reflexes 2, Iron Stamina 2

Willpower: 9

Morality: 7

Virtue: Justice

Vice: Wrath

Initiative: 8 (10 with Fast Reflexes)

Defense: 4

Acting Speed: 5

Running Speed: 12

Weapons/Attacks: Machete (Short Sword), Stake, Heavy Revolver, Shotgun

Armor:

Type	Rating	Initiative Penalty
Reinforced/thick clothing	1/0	0

Health: 8

Ghosts

Ghosts are the ephemeral remains of mortals that linger in the physical world. Some are mere echoes of the dead, the residue of a soul repeating a simple pattern of actions over and over again like a looping videotape. Others are true souls that have become "lost" after death. Unable to continue into the afterlife, they haunt their old homes or workplaces, growing ever more lonely and frustrated with each passing decade. Still others cling to the physical realm through sheer force of will, unable to leave behind unfinished business or an unsolved crime.

This section provides basic rules for including these different kinds of ghosts in your stories, detailing their natures, goals, abilities and powers. The methods that mortals can use to combat these shades or lay them to rest are also covered, as well as a selection of sample ghosts ready for use.

The following rules for handling ghosts are written with mortal, living people – like the players' characters – as their enemies or rivals. Yet these rules could also apply to other supernatural beings whom players can portray, such as vampires, werewolves and mages. Ghosts can turn their powers and tricks on those character types, too, often using the very same rules presented here. Each of **Requiem**, **Forsaken** and **Awakening** also posits other systems and relations that can apply between ghosts and supernatural characters.

Note that ghosts are distinctly different from spirits: the latter are much more frequent around **Forsaken** characters and are unrelated to the ghostly creatures that are discussed here. Both ghosts and spirits are considered ephemeral beings, yet spirits are creatures made of Essence, with an origin specifically in the Shadow Realm. Unlike spirits, ghosts can't be bound into Fetishes and powers that affect spirits don't affect ghosts and vice-versa.

GHOST TRAITS

Ghosts have Attributes similar to living characters, but they are abbreviated to the three general categories of Power, Finesse and Resistance. Power represents a ghost's ability to affect its environment, from throwing objects to opening and slamming doors. Finesse represents a ghost's capability in interacting with or manipulating elements of its environment, from noticing the intrusions of trespassers into its "home" to terrifying someone with horrifying illusions. Resistance represents a ghost's ability to withstand forces that could banish or destroy it, from prayers to exorcisms to physical attacks with blessed objects. These Attributes can potentially range from 1 to 10, although only very old and powerful ghosts have traits higher than 5.

Ghosts do not have Skills or Merits unless they possess a living body (see "Numina," below). Nor do they have a Size trait in the conventional sense. A ghost is a being of ephemera, a sort of spiritual matter. As such, it has a "body" of sorts, but one that is insubstantial to material beings and things. For the purposes of forming this ephemeral body, or Corpus, a ghost's Size is the same as it was at the time of death (5 for an adult human). Rather than Health, a ghost has Corpus dots that represent its ephemeral fortitude. Corpus dots equals a ghost's Resistance + Size.

The only weapons with which a mortal can affect a ghost's Corpus are blessed or enchanted. Blessed items, bearing holy power, deliver aggravated damage to ghosts (see "Blessed Items," below). Some enchanted items (such as an ensorcelled baseball bat) might inflict bashing wounds, while others (a bewitched sword) could inflict lethal.

A ghost's Defense is applied against another ghost's assault. Its Defense trait is equal to its Power or Finesse, whichever is *higher*.

When ghosts or other spirits engage one another in combat, they deliver bashing damage (unless they have Numina that allow them to inflict lethal or aggravated damage). Draw Power + Finesse. Each success delivers one point of bashing damage to the target's Corpus. A ghost's Defense is applied against another ghost's assault.

Ghosts regenerate Corpus in the same amount of time that mortals heal damage (see p. 240). If a ghost suffers as many points of aggravated damage as it has Corpus dots, the ghost is destroyed.

Ghosts have other traits similar to a mortal's. A ghost's Initiative is equal to its Finesse + Resistance. Its Acting Speed is generally 5, but its Running Speed is equal to its Power + Finesse + 10.

Ghosts have a Morality score and Virtues and Vices just like living characters do, reflecting the deceased's sense of morality at the time of death. Ghosts are subject to degeneration just like mortals are (see Chapter 4: Advantages, p. 99), but unlike mortals, they cannot increase their Morality scores. A ghost cannot grow or improve, only decline over the course of time.

Ghosts also possess a Willpower score (Power + Resistance) and Willpower points may be used for them just as they are for mortals. Ghosts regain Willpower by acting in accordance with their Virtues and Vices, just as living characters do. Additionally, they automatically regain one point of spent Willpower at the start of each day.

Finally, ghosts have Essence points which they spend to activate their Numina. Most ghosts can hold up to 10 Essence points (truly old ghosts can hold even more). Ghosts regain spent Essence at the rate of one per day when near their anchors. They can also regain Essence whenever they are remembered by the living, such as when someone lays flowers on their graves, or — even more potent — if their ghostly form is identified by a living person. The Storyteller awards Essence whenever he thinks an appropriate instance of momento mori occurs.

THE NATURE OF GHOSTS

A ghost is an intangible ephemera that exists in the physical world. A ghost with Finesse 1 or 2 is only aware of the area around its anchor (see below), while those with Finesse 3 or more can perceive the rest of their surroundings much as a mortal does.

Ghosts cannot be seen or felt by mortals unless it makes a special effort to manifest (see below). Even when manifested, a ghost is an ethereal, insubstantial presence. Ghosts with a Power of 1 to 3 often appear as little more than an eerie, glowing mist or ball of light. Ghosts with a Power of 4 or 5 might seem as real and substantial as a living mortal — until someone tries to touch them. Ghosts pass effortlessly through solid objects, even when manifested. By the same token, they can't physically touch or manipulate physical objects unless they possess a specific power to do so (see "Numina"). They are immune to all types of mundane damage, and can see and hear clearly regardless of environmental conditions, whether in total darkness, fog or a raging storm.

Players portraying ghosts that are in an unmanifested state should use the "Other Plane of Existence" hand gesture (p. 17).

ANCHORS

Ghosts linger in the physical world because something anchors them there, preventing them from continuing on to the afterlife. Every ghost has at least one anchor rooting it to the physical world. Some powerful shades may have more. The number and nature of a ghost's anchors depends on the individual and the circumstances surrounding its death. In most cases, an anchor is a physical place or object that held great emotional significance to the ghost during its mortal existence. An elderly woman who spent her last years largely confined to her bed might be anchored to the bedroom or to the bed itself. A man who carried a valuable pocket watch wherever he went might be a ghost anchored to the watch, haunting those who come to possess it. Occasionally, ghosts can be anchored to *people* rather than to objects. A father whose last thought was for the welfare of his children may be anchored to them, watching over them in death as he did in life. Or a woman murdered by a jilted lover may find her ghost anchored to him, sustained by a bitter desire for revenge.

Ghosts must remain close to their anchors at all times, whether they manifest or not. A ghost can travel up to 10 steps from its anchor per point of Power that it has. Thus, a ghost with 3 Power can travel up to 30 steps from its anchor. Ghosts anchored to a place instead of a person or object measure this distance from the spot where they died or from where a structure ends. A ghost with 3 Power whose anchor is a mansion can travel anywhere within the mansion, but only up to 30 steps away from the exterior of the building.

Anchors also make it easier for a ghost to manifest in the physical world. If a ghost is within one yard of its anchor it can manifest automatically with no draw required (see "Manifestations," below).

If a ghost has multiple anchors, it can jump from one anchor to another with the expenditure of a single Willpower point, regardless of the distance between anchors. So, the father who lingers in the physical world to watch over his kids can jump from one child to another, even if they are on opposite sides of the world.

If a ghost's anchors are altered (subjected to sanctification or exorcism — see "Dealing with Ghosts") or destroyed, the ghost can no longer remain in the physical world. It passes on into the afterlife and cannot return.

MANIFESTATIONS

When a ghost wishes to interact with mortals or the physical world it must manifest, focusing its energies into a form just substantial enough to allow it a discernible presence. A ghostly manifestation doesn't necessarily have to be visible. A sentient ghost can choose to manifest invisibly if it wishes, but its presence still leaves traces that mortals can detect. Examples of invisible ghostly manifestation include cold spots, strange or intense odors and heightened magnetic fields.

Some areas are more conducive to supernatural energies than others. A graveyard is an extremely easy place for a ghost to manifest, while a laboratory often isn't. As a rule of thumb, locations where mortals frequently express powerful emotions — love, anger, sadness, fear — create conditions that allow a ghost easier access to the physical world. Sterile, emotionless places, or remote areas that have experienced little or no human emotion make it very difficult for a ghost to appear.

Curiously, the presence of mortals creates a cumulative effect that actually inhibits the manifestation of ghosts. This is apparently a phenomenon unique to the modern, scientific era, in which adults are conditioned to disbelieve instances of supernatural activity. The more people gathered in a particular location, the harder it is for a ghost to manifest.

Manifestation requires a successful Power + Finesse draw. Positive or negative modifiers may apply, depending on the location (see chart). If there is more than one mortal present, each person after the first imposes a –1 modifier to the draw. (This last penalty does not apply to other supernatural beings or creatures in the ghost's locale. Their numbers do not affect a ghost's ability to manifest.) If the draw succeeds, the ghost can manifest for the duration of the scene if it wishes. It can make itself visible or invisible at will, and can de-manifest at any time. If the draw fails, the ghost does not manifest and loses one Willpower point. The ghost can continue to attempt to manifest as long as it has at least one Willpower point remaining. If it exhausts all its Willpower, it cannot attempt to manifest again until the following day.

Once a ghost has manifested it can attempt to interact with the physical world by communicating with any mortals present (see "Communication," below), or by drawing on its Numina.

Manifestation Modifiers

Location	Modifier
Graveyard	+3
Battlefield	+3
Church	+2
Hospital	+2
Historic building (100+ years old)	+2
Old building (50–100 years old)	+1
Handmade structure (wooden bridge, shed)	+1
Parking lot	−1
Modern commercial building (grocery store, mall)	−1
Modern industrial building	−2
Modern laboratory	−3

COMMUNICATION

Interaction with the living is difficult for ghosts, even under the best of conditions. Without the proper Numina, a manifested ghost has no voice. It can form words with its mouth and hope a mortal witness can read lips, or it can try to get its message across with gestures. Complicated gestures like sign language are very difficult for ghosts to perform, as they have a hard time translating their thoughts into physical motion. Make a Finesse draw for any such attempt with a –1 modifier for each decade that a ghost has been dead. If the draw fails, the ghost is unable to envision the right signs and gestures to get its point across. Simple gestures (motioning a mortal to follow, pointing to a hidden object) do not require a Finesse draw.

Ghosts with the proper Numina can communicate with mortals in a variety of ways, from speaking directly to writing on objects to imparting visions.

NUMINA

Ghosts have a number of powers at their disposal to interact with or manipulate the physical world. These powers, called Numina (singular: Numen), range from terrifying auras to outright possession of living bodies. The type of Numina a ghost has depends on its nature and personality, its goals and on the circumstances of its death. The number of powers it has depends on its age. Generally, a ghost has one Numen per 10 years since its death. Thus, a ghost that's been dead for 30 years can have up to three Numina. Of course, exceptions are possible in the case of exceptionally potent or willful ghosts. When designing your own ghosts, assign whatever Numina you feel are appropriate to it and to the kind of story you want to tell.

The following are examples of Numina that ghosts can have, along with their costs and effects. Feel free to use these as guidelines to create your own, or alter them as you see fit to suit the needs of your game.

ANIMAL CONTROL

The ghost is able to exert its will over an animal, controlling it completely. Spend one Essence and draw Power + Finesse, subtracting the animal's Resolve from the test pool. Success means the ghost is able to command the animal to perform any task it desires, to the limit of the animal's physical abilities. The ghost can control the animal for the duration of the scene if desired. A ghost can control a number of animals simultaneously (so long as it has sufficient Essence) equal to its Finesse trait.

CLAIRVOYANCE

The ghost can speak to mortals through the body of another living person. Draw Power + Finesse, with the subject's Resolve subtracted from the test pool as a penalty. If the victim is a willing participant, no draw is made. If the ghost fails, no communication is possible. If the ghost wins, it can speak using the victim's vocal cords for a single turn. At the end of the turn, the victim suffers a single point of bashing damage due to the strain of contact. If the ghost wishes to continue speaking through the medium, a further Power + Finesse draw must be made each turn. The medium continues to suffer an additional point of bashing damage at the end of each turn of communication. If the medium is rendered unconscious, no further contact is possible.

COMPULSION

The ghost is able to exert its will over a living person, commanding him to perform actions like a puppet. Spend one Essence point and draw Power + Finesse in a contested draw versus the victim's Resolve + Composure. If the ghost fails or ties the draw (or the mortal wins), the victim is unaffected. If the ghost wins the draw, it seizes control of the victim and can command him to perform any acts it desires, within the victim's capabilities. The victim can attempt to throw off the ghost's control each successive turn with another contested draw. Use the victim's own test pools to determine the outcome of his actions. The ghost can compel a number of victims simultaneously (so long as it has sufficient Essence) equal to its Finesse trait.

GHOST SIGN

The ghost is capable of creating messages or images in malleable forms of media. Spend one Essence point and draw Power + Finesse. If the draw fails, nothing happens. If the draw succeeds, the ghost can create a single message or image. A sentence can be written in the steam condensed on a mirror. A ghostly statement can be heard amid the static of an audio tape. Or an image can be superimposed on a frame of camera film or videotape.

GHOST SPEECH

The ghost is capable of speaking directly to mortals when it manifests. Spend one Essence point and draw Power + Finesse. If the draw succeeds, the ghost can utter a single sentence.

MAGNETIC DISRUPTION

The ghost's manifestation causes electronic equipment to malfunction due to an intense magnetic distortion. No draw is required. If the ghost manifests successfully, it disrupts electronics within a number of steps equal to its Power trait. Radios, TVs and telephones emit static. Appliances stop working. Lights go out. Videotapes and camera film is erased/exposed, ruining any captured images.

PHANTASM

The ghost has the power to create illusory images. Spend one Essence point and draw Power + Finesse. A negative modifier may be applied to the draw depending on the size and complexity of the illusion. Mimicking a person's voice alone or creating a distinctive smell (like perfume) doesn't incur any negative modifiers, but creating the illusion of a person might be subject to a –1 penalty. Creating the illusion of a specific person (down to patterns of speech and mannerisms) that a witness knows might call for a –2 penalty. Creating a complex illusion that seems to have physical substance (the witness is convinced that he can "touch" the illusion and it feels solid) incurs a –3 or more severe penalty. Small, subtle illusions are generally much more effective than large, overt ones. This power can work on only one victim at a time. Other mortals in the subject's vicinity do not see what he does. When a subject witnesses an illusion, draw Wits + Composure (or the Storyteller may allow Composure to be replaced by Occult if your character is aware of ghostly activity). If the draw generates as many or more successes than were achieved in the phantasm draw, the victim recognizes that the image can't be real. If the phantasm draw wins, the subject believes the illusion is genuine, but another Wits + Composure (or Occult) draw is made for him in each successive turn to attempt to see through the power. A ghost can maintain only one illusion at a time, and each illusion remains for the duration of the scene unless dispelled.

POSSESSION

The ghost may attempt to possess a living human being and control his or her body for a short time. Spend one Essence point and draw Power + Finesse in a contested draw versus the victim's Resolve + Composure. If the ghost wins, it gains control of the victim's body for the duration of a single scene. Use the victim's available traits (except Willpower points, which are equal to the ghost's current Willpower points) and test pools for any action the ghost wishes to take. If the mortal wins or ties the draw, the ghost fails its possession attempt. As long as the ghost has Essence points remaining it can continue to make possession attempts against a target. If a possessed body is killed or knocked unconscious, the ghost is forced out and must possess another victim if it still wishes to act.

Attacks using a blessed object against a ghost in possession of a living body damage the ghost's Corpus instead of its physical host. (For more information see "Blessed Items," below.) At the Storyteller's discretion, a player or Narrator may spend a Willpower point for her character to attempt to shake off the possessing ghost at any time during the scene, especially if it attempts to compel the character to perform an act completely out of line with her moral code. Each point allows another contested draw.

TELEKINESIS

The ghost can manipulate physical objects as though it had a pair of physical hands. It can pick up objects, throw them, open and close doors and windows, write messages — basically anything a mortal can do with his hands.

Spend one Essence point and draw Power + Finesse. The number of successes drawn determines the ghost's relative Strength when attempting to lift and/or move an object (see Chapter 2: Attributes, p. 43, for more details on lifting/moving objects). If the successes drawn are equal to the Strength needed to lift an object, the ghost can move it up to one yard. Each extra success allows the ghost to move the object an additional yard. If the ghost wishes to hurl an object at someone and enough successes are drawn to lift the object (and reach the target), the total number of telekinesis successes is drawn as a test pool in an attack against the target. Alternately, the ghost can make a direct attack on a victim, using its raw power to inflict cuts, bruises and bites on the victim's body. Treat this as a normal attack with a −3 modifier. The attack ignores the target's Defense trait, any available cover and any armor worn (unless the armor is supernatural in nature).

TERRIFY

The ghost has the power to strike terror in the hearts of mortals who witness its manifestation. Draw Power + Finesse in a contested draw against the Resolve + Composure of each mortal who witnesses the ghost's manifestation firsthand. (If a crowd witnesses it, draw the highest Resolve + Composure in the crowd for the whole group.) If the ghost loses or ties, mortals in the area are unaffected and are immune to uses of this power for the remainder of the scene. Perhaps their subconscious minds won't allow them to recognize the ghost, or they mistake the intended frightening image for something else such as a hallucination or trick of the light. Mortals who lose flee from the ghost and will not return to the haunted area for at least one day.

DEALING WITH GHOSTS

As antagonists, ghosts are difficult beings to confront or thwart. They are immune to virtually all forms of physical damage, can travel through solid objects and if pressed can literally de-materialize beyond mortal reach.

Generally speaking, the only way for mortals to deal with ghosts is through the people, places and things that anchor them to the physical world. By addressing the ties that bind ghosts to the Earth, it's possible to lay them to rest — or send them to the judgment they richly deserve.

SEVERING ANCHORS

The simplest (but not necessarily easiest) method of dealing with a ghost is to locate its anchor(s) and destroy them. The trouble is, anchors are not immediately obvious. Oftentimes, a ghost itself isn't aware of what ties it to the physical realm. Discerning what object or objects anchor a ghost requires observation, research and careful investigation. Determining the identity of the ghost is the first step. Then comes investigating the circumstances of its death. If the ghost's death does not provide sufficient clues to suggest its anchor, more research is required to identify any personal effects that could possibly act as a tie.

Once an anchor is identified, all that remains is to destroy the object, which is sometimes easier said than done. The anchor must be damaged to the degree that it no longer exists in the form that the ghost knew it. The stone of a diamond ring has to be separated from the band, the band melted down, and the stone split. For more details on damaging objects, see Chapter 6: Dramatic Systems, p. 151.

If a ghost's anchor is a physical location rather than an object, the destruction process can be difficult or even impossible. If the ghost haunts a particular hotel room, how can one completely destroy a single room and leave the surrounding building intact? Such situations require extraordinary measures such as an exorcism.

FULFILLING UNFINISHED BUSINESS

If a ghost exists to fulfill some obligation or desire that it couldn't complete in life, it's possible to lay the shade to rest by identifying what the ghost wants and resolving the situation. Doing so can involve considerable detective work, identifying the ghost and researching its past, or it might require attempts to communicate directly with the ghost to learn what it wants. Once the ghost's needs are met, its anchors disappear and it departs the physical world forever.

ABJURATIONS

Abjurations are prayers or rites meant to banish a ghost from the presence of the faithful, disrupting its manifestation and keeping it at bay for a short time. Abjuration calls for a contested Resolve + Composure draw versus the ghost's Power + Resistance.

Characters can acquire the specifics of an abjuration prayer or rite with a little time and research. What's most important is the knowledge and focus of the person performing the prayer. To perform an abjuration without suffering any penalties, a character must have a minimum Morality of 8 and a minimum Occult or Academics (Religion) of 3. The Morality score reflects the character's purity of thought and intent, while the Skill dots reflect a minimum degree of experience and training in the performance of the rite. For every dot of Morality below 8 or Skill below 3, the abjuration draw suffers a –1 penalty. Similarly, every dot of Morality above 8 or Skill above 3 offers a +1 modifier, reflecting the character's extraordinary focus and experience.

Failure: Your character's faith or capability is found wanting, and the ghost is unmoved by the prayer. Your character can attempt the abjuration again if he wishes.

Success: Your character's faith or capability drives the ghost from his vicinity. The ghost is forced to de-manifest and cannot manifest again within the character's line of sight until the following day.

EXORCISMS

Exorcisms are special rites of sanctification that popular myth has relegated to cases of demonic possession, but they in fact can be used to uproot and banish any form of ephemera from the physical world. Like an abjuration, an exorcism is more about the person who performs the rite than the words spoken, and is primarily a contest of wills between mortal and ghost. A character who performs an exorcism wants a minimum Morality of 8 and a minimum Occult or Academics (Religion) of 3 to avoid incurring penalties on the exorcism draw. For every dot of Morality below 8 or Skill below 3, a –1 penalty is suffered. For every dot of Morality above 8 or Skill above 3, a +1 bonus is gained.

An exorcism is a contested and extended action, with each draw representing five minutes of incantation and prayer. Draw Resolve + Composure for the character performing the exorcism, and the ghost's Power + Resistance. On each draw, the side with the most successes (regardless of total successes achieved) causes the other to lose one point of Willpower. The exorcism draws continue until the character voluntarily abandons the attempt or one side runs out of Willpower. If the character runs out of Willpower, he falls into a catatonic state, ravaged both physically and emotionally. If the ghost runs out of Willpower, it is unable to maintain its hold on its anchor(s) and is banished from the physical realm, never to return.

If neither side gets any successes or both sides get the same number of successes in a draw, the battle continues for another five minutes with no one losing Willpower.

If multiple people participate in an exorcism, treat the effort like teamwork (p. 180). One participant is the primary, and all secondaries may or may not contribute bonuses to the primary's draw in each stage of the rite. The primary loses all Willpower for his "side."

Failure: Your character (or the ghost) comes up short in the battle of wills.

Success: Your character (or the ghost) has energy and determination. The opponent loses one Willpower point if you get the most successes.

BLESSED ITEMS

Like prayers or rites, blessed or sanctified objects that are infused with faith can be used to physically disrupt a ghost, damaging or destroying it utterly. Blessed or enchanted items are among the only means by which a physical attack can harm a manifested ghost. Damage comes from the faith invested in the object rather than from the force of the swing.

A blessed or sacred object can be anything from an ancient wooden cross to a well-worn Qu'ran to a set of Buddhist prayer beads. Blessed items have a ranking from 1 to 5, representing the weight of belief imbued in them. Truly blessed items in the modern world are almost always relics from older, more superstitious times. Such relics cannot be crafted intentionally. Their blessing is a mysterious power afforded by faith. It is entirely up to the Storyteller to determine if an item is blessed or not. A cross that was carried for years by a saintly missionary might come to possess an aura of faith, while a book used by a popular preacher on a nationally televised show might never acquire such resonance. It is impossible to predict where faith will flower into physical manifestation. Likewise, it's hard for mere mortals to know whether a holy relic is infused with faith until it's tested against the supernatural. Certain supernatural creatures can sometimes sense a divine aura, but mortals have no such capability.

To use a blessed item on a manifested ghost, make a normal attack draw as you would with a mundane weapon, but instead of adding a damage rating as bonus points, add the item's blessing rating to your test pool. If the attack hits, each success inflicts a point of aggravated damage.

Example: *Father Sheridan wields a blessed rosary (3 dots), with which he lashes out at a malevolent ghost. His player draws Strength 2 + Weaponry 1 + 3 for the blessed power of the item. The apparition's Defense of 2 is subtracted from the test pool, leaving four points. The draw result is 12 — two successes, inflicting two aggravated wounds to the apparition.*

Blessed items that aren't made to be used in combat do not suffer the usual –1 penalty that improvised weapons normally do (see p. 232). Their power comes from the faith they project, not from their sturdiness or utility.

TYPES OF GHOSTS

The following are examples of general types of ghosts that you can include in your stories. Each profile has its own unique set of abilities. They're listed in general order of power and rarity.

Speed refers to Running Speed; use the ghost's species factor for Acting Speed.

APPARITION

Background: Apparitions are the most common form of ghost, encountered in haunted places across the world. Typically the ghost of someone who met a sudden or violent death, or a lost soul that has become trapped in this world, an apparition has the power to terrify any mortals who encounter it.

Description: Apparitions can come in many forms, from shifting wisps of light to human forms nearly indistinguishable from the living. These ghosts can bear telltale signs of death. The apparition of a murdered man might have bloodstains on his shirt. The victim of a plane crash may be burnt nearly beyond recognition.

Storytelling Hints: Apparitions are generally bound to their places of death, and may appear only when the time of their demise reoccurs (say, sundown each night). In many cases they don't interact with mortals at all, simply going through the motions of their previous existence, but some particularly angry ghosts vent their rage on the living if they can. In rare cases these ghosts are capable of communicating with mortals, often trying to impart dire warnings or to prod an individual into solving the circumstances of their death.

Attributes: Power 2, Finesse 1, Resistance 2
Willpower: 4
Morality: 7
Virtue: Temperance
Vice: Envy

Initiative: 3
Defense: 2
Running Speed: 13
Size: 5
Corpus: 7
Numina: Choose one of Clairvoyance (test pool 3), Magnetic Disruption (no draw required) or Terrify (test pool 3)

POLTERGEIST

Background: The poltergeist, or "noisy ghost," is a ghost that makes its presence known by causing inexplicable sounds (footsteps, slamming doors) and by moving objects, sometimes violently. Plates fly across the room. Pens scrawl messages on notebooks or walls. In rare cases, mortal victims manifest bite marks or scratches all over their bodies. Sometimes these ghosts are angry ghosts who have learned to use their powers to manipulate the physical world. Other times poltergeist activity seems to focus on an adolescent (usually a pre-teen or teenage girl) in a household, possibly suggesting a form of latent psychic power.

Description: Poltergeists are invisible entities that make their presence known by moving physical objects. Mortals occasionally witness glowing balls of light or glowing wisps of smoke, or more rarely see these beings on video recordings as fuzzy, humanoid shapes.

Storytelling Hints: Poltergeists can interact with the physical world only by acting on objects — almost always inanimate objects such as plates, glasses and furniture. Powerful poltergeists can affect living beings directly, punching or biting or hurling them across a room. These ghosts are capable of leaving messages written in a number of ways, but they are rarely interested in communication. Anger and violence are common hallmarks of the poltergeist, which can point researchers to signs of adolescent turmoil in the vicinity of the haunting.

Attributes: Power 3, Finesse 3, Resistance 2
Willpower: 5
Morality: 6
Virtue: Justice
Vice: Wrath
Initiative: 5
Defense: 3
Running Speed: 16
Size: 5
Corpus: 7
Numina: Ghost Sign (test pool 6), Magnetic Disruption (no draw required) and Telekinesis (test pool 6)

DECEIVER

Background: A deceiver is a powerful, sentient ghost capable of terrifying (and even injuring) mortals by tricking them with potent illusions. These entities can be the remnants of an older, more primitive time when human worship lent the beings greater power and insight into manipulating mortal thoughts. In rare cases, deceivers are the malevolent souls of powerful mortals bent on revenge for an injustice committed against them.

Description: Deceivers can assume any appearance they wish, taking the form of a mortal's loved one in one moment and appearing as a nightmarish monster the next. They typically prefer not to reveal themselves at all, relying on indirect illusions that range from the grossly obvious (blood running down walls) to the subtle (the victim fails to see the *Out of Order* sign as he steps into the elevator shaft).

Storytelling Hints: Deceivers are excellent antagonists for a classic ghost story, being able to create any image they wish in order to communicate with (or eliminate) their victims. Unlike apparitions, deceivers can communicate directly with mortals if they wish, through written messages or freakish illusions (a crosswalk sign flashes from "walk" to "run"), or simply by speaking through an illusory form. In many cases these ghosts are malicious entities, delighting in terrorizing or harming victims in retaliation for some past wrong. Others use their power to seek vengeance against specific enemies. The ghost of a boy murdered by local police might visit his own form of justice on those who killed him. Occasionally deceivers are benevolent entities, using their power to shield the innocent and coming to their aid with overt or subtle messages.

Attributes: Power 4, Finesse 4, Resistance 3
Willpower: 7
Morality: 4
Virtue: Fortitude
Vice: Envy
Initiative: 7
Defense: 4
Running Speed: 18
Size: 5
Corpus: 8
Numina: Ghost Sign (test pool 8), Phantasm (test pool 8) and Terrify (test pool 8)

SKINRIDER

Background: Skinriders are rare and very powerful ghosts that can possess the bodies of living people. These ghosts are nearly always malevolent (some say demonic). They use their power to sate physical urges denied them by their intangible forms, or to inflict suffering on victims.

Description: Skinriders occasionally appear as glowing, insubstantial forms that flow like smoke over or into the bodies of their victims. Possession victims can show clear signs of being under supernatural control. Their eyes turn gray and milky or their skin takes on an unearthly pallor. Sometimes a ghost is powerful or subtle enough to operate without revealing itself, unless it is angered or frustrated.

Storytelling Hints: Skinriders are almost always evil ghosts that force their will onto defenseless mortals to fulfill their desires. They enjoy taunting victims, and choose vessels that will suffer the greatest from the consequences of forced actions. A vengeful ghost could also attempt to possess a mortal body if the object of its revenge is nearby.

Attributes: Power 5, Finesse 4, Resistance 5
Willpower: 10
Morality: 3
Virtue: Justice
Vice: Wrath
Initiative: 9
Defense: 5
Running Speed: 19
Size: 5
Corpus: 10
Numina: Animal Control (test pool 9), Compulsion (test pool 9), Ghost Speech (test pool 9), Possession (test pool 9) and Terrify (test pool 9)

INDEX AND TABLES

YOU HAVE BEEN PUT TO SLEEP.
Wake up.

THE WORLD HIDES GREAT MYSTERIES.
Find them.

THE SHADOWS ARE FULL OF DANGERS.
Face them.

MAGIC IS ALL AROUND YOU.
Wield it...
...before someone else does.

MAGE™
THE AWAKENING

ON SALE AUGUST 17TH

WWW.WORLDOFDARKNESS.COM

Mind's Eye Theatre

Name: _____

Player: _____

Virtue: _____

Vice: _____

Faction: _____

ATTRIBUTES

Intelligence	●○○○○
Wits	●○○○○
Resolve	●○○○○
Strength	●○○○○
Dexterity	●○○○○
Stamina	●○○○○
Presence	●○○○○
Manipulation	●○○○○
Composure	●○○○○

MERITS

_____ ○○○○○
_____ ○○○○○
_____ ○○○○○
_____ ○○○○○
_____ ○○○○○

FLAWS

_____
_____

EQUIPMENT

_____
_____
_____
_____

Size: _____

Speed (acting/running): _____ / _____

Initiative Mod: _____

Defense: _____ **Armor:** _____

MENTAL SKILLS
(-3 unskilled)

Academics	○○○○○
Computer	○○○○○
Crafts	○○○○○
Investigation	○○○○○
Medicine	○○○○○
Occult	○○○○○
Politics	○○○○○
Science	○○○○○

SOCIAL SKILLS
(-1 unskilled)

Animal Ken	○○○○○
Empathy	○○○○○
Expression	○○○○○
Intimidation	○○○○○
Persuasion	○○○○○
Socialize	○○○○○
Streetwise	○○○○○
Subterfuge	○○○○○

PHYSICAL SKILLS
(-1 unskilled)

Athletics	○○○○○
Brawl	○○○○○
Drive	○○○○○
Firearms	○○○○○
Larceny	○○○○○
Stealth	○○○○○
Survival	○○○○○
Weaponry	○○○○○

HEALTH

○ ○ ○ ○ ○ ○ ○ ○ ○ ○ ○
□ □ □ □ □ □ □ □ □ □ □

WILLPOWER

○ ○ ○ ○ ○ ○ ○ ○ ○ ○
□ □ □ □ □ □ □ □ □ □

MORALITY

○ ○ ○ ○ ○ ○ ○ ○ ○ ○

Derangements: _____
_____

FAVORED ACTIONS

Action/Power	Traits	Pool
_____ (___ + ___ + ___) =		[ ]
(CONT/RES by _____)		
_____ (___ + ___ + ___) =		[ ]
(CONT/RES by _____)		
_____ (___ + ___ + ___) =		[ ]
(CONT/RES by _____)		
_____ (___ + ___ + ___) =		[ ]
(CONT/RES by _____)		
_____ (___ + ___ + ___) =		[ ]
(CONT/RES by _____)		
_____ (___ + ___ + ___) =		[ ]
(CONT/RES by _____)		
_____ (___ + ___ + ___) =		[ ]
(CONT/RES by _____)		
_____ (___ + ___ + ___) =		[ ]
(CONT/RES by _____)		

CHARACTER TRAITS & POOLS

BASIC TRAITS

Perception Pool
(Wits + Composure) = _____

Defense
(Lower of Wits or Dexterity) = _____

Initiative Modifier
(Dexterity+Composure) = _____

Speed (Acting/Running) = _____ / _____

ATTACK POOLS

Unarmed Attack
(Str + Brawl) =_____ (RES by Def + Armor)

Melee Attack
(Str+Weap +Dmg)=_____ (RES by Def + Armor)

Firearms Attack
(Dex+Firearms+Dmg)=_____(RES by Armor)

MERIT BONUSES

_____

_____

_____

_____

FAVORED ACTIONS

Action/Power	Traits	Pool
_____ (___ + ___ + ___) =		[ ]
(CONT/RES by _____)		
_____ (___ + ___ + ___) =		[ ]
(CONT/RES by _____)		
_____ (___ + ___ + ___) =		[ ]
(CONT/RES by _____)		
_____ (___ + ___ + ___) =		[ ]
(CONT/RES by _____)		
_____ (___ + ___ + ___) =		[ ]
(CONT/RES by _____)		
_____ (___ + ___ + ___) =		[ ]
(CONT/RES by _____)		
_____ (___ + ___ + ___) =		[ ]
(CONT/RES by _____)		
_____ (___ + ___ + ___) =		[ ]
(CONT/RES by _____)		

KEY RULES

ACTIONS & SUCCESSES

Instant Actions: Each character gets one per turn. Consist of a single draw.

Reflexive Actions: Take no time and occur as per the trait's description. Consist of a single draw.

Extended Actions: Take place over several turns or more; and consist of several draws.

CONT(ested) Draws: Both attacker and defender form a pool, draw, and then compare successes. Ties go to defender; otherwise subtract defender's successes from attacker for final number of attacker successes.

RES(isted) Draws: Subtract the defender's traits from attacker's pool before drawing.

Successes: A total of 10 is one success; every increment of 5 above that (15, 20, etc.) is an additional success.

COMBAT SUMMARY

Step 0: Mediate: Can the players resolve things without cards?

Step 1: Initiative: Draw one card + Initiative Modifier; lasts the whole combat

Step 2: Attack: Character with the highest Initiative attacks. A character may choose to hold his action until later in the turn.

Step 3: Resolve: Apply damage or other effects. Damage = attack successes.

Step 4: Repeat: Follow Initiative roster and repeat Steps 2 and 3 for every character until everyone has acted (this is the end of the turn). Then repeat again for the next turn (do not redraw Initiative).

No live organism
can continue for long to exist
sanely under conditions
of absolute reality

for his
purpose

NO ABHORRENCE OF DANGER